Also available at all good book stores

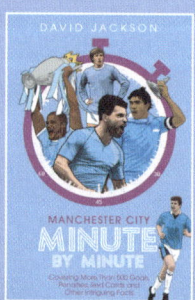

9781785316678

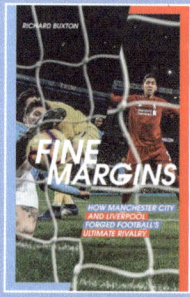

9781785316692

9781785315633

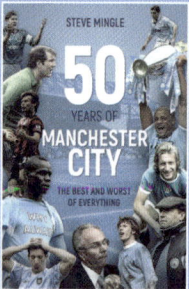

9781785313288

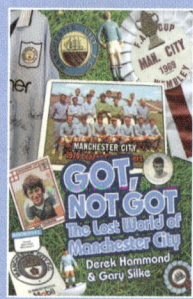

9781909626553

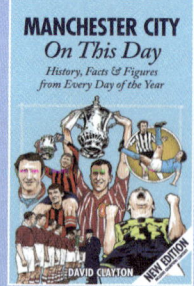

9781908051004

9781909178717

9781908051646

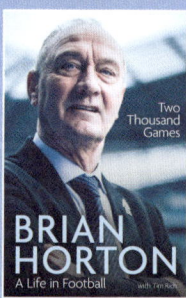

9781785316685

RECORD BREAKERS

To Mum, for a lifetime of support, and to Dad,
for giving me the inspiration to write a football book

RECORD BREAKERS

THE TACTICS BEHIND LIVERPOOL AND MANCHESTER CITY'S TITLE TRIUMPHS AND RECORD POINTS TOTALS

ROB WEAVER

First published by Pitch Publishing, 2021

Pitch Publishing
A2 Yeoman Gate
Yeoman Way
Worthing
Sussex
BN13 3QZ

www.pitchpublishing.co.uk
info@pitchpublishing.co.uk

ISBN 978 1 78531 985 3

Typesetting and origination by Pitch Publishing

Printed and bound by Replika Press Pvt. Ltd.

Contents

Introduction   7

Chapter 1   Guardiola at City and Klopp at Liverpool   19

Chapter 2   City in possession overview   33

Chapter 3   Liverpool in possession overview   50

Chapter 4   Build-up: an end to 'split' centre-backs   64

Chapter 5   The evolution of the full-back   82

Chapter 6   City's wingers versus Liverpool's
               wide forwards   109

Chapter 7   How City accessed one of modern
               football's key spaces   132

Chapter 8   A modern solution to a
               modern attacking problem   149

Chapter 9   Liverpool's full-backs as wing-backs   158

Chapter 10   Full-back underlaps   187

Chapter 11   The concept of 'free 8s'   192

Chapter 12   City's and Liverpool's 'final ball'   204

Chapter 13   Firmino and Agüero –
                modern centre-forwards   231

Chapter 14   A five-man midfield to prevent supply
                to City's front five   252

Chapter 15   Exposing a single pivot –
                midfield rectangles and double false 9s   260

Chapter 16   Liverpool's alternative shape –
                4-2-1-3/4-2-3-1   267

Chapter 17   How did a back five match up against
                City's front five?   271

Chapter 18   Liverpool against a back five –
                isolating the centre-backs   279

Chapter 19   Goalkeepers starting attacks   285

Chapter 20   Why did City and Liverpool high press?   325

Chapter 21   The counter-press: where Guardiola
                and Klopp's philosophies overlap   365

Conclusion   378

Acknowledgements   380

Bibliography   381

Introduction

Table 1

Team	Season	Points
Manchester City	2017/18	100
Liverpool	2019/20	99
Manchester City	2018/19	98
Liverpool	2018/19	97
Chelsea	2004/05	95

Table 2

Team	Years	Points
Manchester City	2017–19	198
Liverpool	2018–20	196
Chelsea	2004–06	186
Manchester United	2011–13	178
Manchester United	2007–09	177

*since start of 38-game format

THE FOUR highest points totals registered in Premier League history were all achieved by either Pep Guardiola's Manchester City or Jürgen Klopp's Liverpool (*Table 1*). Combining their title-winning seasons of 2017/18 and 2018/19, City won an incredible 198 points from an available 228, including the only 100-point season on record (*Table 2*). Combining 2018/19, when they finished second, and 2019/20, when they won the league title, Liverpool registered an equally remarkable 196 points from the 228 available, including 99 in a single season. During these periods, City also won an FA Cup and two League Cups, and Liverpool won the Champions League. These points totals present a strong argument that these were the best two teams the Premier League has ever seen.

For context, let's assess the success of some other great teams of the Premier League era. In the mid-2000s, José Mourinho's Chelsea managed 186 points across two consecutive seasons, a full ten and 12 points shy of Liverpool and City's best totals. None of the best Sir Alex Ferguson Manchester United teams achieved more than 91 points since the beginning of the 38-game format, registering a high of 92 in 1993/94, when they played 42 games. Finally, Arsène Wenger's Arsenal failed to earn more than 90 points, despite going unbeaten throughout the 2003/04 season. Undoubtedly, the City and Liverpool sides of these seasons were special teams.

How much influence do tactics have on the achievement of record points?

It is important to describe what constitutes 'tactics', and assess the level of their contribution to City and Liverpool winning a record number of points. Ultimately, tactics refer to the positions that players take up, the movements they make, and the actions they carry out, both at the team and individual level. These positions, movements and actions may vary depending on the location of the ball, the space, and the positioning and actions of their opponents and team-mates, as well as their strengths and weaknesses. Tactics have the aim of ensuring both the team and its individuals function to their maximum, both in and out of possession, in order to facilitate the two most important controllable factors in winning both an individual match, and subsequently a league: creating goalscoring opportunities, and simultaneously preventing the opposition from creating chances of their own. In possession, tactics do not solely affect the creation of opportunities, but also the prevention, while out-of-possession tactics can influence a team's own creation, as well as the prevention of the opposition's. A team's tactics could be specific to facing an individual opponent or style of opponent, or represent their overall way of playing regardless of the opponent.

But how important are tactics in winning football matches, leagues, and ultimately record Premier League points? Before answering this question, it needs to be made clear that we are describing tactics decided by the manager, not by the players themselves. Even if a manager were to select 11 players and a formation without giving them any instructions, a certain amount of tactics would still take place; players would take up positions, make movements and perform actions which could be considered tactics, based on their judgement of situations occurring during an individual match. In addition, players may discuss among themselves what to do in certain situations as a team, or within a particular section of a team. However, the players' choice of tactics would likely be largely defined by what suits them as individuals. Crucially, it is the inter-related positioning and actions of the team as a whole, or within individual sections of the team, which maximises its potential to create and prevent goalscoring opportunities, and therefore win games. This is where the role of the manager in deciding and implementing a team's tactics is so vital; he instructs his players with the benefit of the whole team in mind, *as well as* for the benefit of each individual, driven both by his particular philosophy and the attributes of the players he has available to him.

The extent to which tactics contribute to winning is a matter of opinion, as it is impossible to measure. Some pundits downplay or even disregard the importance of tactics, suggesting that it is simply the ability of the players which dictates success and failure. This opinion is missing the point. Of course, possessing better players than the opposition is an incredibly important factor in winning football matches and leagues, but the point of tactics is to extract the maximum performance out of a group of players. For example, to enable an inferior team to close the gap on a superior team, to make one of two evenly matched teams superior, or to raise the level of a superior team even higher. Jürgen Klopp discovered the importance of tactics while a player at Mainz under Wolfgang Frank, who used to show his players videos of Arrigo Sacchi's training sessions at AC Milan. In an interview with *The Guardian*, Klopp commented, 'We used to think before then that if the other players are better, you had to lose. After that we learned anything is possible – you can beat teams by having better tactics.' The ability of a group of players is subjective; it is very easy to say in hindsight that the team who wins the league simply has the best players. Perhaps Klopp's assistant manager Pep Lijnders best sums up the relationship between players, tactics and success: 'Without good players there's no collective. But without collective there will never be success.'

Besides, how much is a player's 'ability' related to how he is used by the manager of his team? Would, for example, Sadio Mané and Mo Salah have such outstanding goal records if Klopp's system of play didn't supply them with so many passes close to the opposition goal, from where they could do maximum damage? Would Kevin De Bruyne have the same reputation if Guardiola used him on the wing, where he had played earlier in his career, rather than as a central attacking midfielder, a role which has enabled his talents to flourish? Some people may argue that both City and Liverpool's record points-winning teams contained the best groups of players assembled in Premier League history. But were they better than the Manchester United team of Ronaldo, Rooney, Scholes, Ferdinand and Vidic, or the Chelsea side featuring Cech, Terry, Lampard, Drogba and Robben? Were their players even significantly better than those of their rivals during their record points-winning seasons? Whatever the ability level of the players available to City and Liverpool, the tactics implemented by Guardiola and Klopp arguably *increased* the gap between these two teams and their rivals. Could Guardiola and Klopp have finished first and second without the tactics they implemented? Possibly, but they would not have won as many points; simply having great players is not enough to win points so consistently and achieve the totals they registered.

One reason for some pundits or even managers failing to recognise the importance of tactics may be that when they were playing or managing, detailed tactics were not essential because very few teams used them, at least in English football; instead, any tactics that were applied tended to be fairly basic and similar between teams. Premier League matches from the 1990s or even 2000s do not closely resemble the majority of matches in the modern-day Premier League; they were incredibly fast-paced, with less controlled possession. The ball tended to be passed forwards quickly with both teams constantly fighting for the 'second ball'; there was less time for either the attacking or defending team to form a coherent team shape, or to progress the ball forward in a controlled manner. Other than relying on possessing better players, trying harder than an opponent was the perceived way a team could increase their chances of winning. Therefore, players and managers from previous eras were accustomed to attributing results to the level of effort applied. Television pundit Graeme Souness, who was a Premier League manager in the 1990s and 2000s, once said, 'I'm fed up of listening to people talk bull about tactics and formations and too much football science. Get to the ball first and you've got a chance in football. Simple as.'

Concluding that 'getting to the ball first' is the main key to winning a modern top-level football match, while dismissing the role of tactics, needs questioning. For example, this mantra did not help City or Liverpool break down a deep opposition defensive shape, nor was it the most important factor for City and Liverpool's opponents themselves in preventing them from creating chances; tactics played a vital role. Souness's comments show that he still sees football as it was during his era, when the sport has undergone significant changes. In fact, 'getting to the ball first' itself is not down solely to physical effort, but also related to tactics; the planned positioning of players was a vital factor in City and Liverpool beating their opponents to the ball in various scenarios.

This is not to deny that the effort of the players remains essential in the modern Premier League; for example, there is no doubt that the work ethic of City and Liverpool was extremely high during their most successful seasons. However, the key point is that a team can't win record points without high levels of effort *and* tactics; the importance of one does not dismiss the importance of the other. Yet people both inside and outside the professional game are often too keen to attribute success and failure to one overall factor, when winning consistently in football is multi-dimensional. The ability of the players, their physical capacity, their effort levels, and even less-controllable factors – such as missed chances, defensive mistakes, refereeing decisions, and the timing of key events – all contribute to how many points a team gains during a season, *alongside* the tactics. The more optimal the tactics, the lesser the extent to which a manager has to rely on these other factors; tactics are an element a manager *can* control.

For City and Liverpool, how their players' effort is applied is equally as important as the effort itself. Effort in football isn't so much about which team or player runs the most, nor the fastest; instead the key is to run sufficiently at the correct moments. There is no doubt that City and Liverpool's players sprinted when they needed to sprint and were aggressive when they needed to be aggressive. But this effort and aggression took place in the context of their tactical framework; it was organised. For example, the strategy of pressing relies on significant effort, but its organisation is also vital; it is not simply about randomly sprinting around. Some managers, usually those who give their players limited tactical instruction, often attribute a defeat to a lack of effort or fight from the players. Whether they actually believe this, or they simply use it to blame the players and deflect from their lack of a clear tactical plan, is debatable. Other managers simply can't understand the necessity for detailed tactics. For example, Alan Pardew, following his spell as manager of ADO Den Haag in the Netherlands, a country where tactics are ingrained in football culture, commented, 'The players were needy in terms of wanting to know exactly the game plan, what their role is, that information.' Surely it can only help for the players to know exactly what is expected of them in every scenario. Compare Pardew's quote to the view of Guardiola, who once defined tactics as 'about ensuring that every player knows what he should be doing at all times, and in every position he occupies during a match'.

In *The Mixer*, Michael Cox outlines how more detailed tactics in the Premier League were introduced, evolved and became more widespread over the years. Cox suggests that much of José Mourinho's success in his first spell with Chelsea was due to the fact that he was using more advanced tactics than the rest of the Premier League. He also proposes that Sir Alex Ferguson's Manchester United, a team that dominated the Premier League for many years, were more tactically advanced than their domestic rivals because of what Ferguson had learned from playing in the Champions League, a competition which featured teams with different systems and ideas to the Premier League.

As modern tactics have become more advanced, so have the tactics to counteract them. For example, as teams identified the space between the midfield and defensive lines as important to access in order to create high-quality goalscoring opportunities, opponents began to focus more on staying compact centrally to prevent this. A similar pattern often occurs; a new tactical system or pattern of play is introduced with early success, before opponents find solutions. For example, Antonio Conte's use of a 3-4-3 system in his first season with Chelsea was a significant tactical innovation which opponents struggled to cope with, resulting in an impressive league title win and 93 points. However, in his second season, Chelsea won just 70 points, with many teams coping by matching Chelsea up with a back-three system themselves. Some of City and Liverpool's tactics and even their systems of play themselves had never previously been used in the Premier League. Perhaps the advanced level of City's system of play is well known, as Guardiola has carried the reputation of a tactically innovative manager from his Barcelona days. In the case of Klopp's Liverpool, however, usually their success is heavily attributed to their physical intensity; this book aims to explain why their tactical ideas were equally as important.

Out-of-possession tactics arguably became more widespread earlier than in-possession tactics; in the modern-day Premier League some teams still tend to focus to a greater extent on their out-of-possession game plan than in-possession, which has traditionally been viewed as largely up to players to do what they do best as individuals. The word *shape* for example, is more indicative of how a team sets up to defend than attack. In fact, many managers, such as Diego Simeone, José Mourinho and Rafael Benítez, are considered 'tactically astute' because they excel at organising a team without the ball and creating chances on the counter-attack. However, managers have had to become more and more tactically astute *in possession* in order to break down opponents who allow them the ball and defend deep. Collective tactics are often key to breaking down deep, compact opponents. Some modern managers take inspiration from a concept termed *juego de posición*, which translates literally as 'positional play'. It is complex to define, but in basic terms, it concerns the application of precise positional structure, traditionally only seen when a team is *out of possession*, to *in-possession* tactics. Out of possession, every team has a positional structure and defensive principles, determined by four factors, all designed to ensure necessary superiority in key areas: the position of the ball, the location of space, and the position of both their opponents and team-mates. One interpretation of *juego de posición* is that it concerns having a positional structure and principles *in possession*, using the aforementioned four factors as a reference, with the same goal: to achieve superiority. People often describe teams as *well organised* out of possession, yet rarely do you hear a team described as such in possession. During their most successful periods, City and Liverpool were both very well organised *with* the ball.

The book is an interpretation of the tactics of these two teams, as overall systems, but also broken down into specific scenarios and parts of the pitch. It attempts to explain their effectiveness in the context of the opposition teams' own tactics they came up against. The main focus is on the two seasons when they posted their record points totals: City in 2017/18 and 2018/19, and Liverpool in 2018/19 and 2019/20. As these two teams have continued to evolve their tactics and have bought and sold players since those seasons of unprecedented success, aspects of their tactics have changed; at the time of writing there have been notable differences to City's tactics in particular during certain periods. However, the overall framework and philosophy which forms the basis for the analysis has not changed. On occasions, goals scored by City and Liverpool during these seasons will be used to illustrate particular tactics. Unfortunately permission wasn't granted to use screenshots from Premier League games, but the goals described can be viewed on YouTube by searching for the games in which they occurred.

Glossary

Pockets (also known as half-spaces) – the spaces between the wings and the centre, and between the defensive and midfield lines. For example, against a 4-4-2, the space between and behind the wide midfielder and central midfielder on each side of the pitch

Passing lane – space available to pass between player A and B, without an opposing player 'blocking' the line between the two players

Between the lines – the space between the midfield and defensive lines

'Compact' defensive shape – maintaining short distances between players both vertically and horizontally, in order to limit space and passing lanes between, for example, the defensive and midfield lines

High/mid/low block – where the opposition form their defensive shape; the space they protect, and the areas where they look to close down the opposition's players. Low refers to the area of the pitch nearer their own goal

Transition to attack/defend – the phase of play which occurs following a turnover in possession, when a team changes from attacking to defending, or viceversa

High press – strategy to pressurise high up the pitch

Give and go (also known as a one-two or wall pass) – When player B receives a pass from player A and immediately returns the pass to player A

Second ball – the situation that occurs after the ball has been contested without a team gaining control of it. For example, after the defending team has headed away a cross, both teams compete to win the second ball

Counter-attack – when a team attacks immediately having won the ball back following a period of defending

Pivot(s) – deepest central midfielder(s), traditionally the link between defence and midfield, both with and without the ball

Number 8 – in a 4-3-3, the number 8s are the two central attacking midfielders, placed one each side between the pivot and the centre-forward

The channel – the space between full-back and centre-back, behind both players

Goal side – refers to the player nearest to the goal both vertically and horizontally, when one player is marking another

Position Labels in Figures

Liverpool and City Labels

GK = Goalkeeper

RB = Right-back (right full-back)

LB = Left-back (left full-back)

CB = Centre-back

P = Pivot

R8 = Right number 8

L8 = Left number 8

RW = Right-winger

LW = Left-winger

RF – Right-forward

LF – Left-forward

CF = Centre-forward

Opposition Labels

LM = Left midfielder

RM = Right midfielder

CM = Central midfielder

RWB = Right wing-back

LWB = Left wing-back

Chapter 1

Guardiola at City and Klopp at Liverpool

What changed between their arrivals and their record points-winning seasons?

A fair question to ask would be: if tactics are so integral to what both Liverpool and City achieved, why did Klopp and Guardiola not obtain instant success in the Premier League? Guardiola finished third in his first season, and Klopp fourth in his first two full seasons. The first point to make is that the tactical systems used by both teams during their most successful seasons were not identical to those used during Klopp and Guardiola's early Premier League days. Guardiola's first season involved significant tinkering, changing his system regularly; during 2016/17 he made almost as many formation changes between games as he did during the 2017/18 and 2018/19 title-winning seasons combined. City's manager appeared to be searching for the right players for specific positions and roles within the squad he inherited. For example, Aleksandar Kolarov switched between centre-back and left-back. Fernandinho, who later had so much success as a midfield pivot, played several games at right-back. In one game, right-back Pablo Zabaleta bizarrely featured as one of the outside central midfielders in a 4-4-2 diamond formation.

In Guardiola's first season, City's players appeared slow to take up the positions and make the movements their manager wanted; perhaps the unfamiliarity and complexity of the positioning and patterns being coached was too much for some of them. Many new managers have failed in the short-term for asking players to do things they are not able to do, causing results to suffer. The line between being sacked and being given the time to improve the players' understanding, as well as the resources to bring in more capable or suitable players, is extremely thin – usually it is easier to change the manager. By the time Guardiola's second season came around, the players he retained had a greater understanding of their roles, and City made a huge effort to recruit suitable players for their manager's preferred system and style of play. In came Kyle Walker, Benjamin Mendy, Bernardo Silva and Ederson, followed by Aymeric Laporte in January. Placing too much importance on these signings overlooks the role of Guardiola's training ground work in implementing his tactical system with his existing players. Ultimately, achieving record points came from the combination of the players signed to fit the system, and the development of the system so the players knew it inside out and the movement patterns became more automatic.

However, the aim is not to dispute the fact that the squad City's money enabled them to put together had a significant impact on Guardiola's success; perhaps his style of football requires excellent players more than any other. But that doesn't mean that any manager could have got his group of players to dominate football matches to the same extent as Guardiola. Besides, many of his signings, especially in defence, were necessary to replace ageing players with younger alternatives. To what extent the money spent takes away from his achievements is a matter of opinion, but without doubt he is not the only Premier League-winning manager to have been given a large amount of money to spend. Nor did he simply go and buy the best players in the world; up to the end of the 2018/19 season, when Guardiola won his second title, his record signing was Riyad Mahrez for £60m. During Guardiola's time at City, Arsenal, Chelsea, Liverpool and Manchester United have all spent a bigger fee on a single player than City; in fact, Manchester United have done so three times.

Regardless of money spent, the focus here is on how during a two-season span, Guardiola came up with ways to use his players to maximum effect, resulting in him winning the highest number of points in Premier League history. Following his first season he did not change his principles or style of play, as many people at the time said he must do in order to win the Premier League; he simply improved the implementation of his original plan; building up from the back with control in order supply wide wingers, very attacking number 8s and a centre-forward, all positioned high up the pitch, backed up by conservative full-backs to help prevent counter-attacks.

Klopp's record points-winning Liverpool side did resemble the team early in his reign to an extent, but was unrecognisable in some aspects. Liverpool's counter-pressing, the term given to pressure applied as soon as a team loses the ball, arguably remained as iconic as ever. However, their pressing in the scenario where both themselves and the opposition had already formed an organised shape evolved to become more organised and consistent. Klopp, both during his time with Borussia Dortmund and early on in his Liverpool career, built a reputation as an advocate of 'heavy metal' football and 'controlled chaos', with pressing one of its major components. On Sky Sports's *Monday Night Football* analysis show,

Klopp once stated, 'If you win the ball back high up the pitch and you are close to the goal, it is only one pass away from a really good opportunity most of the time. No playmaker in the world can be as good as a counter-pressing situation.' However, this was often poorly interpreted to mean that his teams didn't value possession football, nor attempt to use it to create goalscoring opportunities. Klopp himself felt that his philosophy had been misjudged, once commenting to Spox.com, 'We do not claim that counter-pressing is the only way to play. It has been proved to be very useful to us and remains a very important part of the game. However, we would like to have 90 per cent possession every game. Our own footballing approach is underestimated in my opinion.'

The Liverpool manager did not arrive at Anfield with the level of in-possession tactical understanding he later gained; one of the factors behind Liverpool's transformation from a very good team to an outstanding team concerned their tactical evolution *with* the ball, which stemmed from their manager's own evolution of ideas. It is interesting to compare his more recent quote promoting the value of possession with a previous quote while manager of Borussia Dortmund. Ahead of a Champions League clash with Arsenal, Klopp said of Arsène Wenger, 'I think he likes having the ball, playing football, passes, it's like an orchestra. But it's a silent song. I like heavy metal more.'

The mistake some people make is thinking that a team has to be *either* counter-attacking *or* possession-based, when the reality is that the Liverpool team of 2018/19 and 2019/20 were both – this flexibility evolved Klopp and Liverpool into a manager and team capable of winning so many points. Even Guardiola's City, who every season under Guardiola ranked first in the possession statistics, scored a significant number of their goals from counter-attacking situations, as they possessed so many players who thrived in the space which is only really available on the counter-attack, before the opposition has recovered its defensive shape. This is possible because teams who have a large volume of possession still have a significant number of turnovers of possession which they can use to counter-attack.

Football statistics expert Tom Worville explained in an article in The Athletic, 'Teams actually have an equal number of distinct possessions per game. The only reason that percentage possession differs in a game is that one team spends more time on the ball.' This means that if one team has 70 per cent possession and the other 30 per cent, the opportunities to score on the turnover are equal in number, if not necessarily in level of difficulty. Notably, fairly early on in Klopp's Liverpool career, some pundits thought that for Liverpool to improve they should let their opponents have more of the ball. The pundits reasoned that it would enable them to use their pressing and counter-attacking strategy instead of having the majority of possession in games, therefore allowing the opposition to defend deep with a compact shape.

Previously it was true to say that Liverpool under Klopp struggled to break down compact, well-organised teams, and that they were susceptible to the counter-attack themselves. However, rather than give up more possession in an attempt to increase their opportunities to press and counter, Klopp and his staff had a different solution: to redesign and improve their in-possession system in order to create more chances that way. In Raphael Honigsteins biography of Liverpool's manager, *Klopp: Bring the Noise*, Liverpool assistant coach Peter Krawietz recounted how the Liverpool coaching staff realised they needed to introduce into their system the ability to use complex attacking patterns in order to adapt to the more conservative strategies of their opponents.

In other words, in games where there were limited opportunities for the counter-press to be 'the best playmaker' – or, regardless of their opponent's tactics, simply to increase their ability to create opportunities in other ways, alongside those which they created from counter-pressing. Either way, Klopp and his staff successfully enhanced Liverpool's in-possession system and tactics. The Liverpool side who won record points were able to attack *either* from a base of controlled possession, *or* by using 'heavy metal', intense football.

The signing of Fabinho, a midfield pivot more associated with controlled possession than counter-pressing, at the beginning of the 2018/19 season, was a clear indication of a slight change in direction. Equally, in the summer of 2020, the edition of playmaker Thiago Alcântara further confirmed the wish to control the ball to a greater extent. In addition, the redesign of the system made Liverpool less susceptible to counter-attacks, with their full-backs' starting positions more conservative, their centre-backs positioned closer together in possession, and with a greater focus on not attacking with too many players in advance of the ball, too early. Klopp's team continued to progress every season at breaking down teams who defended deeper and more compactly in order to avoid the kind of open game in which Liverpool traditionally excelled.

Like City, Liverpool also improved their playing squad. The departure of Philippe Coutinho combined with the arrivals of Sadio Mané and Mo Salah, both of whom possessed electric pace, altered the way their entire system functioned in attack: their wide forwards were positioned higher than previously, from where they made dangerous runs in behind the opposition defence, whereas when Coutinho had filled one of these wide forward positions, Liverpool looked to supply him with passes to his feet between the lines. Equally, Coutinho often played as a number 8, yet his attributes were very different to those of the more physical and energetic number 8 options later available to Klopp – players who gave their front three licence to play higher. Finally, the addition of Andy Robertson and the emergence of Trent Alexander-Arnold added to Liverpool's attacking weapons in a way that none of the full-backs previously available to Klopp could.

In addition to enhancing their tactical systems and signing more optimal outfield players to implement them, another factor in both teams' subsequent success was Klopp and Guardiola addressing a problem they had previously failed to fix; or in Guardiola's case one that he arguably created himself: possessing a goalkeeper who could keep the ball out of the back of the net! Early on in their tenures, both men attempted to improve on the goalkeepers they inherited – Joe Hart in the case of Guardiola, and Simon Mignolet in the case of Klopp. Guardiola appeared to change his goalkeeper with the specific aim of bringing in one with more suitable in-possession attributes: Claudio Bravo. But although better than Hart with his feet, Bravo simply let in too many goals which he should have saved. Similarly, Klopp also brought in a goalkeeper who struggled with this fundamental function: Loris Karius. Before both teams' record points-winning seasons, the two managers fixed their mistakes with the signings of Alisson and Ederson. Later we will assess the changes that occurred with the addition of these two Brazilians *with* the ball, but their impact in terms of preventing goals was clearly an important factor in those record points totals.

Perhaps an explanation for City's more meagre points totals since their record seasons may also be required (at the time of writing it is not possible to say with confidence how Liverpool will fare following their title-winning season, although clearly they were heavily affected by injuries to centre-backs). In Guardiola's fourth season City finished second, a full 18 points adrift of Liverpool. City were, however, as productive as ever in terms of chance creation, ending the season with their highest Expected Goals (xG: a measure of how many goals a team would be expected to score based on the quality of their shots) of the Guardiola era. However, in terms of actual goals they out performed their xG by a smaller margin than in their two record seasons, which demonstrates their greater tendency to miss chances. Another problem occurred at the other end of the pitch, where City's xG against increased significantly during the 2019/20 season, in line with their actual goals conceded. Arguably this was down to both system and personnel changes. The absence of their best defender, Aymeric Laporte, for more than half of the games hit City hard defensively, especially following the departure of fellow centre-back Vincent Kompany, and the loss of form and injury problems of John Stones. Fernandinho, naturally a midfielder, was used as a centre-back for much of the season. In addition, the system of play was not identical – at least one full-back tended to play high, which meant City didn't usually play with two wide wingers, and City did not press in the same manner nor with the same intensity. Following a poor start to 2020/21, Guardiola returned to his original idea of conservative full-backs, and high and wide wingers. After City's subsequent upturn in form, he commented, 'I didn't like the way we were playing. In previous seasons the wingers were wider and higher so we came back to our principles. In the end, I felt having the wingers wide and high helped us to be more stable.' Ultimately, how much responsibility Guardiola should take for City's drop in form during the 2019/20 season is a matter of opinion; there were arguably problems he couldn't control, and others which he created himself.

How did City and Liverpool directly compare?

Arguably one of the most interesting aspects of the comparison between City and Liverpool is that they won record points in the same era, yet they did not play the same way; their systems of play, styles, and the attributes of their players were significantly different, even if their formation was the same in name. During their most successful seasons, both City and Liverpool predominantly played 4-3-3, so their structures and patterns of play within this formation are the main focus. However, their alternative formations contained similar positional structures and principles; the formation itself was not fundamental. This is a trend of modern football – the formation is just a framework. On this subject, Guardiola once commented, 'Football is a question of space and how to use it. Numbers and formations aren't the central point at all. The crucial thing is space, how to adapt to your opponent's movements and then to anticipate them and break into the spaces they leave.'

This philosophy is abundantly clear when analysing City and Liverpool. They positioned their players where they could cause maximum problems for opposition teams, either to receive the ball themselves, or to move an opposition player out of the way in order to create space for a team-mate. City and Liverpool both played very attacking versions of 4-3-3; Guardiola and Klopp's teams ranked first and second in the Premier League for goals scored in 2017/18, 2018/19 and 2019/20, earning their record points by taking the game to the opposition. But this did not mean that City and Liverpool neglected the defensive side of the game. Both teams' defensive records were exceptional; City and Liverpool ranked first and second for fewest goals conceded during their record seasons. These achievements would not be possible without a clear focus on their out-of-possession tactics, but also on their ability to attack without leaving themselves vulnerable to the counter-attack – this was the principle situation their opposition would target to score a goal.

In terms of style of play, the main difference between the two teams was the necessity for *control*. It was clear that Guardiola's City were always desperate to maintain control, aiming to avoid random, 'second ball' scenarios as much as possible, and to progress the ball with limited risk of losing it or having to recontest it. Every season under Guardiola, City averaged the highest pass completion percentage in the Premier League, as well as the lowest percentage of long passes (*Graph 1*). During their record points seasons they also ranked either first or second for per cent long passes completed, which shows that when they did pass longer, they selected passes which had a high likelihood of completion. Key to achieving control was the disciplined positioning of the players within the system; they were spaced optimally in order to create consistent passing options, as well as to sufficiently move the opposition with the

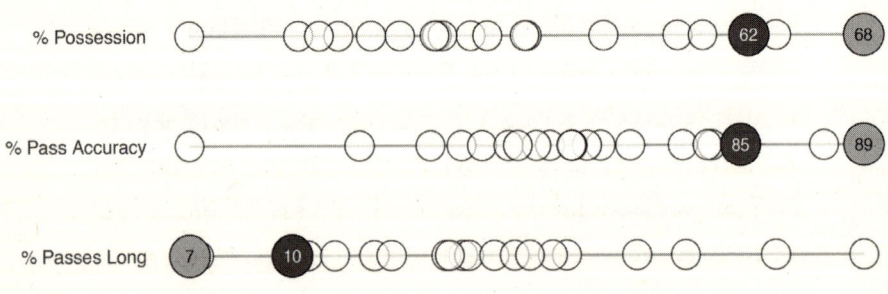

Both teams controlled possession in 18/19

Manchester City had the most possession and the lowest % of passes long; **Liverpool** also had high possession but passed long slightly more often.

Note: Each point represents a PL team that season, lowest ranked to the left and highest to the right.
Values are shown in the circle for the highlighted teams.
Source: Stats Perform

Graph 1.

aim of opening up space, or creating superiority, whether that be a numerical overload, or a favourable one versus one situation. The superiority was not used simply to keep possession but to progress the ball forward with control; this is the aim of the positional game, not possession for possession's sake. Short passing, or possession-based football, especially when used by Spanish managers, has lazily gained the label 'tiki taka'. However, Guardiola himself once distanced himself from this term, dismissing tiki taka as 'passing for the sake of it'. In an interview with canofootball.com, he said, 'If you do nothing with the ball then what's the point? Everyone in the world knows when you're playing with meaning or when you're just playing because you like having the ball.'

The Liverpool record points team, on the other hand, were the ultimate modern football side in terms of their flexibility in style of play, making them equally difficult to defend against. While they were, like City, a possession-based team, Klopp's side were prepared to use a greater range of styles of play and weapons to hurt opposition teams than City. This meant that if the opponent set up to nullify one strategy they simply switched to another, often within the same passage of play. For example, they frequently began to build up with short passes in their own half, before playing a defence-splitting long pass which caught the opposition defensive line off guard. Although as already mentioned Liverpool took steps to increase their ability to progress the ball forward with control, they were less bothered about attacking with *complete* control as City, as long as the opposition themselves weren't in control. At times they played passes which encouraged randomness, with their players positioned and trained to to take advantage of these situations. Whereas City were aiming to maximise the *quality* of their attacks by ensuring the ball arrived with their front players with complete control and following a pre-planned movement pattern, Liverpool were aiming to maximise the *quantity* of their attacks, by ensuring the opposition defence was constantly put under pressure. This was reflected in Liverpool's pass completion percentage averaging out at four to five per cent lower than City's, a statistic which tends to be an indicator of style, in terms of the length, and therefore usually difficulty, of passes attempted. However, this more direct style must be put in context – Liverpool could only be considered a more direct team compared to City; they were still a team which relied on controlled possession and intricate build-up to a greater extent than the majority of Premier League teams, with their possession and pass completion percentages either the second or third highest in the Premier League during their record seasons.

Of course, neither City nor Liverpool's style of play can be adequately described without mentioning their out-of-possession pressing strategies, both in the seconds following their own loss of possession, and in situations when the opposition had formed their build-up shape. Both teams used their ability to win the ball back high up the pitch as a way of creating goalscoring opportunities, but also as a means of preventing the opposition from creating opportunities against them. Defending against City and Liverpool required significant energy, but there was no let-up having won the ball back; Klopp and Guardiola's sides immediately put the opposition under pressure, making their task of holding on to the ball or starting an attack themselves, and therefore relieving pressure, extremely challenging. Winning the ball back quickly allowed City and Liverpool to dominate the ball and become the protagonists in games. As Leicester's 2015/16 Premier League title win showed, being the protagonists every week is not the only way to win the title; but earning record points without being the protagonists is another matter.

One thing that becomes very apparent when analysing both City and Liverpool is that neither side tended to significantly change the fundamentals of their tactical systems between games; a large proportion of what these two teams did both with and without the ball was consistent regardless of their opponents. Guardiola and Klopp did of course have specific game plans which featured subtle changes to how they defended and attacked, or to the formation, but these alterations were small details which were fairly easy for their players to adapt to. Equally, any changes made tended to follow consistent patterns against similar types of opponents or formations, so any tweaks usually involved a previously used tactic which the players were accustomed to.

When managers are described as 'tactically astute', this is usually a reference to the fact that they are able to come up with very different plans for individual games, adapting to the strengths and weaknesses of opponents. José Mourinho, for example, has often been credited with successfully altering his team's system and style of play between games, attacking with a possession-based strategy one week against a weaker opponent, then defending deep and counter-attacking the next week against a stronger opponent. However, in the cases of Guardiola and Klopp, perhaps their most impressive achievements were that they didn't need to alter their philosophy between games. The belief appeared to be that their overall structure and principles of play would dominate every game, so if they stuck to these structures and principles they would win. The consistency of their tactics gave their players a familiarity with when and how their managers wanted them to carry them out. Arguably, the ability to implement consistent, complex patterns of play with the ball is the main aspect in which the top coaches in the modern game differ to their counterparts from ten-plus years ago. Guardiola and Klopp designed and implemented systems which their players came to know inside out, enabling them to carry out their roles to the maximum level both as individuals and within their relationships with their team-mates.

Chapter 2

City in possession overview

WE'RE GOING to begin by analysing City's 4-3-3 both as a whole unit and in its sections, before going into more detail in terms of specific patterns of play within the system. Later we'll discuss their build-up play from the goalkeeper, but first we're going to refer to Guardiola's system for when his team faced their most common scenario during a game; possession in the middle third, facing an opposition who had formed a mid-to-low defensive block. The first clear aspect was that they usually built up with five outfield players, whose task it was to supply the other five outfield players with the ball in advanced positions. This five-plus-five balance was fundamental to how the system functioned as a whole. When beginning their build-up play in the middle third, their structure was at its strictest or most rigid (*Figure 1*). The five players who built up were more often than not the two centre-backs, two full-backs, and midfield pivot. In turn, the front five, consisting of the two number 8s, the two wide players (which in City's case we'll term 'wingers'), and the centre-forward, were positioned in five distinct vertical zones. Specifically, City positioned their two wingers in each outside vertical lane. Each of their number 8s

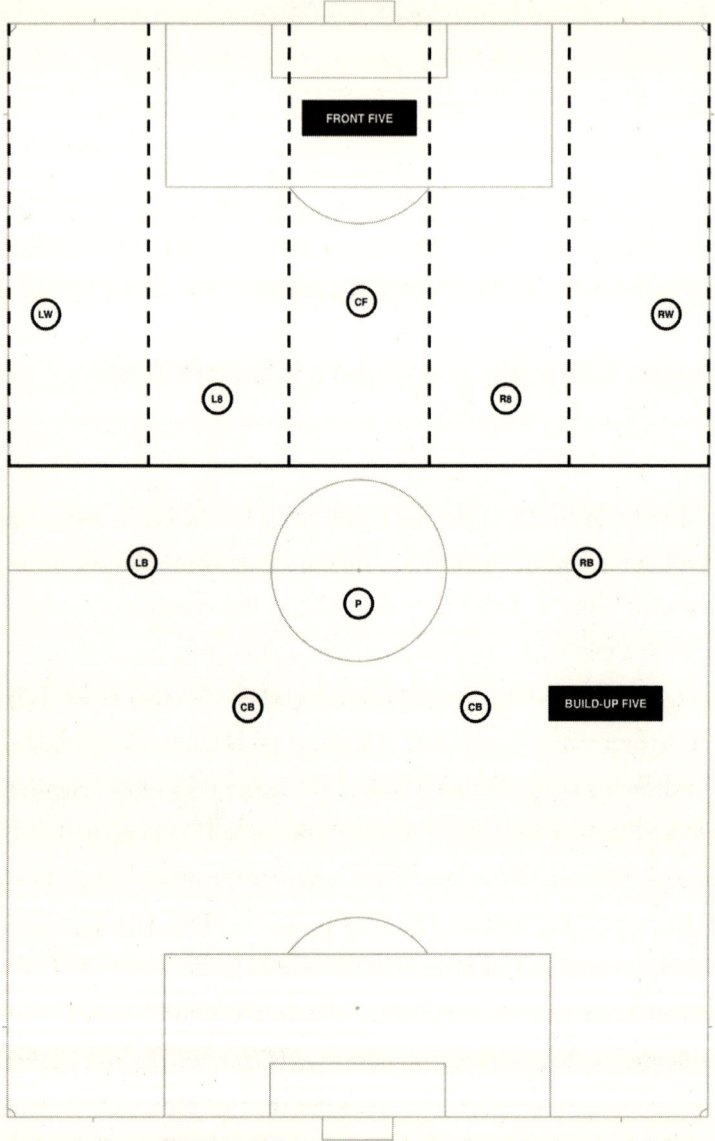

Figure 1. The five players City used to build up, and five more positioned higher, in five distinct vertical zones

occupied the next lane inside on each side, in the pockets between the opposition midfield and defensive lines. Finally, their centre-forward occupied the middle vertical lane.

One of the keys was that their five front players possessed the positional discipline to hold their assigned position as the team built up; this is a fundamental requirement of the positional game. Thierry Henry tells a story from his playing days as a winger for Guardiola at Barcelona. Having not touched the ball for a few minutes, he decided to cross over to the other side of the pitch to get involved in the play, and despite having scored a goal, he was taken off at half-time for a lack of positional discipline! It wasn't necessary to roam around looking for the ball; instead, the attacking players held their shape, because the system was designed to find them and give them the most favourable conditions possible to expose the opposition.

This may be at odds with the impression many casual observers have of Guardiola's players constantly moving around to create space. When they did rotate, it was off a structure, which ensured that the pre-planned optimal shape was maintained. For example, their wingers, number 8s and full-backs had to follow the system's structure; one provided width high up the pitch, one filled the pocket, and one was positioned deeper to assist with build-up, ensuring that optimal spacing and angles were maintained between players. With this structure, as their front five held their positions, City's build-up five barely had to look before passing, as they knew where their team-mates were going to be. To reiterate, simply maintaining possession was not the aim; instead, the objective was always controlled forward ball progression.

But why did Guardiola design his system in this way, with five front players in the five vertical lanes, and five players positioned deeper to supply them? The answer must lie in the game plans of the Premier League teams City faced. Their main defensive strategy was to allow City to have possession in front of their defensive block and prevent them from playing through the centre between the lines where David Silva and Kevin De Bruyne, City's regular number 8s, were positioned. In addition, the opposition's main attacking strategy was the counter-attack. Guardiola therefore designed a system that had two fundamental functions: 1) To facilitate breaking down a mid-to-low centre-focused block in order to create goalscoring opportunities. 2) To prevent counter-attacks in order to limit opposition goalscoring opportunities.

Beginning with the first function, one of the great misconceptions some pundits and even opposition managers had about City, at least in the early Guardiola years, was that their strategy was focused principally on directly attacking the central areas. Clearly, the vast majority of teams they faced were compact enough to limit this space on the inside of their defensive shape to a minimum, with almost every manager in the league working on this plan throughout the week before a game against City. Guardiola therefore positioned his players and implemented patterns of play accordingly to ensure that City were equally as effective using the space and favourable situations (for example one versus ones) more readily available to them on the outside of an opposition defensive shape. The genius of City's front five was that the high positions of their number 8s would pin a back four extra narrow, giving more space to their two wingers. Thierry Henry once explained, 'If you stand between the right-back and the right centre-back and another player does the same on the other side, suddenly you hold four players alone: you are freezing four players.' Conversely, if the opposition team didn't prioritise defending the centre, the

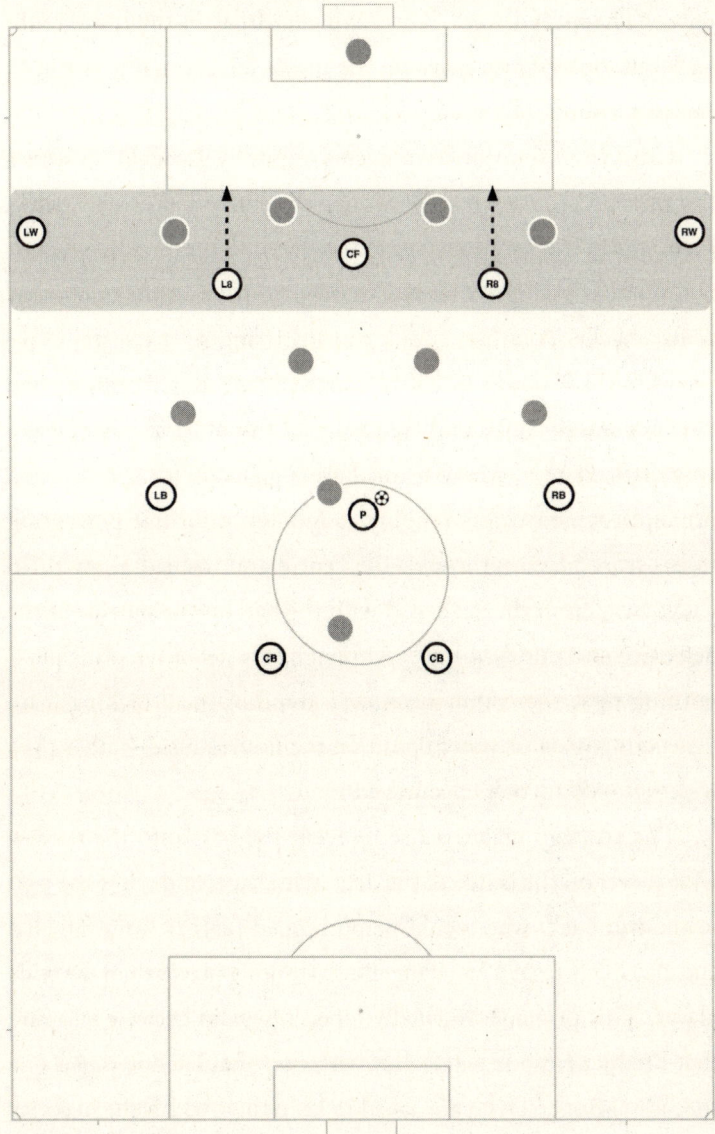

Figure 2. City's 'front five' created a five versus four situation against the opposition back four. If the back four shifted to the left or right, City's winger on the opposite side of the pitch was free. Alternatively, if one of the full-backs moved too early towards one of City's wingers, City's number 8 was potentially available between the full-back and centre-back

opposite happened; one of City's wingers drew the opposition full-back out, opening up space on the inside for City's number 8s or centre-forward.

City's front five caused problems simply by the fact they were a front five. As the five players covered the entire width of the pitch, there was in theory a constant option for a pass into either pocket, out to either wing, or directly between/in front of the opposition centre-backs. Against a back four, this meant a constant five versus four advantage in City's favour (*Figure 2*). City always had a spare man, so consistently blocking all five of these passes was a very difficult task. Many teams have a general out-of-possession principle, which works roughly as follows: prioritise preventing teams from playing through the centre and instead allow them wide, away from the goal, and with the ball on the outside of the defensive and midfield lines. Although this defensive principle is nothing new, the common modern trend of the attacking team instructing wide players to position themselves inside rather than wide has only further encouraged it.

The strategy makes sense: prevent the pass into the narrow wide player on the inside of the defensive shape, and allow the pass to the full-back, who would be positioned further from the goal and also likely to be a less dangerous attacking player than the wide player. This principle is usually especially valid because it is rare that Premier League teams play with two genuine one versus one specialist wingers, who are asked to keep their width the majority of the time. Even with the knowledge that City *were* a team who played with one versus one specialist wingers, many teams still decided that as long as they possessed a full-back who was a good one versus one defender, and a clear strategy of having a support player near enough to be able to assist their full-back and 'double up' two versus one, it was still a more favourable scenario for City's wingers to have the ball near the touchline, than allow City to play through the centre. But the damage City were able to do following a pass out wide meant that although a team needed to be compact centrally, they could not be so narrow that they struggled to defend the wide areas. Finding the balance was difficult.

In line with the rise in wide players tending to play more narrowly, the trend over the last few years in football has been for teams to play with attacking full-backs, positioned high up the pitch. The 'modern' full-back tends to possess some of the qualities traditionally seen in wingers: pace, the ability to run with the ball, and to deliver crosses. Their function in possession is to provide the team's width in an advanced position, either to create chances themselves, or to stretch the opposition in order to create space on the inside for team-mates. However, this has led to a rise in the opposition strategy of counter-attacking using the space between the attacking team's centre-back and full-back, when the full-back is caught forward, leaving his centre-backs unprotected. In contrast, Guardiola flipped the modern full-back trend on its head – he asked his full-backs to play deep and narrow, or 'inverted' – there was no need for them to play high and wide, as that was the role of the wingers.

Pundits often referred to Kyle Walker's attacking threat from right-back as one of City's attacking weapons. While Walker did occasionally use his electric pace to burst forward and claim an assist, when considering City's prolific chance creation, his forward runs were a long way down the list of frequently occurring threats (*Graph 2*). In fact, much of the time Walker moved deep and narrow to become a third centre-back or second central midfielder (pivot) as City built up. In the majority of games during City's two record

City's full-backs have created a relatively low proportion of their team's expected goals

Note: Statistics are on a per-90 basis unless specified. Data are from full-back or wing-back starts only.
Each point represents a Premier League full-back in a season between 16/17 and 19/20 with minimum 10 starts, ranked from lowest up to highest for each statistic.
Data source: Stats Perform

Graph 2.

seasons, two left-footed central midfielders, Fabian Delph and Oleksandr Zinchenko, shared the left-back role. They could play in this unfamiliar position because Guardiola required his full-backs to be part of the build-up five, performing roles where they could use their natural attributes as central midfielders. The roles of Walker, Delph and Zinchenko are clearly reflected in their chance creation statistics. They created 6.9 per cent, 4.3 per cent and 7.7 per cent of City's chances respectively when they were on the pitch. In comparison, 47 Premier League full-backs who played more than 15 games during the 2017/18 and 2018/19 seasons created a greater proportion of their team's chances than Zinchenko.

The proportion of crosses which came from City's full-backs gives a further indication of their limited involvement in chance creation. Walker, for example, went from delivering 22.1 per cent of Tottenham's crosses during the 2016/17 season, the joint highest proportion in Mauricio Pochettino's team, to 14.2 per cent of City's in his first two seasons under Guardiola. On City's left, however, there was sometimes a big exception. Benjamin Mendy was asked to play higher and wider in order to take advantage of his attacking attributes. For example, he delivered a huge 38.4 per cent of City's crosses in the games he played, but due to injury he only started 17 of the 72 games, so did not represent the norm of how City's left-backs were used.

A full-back's most important relationship in possession is with the winger on his side. Coaches often insist that these two players should not be on the same vertical line as each other, but instead be positioned at an angle – for example, one providing width, with the other narrower. City's full-backs were almost always positioned on a different vertical and horizontal line to the winger, and therefore at a diagonal angle (*Figure 3*). Because of this it was much more difficult for the opposition full-back to prevent the winger's supply by moving wide early, and potentially intercept the pass. This is because one of the reference points for where the opposition full-back had to position himself was the location of the ball. When the City full-back received a pass in a narrower position, the ball was more central than the winger. This meant the opposition, and more specifically their full-back, had to mirror the ball position and remain significantly more central than the winger himself, as a more central pass to City's number 8 was still potentially available. Crucially, the opposition full-back wouldn't have known for sure the ball was definitely going wide at that point, so he had to prioritise defending the inside pass first; it is a cardinal sin as a full-back to move too wide too early, allowing a pass on his inside. This is simply because he must remain horizontally between the ball and the goal in order to protect it. If City's full-back were

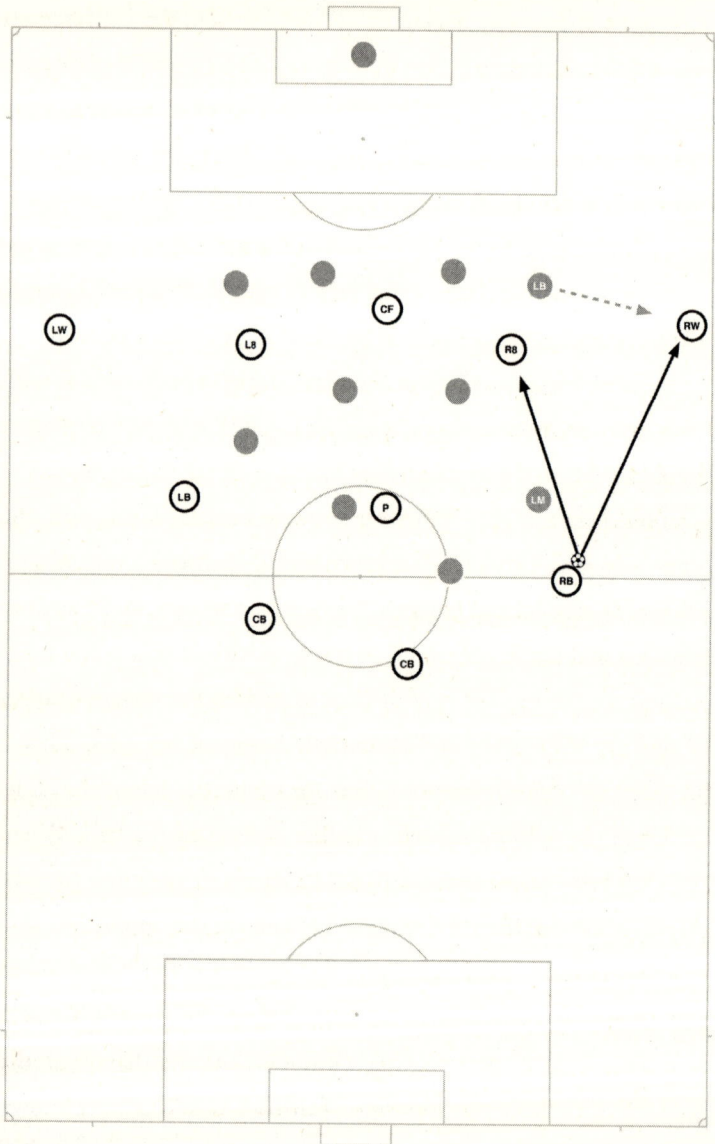

Figure 3. *The opposition left-back had to remain narrow before the ball was passed wide, otherwise a pass could be played on his inside to City's right-sided 8. The left-back had to mirror the ball's position, waiting for the pass wide before releasing to close down*

positioned wider, on a similar vertical line to the winger, it would have been more difficult for him to play the pass to the winger, because the opposition, and crucially their full-back, would already have moved wide as City's full-back received, as the opposition full-back's positional reference would have been the ball's wider location (*Figure 4*). This meant the opposition full-back would have had the time to get tight enough to City's wide player to either force him very deep to receive unchallenged, or risk an interception if the pass was played to him in a higher position.

Secondly, from a straight pass from City's full-back to the winger, due to being on the same vertical line as the full-back it would have been much more difficult for the winger to receive the ball *open*. Open in this context refers to a body position facing towards the opposition goal or at least the inside of the pitch, in order to run or pass forward or inside more easily. By being on the same vertical line as his full-back, a winger's body position is *closed* to the play, due to the direction from which the pass arrives. If, however, the pass is at a diagonal angle, the winger can naturally receive the ball open, as he would already be facing the inside of the pitch/opposition goal due to the the passer's location. The split-second difference between having to turn before being able to run forward or pass the ball and immediately being able to do so could be enough to cause the winger to be trapped and forced to play backwards, or to be dispossessed as he turned. Although this example uses the pass between full-back and winger, the same concept applied for a diagonal pass from City's number 8 to the winger, enabling him to receive open. Alternatively, the pass wide to the winger could come from one of City's centre-backs, missing out the pass from the full-back completely, giving the opposition less time to adjust. But ultimately, whichever player the City winger

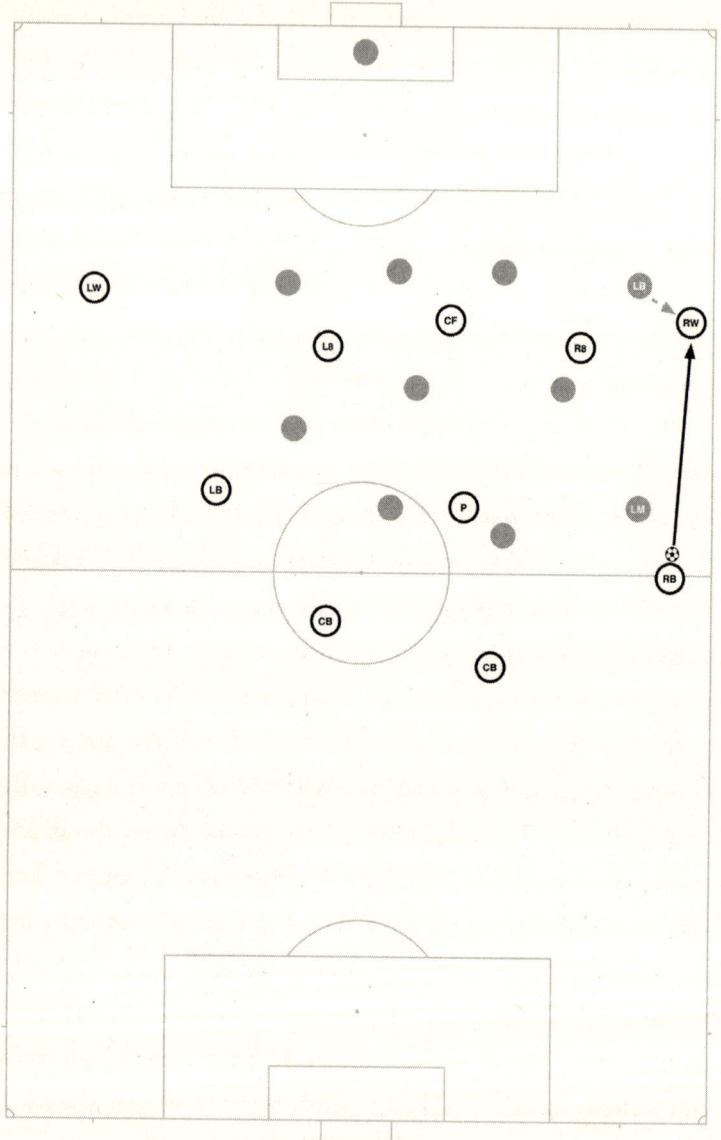

Figure 4. If City's right-back received wider, the opposition left-back could mirror the ball and move wide early, closing down the City's winger's space to receive, and reducing his time to turn

received a pass from, the theory was that for the winger to receive open and in sufficient space, he needed to be accessed with a pass from a central position, rather than after the ball has already moved wide.

As City's full-backs were positioned deep and inside, there was no requirement to use a number 8 deep alongside City's pivot as there were already a sufficient number of players to assist with build-up play and to cover counter-attacks. In contrast, with wide wingers and only one centre-forward, there was a requirement for the number 8s to fill the two pockets each side between the defensive and midfield lines. Out of all the teams who played 4-3-3 in the Premier League, the starting positions of De Bruyne and Silva as a pair of number 8s, were arguably the highest. When the ball was on their side they operated more as second forwards or number 10s than as central midfielders.

Other than receiving the ball between the lines themselves, or freeing up space for City's wingers by forcing the opposition to defend extra narrowly, the high positions of City's number 8s served several functions. Firstly, their positions prevented many opposition teams from sending central midfielders higher to reduce City's numerical superiority when building up. This is because the central midfielders were needed deeper in order to block passing lanes into De Bruyne and Silva, to close them down should they receive a pass, and to track their forward runs. Secondly, their high, 'second forward' positions meant that as soon as a gap appeared in the opposition defensive line, they were in an optimal position to exploit it. For example, when the full-back left the defensive line horizontally to close down City's winger, De Bruyne and Silva would either run into the newly available space between full-back and centre-back, or play a full-back into the space. Equally, as soon as an opposition centre-back stepped out vertically to close down City's centre-forward, who would often drop off to receive, City's number 8s were in an optimal position to attack the space behind the centre-back, again, with either a run or pass. Later on, we will analyse in detail how City's number 8s interacted with their wingers, full-backs and centre-forward, both with and without the ball. But the key point is that their high positions allowed them to be connected to the wingers and centre-forward, and actively affect and attack the opposition defensive line.

Now we have described the positioning of all City's outfield players, their exact shape can be broken down into more detail (*Figure 5*). More specifically than a build-up five and front five it was often a 3-2-2-3, in which the first line consisted of the two centre-backs and right-back, the second consisted of the left-back and pivot, the third consisted of the two number 8s, and the fourth consisted of the two wingers and the centre-forward. Alternatively, depending on the scenario or the opposition set-up, City's right-back sometimes moved forward to join the second line, forming a 2-3-2-3. These set-ups consisted of the optimal spacing of players in order to bypass each opposition line vertically *and* horizontally, crucially with short passes, and therefore control.

The second function of City's five plus five system was to prevent the main opposition strategy of creating chances against them; namely, the counter-attack. Once City progressed the ball into an advanced position, the majority, if not all of their five build-up players thought less about supporting the attack and more about how they could position themselves to trap the opposition in their own half, in order to sustain the attack for themselves, and subsequently prevent the opposition from counter-attacking against them. The two functions of the system were therefore inter-

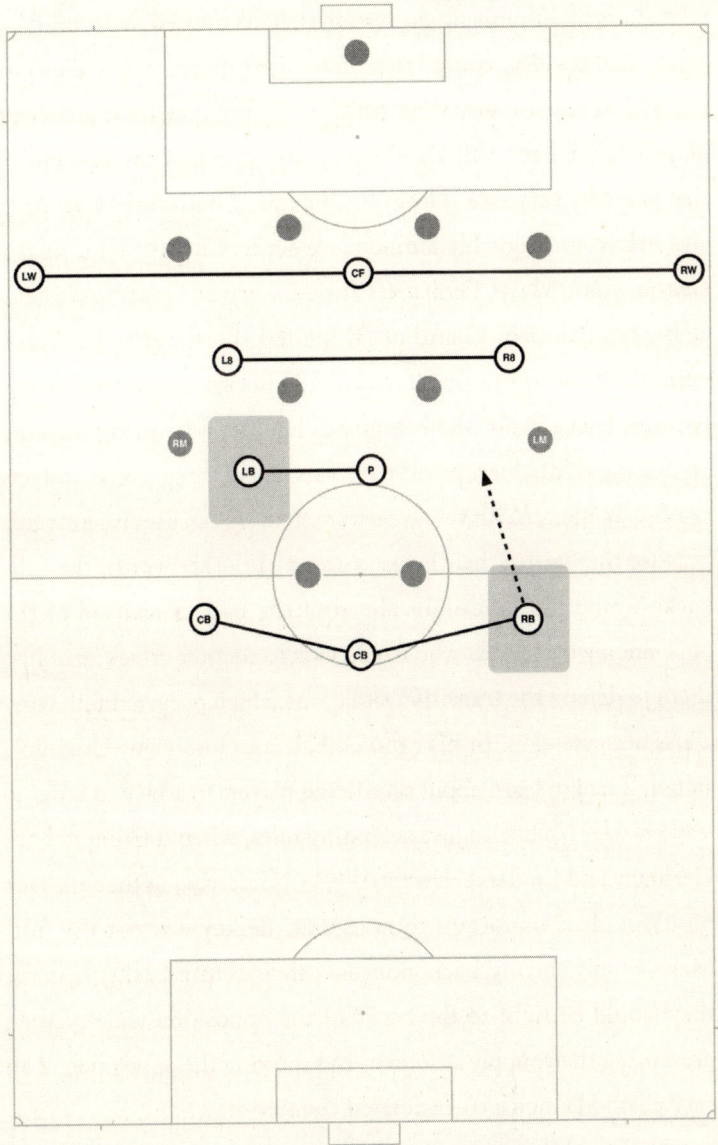

Figure 5. Example of how City usually positioned themselves in possession, forming a 3-2-2-3 or 2-3-2-3 shape for the purpose of build-up. Note the positions of the full-backs, neither of whom were caught ahead of the opposition wide midfielders as City attacked

related: the positioning in possession that maximised their ability to create chances also reduced their defensive exposure when they lost the ball. It is not unusual for teams to ensure they have sufficient players behind the ball should they lose it, nor is the concept of five plus five very rare. However, the use of both full-backs deep and inside was arguably a unique aspect to City's system. In *Pep Confidential*, Martí Perarnau's inside story of Guardiola's time at Bayern Munich, Guardiola is quoted shortly after he struck upon the plan to use five 'forwards': 'This system hinges on the two full-backs, who when in possession are close in tight to the organising midfielder [pivot] to form a line of three which protects against counters. With this security system we can use five forwards because they've got their backs covered.' In other words, the full-backs would not be caught ahead of the ball, nor ahead of the opposition wide players who would look to counter-attack, enabling them to defend the transition situations which occurred following a loss of possession. In his canofootball.com interview, Guardiola stated, 'I had to learn about sacrificing players in attack in order to leave players back with just defending roles, when starting in both Germany and England.' Essentially, he is referring to the full-back positions. It is important to note that the key was not the full-backs simply staying back alongside their centre-backs. Instead, they would be tight to the backs of the opposition wide players, preventing their supply at source, and starving the opposition of an easy pass to launch a co-ordinated counter-attack.

At the risk of stating the obvious, a manager would generally want all his defenders to be in a position to defend every time the opposition attacks. However, the one scenario when a team's defenders are often *not* in a position to defend is when they are being counter-attacked, due to the tendency for full-backs to be positioned ahead of, and much wider than, the ball. However, by keeping his full-backs *behind* rather than ahead of the ball, Guardiola was usually able to ensure that when his team lost possession his entire back four were in a position to defend. This was especially important during build-up play in the middle third, an area where a loss of possession would result in a counter-attack over a relatively short distance to City's goal. There were exceptions where they conceded goals on the counter-attack despite their system. In fact, during Guardiola's post-record points-winning seasons one full-back often played higher, depending on the personnel and the opposition. However, during the two record seasons, it was rare to see the City full-backs in advanced positions, especially before the ball was progressed into the final third. Because of this, it was much more difficult to attack 'in behind' City's full-backs, significantly blunting one of many opposition teams' major strategies. Considering how often teams attempted to counter-attack City as their main goalscoring strategy, City managed to restrict the chances created against them to very few. The system allowed them to play with five 'forwards' (most commonly Sergio Agüero, Raheem Sterling, Leroy Sané, David Silva and Kevin De Bruyne) attacking together high up the pitch where they could do maximum damage, without leaving themselves open at the other end.

Chapter 3

Liverpool in possession overview

IN THE case of Liverpool, it is not as simple to break down their 4-3-3 system in terms of the exact number of players they used both to build up and to be positioned high, nor specifically which players they always used for each function. This is because there was more freedom in terms of their players' positioning, especially with regards to their full-backs and number 8s, who regularly performed different roles both within games and from one game to the next. Their roles depended on the opposition defensive set-up or the attributes of the individuals selected by Klopp for a specific game, but Liverpool's number 8s and full-backs were also actively encouraged to take part in build-up play one minute, before moving high up the pitch the next.

In *Klopp: Bring the Noise*, Peter Krawietz revealed that the coaching team wanted to 'implement a footballing idea that could be produced in a flexible manner under pressure'. In other words, in contrast to Guardiola's idea that the consistent optimal positioning of players leads to patterns of play being carried out more automatically, Klopp saw greater flexibility in his players' positioning and movements as a positive, as long as their movements followed the guidelines. Krawietz also spoke of 'using agreed procedures for creating space in areas where opposition teams were perceived to be most vulnerable'. These words demonstrate overlap between both Klopp and Guardiola's systems, with Liverpool, like City, looking to target specific opposition zones with well-rehearsed patterns.

The most interesting contrast between City's 4-3-3 and Liverpool's 4-3-3 was that both teams' wide players were generally positioned completely differently. Liverpool's wide players (whom we are going to label wide forwards), Sadio Mané and Mo Salah, would usually take up very narrow starting positions – it is ironic that Liverpool fans sing the lyric 'Mo Salah – running down the wing' in their tribute song to the Egyptian, yet he spent relatively little time actually out on the wing. Perhaps 'Mo Salah – running in behind' didn't have the same ring to it. As alluded to when noting the unusual wide positions of City's wingers, in terms of modern football trends it is fairly common to see wide players positioned narrowly. Crucially, however, Mané and Salah were positioned *high* and inside where they were always available to attack the defensive line by making a run in behind.

It is by no means rare for teams to position at least one of their wide players high as more of a wide forward, on the outside shoulder of the opposition full-back, ready to make a run in behind. But the striking aspect of Mané and Salah's positioning was just how high and inside they played, much of the time appearing more like two centre-forwards than wide players. From these narrow positions they were effectively able to attack the opposition's defensive line in three ways: 1) A diagonal inside run into the space behind the centre-backs. 2) A diagonal run outside into the space behind the full-back, often termed the 'channel'. 3) By receiving a pass to feet, either up against the full-back, or having dropped off into the pocket to receive. Which movement Mané and Salah chose depended on the location of the ball, the location of the space, and how the opponent defended. They were in the optimal positions to punish any positional mistakes made by the opposition defenders, both on an individual level or as a unit.

It is not true to say that Mané and Salah were always inside; in fact, Liverpool increased their system's flexibility even further throughout 2019/20 to enable their wide forwards to play more like wingers as a variation. But we are going to focus on their more regular and iconic starting positions. When Mané and Salah were positioned inside, they were not providing the width high up the pitch needed to stretch the opposition when they were narrow and compact. With Liverpool, three scenarios occurred concerning the provision of width (*Figure 6*), which we will explore in further detail in future chapters: 1) One or both of Liverpool's full-backs moved high and wide. 2) One of Liverpool's number 8s vacated the centre to move wide on the side where the full-back remained deep. 3) Liverpool didn't bother with width high up the pitch, at least on one side.

The first option was the classic modern trend of full-backs playing like wingers, a role in which Trent Alexander-Arnold and Andy Robertson excelled. Guardiola had number 8s of the quality of De Bruyne and Silva to assist the rest of the attackers with chance creation. Liverpool, on the other hand, were reliant on their full-backs for this function (*Graph 3*), as they did not possess such creative number 8s. In a similar reciprocal relationship to the one between City's number 8s and wingers, the narrow positions of Mané and Salah helped create space for Alexander-Arnold and Robertson, and vice-versa. However, Liverpool's full-backs were

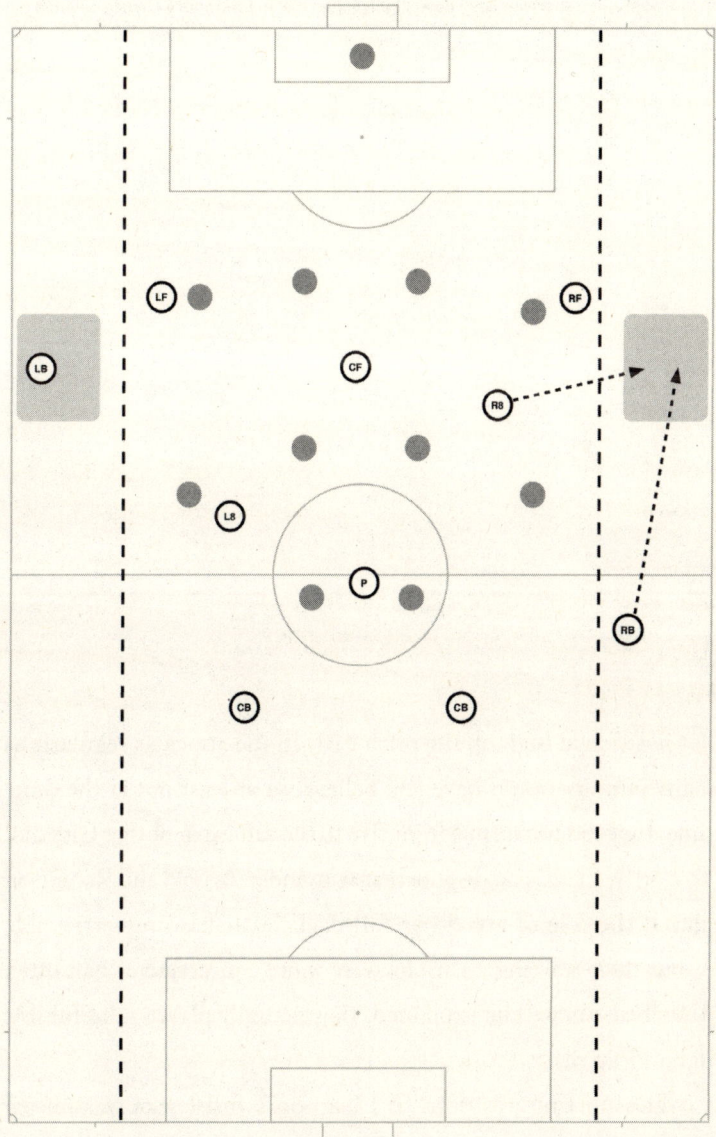

Figure 6. Examples of how Liverpool provided width high up the pitch each side. On the right, either Alexander-Arnold (RB) or Henderson (R8) could move into the space on the outside of the opposition full-back. On the left, Robertson (LB) would usually provide the width high up the pitch

Alexander–Arnold and Robertson have been highly influential in Liverpool's chance creation since 18/19

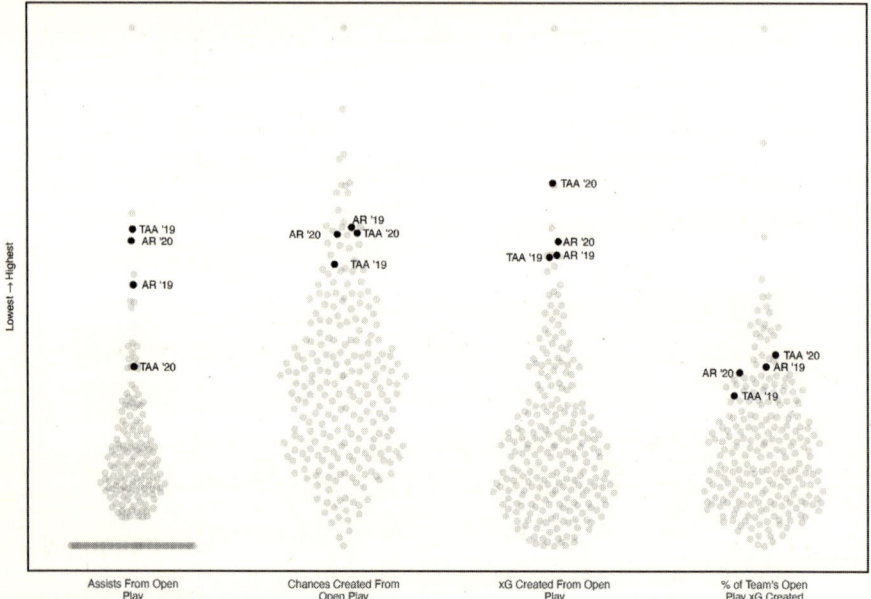

Note: Statistics are on a per–90 basis unless specified. Data are from full–back or wing–back starts only.
Each point represents a Premier League full–back in a season between 16/17 and 19/20 with minimum 10 starts, ranked from lowest up to highest for each statistic.
Data source: Stats Perform

Graph 3.

not positioned high up the pitch early in the attack as regularly as many pundits would have you believe, or at least not at the same time; they did not form a front five to the same extent that City did. To clarify, there is no dispute that Alexander-Arnold and Robertson played the role of attacking full-backs – that is unquestionable – but their starting positions were more conservative than often described. As will be explained, they actually played a useful role in build-up play.

The starting positions of Liverpool's full-backs was one of the differences between the Liverpool of Klopp's early seasons at Anfield, when both full-backs would regularly be very high up the pitch, and their record points-winning seasons, when their more conservative positions meant that counter-attacking behind the full-backs was not as readily available an option. There were also attacking advantages of starting deeper. Both Liverpool's full-backs often excelled in the attacking third having come on to the ball from a slightly deeper position. Their strength in the attacking third was crossing, either from deeper where they couldn't be closed down in time, or higher but having run on to the ball from deeper to cross early, often first time. Their other favourite move in the opposition's half was to pass inside to Mané and Salah, usually down the side of the centre-backs into the channel. This pass was more optimal from deeper, as the higher position of the opposition defensive line meant there was space to play the pass without running out of pitch.

The second option for creating width was for one of Liverpool's number 8s to move wide, on the outside of Salah and Mané. This was a fairly novel and interesting tactic as it involved a very non-traditional movement. Usually the role of a number 8 is to either play deep to help with build-up play, or higher between the midfield and defensive lines. But in both these scenarios, to play centrally – a number 8 is a type of *central* midfielder. The reason for moving wide was probably that if Liverpool's number 8 provided width higher up, neither Liverpool's wide forward nor full-back needed to, which was an especially favourable situation on Liverpool's right, as it meant that Salah and Alexander-Arnold's attributes could be used in different areas. Salah could be narrower in a position from where he could attack the defensive line, and Alexander-Arnold deeper, in a position from where he transformed into a playmaker from full-back. The fact that Liverpool's number 8s made these non-traditional movements meant that the opposition either had no solution, or they had to defend in an unnatural manner themselves; in wide areas they were used to defending against wide players or full-backs, not number 8s. Later on we will discuss which specific players tended to be used for this wider role, in which scenarios the movement occurred, and the confusion it caused for the opposition.

The third option, of not needing width higher up the pitch, was an exception to the rule that there must be a player wide at all times – a player providing width each side is an important aspect for most teams' in-possession systems. The main reason why Liverpool didn't always need a player wide was their willingness to play directly in behind the opposition defensive line early in the attack. There was no need to attack wide or to stretch teams horizontally if there was space to attack them vertically. It's not true to say that City never used this early vertical pass, but they tended to only do so when there was a high percentage chance of completing it – when there was clear space for their winger to run into behind the full-backs, either because the opposition defensive line was too high, or because there were large gaps between defenders. Usually, however, City wanted to access the space in behind by using a pass from the pockets, with a shorter through ball along the ground. In addition, City's principle solution if they couldn't play through a team was to play wide first, drawing the opposition out, before attacking the newly vacated space on the inside. The key for City was that these movements involved more control in terms of the likelihood of the pass being completed.

Liverpool, on the other hand, were not so concerned by control, which meant they were prepared to play long passes from deeper, regardless of whether they had a high percentage chance of completion. If they didn't win the first ball, they competed aggressively for the second ball and attacked from there, before the opposition could reorganise. There has arguably been no other Premier League team that peppered an opposition defensive line with passes in behind for their wide forwards making runs from the outside to the inside to the extent that Liverpool did, bucking the modern trend of favouring passes to feet. Guardiola himself once commented, 'Maybe Klopp is the best manager in the world at creating teams who attack the back four with so many players, from almost anywhere on the pitch. I don't think there is another team in the world attacking in this way with so many players capable of launching moves in an instant.' Liverpool possessed all the factors to make it a successful strategy: the passing ability of the likes of Virgil van Dijk and Alexander-Arnold, the pace of Salah and Mané, and the optimal timing of the run and pass, which came from practising this tactic over several seasons. This combination of factors significantly increased the chance of success, which often resulted in a one versus one with the goalkeeper; a very high reward.

The other consistent aspect of Liverpool's 4-3-3 was the role of Roberto Firmino, their centre-forward. There was little requirement for Firmino to make runs in behind, or even to remain high to occupy the opposition defensive line and prevent them from stepping forwards to close down between the lines; Mané and Salah's high, narrow positions did that for him. Instead, rather than push the defensive line back, one of his tasks was to bring a defender forward. Firmino dropped deeper, sometimes by just a few yards, and on other occasions all the way into central midfield. His movement was usually followed by a movement in the opposite direction from Mané or Salah; as Firmino dropped, Salah or Mané made a run in behind.

Later on we will discuss this interaction in greater detail, but for now it's important to highlight the two scenarios which occurred as a consequence of the opposite movements of Liverpool's front three (*Figure 7*): 1) Firmino's run deeper dragged at least one defender with him, opening up space in behind the defensive line for Salah/

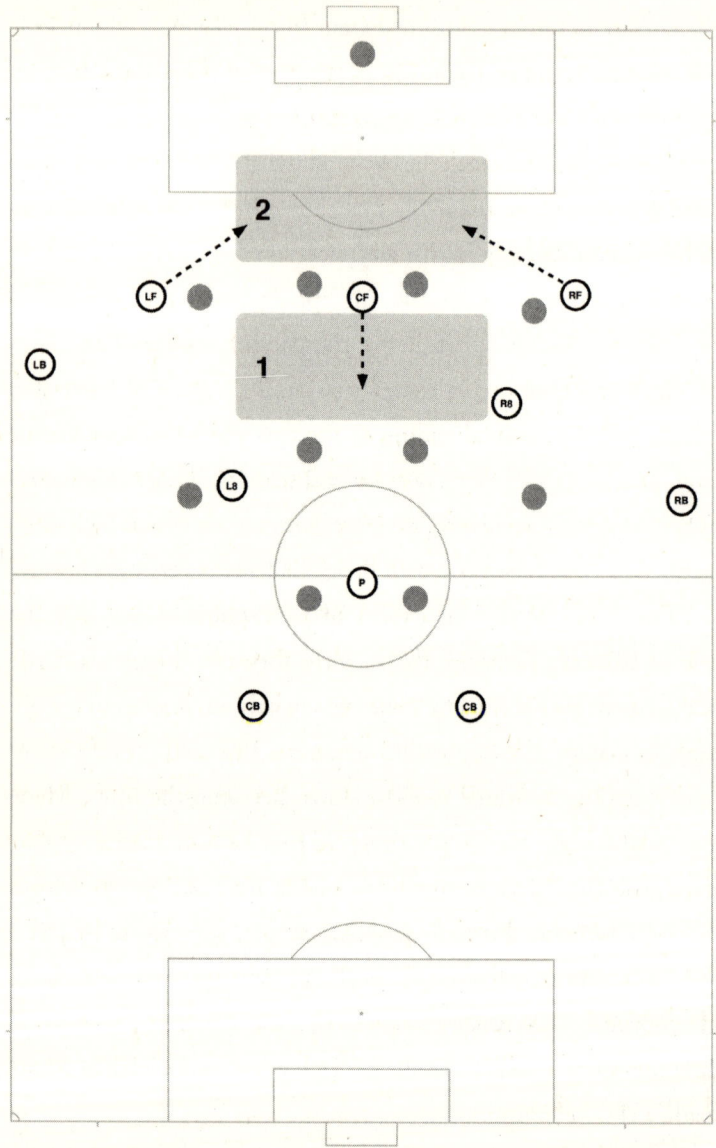

Figure 7. The shaded areas indicate the spaces which would open up due to the 'opposite' movements of Liverpool's centre-forward and wide forwards. 1) Space between the lines for Firmino (CF) to receive due to Salah (RF) and Mané (LF) pushing the defensive line back. 2) Space in behind for Salah and Mané due to Firmino pulling the defensive line forwards

Mané to run into. 2) Salah/Mané's run higher took the defensive line back with them, creating the space and time for Firmino to drop to receive the ball and turn. When Firmino dropped off even further into midfield to receive passes himself, he was usually doing so to fill a space that the opposition had vacated, or to create an overload effectively as a fourth midfielder. The main challenge for the opposition was how to mark a centre-forward who didn't actually play as a centre-forward, almost having a free role to take up undetectable positions, a role often termed a *false 9*. Firmino was such a problem because he rarely stayed in the same position, so could never fully be designated the responsibility of a specific opposition player.

The interaction between Liverpool's number 8s and full-backs was important for how the system functioned in terms of ensuring there were enough players to help build up and simultaneously protect against counter-attacks, but also enough players to attack higher up the pitch. One principle was for the full-back and number 8 each side of the pitch to adjust their positions using each other as a reference for where they needed to be. For example, if the number 8 one side was well in advance of the ball, Liverpool's full-back that side was usually more conservative. Equally, if Liverpool's number 8 had dropped deep to help with the build-up, the full-back on his side had licence to move higher. Or, at times both number 8s were positioned high which meant both full-backs needed to remain deep, or vice-versa. Of course, the specific counter-attacking threat of the opposition would also be taken into account. Left-back Robertson, in an interview with The Athletic, explained some of the process behind deciding when to move higher: 'It all depends what's happening around me. Sometimes it's on for the midfield to drive forward, sometimes it's on for us to drive forward. As long

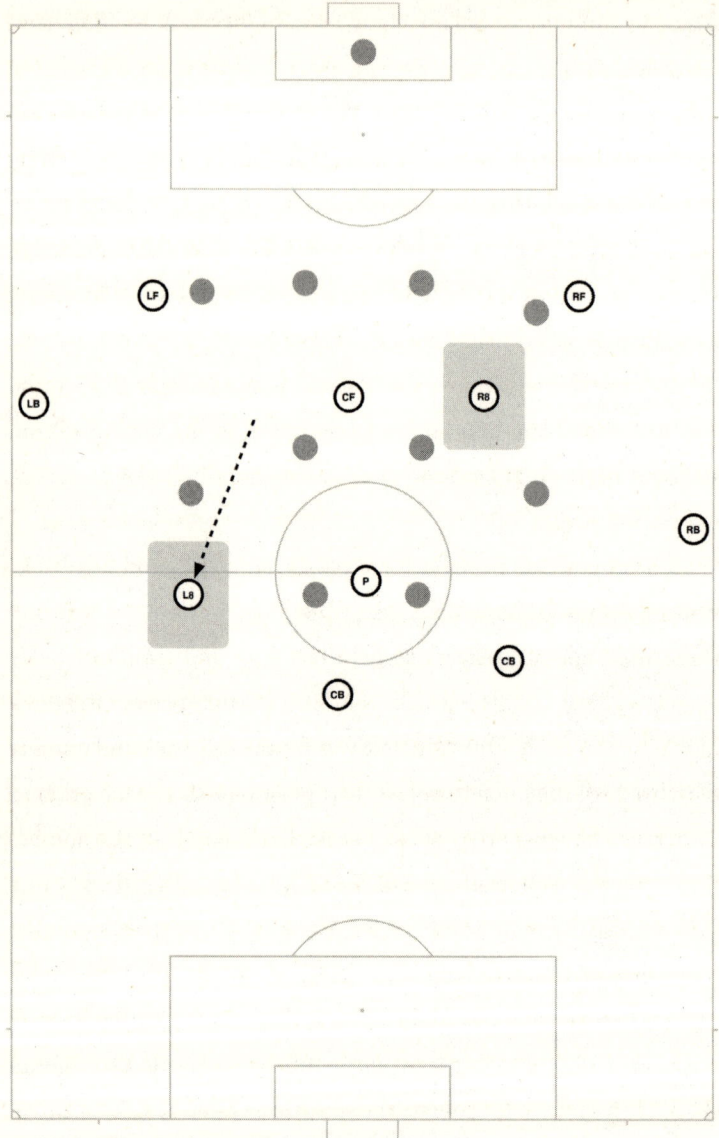

Figure 8. *Liverpool's number 8s often played lopsided. Wijnaldum (L8) tended to drop deep and wide to enable Robertson (LB) to move forward. On the other side, Henderson (R8) played high between the lines, and Alexander-Arnold (RB) was more conservative*

as the protection is right, that gives us the freedom to both go at the same time. If it's not, then whatever Trent does impacts on my decision-making and vice versa.'

Although there was plenty of flexibility, the general pattern, especially during 2019/20, was for Liverpool's number 8s each side to play designated alternative roles, in a 'lopsided' system (*Figure 8*). During build-up play, the tendency was for the right-sided number 8, usually Jordan Henderson, to move high, and for Alexander-Arnold to be a little more conservative, so he could drop deep and use his range of passing to help Liverpool progress the ball. Then on the left side, the tendency was for Liverpool's number 8, usually Georginio Wijnaldum, to drop deeper as a second pivot and for Robertson to move higher. However, in every game there would be multiple examples of both number 8s and full-backs performing different roles; it was not a rigid system.

So how could Liverpool's in-possession shape be defined in more detail than as a 4-3-3 where the number 8s and full-backs played lopsided? It was clear that City formed a build-up five and a front five. However, Liverpool's full-backs were neither consistently high enough to form a constant front five, nor consistently deep enough to form a constant build-up five. In Liverpool's lopsided 4-3-3 system, the players' positions through the middle of the pitch formed four lines of two players (*Figure 9*). The centre-backs were the first two, the pivot and the left-sided number 8 the second two, the right-sided number 8 and Firmino (the centre-forward) the third two, and Salah and Mané (the wide forwards) the final two. The full-backs started in varied vertical positions on the outside, making two of the twos into threes, depending on what the game situation, or the game itself, required. For example, Robertson could be positioned in line with Firmino and Henderson, or sometimes

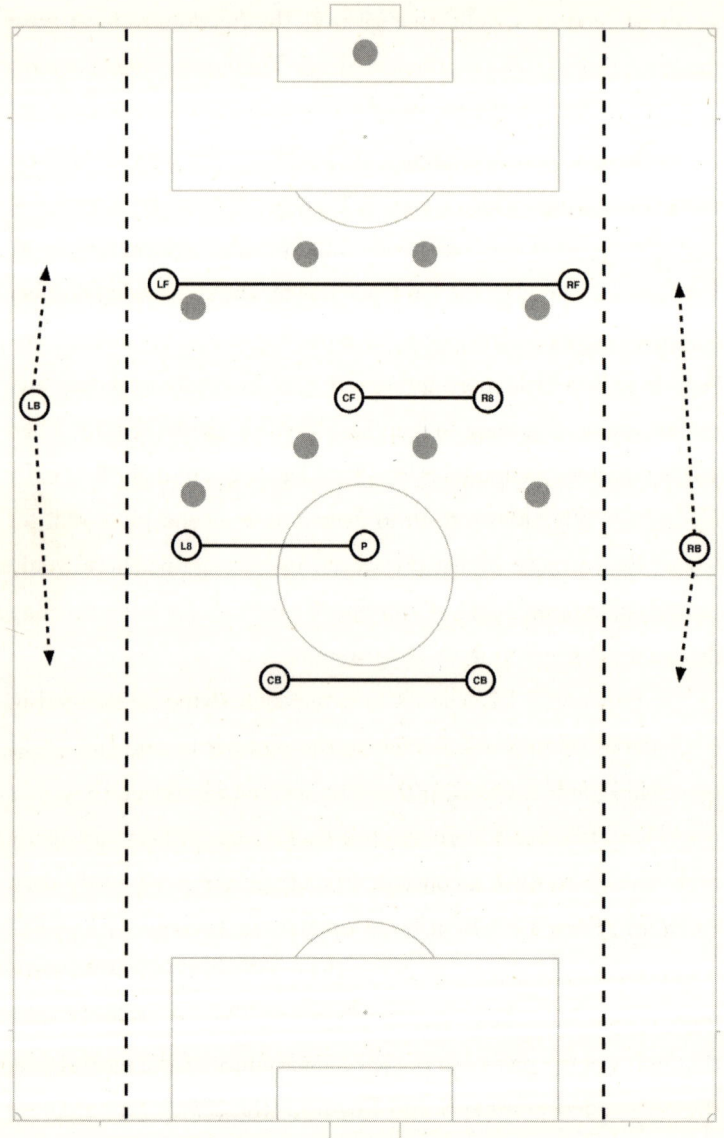

Figure 9. An example of Liverpool's regular shape in possession. Four lines of two through the middle, with the full-backs varying their positions to make two of the lines of two a three

even higher in line with Mané and Salah, while Alexander-Arnold could be positioned in line with Liverpool's pivot and Wijnaldum, or even deeper in line with the centre-backs.

In summary, Liverpool's players adhered to a general structure, but with significant flexibility to rotate and move into different spaces. This poses an interesting question: which team was more difficult for the opposition to defend against? Liverpool, whose strength was the ability to constantly vary their positioning and style of play fairly seamlessly? Or City, whose strength was the consistency of their system and style, which enabled them to carry out their movement patterns so fluidly and automatically?

Chapter 4

Build-up: an end to 'split' centre-backs

HAVING OUTLINED City and Liverpool's systems, it's time to move on to the specifics of how these two teams aimed to construct attacks. Build-up play has always been a vital aspect of Pep Guardiola's philosophy, with many of his ideas adapted from the work of his former manager and mentor at Barcelona, Johan Cruyff, while for Jürgen Klopp it appeared to become more and more important as his career progressed. To recap, City usually used both full-backs, their pivot, and of course their centre-backs, to build up, while Liverpool tended to use one of their number 8s deeper, enabling at least one of their full-backs to be positioned higher, but there was flexibility. When an opposition attempts to disrupt the build-up, being able to progress the ball beyond the first line of the pressure requires numerical superiority, high-tempo ball circulation, and, crucially, players positioned at optimal distances and angles to each other.

To be clear, we are not analysing situations deep in City and Liverpool's own half, as in these situations their goalkeepers were able to be involved in the move, so City and Liverpool's patterns were different to when building up higher up the pitch. In fact, City and Liverpool's goalkeepers would often move outside of their own penalty areas to assist with build-up. Intriguingly, City returned from their COVID-19 break during the 2019/20 season keen to involve Ederson in build-up play even higher up the pitch, well outside of his area. However, this tactic ended abruptly when City lost the ball with their goalkeeper way out of his goal against Southampton in July 2020, allowing Che Adams to score into an empty net.

However, in the seasons we are analysing, generally City and Liverpool's goalkeepers did not significantly get involved in the build-up when the ball was being circulated much higher than their own penalty areas, i.e. in the middle third. Rather than analysing various different types of build-up play against several different opposition set-ups, we're going to concentrate on a specific method used by City and Liverpool, which is perhaps the most interesting. The two teams formed the build-up shape we are going to analyse when faced with several different opposition set-ups, but perhaps to a greater extent against teams who used two players as the first line of their defensive block, rather than one or three, as it was most effective against a two-man first line of the block. For example, a team playing 4-4-1-1, 4-4-2 or 5-3-2 out of possession tends to use two players to disrupt the build-up. Before we outline the specific shape that City and Liverpool used to progress the ball beyond the first line of an opposition two-man block, it is necessary to assess previously used methods, many of which are still common practice for other Premier League teams.

A history of three versus two build-up

It is not uncommon to play with three central defenders in a back three against teams who play with two forwards, in order to maintain a three versus two overload, or spare man. This is often justified from a defensive point of view, but it can also be important from an attacking perspective in terms of bringing the ball out using the numerical advantage, with the idea that the opposition two find it difficult to adequately cover the three. However, clearly not all teams want to play with three central defenders whenever they face an opponent with a two-man first line of the press. Instead, teams playing with two central defenders in a back four began to form a back three by a central midfielder, the pivot, dropping deeper for the specific scenario of build-up play. To help explain why forming a back three is desirable, let's first assess how opposition teams generally look to disrupt the build-up with a two-man first line of the press against a 4-3-3, should the in-possession team not build up with a back three. If the pivot is in his orthodox position in front of the centre-backs, at a diagonal angle to each, there are several means by which the two opposition players could prevent ball progression.

In a common example (*Figure 10*), both opposition forwards start close together either side of the pivot, preventing the centre-backs from passing to him. Then, as the ball is passed, for example, from the left centre-back to the right centre-back, the opposition forward nearest to the right centre-back moves to close him down. His angle of approach should naturally prevent the centre-back from dribbling past him, while at the same time block the passing lane to the pivot, who, regardless, is still marked by the other opposition forward. He may even be able to simultaneously prevent the square pass back to the left centre-back, keeping the centre-back on the ball playing down his side.

However, at worst for the defending team, this square pass remains available. As the ball is passed back from the right centre-back to the left centre-back (*Figure 11*), the opposition forward

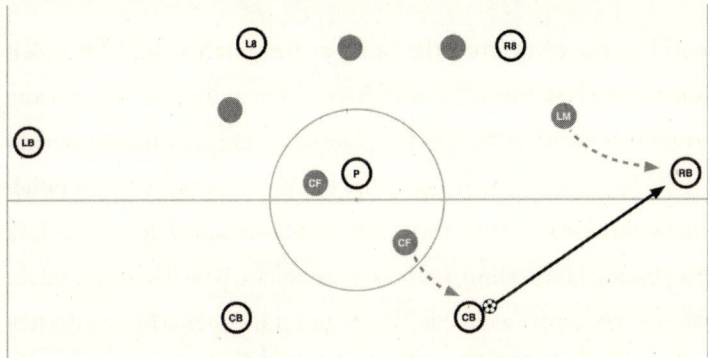

Figure 10. One forward marks the pivot, the other closes down the centre-back, who is offered the pass to the right-back, at which point the opposition wide player (LM) closes down and traps the in-possession team out wide

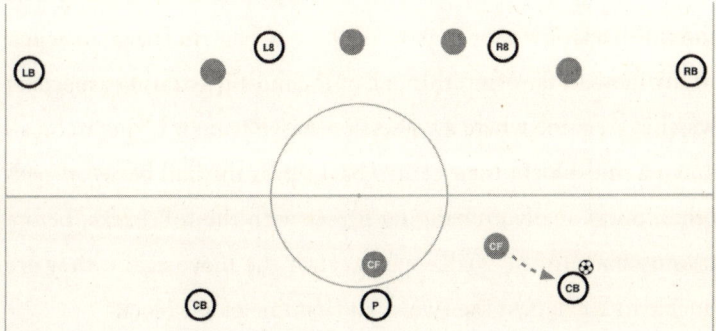

Figure 11. When the pivot drops between to form a back three, the two forwards can work together to prevent the pivot becoming the link to find the spare centre-back on the opposite side

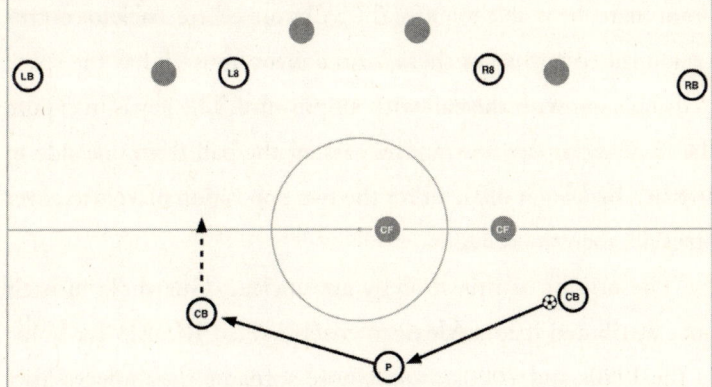

Figure 12. The pivot drops deep to form a triangular back three. In his deeper positions the pivot is more difficult for the opposition to press, enabling him to be used as the link between the two centre-backs, one of which can then 'exit' without pressure. However, the pivot ends up playing very deep, and the centre-backs have a big gap between them

marking the pivot does the same as his partner did previously, moving to close the left centre-back down and prevent him from dribbling out, or passing to the pivot. Suddenly, with both centre-backs closed down the scenario has become a two versus two rather than a three versus two; the pivot can't be accessed due to the lack of a passing lane to him, and even the square pass between centre-backs is no longer available. Without taking a risk by the centre-back trying to dribble past his man, the only realistic options would be to pass to the full-back, potentially leading to the team being 'trapped' deep and wide as soon as the opposition wide player closes the full-back down, or to pass all the way back to the goalkeeper. Many football fans find this one of the most frustrating aspects of watching a game where a possession-based team is trying to break down a mid-block; their centre-backs pass the ball between each other, occasionally exchanging passes with the full-backs, before passing back to the goalkeeper to start the move again; they are unable to break past the two-man first line of the block.

A solution emerged where the two centre-backs 'split' wider apart, enabling the pivot to drop in between them to form a three. From there, he is able to move the ball from centre-back to centre-back until either one of them, or the pivot himself, has the space to dribble out with the ball without pressure. The key is to expose the *three versus two overload* by passing the ball from one side to another, making it difficult for the two opposition players to cover one side, then the other.

The origins of this strategy are unclear; Guardiola himself once attributed it to a Mexican coach named Ricardo La Volpe in the 1990s and 2000s, from whose surname the unnecessarily fancy term 'La Salida Lavolpiana' was coined; the translation of the Spanish word *salida* is exit. The only real benefit of using this fancy term instead of calling the situation a *three versus two overload* is to emphasise that the function of the overload is to 'exit' the newly formed back three by stepping into space with the ball or completing a forward pass; the overload is not intended to retain possession between the three players for the sake of it. This method of forming a back three is especially common in teams who want to push their full-backs forward; the full-backs don't need to occupy their traditional space deep and wide because the centre-back nearest to them all but covers it by spreading wider. As a back three is formed behind them, the full-backs essentially become wing-backs in a back five. However, as with any tactic, the more widespread it became, the more teams developed solutions against it. If the pivot drops on to the same parallel line as the centre-backs, there is no reason why the two opponents cannot make the three versus two a two versus two, by one forward closing down the centre-back on the ball, and the other tracking the pivot, preventing him from receiving a pass in the first place, or should he receive, closing him down at an angle which blocks the pass to the left centre-back.

Naturally, a counter-solution emerged (*Figure 12*), in order to prevent the opposition from disrupting build-up in this manner, which is used both by teams who play with three central defenders in an orthodox back three, and by teams who play with a back four but use a back three to build up. The pivot, instead of only dropping as far as to be parallel with the two centre-backs, drops off a further five to ten yards, creating a diagonal backwards passing angle between himself and the two centre-backs, forming a triangle shape. Firstly, this gives the centre-back on the ball a backwards pass, making it impossible for the player closing him down to force him to only pass down his side of the pitch, or back to the goalkeeper. Secondly, this gives the opposition player marking the pivot more of a problem; if he follows the pivot deep before he has received the ball, he may allow himself to be bypassed by a pass on his inside from right to left centre-back. Or, if he remains deeper before the ball has been passed, ensuring that he blocks the passing lane between the two centre-backs, he will not be able to stop the pivot from receiving the ball; the increased distance to run to close him down from deeper once the pass to the pivot has been played makes it very difficult for him to affect the pivot's next pass to the left centre-back in time.

The other advantage to creating this triangular shape is that the pass from the pivot to the spare centre-back is an angled pass. While a square pass may break the first line of the block horizontally, an angled pass breaks it horizontally *and* vertically; in other words, it is also a forward pass. This means that by receiving the ball further forward than the first line of the block, or at least parallel to it, the centre-back has already 'exited'. This is true for a triangle which creates angled passes anywhere on the pitch; the keys to angled passes are simultaneous vertical and horizontal ball progression, which is more difficult for the opposition to disrupt.

During Guardiola's first season at City, his team would often build up with their pivot dropping deep between, or, when necessary, deeper than the centre-backs, forming the 1-2 shape described. Up until the end of the 2017/18 season, Klopp's Liverpool would build up in the same way. It is worth nothing that Liverpool still used this method during their record points seasons, but as a variation, rather than as their principle strategy. However, both City and Liverpool adapted their systems to ensure their pivot didn't need to drop so deep, and their centre-backs didn't have to play 'split' wide apart.

These are the two main disadvantages of building up with the pivot between the centre-backs. With the previous method, the pivot has to play so deep in possession that his passes are not able to have an impact in positions where they can cause the opposition significant damage. When a pivot drops so deep, often the opposition decide he is not in a dangerous enough position to close down, so he is allowed to have the ball, with the two opposition players instead spreading wider to concentrate on preventing the centre-backs from dribbling out. Secondly, the centre-backs playing wide apart is less than ideal for defending counter-attacks – the priority in these situations is protecting the centre of the pitch and therefore the goal. This means their recovery runs are often too large, leaving gaps between the two of them for the opposition to exploit. The pivot is not a defender, yet due to his deep, central position, on transition he has to defend as if he were a centre-back. Finally, City and Liverpool's pivot was often needed to press relatively high when City and Liverpool lost the ball, which he couldn't do from his deep position if his team lost the ball soon after having progressed it beyond the first line of the block.

Creating a diamond, four versus two build-up shape

We can now move on to how City and Liverpool tended to create their three versus two overloads in a triangular shape, while keeping the pivot in his traditional position, rather than have him drop between two centre-backs positioned wide apart. Both teams' build-up play was fundamental to their attacking play as it enabled them to attack with short, controlled passing, which in City's case was especially critical to how they progressed the ball to their front players and ultimately created chances. For Liverpool, who implemented the pattern described more and more fluidly as the 2018/19 and particularly 2019/20 seasons progressed, it could be suggested that there was a second function: to allow them enough time and control to play their classic long pass in behind at moments when Mané and Salah were in the optimal positions to make the runs, as opposed to being forced to play the long pass because the player on the ball was under pressure. Rather than relying on Fabinho, their usual pivot, to play this pass, Liverpool's build-up shape gave the likes of Trent Alexander-Arnold and Virgil van Dijk, the best long passers in the team, the time to use their passing ranges to great effect.

Following the common theme of the comparison between City and Liverpool, City tended to build up in a more set structure, whereas Liverpool varied the players they used. City's third player in the first line of the build-up was usually right-back Kyle Walker (*Figure 13*). The positioning was as follows: the right-sided centre-back, for example, Nicolás Otamendi, dropped slightly to become the deepest player in a central position, almost like a sweeper, leaving the left centre-back, often Aymeric Laporte, further forward to

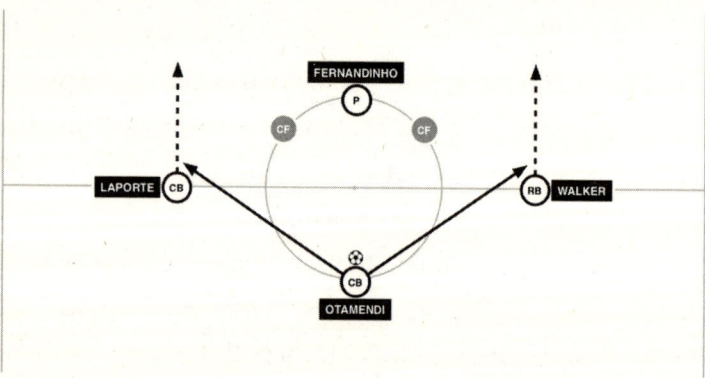

Figure 13. Deep, central position of Otamendi enabled him to pass in either direction, for either Laporte or Walker to 'exit' with the ball. Fernandinho's central position 'pins in' at least one of the two forwards, enabling Otamendi to choose which side to pass to. If one forward moved to close down Laporte and the other covered Fernandinho, Walker would be free the other side

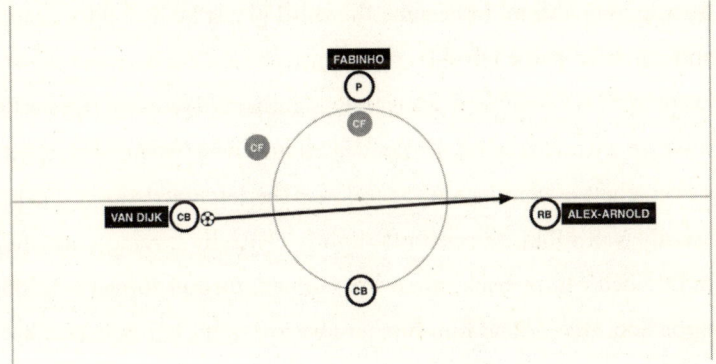

Figure 14. Alexander-Arnold would sometimes form the three, receiving inside where he could use his fantastic passing range, from a space where the opposition often didn't close him down. Often the other centre-back was missed out, enabling quicker transfer to the other side, giving the opposition less time to readjust

Otamendi's left side, and Walker further forward to his right side, parallel to Laporte. On occasion Liverpool would also use one of their full-backs, most frequently right-back Alexander-Arnold, to drop off to become the third player (*Figure 14*). However, an equally common method Liverpool used was for their left-sided number 8,

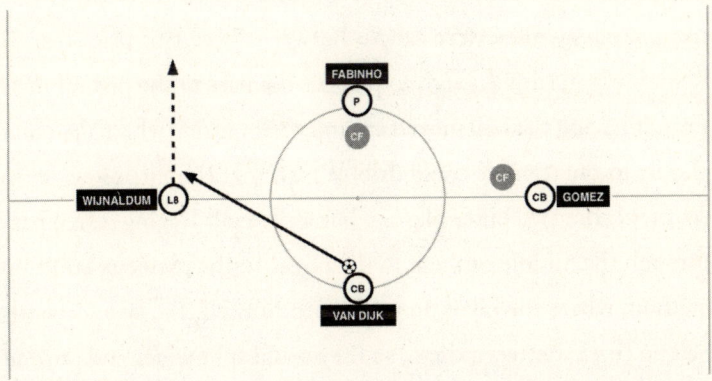

Figure 15. In this example the ball has just been passed back from Gomez to Van Dijk. Wijnaldum would drop to the side of the two forwards to form the back three and receive in space. From his slightly deeper, central position, Van Dijk was often given the time on the ball to pass forwards, often looking for Mané or Salah in behind

usually Wijnaldum, to become the third player by dropping deep, and crucially, to the left side of the centre-backs, not between them, keeping the two centre-backs closer together (*Figure 15*). If, as was the case with Liverpool, it was Wijnaldum who became the third player, the positioning was as follows: the left sided centre-back, usually Van Dijk, dropped off slightly centrally leaving both the right-sided centre-back, often Joe Gomez, further forward to his right side, and Wijnaldum further forward to his left side, parallel to Gomez.

In addition to the previously mentioned advantages to forming a triangular shape to build up (the constant availability of a backwards pass, and the ability to bypass the two forwards vertically as well as horizontally), there was another benefit. As the pivots, Fabinho and Fernandinho, could remain in higher, more orthodox positions, the shape formed was more of a 'diamond' 1-2-1, and the overload became a four versus two. This four versus two overload and the diagonal angles between each player made it extremely difficult for the two forwards. If they attempted to use their 'press and cover' strategy, they were caught between these two priorities: 1) Remaining narrow enough to prevent the pass to the pivot, but as a result having the ball moved around their outside where the outer players in the triangle could dribble forward. 2) Splitting wider to deal with the two outer players, but as a result leaving a free pass through the middle of them to the pivot. In the previous build-up method, where the pivot dropped deep himself, the two forwards had no threat between them, so they could split wider and prevent the two wide centre-backs from dribbling out. With the newer method, however, the outer player in the triangle whose nearest forward remained with the pivot was free to dribble out. If the forward did manage to close him down, he simply passed back to the deeper central centre-back, and the process was repeated the other side.

If the two opposition players did manage to split wider to cover the two outer players but also remain close enough to the pivot to make the pass to him risky, the dropped-off middle centre-back would often dribble forwards, forcing at least one of the forwards to move extra narrow to block the pass to the pivot, which was now a shorter pass (*Figure 16*). City's John Stones in particular did this very effectively, often pointing in front of him to make the forwards think he was instructing the pivot to move closer to receive. Due to these actions, space would open up for a pass to one of the outer players in the triangle. Some teams attempted to disrupt ball progression by placing one player around the pivot, and moving the other higher in an attempt to disrupt the triangle, forming more of a 4-4-1-1 shape. In this scenario, essentially the higher of the two opposition players could be bypassed in two ways. Firstly, if he positioned himself so he could block the passing lane between the two outer players in the triangle, the dropped-off centre-back, from his deeper central position, could be used as the passing link

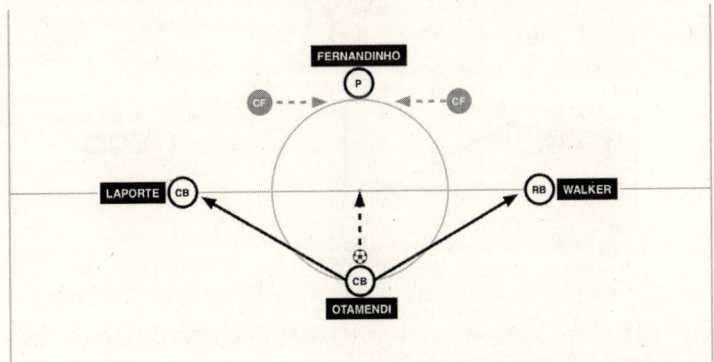

Figure 16. *If the two forwards split wide to cover the two outer players in the triangle, the middle centre-back would dribble towards them, forcing at least one of the forwards to move extra narrow, which gives more space for the outer player in the triangle to dribble out with the ball*

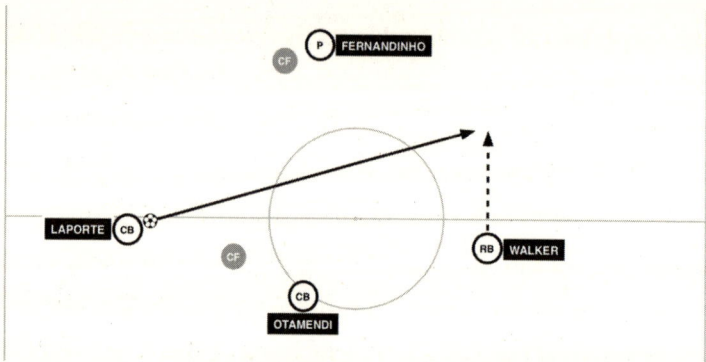

Figure 17. In this example the opposition is set up in more of a 4-4-1-1, with one forward between the two centre-backs, and the other forward around Fernandinho. A pass is still available between the two opposition forwards to Walker, who would often step forward to make an angle to receive, and to help transfer the ball from one side to the other. If the deeper forward moved higher to block the pass, Fernandinho would become free behind him

between the two outer players, enabling the ball to be progressed around the forward. Alternatively (*Figure 17*), if the forward moved higher in an attempt to prevent the use of the central centre-back as a passing link, the two outer players would be able to pass between each other on the forward's inside. Walker in particular was very adept at adjusting his position slightly further forwards to give

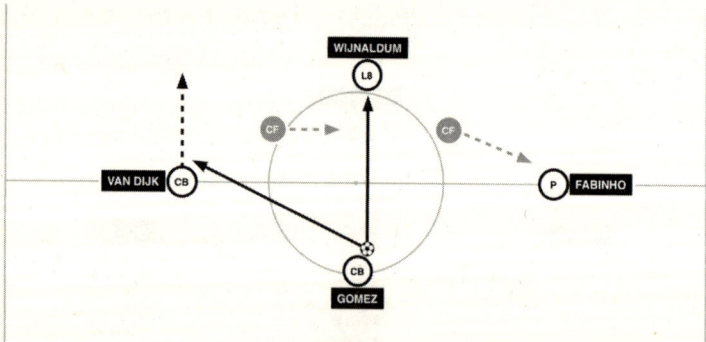

Figure 18. One of Liverpool's variations was for Fabinho to move to the right-side to become the third centre-back. Wijnaldum would then move to the centre to replace Fabinho as the pivot, either to maintain the option of a pass between the forwards (previously offered by Fabinho), or to occupy the other forward, which would then leave Van Dijk free. Crucially, the same 1-2-1 shape was maintained

an option for Laporte to bypass the higher of the two opposition players, who moved high early to anticipate the backwards pass to the central centre-back. By using Walker or Alexander-Arnold as the third player in the triangle, they were often given free possession simply because the opposition forwards did not see it as their job to close a full-back down, even if effectively the full-back had become a third centre-back.

Liverpool even had another variation of this 1-2-1 build-up shape (*Figure 18*). Their pivot moved to the right to become the third player in the triangle, and Wijnaldum moved centrally into the position the pivot vacated, maintaining the 1-2-1 shape and therefore the option of passing through the middle of the two forwards. With Liverpool, this was a very clear principle; when a central midfielder moved wider, another central midfielder had to fill his position centrally. These rotations within their structure made it difficult for the opposition to form a consistent pattern in how they looked to disrupt Liverpool's build-up play, as the picture kept changing around them.

The extent to which the central centre-back needed to drop off was pressure-dependent. If attempts to apply pressure to him were limited, there was no real need for the centre-back to drop too deep to receive and progress the ball. When there was pressure, the increase in depth to the build-up created by the central centre-back dropping off facilitated moving the ball to the other side, which meant the opposition players behind the ball had to do a great deal of running from side to side, tiring them out to the extent that a gap would often appear. The choice of which players to use to form the triangular shape was down to how the system functioned as a whole and the profiles of the players. As mentioned, for Liverpool this shape also had the function of increasing the opportunity to play their classic long pass in behind for Salah and Mané, because the increased control of the ball at the back allowed them the time to look up and execute the pass, without being rushed into it by pressure. Van Dijk in particular took advantage of this shape because, regardless of which position he took up in the triangle at a particular time, his position was often more central than if the pivot were deep in between him, causing him to spread wider. Making this pass from central areas meant Van Dijk could play an angled pass for *either* Salah *or* Mané, without being dictated to by any pressure on him.

This triangular back-three shape is fairly common in an orthodox back three system, i.e. one composed of three centre-backs. Nuno Espírito Santo's Wolves, for example, often used Conor Coady as a deep-lying middle centre-back, enabling him to spray passes all over the pitch under little pressure. David Luiz, too, excelled in this central dropped-off centre-back role in Antonio Conte's title-winning Chelsea team. Midfield pivots who are able to strike accurate long-distance passes have long been described as playing the 'quarterback' role. In American football, the quarterback receives a backwards pass before distributing to the best option he sees in front of him. With the rise of the deep-lying central centre-back, the likes of Coady, Luiz and Van Dijk have arguably become the quarterbacks, passing from positions which give them extra time to get their head up and execute the pass, and the ability to distribute to either side.

For City, using Walker as a third centre-back suited their whole in-possession 4-3-3 system. If Walker was going to take up these positions on a regular basis, it was vital that City's right-winger provided width. This was of course a fundamental positional requirement of City's right-winger regardless, so no matter how narrow or deep Walker was positioned, the right-winger always an option wide. The other advantage of using Walker as a third centre-back was his ability to travel with the ball at pace to 'exit' the first line of the opposition block, giving the opposition player tasked with shifting across to prevent him from coming out with the ball a really difficult task. Equally, having travelled further forward with the ball, an opposition player from the second line of the block would eventually have to close him down, vacating space or leaving one of Walker's team-mates unmarked to do so. Teams look more and more to find ways to access the space either side of the opposition first line of pressure, by placing a full-back or central midfielder there, as it is a space usually left vacant by the opposition. City and Liverpool's record points teams were not unique – many Premier League teams form shapes similar to those described in this chapter, using various different players. However, perhaps no team has done it as effectively by using a full-back as City did with Kyle Walker, nor as flexibly as Liverpool, who were able to smoothly transition from number 8 to full-back to pivot in the space to the side of the two forwards.

City consistently had a fifth player deep to assist with build-up: their left-back. We have already outlined that he was part of the build-up five, yet he has barely been mentioned so far when describing City's build-up play. This is simply because he didn't tend to become a third centre-back, as Walker performed this role from right-back. His exact positioning when City built up varied substantially depending on the opposition set-up. When Zinchenko and Delph were selected, they were almost always narrow, often to the extent that they could be considered a second midfield pivot. This meant that with the City pivot almost always marked, the left-back was positioned to the side of him, creating a 1-2-2 shape, and making him available to receive a pass to bypass the first line of the opposition's block. In this situation, City's left centre-back often didn't need to dribble out with the ball himself, as he had a simple pass available to City's left-back, positioned narrowly. On occasion, the left-back fulfilled the same function as the pivot; his presence would force one of the opposition forwards to drop back on to him, rather than attempting to disrupt City's back three build-up. This created a scenario whereby both opposition players in the first line of their block were occupied (by City's pivot and left-back), enabling City's back three (Walker plus the two centre-backs) to pass the ball from one side to the other and 'exit' with no pressure on the ball, often passing directly into City's wide wingers, who essentially took up the positions of very attacking wing-backs in a back five. As stated in the overview of City's 4-3-3 system, much of the time City's shape in possession was an artificially created 3-2-5, for example: Walker, Otamendi, Laporte; Fernandinho, Delph; Sterling, De Bruyne, Agüero, Silva, Sané. Next, we are going to analyse the role of City's left-back in more detail, and explain how Liverpool joined City in flipping the role of the modern full-back on its head.

When facing City and Liverpool's 1-2-1 shape, the only way to ensure consistent disruption of their build-up was to press with three players in order to reduce City and Liverpool's numerical superiority. For example, in a 4-4-2/4-4-1-1, one of the central midfielders could step on to Fernandinho/Fabinho, releasing the two forwards higher and wider as they wouldn't need to cover the pivot. Or, one of the wide players could move forward to form a three and press, for example, Walker, enabling the forward on the opposite side of the wide player to spread wider to cover the outer player in the triangle, and the other forward to press the dropped-off middle centre-back, while simultaneously blocking the pass to the pivot. The opposition had to weigh up whether committing an extra player to build-up was worth losing a player to defend deeper; if City or Liverpool were able to bypass the three-man block (of course, City and Liverpool had alternative build-up shapes and strategies against three-man blocks), they would take advantage of the increased space beyond it.

Chapter 5

The evolution of the full-back

CITY AND Liverpool using their full-backs as auxiliary central midfielders or centre-backs demonstrates how the role of the full-back has begun to come full circle. Until relatively recently, at least in English football, full-backs were seen as 'defenders first', who would support their wingers from behind before simply delivering crosses into the box, usually from fairly deep. The full-back was perhaps seen as the least important position in a team. As Jamie Carragher famously once remarked in a dig at his fellow *Monday Night Football* pundit Gary Neville, 'Full-backs are either failed centre-backs or failed wingers. Nobody grows up wanting to be a Gary Neville.'

More recently their role evolved, as coaches converted full-backs into a more attacking, wing-back style of player, who needed athleticism to get up and down the pitch, as well as the ability to either run with the ball and/or cross with quality. As wingers tend to possess these attacking attributes, coaches began to convert them into full-backs, especially as the attacking full-back role meant that they would tend to receive the ball in positions similar to a traditional winger. In his first season at City, Guardiola himself occasionally used natural winger Jesús Navas as a right-back, a role he continued to play with distinction, for Sevilla, after leaving City. However, the role of this position as a whole may be evolving again, with full-backs beginning to be seen as players who help to construct the attack.

In the case of Trent Alexander-Arnold, he helps build the attack to the extent that he could be considered a playmaker. Liverpool's right-back himself commented that he and Robertson 'want to change the way the position has previously been thought about'. Using full-backs to help construct the attack makes sense. The perception exists that full-backs, especially when receiving passes in fairly deep areas, are not players who need to be prioritised by the opposition, so they tend to be given more time on the ball. An evolution already happened with centre-backs for the same reason: modern centre-backs are required to have the ability to start attacks, partly because the opposition usually allows them to have plenty of the ball, in locations deemed to be less dangerous. Concerning full-backs, the instruction for many wide players out of possession is often along the lines of: stay narrow to protect the pass inside of you between the lines, and allow the ball to go their full-back. So if full-backs are likely to be given more time on the ball than other players, why not select a player at full-back who has the attributes of a playmaker? The counter-argument to this is that for most teams the first priority of a full-back is defending – being good with the ball is a bonus. However, for teams like City and Liverpool, who spent the majority of the game with the ball, attempting to break teams down, could they afford to select full-backs who weren't excellent in possession?

City – full-back as a central midfielder
From the beginning there was a clear indication that Guardiola wanted his full-backs to play very narrowly in positions usually

filled by central midfielders. City would often form the 2-3-5 shape which he developed at his previous team Bayern Munich where he inherited technical, tactically intelligent full-backs such as Philipp Lahm. However, he soon abandoned this idea at City, where he didn't inherit full-backs with the necessary attributes. In his first season the left-back role was mainly filled by Gaël Clichy, who was more of a classic modern attacking left-back, unsuited to an auxiliary central midfielder role. Following his first season, Guardiola was given the chance to sign full-backs more suited to the roles he wanted them to perform. However, by bringing in Kyle Walker and Benjamin Mendy, Guardiola's intentions were unclear, as both had previously played very attacking roles at Tottenham and Monaco respectively. The subsequent conversion of Walker into a deeper role was successful to the point that England used him as a centre-back in a back three during the 2018 World Cup. In the case of Mendy, however, he was unable to have a major impact during City's record points seasons. Firstly, due to multiple injuries, at the time of writing he is yet to have had a sustained period of availability. Secondly, because of how successfully Guardiola converted two natural central midfielders with completely different attributes to Mendy, Fabian Delph and Oleksandr Zinchenko, into left-backs.

When Mendy did play, although there were occasions on which he did take up very narrow positions, the majority of the time, and especially during Guardiola's fourth season, he was used in an wider attacking role which enabled him to use his pace and crossing ability to create chances. Whether or not this was because Mendy was not suited to playing a narrow, almost central midfield role is unclear; did Guardiola only discover this following his arrival? If not, then why did Guardiola sign him specifically? Perhaps

Guardiola had a desire to have an option to attack in a different way on City's left than their right. City's manager hinted towards this in an interview between the 2017/18 and 2018/19 seasons, commenting, 'Mendy has the energy to go up and down so we can attack in different ways.'

Using Mendy higher enabled City to position their left-winger more narrowly when it was appropriate to do so. Consequently, this enabled the team to play with a number 8 deeper as a second central midfield pivot instead of two high number 8s when required. Alternatively, Mendy enabled them to attack with six players ahead of the ball instead of five, while building up with four not five. The latter certainly seemed to be something Guardiola moved towards following his record points seasons. This may have been influenced by teams showing a greater tendency to defend deep against City – perhaps Guardiola felt they required a sixth player in the opposition third when attacking, and a maximum of four players deeper to build up and prevent counter-attacks.

With Mendy largely injured during City's record seasons, the use of Delph and Zinchenko as left-backs, either by accident or design, enabled Guardiola to revert to his original idea when taking over at City: that the left-back moves narrow to become a left-sided second midfield pivot. This is the role that João Cancelo excelled at during 2020/21, as both a right-back and left-back. During City's earlier seasons, at times, Walker also advanced into central midfield positions alongside the pivot, especially if the opposition left a passing lane between him and Laporte, enabling the ball to be transferred to him more quickly, rather than via the right-sided centre-back. How the opposition defended was the key; sometimes Walker needed to be deeper to form a back three, but on other occasions higher to form a central midfield three. By stepping either forwards or backwards, Walker adjusted his position to where he could receive a pass, enabling City to transfer the ball from their left to their right with controlled possession. However, when Delph and Zinchenko played, it was predominantly City's left-back who took up a position in central midfield, alongside Fernandinho.

But why use a left-back in a central midfield position? We have already discussed how the traditional wide position of a full-back was redundant for City because their wingers provided the width. It has also been explained how, in order to create the optimal angle to supply their wingers, the full-backs had to be positioned more narrowly than the winger. But why so narrow that they were effectively in central midfield positions? Two reasons could be suggested, both relating to the principle of numerical superiority in the centre of the pitch: 1) In these ultra-narrow positions they could usually receive without pressure, as they were the spare man. 2) Their position made the opposition defend ultra-narrowly, moving players away from City's wingers, aiding both the winger's supply and the situation he faced when receiving.

When you consider the fact that Delph and Zinchenko were naturally central midfielders, and were therefore accustomed to receiving and passing from central positions, their roles made sense. Usually the only natural opposition player to close them down was their wide player, because everybody else had a job to do against City's front five and midfield pivot. When, for example, Delph wandered inside alongside City's pivot, could the opposition wide player follow him in so far? If he did then the opposition's midfield line would immediately lose a player, opening up space. For example, if the wide player followed Delph all the way inside, Laporte had a free pass to Sané, or even to Silva, who could move slightly wider to receive from his position in the pocket (*Figure 19*).

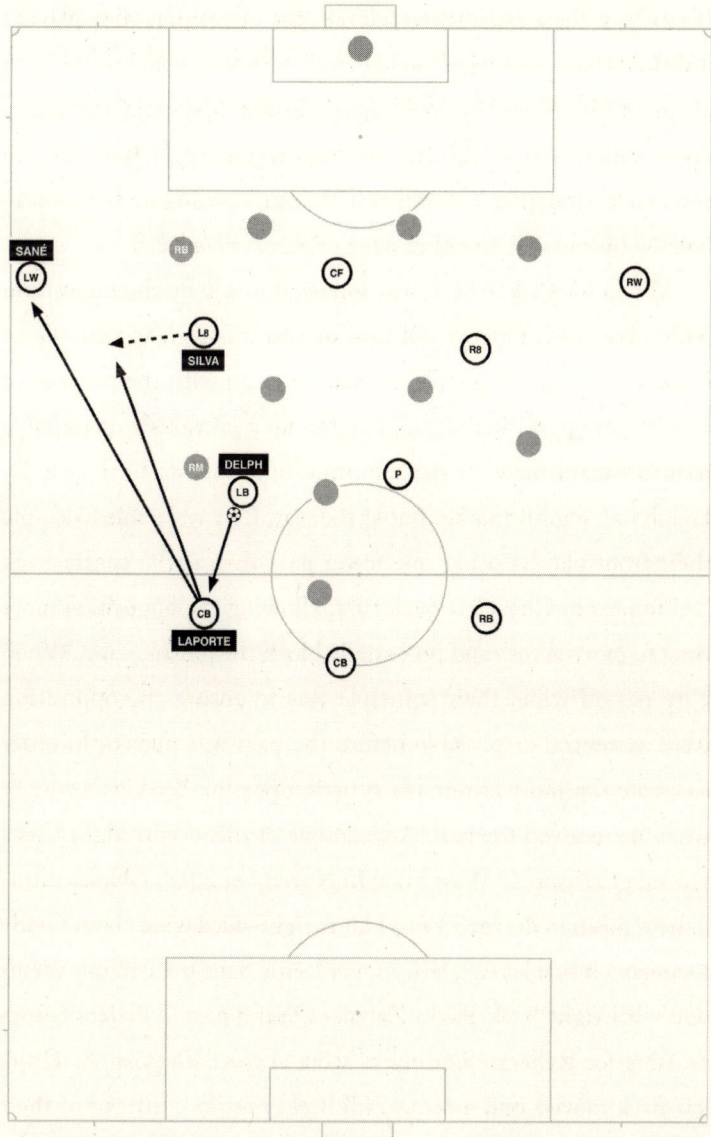

Figure 19. In this example the opposition wide midfielder has moved narrow to close down Delph in his central midfield position, meaning Laporte has an available passing lane to Sané. Alternatively, Silva would often move on the outside of the opposition wide player to receive in the space vacated by the opposition wide midfielder

If either of these passes were played, the opposition wide player's position would have been too high and narrow to help his full-back against City's winger by doubling up, leaving a potential one versus one situation. You would often see this exact move; Delph made the run inside, dragging his marker with him, opening up the passing lane on his outside, to either Sané or Silva (*Figure 20*).

When City's left-back was followed inside by the opposition wide player, his narrow position or run was a clear example of the City concept of one player making a run with the purpose of moving an opposition player, to open up a previously unavailable pass to a team-mate, or space for him to move into to receive. By Delph moving his marker out of the way, City were able to supply their front players using one fewer pass than if the centre-back had to pass to City's left-back first, allowing the opposition more time to move across and potentially block the passing lane. When City passed wide, their principle was to ensure the opposition were as central as possible before the pass was played, in order to create the most favourable situation possible for City's winger when he received the ball. An example of this occurred for City's second goal away to West Ham in November 2018. Delph's ultra-narrow position dragged West Ham's right-sided wide player Grady Diangana inside leaving left-winger Leroy Sané isolated one versus one with right-back Pablo Zabaleta. Sané beat Zabaleta before crossing for Raheem Sterling to score at the back post. As City's left-back moved into a central midfield position, instead of their wide player being dragged inside to close him down, could one of the opposition's central midfielders move higher to close down? In theory yes, but in doing so he would leave City's number 8 free in the left pocket, a problem which we will discuss in more detail later on.

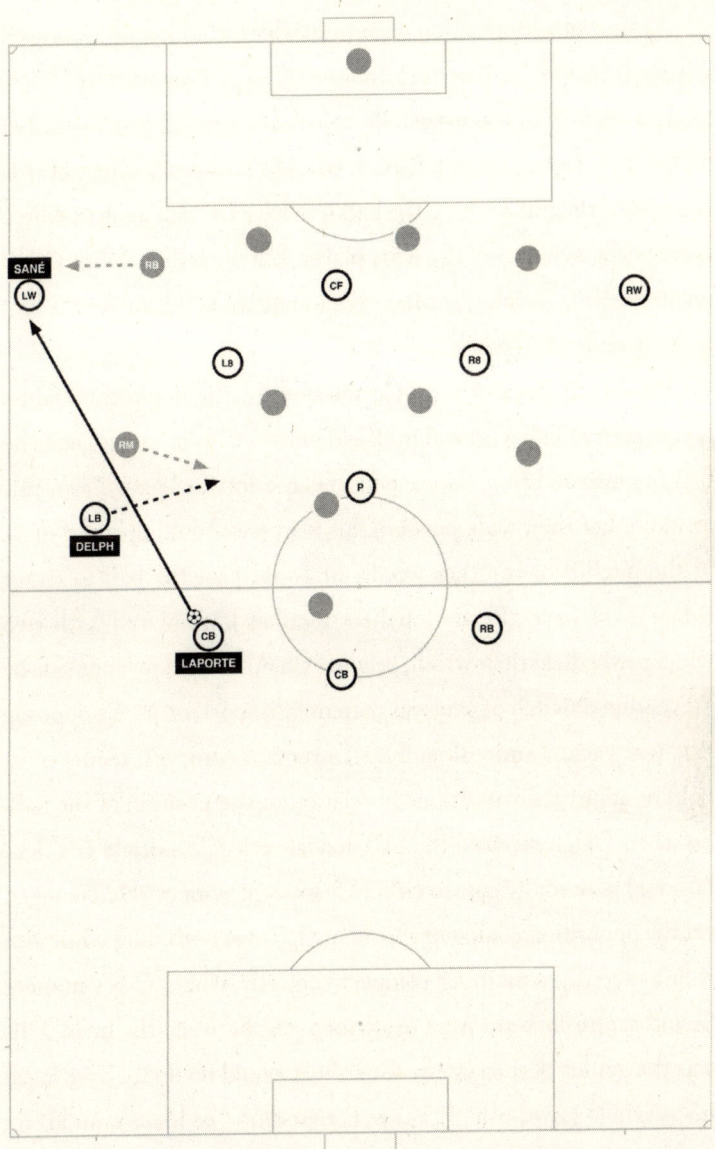

Figure 20. In this example the ball has been passed from City's right to Laporte. Delph makes a run inside, taking the opposition wide player with him, which creates a passing lane straight from Laporte to Sané, who finds himself one versus one with the opposition right-back

At times the opposition wide midfielder wouldn't follow City's left-back inside, leaving him free to receive. This idea of Delph being a spare man was especially apparent when City had attacked down their right. City's left-back would often cross over towards the side of the pitch where the ball was located, into an area where there was no chance of the wide player following him. With City's pivot marked, Delph was often free to receive and transfer the ball to Sané wide on the left.

Due to the lack of a simple solution for the opposition, when Delph moved into a central midfield position, on most occasions he had the required time on the ball to play a forward pass. From this inside rather than wide position, his next pass could open up more of the pitch – or in other words, he could pass the ball to either side. As we have already touched upon, as City played with two wingers who held their width, keeping City playing down one side by preventing a switch of play was extremely important, as the opposite side was vacant and vulnerable. To remain compact, teams must hold or adjust their positions in relation to the position of the ball. So when Delph received the ball in a left central midfield position, he could potentially pass to either City's right-winger *or* left-winger, yet the opposition could not spread out to cover both sides while also simultaneously remaining compact centrally, where City's number 8s and centre-forward were ready for a pass between the lines. This was the genius of the system: Guardiola would no doubt have loved his midfield pivot, usually either Fernandinho or İlkay Gündoğan, an excellent passer of the ball, to frequently play forward passes from central midfield during the build-up phase, but every opposition team concentrated on marking the pivot very tightly.

But why use the full-backs as alternative second pivots when the pivot was marked, instead of asking Silva, City's left-sided number

8, to drop deep to receive? This would be a more natural pattern for the opposition to cover, as a number 8 dropping deep to receive is a common pattern, and the opposition central midfielder covering him would not see it as unusual to track the movement. Even if Silva did manage to lose his man and drop to receive a pass, it would result in City converting from a front five to a front four, with nobody in the pocket which the number 8 vacated. Or, to maintain the front five, Delph would have to move high and wide and their winger narrow. While this would have been an effective alternative strategy, it would have taken away the advantages of City's version of 4-3-3 which we have already highlighted: that the full-back didn't need to move beyond the ball during the build-up phase, so he was in a better position to defend counter-attacks. In addition, City's winger being able to maintain width was an important aspect of the system, in terms of the problem it gave the opposition in adequately defending both sides of the pitch.

On occasion, there was another variation that City used which enabled Silva to drop deeper while maintaining a front five, without the winger needing to move more into the pocket. Following a pattern regularly seen during Guardiola's spell with Bayern Munich, City's left-back would move into a narrow position *higher up* the pitch, in the pocket as part of the front five. The aim here was the same as previously: to act as a decoy to keep the opposition extra narrow in order to create space for City's winger. Mendy would often make this run when he played as his attributes were more suited to this higher position, from where he could make an underlap on the inside of the winger, than to assisting building up as a pivot. Instead of enabling the number 8 to play deeper, on occasions this pattern was used to allow the number 8 to play more centrally, as part of the strategy mentioned previously, to move a sixth player higher.

Instead of their number 8s dropping deep, selecting a left-back with the qualities of a central midfielder allowed City to effectively play with four midfielders (the left-back, pivot, and two number 8s) around the opposition's two or three central midfielders, while simultaneously maintaining a two-winger system. A counter-argument against the idea of selecting a central midfielder at left-back is that the most important thing for a full-back is to be able to defend. There is no doubt that Delph and Zinchenko did cost City goals with their lack of knowledge and attributes to play the position (Delph, for example, was at fault for Son Heung-Min's goal in the Champions League quarter-final first leg against Tottenham Hotspur in April 2019), but these moments were few and far between, because City didn't have to defend deep very often. As Guardiola once said about his strategy with Barcelona, 'We want to dominate the ball because without it we are a horrible team.' Therefore, with their high percentage ball possession and high pressing strategy, neither his Barcelona team, nor his City team, had to do a great deal of defending in deep areas as a back four unit, where their left-back could potentially cost them a goal with, for example, poor positioning or marking in his own box. Besides, arguably Delph and Zinchenko were no poorer defensively than many 'modern', attacking full-backs; Mendy being one of them.

As we transition from City's build-up phase to attacking phase, it is an appropriate time to analyse the specifics of some of the alternative 'formations' Guardiola used during his time at City, as they were actually very similar to the 4-3-3, *in possession*. These alternative formations highlight the fact that with the ball it was the positioning of the players, rather than the formation itself, which was the important aspect. As mentioned previously, when Walker dropped to become a third centre-back, the 4-3-3 could be labelled a 3-2-5 (or 1-2-2-2-3) to be more specific. When Guardiola changed to an orthodox back three using three 'traditional' centre-backs, the in-possession shape they took up was usually identical – a 3-2-5 (1-2-2-2-3); the only difference was the out-of-possession shape was a clear back three with wing-backs, whereas City's 4-3-3 featured a back four. Guardiola even once played a back-three system without traditional full-backs in the wing-back positions, out of possession, instead using wingers Sterling and Sané as wing-backs. For Guardiola, the 3-2-5 was a desirable in-possession shape. Arguably, much of the increase in popularity of the 3-4-3 system (basically a 3-2-5 in possession) is due to the the natural shape this formation enables. A 3-4-3 provides a useful spread of players in different horizontal and vertical lanes that is awkward for the opposition to defend. Antonio Conte's title-winning Chelsea side, for example, played a 3-4-3 which merged into a 3-2-5 in possession, with the wing-backs pushed on high to form the front five. In possession it was a very similar shape to City's version of 4-3-3. In fact, Chelsea's use of right-back Cesar Azpilicueta as a right-sided third centre-back has parallels with City's use of Kyle Walker in this role, in possession. Instead of playing a conventional 3-4-3, using three orthodox centre-backs, forcing City to defend as a back three out of possession, Guardiola found a way to play a 3-2-5 in possession, but while maintaining a back four defensive system.

Another alternative formation Guardiola used with City, albeit not in their two record points seasons, was 4-2-3-1, yet the way City built up was very similar – 1-2-2-2-3, or 3-2-5. The only difference was that in the 4-2-3-1, the 3-2-5 in-possession shape was formed by alternative players; Guardiola played two traditional central midfielders as the double pivot and one of the full-backs higher, allowing the left-winger to play in one pocket and the number 10 to play in the other. The other winger still played wide, which meant the full-back on his side became the third centre-back. The similar way in which Guardiola's City built up across all systems demonstrates that for City's manager, it was the positioning of the players in possession, rather than the formation's broad label (3-2-5, 4-3-3, 4-2-3-1), which was of primary importance.

The questions many modern managers seem to ask themselves before picking a team or choosing a formation to play, appear to be along the lines of: 1) How many players do we need to build up with, and how do they need to be positioned, in order to create the required numerical superiority to progress the ball? 2) Who are the best players/positions to place between the lines, and in which specific spaces to do they need to be positioned? 3) Which player/position should provide the width each side to stretch the opposition horizontally and take advantage of space in wide areas? 4) Which player/position should be high, stretching the opposition vertically and providing an option to attack in behind?

Trent Alexander-Arnold – the David Beckham of full-backs?

While full-backs performing midfield roles is a fascinating development, arguably Trent-Alexander-Arnold's transformation into a unique playmaker from right-back was even more of a role change for a full-back. Later we will analyse the threats of both Alexander-Arnold and left-back Robertson higher up the pitch, but first let's assess the Liverpool right-back's deeper role, which helped Liverpool transition from build-up play to attack. As already outlined, he frequently moved inside as more of a third centre-back or central midfielder, but even when he retained more of a traditional right-back position slightly wider and higher, he in effect acted as a playmaker.

There was no apparent benefit for Liverpool in terms of their system of play for Alexander-Arnold to receive the ball deep and/or narrow like Kyle Walker did for City, because Salah, unlike City's right-winger, was not usually positioned wide. However, due to the incredible range and accuracy of Alexander-Arnold's long-distance passing, even from deep on the touchline he could in theory pass to anybody on the pitch. On occasions he even attempted to play Sadio Mané through on goal, striking a pass which no other Premier League right-back would dream of attempting. Alexander-Arnold also regularly managed to fire difficult passes to Roberto Firmino between the lines, even when a passing lane didn't appear to be available. Here we are going to analyse two of his most common, effective passes from deep: 1) A switch of play to left-back Robertson. 2) A pass into the channel between the opposition left-back and left centre-back for Salah. Note that Robertson would also drop deeper at times, from where he passed into the channel for Mané, and switched play to Alexander-Arnold. However, there is no doubt that Alexander-Arnold executed these passes with an unrivalled regularity and quality, so we're going to use him as the example.

Full-back to full-back – a unique switch of play

A switch of play to a full-back is a widely used pass in football. The interesting aspect to this pass, however, is that it moved the ball directly from one full-back to the other. This particular pattern of play between Alexander-Arnold and Robertson developed into a trademark, possibly unique tactic, at least in Premier League football. It is not unusual to play with both full-backs advanced, occasionally crossing the ball to each other, but that is a scenario which has different requirements in terms of the opposition's positioning, because it takes place nearer to the opposition goal. In 2019/20, Alexander-Arnold ranked first in the Premier League for successful crossfield passes from one full-back to the other full-back, and Robertson ranked fourth. It wasn't the volume of these passes which was a problem for the opposition – just four per cent of Alexander-Arnold's successful passes were to Robertson – but the effectiveness of the pass when it occurred. To explain why, let's reiterate the principles of defending. When Alexander-Arnold received the ball on the right, the opposition had to move across accordingly to a certain extent, in order to remain compact; any team who wants to remain compact must move across when the opposition right-back has the ball. When Alexander-Arnold received near the touchline, the furthest opposition players on the opposite side of the pitch to Alexander-Arnold would usually be roughly in line with the furthest point of the six-yard box, or maybe even narrower, in line with the far post, in order to maintain compactness both centrally, and on the side of the ball.

Against every other team in the Premier League, the left-back on the far side of the pitch would be irrelevant, because he couldn't be reached without a shorter pass from the right-back to a team-mate inside of him, who would then switch the play himself. The principle here is that as the ball is passed inside to, for example, a centre-back or central midfielder, the opposition lines shift across with it, enabling their furthest players on the opposite side to be closer to the left-back should a switch of play occur. However, the ability of Alexander-Arnold to strike this switch of play *directly* from right-back, close to the right touchline, meant that the opposition were likely to be caught too far over the other side to get to Robertson in time. This is why the variation in Alexander-Arnold's passes was so effective; the opposition didn't know if he

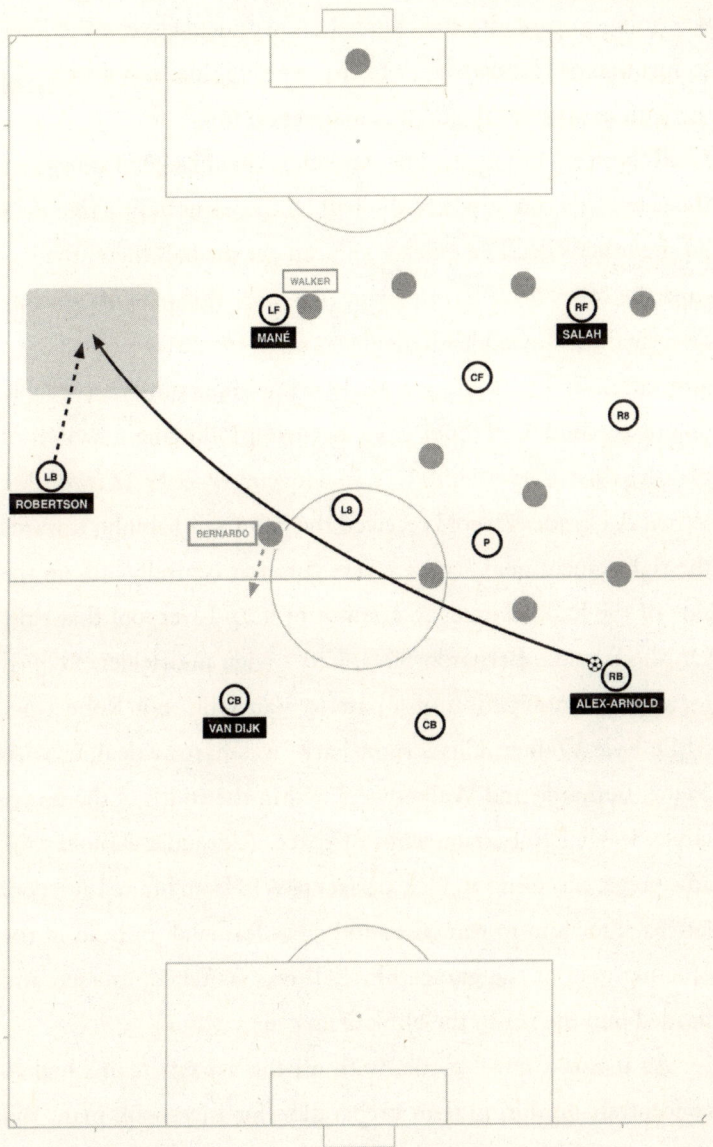

Figure 21. *The situation for Salah's goal against City in November 2019, following a switch of play between Alexander-Arnold and Robertson. City wide midfielder Bernardo took a couple of steps forward anticipating a pass to Van Dijk, enabling Robertson to be found untracked with a left-footed switch of play. City right-back Walker was occupied inside with Mané, which meant he wasn't able to get out and prevent Robertson's cross in time*

was going to pass into the channel on his side, between the lines to Firmino or Henderson, or to the opposite side, and it was very difficult to position themselves to cover all three.

Robertson, talking to The Athletic, explained, 'As teams press the side of the pitch where the ball is, there's usually a free man on the other side. The quicker you can get the ball there, the less time the other team has to adapt.' The fact this pass often came directly from Alexander-Arnold was often the difference between adaptation and conceding a goalscoring opportunity. Arguably one of the best Liverpool goals occurred following a switch of play, against City themselves in November 2019 (*Figure 21*). When Alexander-Arnold received the ball from Fabinho towards the right touchline, City were very compact centrally and on the side of the ball, in order to attempt to keep Liverpool that side. On the far side, Bernardo Silva, City's wide midfielder, stepped forward in anticipation of a pass to Van Dijk, not Robertson, while Kyle Walker, City's right-back, was narrow dealing with Mané. Bernardo and Walker were within the width of the centre circle, leaving Robertson acres of space. Alexander-Arnold took advantage, executing an inch-perfect pass in front of the Liverpool left-back for him to run on to and cross for Salah to head in the opening goal of the game. The ball was switched, crossed and headed into the net in the blink of an eye.

As it was a novel tactic, with all the aspects teams had to concentrate on during their preparation for Liverpool, many did not appear to have a plan specifically for preventing the switch of play from full-back to full-back, and so they were caught out fairly regularly as Liverpool's full-backs perfected the move. The solutions which some teams came up with consisted of two parts (*Figure 22*): 1) Preventing the pass in the first place. 2) Adapting

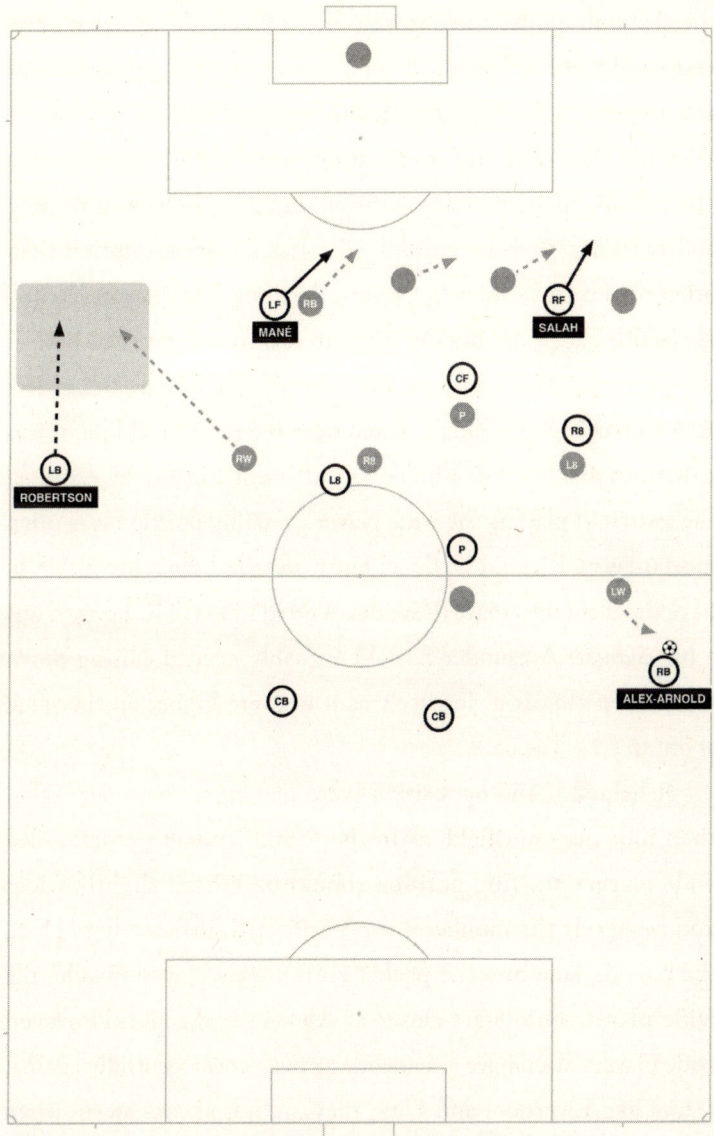

Figure 22. *The location of the ball and the runs of Mané and Salah meant the opposition back four had to be across towards Liverpool's right side. This placed reliance on the opposition's left-sided wide player to pressurise Alexander-Arnold, with his angle of approach preferably blocking the pass to Robertson, and the right-sided wide player to be wide enough to track Robertson or intercept the switch of play. Both of these outcomes were easier to achieve in a five-man midfield, which could spread wider*

the shape to ensure there was always a player to defend slightly wider and therefore remain closer to Robertson. So how were teams able to prevent the pass at source? Many coaches tend to promote allowing opposition full-backs to receive the ball when in deep areas. Both their receiving location and relative lack of passing ability means they are considered a less dangerous option than other players. Instead, wide players, the designated players to close down full-backs, are usually asked to tuck in narrowly, to protect the pockets inside of them. This meant that when Alexander-Arnold received the ball deep and near the right touchline, it was a difficult task to close him down sufficiently before he executed the switch of play, as the wide player's starting position was often too far away. It could be done, but it required the wide player to have the mentality that Alexander-Arnold's pass to Robertson was a big danger; Alexander-Arnold arguably needed closing down when deep almost as intensely as if he were higher up the pitch about to cross the ball.

It helped if the opposition were playing a five-man rather than four-man midfield, as in the former system the left-sided wide player's starting position should have been slightly wider and higher. If the number 8 was positioned sufficiently to block the passing lane into the pocket on the wide player's inside, the wide player could start closer to Alexander-Arnold. However, wide players often have a tendency to 'over-cover' centrally against teams like Liverpool and City; they are not always aware when they have sufficient central midfield cover on their inside to move wider. Mauricio Pochettino's Tottenham played with a five-man midfield at Anfield in October 2019, with left-winger Son Heung-Min tucked in narrowly and relatively deep to ensure compactness centrally. Yet this simply freed up Trent Alexander-Arnold to become the playmaker, passing and crossing without sufficient pressure; in this game Liverpool's right-back completed 68 passes, attempted 11 crosses. In addition, Alexander-Arnold completed seven long cross-field passes to Robertson, the most long passes from full-back to full-back in any Premier League game from the start of 2016/17 to the end of 2019/20. In only 11 games during these four seasons did a full-back complete four or more; nine of these 11 were Alexander-Arnold.

Equally as important as the intensity with which the wide player closed down was the angle at which he approached Alexander-Arnold. If the wide player bent his run to show the Liverpool right-back the outside, he could block the line of the pass to Robertson, enabling the rest of the team to remain compact and move over to 'close' the channel on his side of the pitch. To my knowledge a team has never taken the drastic measure of designating a player to man-mark Alexander-Arnold in the way they would if he was a classic central midfield playmaker, with the exception of Marcelo Bielsa's Leeds United during the 2020/21 season, who man-marked almost every opposition player, in every game. Interestingly, against Leeds, Alexander-Arnold created zero open-play chances, completed just 22 passes, his fourth-lowest total in a 90-minute Premier League game, and attempted just three crosses from open play, and none until the 68th minute. Compare these figures to those from the Tottenham game, where Son got nowhere near him, and the difference in the amount of freedom he was given was striking. Man-marking would mean sacrificing a degree of compactness, but as he was arguably Liverpool's main playmaker, it made sense to consider it.

The second possible solution to the the switch of play between full-backs involved designating either the right-back or right-sided wide player to defend slightly wider, starting horizontally closer to Robertson. Some teams were even known to select a natural full-back as a right-sided wide player to track the Liverpool left-back. When a switch of play to Robertson was struck from a more central area, it was definitely possible for the opposition wide player to move wide enough to discourage the switch of play, yet still be narrow enough to retain the required compactness centrally, as the distance between the location of the ball and the left touchline, the widest point of the pitch where Robertson was positioned, was not huge. However, when the ball was with Alexander-Arnold near the right touchline, the scenario was not the same, as the distance between the location of the ball and the left side, where Robertson was positioned, was at its maximum. If the opposition right-sided wide player moved wider with a view to discouraging the switch of play, or at least to be close enough to Robertson when he received the ball, a problem was potentially created centrally; if instead of being switched to the other side, the ball were to be passed back inside, passing lanes into Mané or Firmino between the lines would potentially open up.

In effect, the position of Robertson would serve as a means of stretching the opposition horizontally, enabling Liverpool to take advantage of the resulting space. The instruction to remain wide on the opposite side when Alexander-Arnold was in possession would go against the constant message wide players are given by coaches: when the ball is on the opposite side, tuck in narrowly to help the team remain compact horizontally. That being said, the opposition wide player had to be wider than usual, otherwise he would get nowhere near Robertson. Even if he were positioned wider, the wide player still had a problem – he had to face the ball, which meant he couldn't see the exact position of the Liverpool left-back behind him, nor know the exact timing of his run, putting him at a disadvantage. This problem of having to face the ball when attempting to track 'blind side' movements will come up time and time again as we analyse the different passes and movement patterns of City and Liverpool. In addition, in order to face the side the ball was coming from, the wide player had to have his back to the final destination of the ball. Due to his forward-facing body orientation Robertson could accelerate forwards to meet the ball, whereas the opposition wide player had to turn his body before he could run forwards; the resulting split-second delay would often enable Robertson to receive having bypassed the wide player vertically, or give him enough time to perform an action before the pressure came. The task of tracking a full-back with the energy and pace of Robertson was extremely difficult.

With these drawbacks in mind, in many situations some teams attempted to share the responsibility between the right-back and right-sided wide player. However, from a switch of play from near the right touchline it was difficult for the opposition right-back to take any responsibility due to Mané's position. Mané was always narrow, ready to make a run in behind across the defensive line, following a short pass back inside. Or, should Liverpool progress up the right side, his narrow position would enable him to move into the box for a cross. Mané could not simply be passed on to the right centre-back because he himself needed to be across towards the side of the ball, maintaining the distance between himself and the left centre-back and left-back, who needed to close off the channel on the left side of their defence, in case Alexander-Arnold chose that pass instead (more on this in the next section). The problem was that the opposition defensive line didn't know where the pass was going to be played, so the priority had to be preventing the more dangerous pass to Mané, because he was closer horizontally to the goal than Robertson. After the ball was switched to Robertson, the opposition right-back would be able to pass Mané on to the centre-back and sprint out to close down the left-back because by that stage he would have known the ball was definitely going to Robertson not Mané. However, from such a narrow position it was practically impossible for the right-back to sprint out in time to effect Robertson's next action; he was effectively pinned in by Mané's position.

It would be interesting to know how much credit Klopp deserves for the development of the switch of play between full-backs. Is it something that Alexander-Arnold and Robertson came up with themselves and that Klopp simply encouraged or enhanced? Or did it develop from deliberate instructions from the coaching staff? Either way, Alexander-Arnold was clearly given the freedom to attempt very difficult passes; he actually failed to complete passes on a regular basis, but as already mentioned, Liverpool wanted to maximise their volume of attacks, pressing hard to win the second ball should a pass fail. With the one or two remarkably difficult passes which Alexander-Arnold completed a game, Liverpool would create a golden chance to score.

A more optimal 'channel ball'

A channel ball is traditionally associated with old-fashioned English football, so it would be reasonable to ask what is so impressive or sophisticated about this type of pass. However, the Liverpool channel pass was not a straight pass from the back for a forward to chase, with the aim of 'turning' the opposition to win the second ball or throw-in, from which a cross, traditionally seen as a favourable outcome, may occur. In reality, the likelihood of this type of pass resulting in a direct opportunity to score is fairly small. However, the Liverpool channel pass had significantly more optimal characteristics. Firstly, it was enhanced by the fact that Alexander-Arnold and Robertson struck the ball with incredible pace and accuracy, whereas the majority of centre-backs or full-backs playing this pass do not have their passing ability. Secondly, the electric acceleration possessed by Salah and Mané gave them an advantage in beating the defenders to the ball. Thirdly, the technique, in particular that of Alexander-Arnold, was reminiscent of a whipped cross or shot at goal from a free kick, which meant the ball trajectory curved back towards the goal. It was similar, for example, to David Beckham's classic curved striking of a ball. This enabled the trajectory of the ball to be wide enough for the opposition full-back not to be able to intercept, but then curve back centrally, where Salah or Mané could receive and instantly attack the centre-back and the goal. Add the acceleration of Salah and Mané to the pace, accuracy and trajectory of the pass, and the likelihood of it resulting in a goalscoring opportunity was much higher than for a traditional channel ball.

Firstly, it was important for the defending team to consider Salah as one of two centre-forwards, Mané being the other, almost as if Liverpool played a 4-4-2 diamond formation (Firmino, as already mentioned, was positioned deeper than a traditional forward, as if he were at the tip of a diamond midfield). Considering the Liverpool wide forwards as forwards rather wide players is a common theme we will revisit when assessing how opposition teams attempted to deal with the two of them. If he were to be considered a wide player, Salah would be seen as the left-back's opposite number to mark or track. However, when Salah made a run into the channel he was so narrow in relation to the position of the ball that he was often as close as, if not closer, to the left-sided centre-back than the left-back (*Figure 23*). In addition, the ball's trajectory meant that Salah was likely to receive the pass on the inside of the left-back, who would consequently be unable to stop the Egyptian from heading towards goal.

It was really important that when the ball was passed wide to Alexander-Arnold, the opposition defensive line, and crucially the left centre-back and left-back, moved across to 'close off' the channel. In the Amazon documentary on City's 2017/18 season, Guardiola himself was heard instructing his defensive line to do as described against Salah and Mané. Closing off the channel is a widely used tactic across the Premier League against teams who look to play this type of pass. If the defensive line moves across as a unit, the left-back himself is able to move wider, resulting in less space on his outside for the pass to be curved around him. The same applied to the left centre-back. If he moved over closer to the line of the ball before it was passed into the channel, he would have less distance to run to intercept the pass, or he would at least be close enough to Salah to ensure he could not turn.

However, it was never a simple task for a defensive line to get their positioning spot on and close off the space into where the pass could be played. If their positioning was poor, a potentially disastrous situation could occur where Salah was faced up one versus one with the left centre-back, or even goal side to the extent that the centre-back could not block his path to goal. The addition of a high-quality channel pass to Liverpool's game is rare to see in a possession-based team. It is an example of how Liverpool were prepared to attack in mixed, unpredictable ways.

It has been suggested that one day Alexander-Arnold may move into central midfield, where he played at academy level. However, Alexander-Arnold himself once remarked, 'From right-back I get

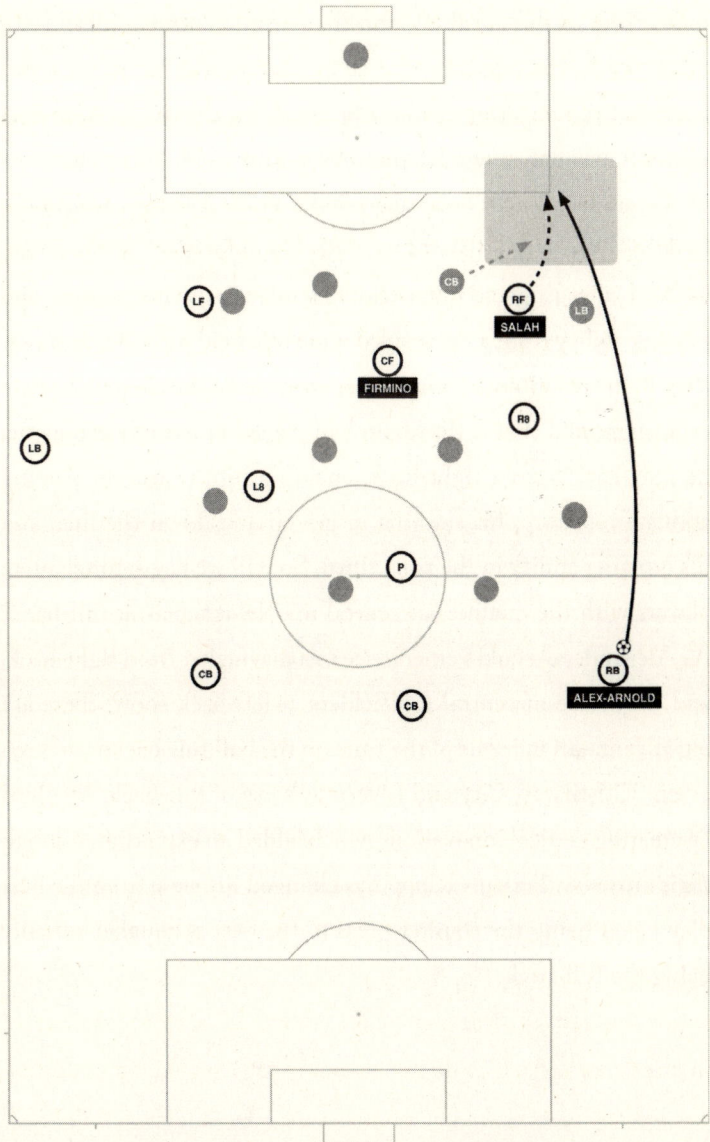

Figure 23. *Alexander-Arnold attempted to bend passes over or around the left-back into the channel for Salah to receive on the left-back's inside. With Firmino usually deeper it was important for the opposition left-sided centre-back to consider Salah a centre-forward, and move across to 'close off' the channel*

more time to dictate the game than from central midfield.' In other words, the relative space he has had on the ball from right-back and the resulting damage he has been able to do from that position may encourage Klopp to keep him there. Some observers of Alexander-Arnold have suggested that his role for Liverpool is strikingly similar to that of David Beckham for much of his career, as the former England international tended to use his crossing and passing ability from a right-sided wide midfield position; at times, Beckham was almost a playmaker from wide. Some people have even suggested that if Beckham had played in the modern game, he may have been a right-back, enabling him to use his passing ability from deep, his stamina to get up and down the line, and his crossing ability in the final third. So will we begin to see more players with the qualities of central midfielders play at full-back? As Alexander-Arnold's emergence as a playmaker from right-back, and City's use of central midfielders at left-back show, there are big advantages in terms of the time on the ball full-backs are often given. Either way, City and Liverpool's use of full-backs involved fascinating tactical innovations which added an extra dimension to their armoury. Perhaps Klopp has changed his view from the best playmaker being the counter-press to the best playmaker actually being the full-back.

Chapter 6

City's wingers versus Liverpool's wide forwards

AS SHOULD already be apparent, 4-3-3 is a formation which can be played in several different ways in terms of the roles of the full-backs, number 8s and wide players. Raheem Sterling, Leroy Sané, Sadio Mané and Mo Salah were some of the superstars of the City and Liverpool teams that won record points, yet the City pair were used very differently to the Liverpool duo in terms of their positioning. Salah and Mané registered 48 per cent of Liverpool's Premier League goals during their two record seasons. Sterling and Sané were slightly less prolific, scoring 28 per cent of City's goals, but they contributed 29 per cent of City's assists, compared to 21 per cent for Salah and Mané.

These basic statistics give some indication as to their contrasting roles in Guardiola and Klopp's systems; Salah and Mané attacked the goal more directly, reflecting their higher number of goals, while Sterling and Sané attacked the wings before supplying their team-mates centrally. However, both teams looked to transition from build-up play to attacking play by supplying their wide players with a similar pass: the diagonal ball. These passes could be devastating, resulting in a goal being scored before the opposition managed to adjust to the forward pass.

City – switches of play to wide wingers

Against the situation City faced during the vast majority of Premier League games – a narrow, compact, mid-to-low block – a diagonal switch of play to their winger on the opposite side was an important weapon they used to expose opposition teams. The theory was that with the majority of opposition players congregated towards the side of the ball's location, there was always space to exploit on the opposite side. Guardiola, in an interview with canofootball.com, explained the role of his wingers in over-simplistic terms: 'If they're defending with all the bodies in the centre then we will look to the wingers in wider spaces.' Later we will analyse what City did once their wingers received the ball, but first let's continue to assess their supply. We have discussed how every opposition team prioritised preventing City's pivot from receiving the ball as City built up by marking him tightly, so the responsibility of playing the diagonal pass to City's wingers often fell to one of the other build-up five. Later we will assess how higher up the pitch City's pivot regularly did become free to play a diagonal switch, but from deep he was often too well marshalled.

If the pitch were to be split into five vertical lanes, many of City's switches of play were struck from the second widest lane from the touchline each side. This location was optimal because the player on the ball was central enough to be able to comfortably complete the pass to the winger on the far side, yet far enough to one side for the opposition to have adjusted their position towards that side, meaning the receiving winger had more space between himself and the opposition full-back. Both these factors were crucial to being able to find the winger without the pass being intercepted by the full-back. A successful switch of play was likely to result in a one versus one situation, whereas an incomplete pass either resulted in a loss of possession, or potential loss of control in terms of the resulting second ball situation which occurred. A one versus one for City's wingers, Sterling and Sané, was not a situation of *numerical* superiority. However, when considering the outstanding attacking attributes of the two players, against most opposition full-backs, superiority still existed. This is a goal of *juego de posición* – to create a situation where specific players could receive the ball isolated against a perceived inferior player – the superiority didn't have to be numerical.

Due to City's clever build-up shape, and their numerical superiority around the ball, one of their five deeper players usually had time on the ball to execute the switch of play to the winger. Kyle Walker, for example, developed this part of his game significantly; he would dribble forward from his third centre-back position, and with the opposition concentrating on City's right-winger out wide and right-sided number 8 in the right pocket, switch play to City's left-winger. For example, against Liverpool in January 2018, Walker picked out Sané with a brilliant diagonal ball, enabling the City winger to beat right-back Joe Gomez and score (*Figure 24*). However, often one of City's centre-backs was the player who hit the diagonal pass, more often than not their left centre-back, as he tended to receive possession in the optimal position more often, as the left of the artificially created back three.

Ideally this pass was executed by a left-footer from City's left side and a right-footer from City's right, because it enabled more disguise before the pass was executed. In Guardiola's first season at

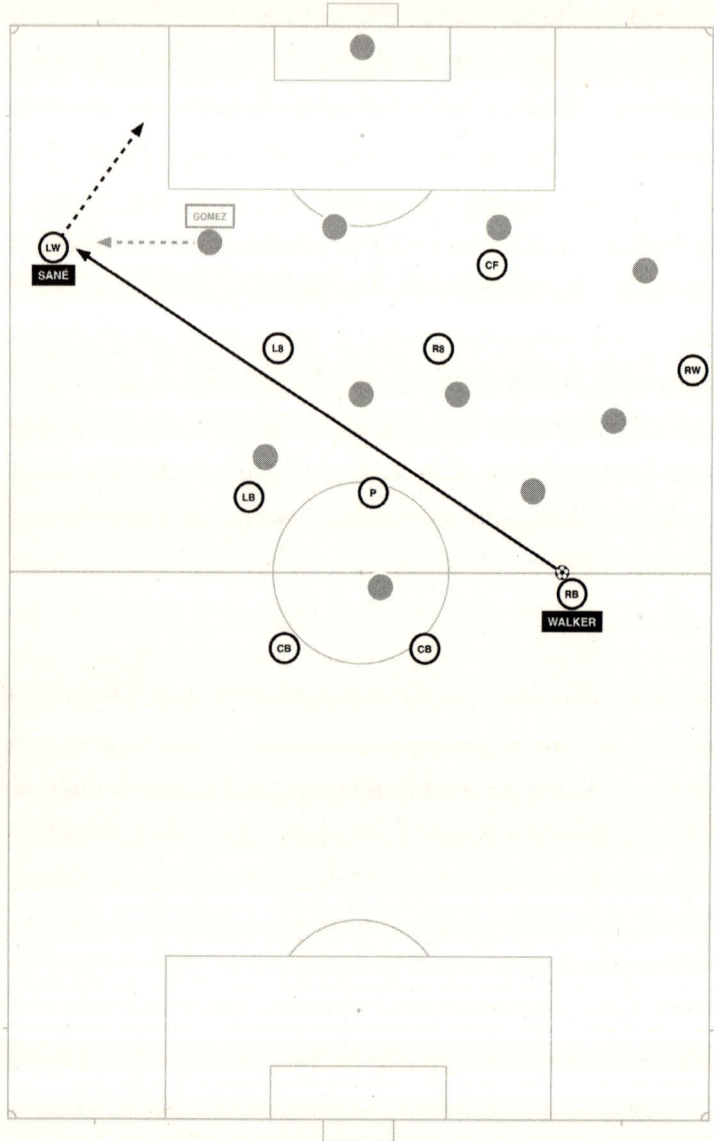

Figure 24. *The situation for Sané's goal against Liverpool in January 2018. Walker stepped forward into the space in front of him unchallenged and switched play to Sané. Liverpool right-back Gomez attempted to intercept, but the pass was too wide for him, enabling Sané to take the ball past Gomez with his first touch*

City, left-footed defender Aleksandar Kolarov was very effective at striding out with the ball before switching play to Sterling on City's right. If, on the other hand, the right-footed Nicolás Otamendi were playing at left centre-back, he would have to open his body in order to manoeuvre the ball on to his right foot before striking it. This gave the opposition left-back the crucial split second he needed to adjust his own body to sprint out to and reach the ball before City's winger, or at the very least make a challenge off his first touch. In contrast, a left-footed centre-back only needed to adjust his body shape fractionally in order to strike the pass with his left foot. Often he didn't even need to look to check the right-winger was wide, as it was a requirement of the winger's role in the system.

Following Kolarov's departure for Roma in the summer of 2017, City finally signed another left-footed centre-back in January 2018, Aymeric Laporte from Athletic Bilbao. Laporte perfected the art of dribbling forward with the ball before finding City's right-winger with a disguised diagonal pass; the opposition often didn't know if he was going to attempt a short pass on his side of the pitch or a diagonal pass to the right, until the split second before he struck the ball. With the diagonal switch of play there was minimal risk for City; the fact that the switch was almost always to a winger not a full-back meant that if intercepted, City's full-back wasn't ahead of the ball, and was therefore in a position to defend from behind.

For the first time, we're now going to touch on an incredibly important relationship in Guardiola's City team – the role of City's number 8s, Kevin De Bruyne and David Silva, in giving their wingers the time and space to receive the ball and attack the full-back. The movements of City's number 8s are used by other teams who play 4-3-3, but the extra-high, aggressive starting positions of

De Bruyne and Silva enabled them to stay connected to the wingers to a greater extent than the number 8s of other teams. In addition, the automatic, almost robotic nature of De Bruyne's and Silva's movements really stood out. Previously we have demonstrated why the opposition full-back couldn't move out too early towards City's winger in the anticipation of the diagonal pass; this would have created a gap in the defensive line between himself and his nearest centre-back. This problem was exacerbated by the high position of City's number 8s; almost without fail they were high enough to make a run on the inside of the opposition's left-back (*Figure 25*). A basic key defensive principle is that it's better to allow a pass on the outside, rather than on the inside, where the attacking player can receive the pass closer to the goal and has fewer defenders to beat to score.

Shortly before City executed the switch of play, their number 8 on the opposite side to the ball made sure the opposition full-back was as narrow as possible in order to give their winger more space; in effect the full-back was 'pinned in' by City's number 8. Another word that football coaches use to describe this action of City's number 8 is *fixed*. For example, Laporte would dribble forward and see Sterling wide on the right available for a switch of play. De Bruyne made a run in between the opposition centre-back and left-back, causing the left-back to move inside to close the space between him and his nearest centre-back, but instead, the pass was played on his outside, to Sterling. De Bruyne's run was usually a decoy but the left-back couldn't take that risk as he had to prioritise protecting the inside and therefore the goal.

To facilitate the defending of the situation, a competent full-back would open his body so he would only have to turn marginally to sprint out towards the winger as soon as the ball was on its way.

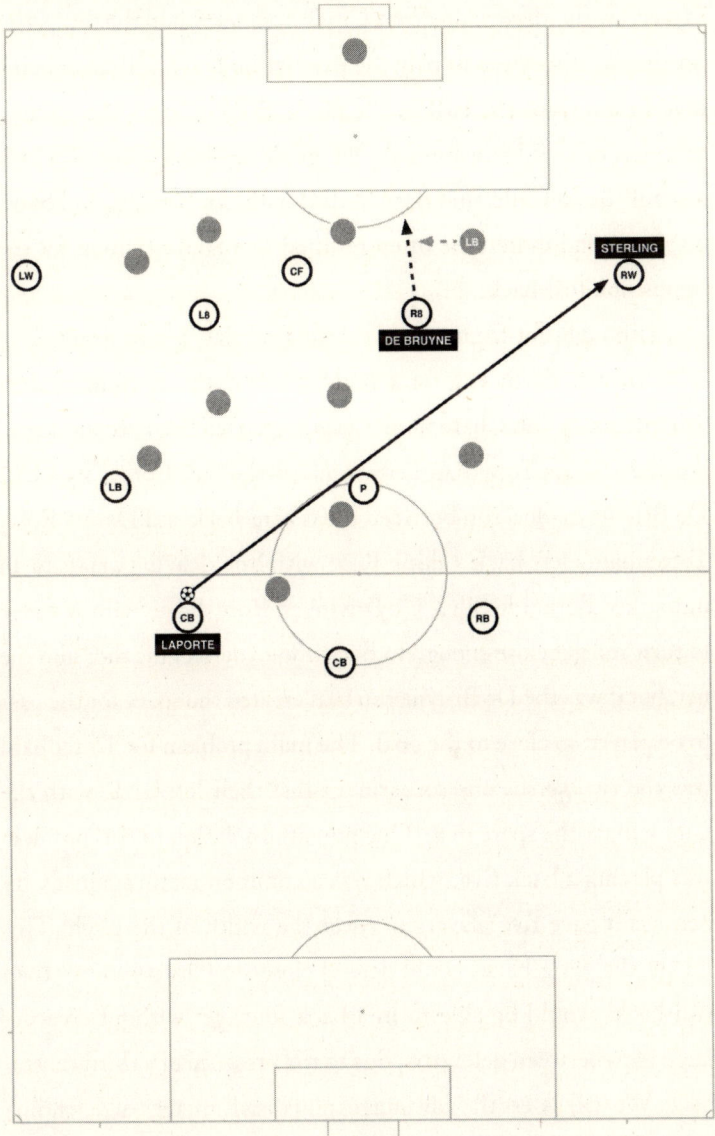

Figure 25. De Bruyne's runs would 'pin in' or 'fix' the opposition left-back, creating more space and time for Sterling to receive a switch of play from Laporte. The left-back had to cover the run of De Bruyne first, as a pass to De Bruyne was more dangerous than a pass to Sterling

However, the decoy run from City's number 8 bought the player on the ball the space to play the pass without the full-back being able to intercept the ball in the air, and the winger the time to take a touch and run towards the goal, reaching a speed which any full-back would find hard to deal with; for Sterling and Sané, a split second more time often resulted in a fatal situation for the opposition full-back.

Although not from a direct switch of play, a nice example of a De Bruyne decoy run for a goal by City's winger came against Tottenham in the Champions League quarter-final second leg in April 2019. As Sergio Agüero received the ball from City's left, De Bruyne made a run between the centre-back and Danny Rose, Tottenham's left-back, taking Rose with him, leaving a pass to an unmarked Bernardo Silva, City's winger. Rose did actually manage to turn and get close enough to Bernardo to deflect his shot into the net, but it was the De Bruyne run that created the space for the pass to be played so close to the goal. The main problem for Tottenham was the two versus one scenario against their left-back, with the City winger the spare man. One potential solution to this problem was playing a back five, which was a common tactic against City because it gave five players to cover the width of the pitch. This meant the wing-backs could defend closer to City's wingers than full-backs would be able to in a back four, yet without creating large gaps between defenders, due to the presence of a third centre-back. We will assess the advantages and disadvantages of defending against City with a back five in a later chapter.

As well as stretching teams horizontally, the threat of this diagonal pass was often a factor in preventing teams from defending higher up the pitch against City, combined with a lack of pressure they were often able to get around the ball due to City's numerical superiority – pressure on the ball is key to holding a high defensive line. As well as a narrow, compact midfield, a high defensive line is another strategy which prevents teams from being played through. If the midfield is compact, and the defensive line is high, it almost doesn't matter how many players a team places between the lines; there is simply no space to find a pass. The higher the line, however, the more space there would be for City's diagonal pass to bypass the defensive line vertically as well as horizontally, potentially putting Sterling or Sané through on goal. Or, having received the ball parallel with the opposition full-back, the more space there would be for Sterling or Sané to use their pace to attack the full-back down the outside, without running out of pitch. There would then be a greater area to cross the ball into before the centre-backs could recover; the early cross was a regular source of City's goals. A diagonal pass which bypasses the defensive line vertically, as well as horizontally, brings us on to Liverpool, as it was their speciality.

Liverpool – long passes to wide forwards in behind

Due to the significantly narrower positions of Liverpool's wide forwards, Salah and Mané, compared to Sterling and Sané, the destination of Liverpool's diagonal passes were usually more central, with the aim of bypassing the defensive line vertically, often removing the need to win a one versus one duel completely. In addition, the decoy run to create space tended to come from Liverpool's centre-forward, Roberto Firmino, not their number 8s. Furthermore, Liverpool were not as concerned as City whether the pass was completed or not, as they were often able to take advantage of the chaos that it caused, by attacking having won the second ball. Liverpool used the diagonal pass in behind very regularly, and with a relatively high success rate, not only to score goals directly but to

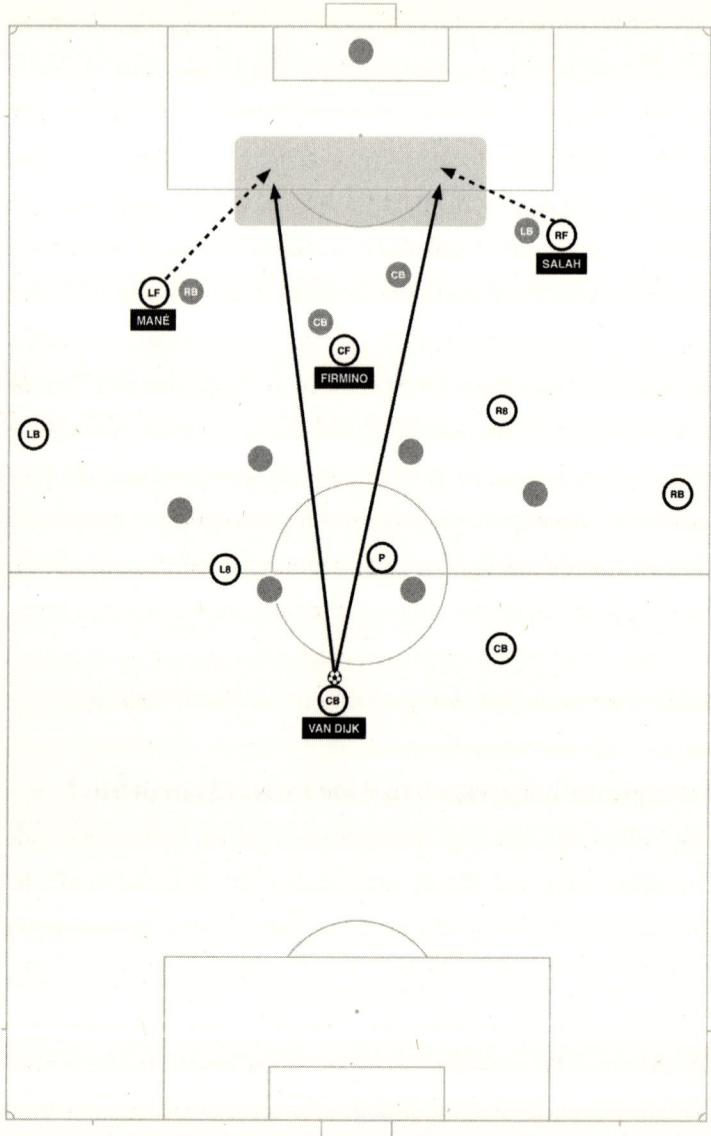

Figure 26. Two ways in which space could be created for Mané and Salah in behind the opposition centre-backs. The opposition right-back has been left exposed by the right-sided centre-back stepping forwards to track Firmino between the lines. The opposition's left-back has dropped deeper than the rest of the defensive line to anticipate Salah's run, but by doing so he enables Salah to begin his run from behind the left-sided centre-back, allowing him to reach a pass in the space behind the centre-back

get themselves into the opposition's defensive third and attack from there. There are other teams who play long passes in behind on a regular basis, but they tend to play with two central forwards, not wide forwards in a front three. The disadvantage for teams who play this pass for one of two forwards is that the receiver makes a run from the inside to the outside; these passes are generally less dangerous because the receiver is running away from goal, into the channel. We have already discussed how Liverpool themselves played this channel pass for a run from in to out, but for them it was a variation, not their principle pass.

In addition, Mané and Salah were usually positioned on the outside shoulder of the opposition's full-backs before they made their runs, not between the full-back and centre-back, so that they could make an angled run from the outside of the defensive line to the inside, towards the goal. There was a targeted space in behind the defensive line, where the pathways of the run and ball met (*Figure 26*). Clearly the pace of Mané and Salah was an advantage, but the run was often a short one: the timing of the run and quality of the pass were equally important factors. The purchase of Virgil van Dijk gave Liverpool a centre-back who possessed exceptional long passing ability. However, as described in detail, the build-up shape Liverpool formed, with one of the centre-backs often dropping off and a central midfielder or full-back moving to the side, enabled these players to move the ball between each other until one had enough time on the ball to execute the pass when they felt it was on to do so, not only because they were being closed down and needed to play forward.

As Van Dijk's influence grew, teams focused more attention on closing him down. But the two different positions he took up in Liverpool's triangular build-up shape (either deep and central or further forward to the left side of the first line of the opposition pressure) gave him more time on the ball than if he were simply parallel to Liverpool's right centre-back, making it easier for the opposition first line of the opposition press to close him down from a square pass from his centre-back partner. Equally, with the centre-backs close together, not split wide apart with Liverpool's pivot between them, the passes tended to be from more central positions, opening up the possibility of Liverpool passing diagonally to either Mané *or* Salah, consequently making the direction of the pass more unpredictable for the opposition. The rewards of timing the pass and run perfectly were very high; effectively Mané or Salah would be through on goal with only the goalkeeper to beat. As their runs were diagonally towards the goal, their first touches, assuming they followed the same direction as the run, would usually take them on to their stronger feet without having to break stride; the right-footed Mané played on the left and the left-footed Salah on the right. If Salah, for example, had played on the left, he would either have had to take the ball on to his right foot, or break his stride to work it on to his left. Mané and Salah's first touch often took them across the defender, meaning that if he made a challenge there would be a risk of bringing the Liverpool wide forward down and conceding a penalty.

With Mané and Salah positioned narrowly, ready to make their diagonal runs at any moment, the opposition defensive line needed to maintain constant focus, making sure they were in the correct positions to defend a potential pass at all times. Arguably against no other team was there such a constant threat to the defensive line, regardless of the position of the ball. Other than the quality of the pass, the pace of Mané and Salah, and the fact the pass was potentially available to be played at any point in time, it's worth analysing why it was so difficult to defend, and how Roberto Firmino looked to swing the chances of success further in Liverpool's favour. The first thing the opposition team had to establish was who had responsibility for Mané and Salah, the full-backs or centre-backs? Technically, as wide rather than centre-forwards, they were the full-backs' 'man', yet they were making a run into the zone of the centre-back. Or, if it were to be a shared responsibility, the more horizontally compact the defensive line the better, in order to minimise the gaps between defenders. Before this pass became so well highlighted, full-backs would get caught out simply because they were watching the ball and weren't expecting the run, or because they were too wide and therefore too far apart from the centre-backs, creating more space for Mané and Salah to run into. However, after several seasons of this tactic, full-backs would go into games against Liverpool fully aware that they were going to face the situation, ensuring that they tucked in narrowly and were checking their shoulders for Mané and Salah's positioning and runs.

This increased awareness of the run created a different problem: full-backs began to worry that if they didn't track Mané or Salah's runs, resulting in a goal, they were going to get the blame; as mentioned, Mané and Salah were naturally seen as the full-backs' 'man'. They knew that both these players were extremely quick, so once they got goal side, it would be difficult to catch them up. Due to this anxiety, many full-backs began dropping deeper than their own centre-backs, anticipating the pass and attempting to give themselves a head start to get to the ball first – but, crucially, before the pass had been struck. This hindered rather than helped the situation, as Salah or Mané could now move deeper than the centre-backs and remain onside, because the full-back would be playing them on. By dropping deeper, a full-back exposed himself to a greater extent by reducing the possibility of the nearest centre-back being able to drop back and intercept the pass, because the ball could now be passed deeper behind the centre-back; Mané or Salah could reach the ball, due to their vertical starting position closer to the ball's destination than that of the centre-backs. Regardless of the opposition they are facing, every defensive line has the golden rule of full-backs never dropping deeper than their centre-backs.

If the centre-back and full-back did remain in line with each other before the pass was struck, however, Salah and Mané would have to begin their runs from level with the centre-back to stay onside. In this situation there would be no advantage in terms of vertical distance between the Liverpool wide forward and the nearest centre-back, enabling the centre-back to potentially drop back and intercept. The centre-back already had the disadvantage of having to run backwards to meet the ball, whereas Mané and Salah would be accelerating forwards. Another problem for the centre-backs was that they had to face the ball, which meant they could not see if their full-backs had dropped, nor Mané or Salah's exact position – this made it more difficult for them to adjust their own position to that of the full-backs. If a full-back had dropped too early and isolated himself, it was essential for him to get to the ball first without the help of his centre-back. However, apart from the likely disadvantage in speed versus Salah and Mané, this was difficult because the full-back had the same problem as the centre-back: he was facing the ball, so needed to either run backwards or turn before accelerating forwards. Mané and Salah, on the other hand, were already facing forwards, giving them a crucial split second advantage in terms of momentum.

So, it was essential that the full-back did not drop too early to ensure that his nearest centre-back could potentially move backwards and intercept the pass. Liverpool used a strategy to try to artificially create this situation where the opposition centre-back ended up higher than Mané or Salah, without relying on a full-back dropping. Liverpool's centre-forward, Roberto Firmino, would make a movement in the opposite vertical direction to Mané and Salah shortly before the pass was struck, dropping off a few yards to provide an option for a pass into his feet between the lines. As Firmino began his run from the centre-backs' zone, the centre-backs would often see it as their job to follow him in anticipation of him receiving a pass; usually due to the fact that he was Liverpool's centre-forward. If any centre-forward was allowed to receive to feet before turning and executing a through ball to one of the wide players, it would normally be perceived to be the centre-backs' fault. Firmino excelled as a creator of chances, so it is no wonder that centre-backs attempted to prevent him from receiving the ball. If anything, they may have felt encouraged to stay tight to him, knowing that he would be unlikely to turn and run in behind them; many centre-backs would want to play against a centre-forward who is constantly asking for a pass to feet rather than running in behind. However, most centre-forwards do not have two wide forwards like Mané and Salah to do the running in behind for them; without this threat it may have been a more obvious and safer strategy for one of the centre-backs to stay tight to Firmino when he dropped off a few yards.

On other occasions, the Brazilian would drop much deeper into areas where a centre-back simply could not follow him (unless he is a centre-back in a Marcelo Bielsa team, of course!). Firmino wasn't an orthodox forward; he was the definition of a 'false 9'. We will describe his role in more detail in a later chapter, but for now it is really important to state that the defensive team needed to consider him at least partially the responsibility of the midfield pivot(s), not the centre-backs (*Figure 27*). As soon as a centre-back departed the defensive line to follow Firmino, the pass could be played into the newly vacated space behind him. This put the reliance on the full-back to beat Mané or Salah to the ball. In addition, if the pass was played at the same moment as the centre-back moved forward, it was even more difficult for him to reverse his forward motion and run backwards. The important thing for the opposition centre-backs was not to go with Firmino *before* the action of the pass, but to wait until they were sure that the pass would be played to him and that his run was not intended as a decoy.

A movement of just a yard or two could be the difference between a last-ditch interception and Mané or Salah running through on goal. One of the best examples of a goal resulting from a Van Dijk diagonal pass for a wide forward diagonal run in behind was Liverpool's first goal in the Champions League second round second leg in March 2019 versus Bayern Munich. As well as the textbook execution of the move, the level of the opposition and the importance of the game make it really stand out; Liverpool went on to win the competition. The situation occurred as follows: Liverpool's build-up shape allowed Van Dijk the time on the ball to look up and execute the pass. Bayern's right-sided centre-back, Niklas Süle had more of an eye on Firmino, who was positioned several yards in front of him, than Mané. Anticipating Mané's run, Rafinha, the Bayern right-back, began to drop, which meant the Liverpool wide forward could begin his run from behind Süle, removing him from the move, and putting a reliance on Rafinha to beat Mané to the ball. The angle of the pass, struck from just left of the centre circle, made it difficult for goalkeeper Manuel Neuer, an expert 'sweeper' behind defensive lines, to intercept, with Mané

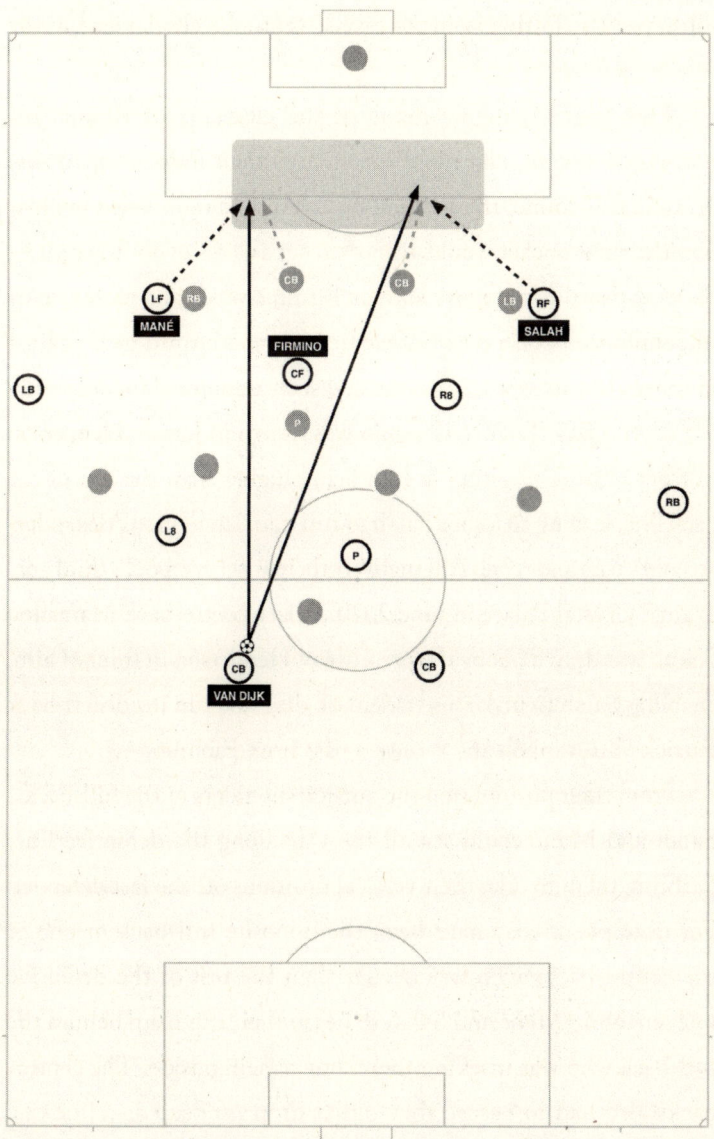

Figure 27. *In this example Firmino has been passed on by the opposition centre-backs to their deepest midfielder, the pivot, and the full-backs haven't dropped too deep before the pass has been struck. The opposition centre-backs are able to drop back and intercept the passes in behind, as Mané and Salah can't begin their runs from behind the centre-backs and remain onside at the same time*

subsequently slotting home to give Liverpool a crucial lead in the two-legged tie.

This goal highlights many of the elements of Klopp's in-possession system, and more specifically their most iconic move. As well as Firmino, the position of Liverpool's right-sided number 8 in the right pocket would also often act as a decoy for the centre-backs, especially in scenarios where Firmino was being picked up by the opposition's deepest midfielder. Liverpool's third goal against Huddersfield in April 2019 was one such example. Huddersfield's left centre-back Terence Kongolo was drawn to Jordan Henderson in front of him, resulting in him being higher than the rest of the back line, leaving space for Salah to run into, latch on to Alexander-Arnold's pass and score. Alternatively there was Liverpool's third goal against Crystal Palace in June 2020. Palace centre-back Mamadou Sakho was drawn out by the presence of Henderson in front of him, enabling Salah to make his trademark diagonal run inside left-back Patrick Van Aanholt and receive a pass from Fabinho.

From their positions on the outside shoulders of the full-backs, Salah and Mané could see all the way along the defensive line, enabling them to take their vertical positions off the last defender. For example, it may have been the opposite full-back or one of the centre-backs who was deeper than the rest of the defensive line, enabling Mané and Salah to begin their run from behind the full-back who was marking them, but remain onside. The centre-backs also had to ensure they didn't drop *too* deep as a line due to their anxiety over the passes in behind, leaving space between the lines for Liverpool to pass into the feet of Firmino, or even Salah or Mané themselves, who were also prepared to show for the ball deeper. But it was a catch-22 situation: the higher they played as a defensive line, the more space there was in behind them for Mané and Salah to attack. Whether deep or high, the crucial factors for the opposition were the compactness of the defensive line both horizontally and vertically, not becoming disconnected by Firmino's decoy run, and using the shared responsibility of the centre-back and full-back two versus one against Liverpool's wide forward. A higher but connected defensive line was better than a deeper, disjointed defensive line.

There was another advantage Liverpool gained from passing in behind for Mané and Salah. By the 2019/20 season centre-backs tended not to be fooled by Firmino's decoy run, but to anticipate the pass in behind by dropping back to head the ball clear. However, arguably this did not lead to a reduction in the frequency to which Liverpool passed in behind; as long as Liverpool won the second ball, the pass still resulted in a favourable outcome, so they continued to regularly attempt it. This demonstrates a key difference between City and Liverpool: Klopp's team did not need controlled possession to attack to the same extent – they were content with having enough control to execute the longer pass with quality – nor were they bothered by pass completion statistics.

For all their tactics, brilliant moves and outstanding players, Liverpool showed an intense desire to win second balls. This was not the same as simplistic 'second ball' football where a team plays up to a target man forward who looks to knock it down for a team-mate; Liverpool usually did not compete for the first header. Although they favoured Mané or Salah getting to the ball ahead of the centre-back, they realised that against compact teams, the second ball following a failed pass in behind was a potentially advantageous situation in itself; by playing the pass in behind, a gap opened up between the opposition defence and midfield. Even though the centre-back could often drop back to head the

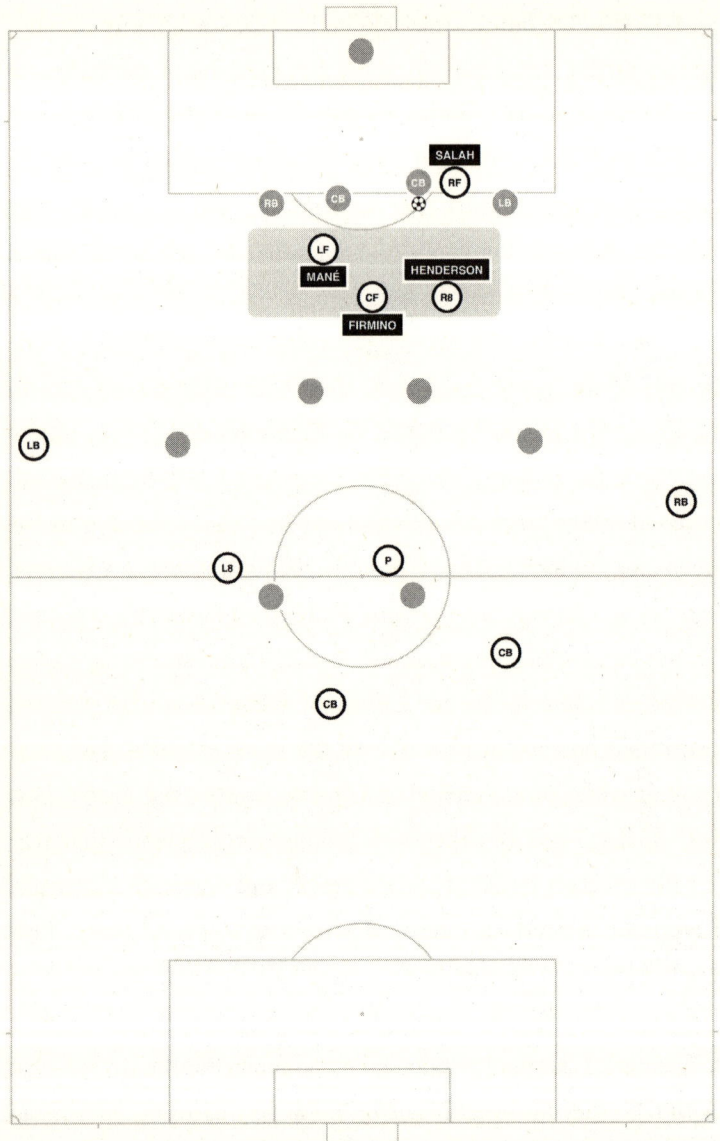

Figure 28. Following the long pass in behind, the back-pedalling centre-back would often head the ball back into the space in front of him, where Firmino, Henderson and one of Liverpool's wide forwards looked to win the second ball, often having sprinted forward more quickly than the opposition midfield had sprinted back once the ball has been passed over their heads. In this example, the pass is for Salah, so Mané had moved more centrally to compete for the second ball

ball, he was often heading it on the stretch, which made it very difficult for him to get much power on the header. Liverpool were incredibly well-rehearsed in this situation; the majority of the time they would react to reach the second ball more quickly than the opposition midfielders reacted to run back. The clever positioning of Firmino helped Liverpool in that his deeper position often meant he was ideally placed to pick up the second ball between the lines. In addition, the higher of the two number 8s was also in a great position to compete for the second ball (*Figure 28*). If Liverpool did manage to win the second ball, they bypassed the opposition midfield, enabling their front players to attack the newly disjointed defensive line. When a team is sat in a compact shape, playing through the defensive block to access the space behind the opposition midfield is difficult to achieve; Liverpool's ability to win second balls following a long pass enabled them to do get behind the opposition midfield in another manner.

The key was the variation in style; if it had been Liverpool's predominant tactic, the opposition would have been much more prepared for the long pass when Liverpool had the ball in deeper areas. However, it was just one of their many alternative strategies and patterns of play. It is surprising that more possession teams are not prepared to adapt their style to include this type of pass for their wide players, as giving the opposition something else to think about would likely enhance the effectiveness of their more intricate build-up play. Instead, the trend for wide players is to make their movements either between the lines or to stay wide with the aim of isolating full-backs one versus one; in general, the modern tendency is for players to want to pass and receive to feet.

Commentators often remark that a team is failing to create chances because they are passing the ball 'in front' of the entire opposition team. Liverpool could very rarely be accused of that. The 'sell' for a manager to get a wide player to make these runs is that it results in them receiving the ball closer to the goal, giving them more opportunities to score. It is not effective solely because of Salah and Mané – on the rare occasions that either man was injured, their replacements, often Alex Oxlade-Chamberlain and Divock Origi, scored goals by making similar runs to those made by the regular wide forwards. In Liverpool's win over Bournemouth in December 2019, Oxlade-Chamberlain made a Mané-esque run across Bournemouth's defensive line, latching on to a Henderson pass before finishing with a first-time volley. This goal was especially notable for the fact that Bournemouth instructed forward Callum Wilson to man-mark Van Dijk, presumably in an attempt to prevent his long passing. However, Wilson's position on the opposite side to the ball gave right-sided centre-back Dejan Lovren the space to find Henderson, who was playing as the pivot, unchallenged.

There is another undervalued aspect to the run and pass in behind, even if the wide player receiving doesn't manage to get goal side of the full-back to the extent that he can run through on goal, which is that any one versus one takes place in a position the opposition wide player or central midfielder will have trouble getting back to in time to double up. With this in mind, let's now assess the other type of diagonal pass Liverpool played for Mané and Salah. When an opposition's defensive line was very narrow and compact, or perhaps fairly near to their own goal with no available space behind the centre-backs, Liverpool would often play a diagonal pass on the outside, or directly over the head of the opposition full-back, rather than on the inside. Alternatively, on other occasions, the intention was to play a pass more centrally, but the execution wasn't perfect. However, it remained a dangerous situation. From this position, if Mané and Salah could get to the ball first, it was unlikely that an opposition player would be able to get there in time to help out the full-back, leaving a one versus one scenario in a dangerous position. Even if the full-back did manage to recover goal side himself, on many occasions Mané or Salah instantly cut inside the full-back before bending the ball into the far corner of the goal. Positioning Mané and Salah on the outside shoulder of the opposition full-backs, giving them the option to receive *either* behind the centre-backs *or* over the heads of the full-back, enabled Liverpool to create two favourable situations.

Like City with their own patterns of play, Liverpool persevered with the diagonal pass in behind, knowing that the opposition only had to lose their concentration once for Liverpool to be presented with a potential goalscoring or even match-winning opportunity. An example of this was their 1-0 win over Norwich in February 2020. Norwich had kept Liverpool's goalscoring opportunities to a minimum for 78 minutes, before one diagonal pass from Henderson for Mané evaded the Norwich defenders, enabling Liverpool's wide forward to win his team the game.

Chapter 7

How City accessed one of modern football's key spaces

WHILE LIVERPOOL came up with a way to break teams down by passing over the top of opposition defences, City designed a system to go around them. This chapter attempts to dismiss the idea that stopping the City of 2017/18 and 2018/19 was mainly about remaining compact to prevent them from playing through the centre. Guardiola knew that every team they faced would defend with this priority. His system was designed with the knowledge that City were going to be forced to use the wide areas more often than not, so they were going to make sure the opposition would encounter maximum problems when defending these zones. Of course, goals are scored in the middle, not out wide, so City needed to find ways to score having moved the ball outside of the entire opposition team, horizontally further from the opposition goal than where the move often began. We have already discussed City's strategies to help the winger when he received the ball: the number 8 making a run to ensure the opposition full-back had to stay narrow until the ball was on its way wide, and ensuring the pass into City's winger was played at an angle, so he could receive the ball with an open body shape, enabling him to attack without having to turn.

Ideally, nothing special needed to happen when either of City's wingers received the ball. Often Sterling and Sané would simply use their change of pace to beat the full-back, and either take a shot themselves or pass or cross into the area. Sané's previously mentioned goal against Liverpool in January 2018 is an example of this. Collecting a diagonal pass from Kyle Walker, Sané took the ball past right-back Joe Gomez with his first touch and used his pace to drive away, before firing past the goalkeeper.

It is interesting to note that when they both played in the same team, Sané, a left-footer, played on the left, and Sterling, a right-footer, played on the right. This used to be the tradition for teams who played with wingers, at least in English football, due to their requirement to beat the full-back on the outside before crossing. However, a modern trend has been for teams to play with 'inverted' wingers: a left-footer on the right, and a right-footer on the left. As explained in the previous chapter, this was how Liverpool used Salah and Mané. The benefit of inverted wingers is that as they dribble inside towards the goal they are able to shoot, cross or pass with their stronger foot, essentially 'opening up' the inside, or opposite side, of the pitch. Alternatively, by attacking the inside of the full-back, an inverted winger creates space on the outside for his own full-back to overlap.

However, during City's two record points seasons, the majority of time Guardiola's wingers were not inverted, instead attacking the outside in order to get behind the opposition's defence, and there were few occasions when Guardiola's full-backs overlapped, as if they did so they would kill the winger's space. Every Premier

League team was aware of the threat City's wingers posed, so they had a plan to prevent them easily beating their full-back. Several scenarios could occur which could reduce the winger's effectiveness. As the ball travelled wide, often the full-back was able to get tight enough to City's winger to prevent him from running with the ball. Perhaps the full-back had the pace to match City's winger. Maybe the full-back 'showed' the winger inside where there was no space for him to run with the ball. Or, an opposition central midfielder or wide player was able to sprint across to support his full-back and prevent the dangerous one versus one situation.

In these scenarios, the wingers' combination play with the number 8s was vital. It is necessary to refer again to Guardiola's comment, 'The crucial thing is space, how to adapt to your opponent's movements and then to anticipate them and break into the spaces.' For City, this 'adaptation' to their opponents' movements was easier simply because it was their own pattern of play which would make the opponents move in a predictable manner. In other words, City would force an opponent to vacate a space, and have a player positioned ready to instantly exploit it. We have just analysed this exact principle with regards to Firmino's movement for Liverpool in dragging the opposition centre-back out, creating space for Mané and Salah in behind. In City's case, this is what happened when their winger received the ball and the opposition full-back moved horizontally to close him down; by doing so, the full-back always left potential space between himself and the nearest centre-back. Many people consider an alternative space, the area between the defensive and midfield lines, to be a crucial 'red zone' which the defending team must prevent the attacking team from accessing. Perhaps more specifically, this 'red zone' is the central area directly in front of the centre-backs, where a number ten would traditionally operate. This is because when a team finds this space it means only the defence remains to protect the goal; it effectively means that the midfield, whose job it is to protect the defence, has been bypassed.

Although it remains very advantageous to access this space, arguably in the modern game the difficulty in doing so has led to teams focusing their attention more and more on the space on the inside of and behind the full-back, between him and the nearest centre-back, often termed the 'channel', which is created when a full-back moves horizontally to defend out wide. This space is equally as dangerous as the traditional 'red zone', but often more accessible. Against City, if a team didn't take measures to prevent them from accessing this space, more often than not they conceded multiple clear goalscoring opportunities (*Figure 29*). This was one of the fundamental functions of City positioning their wingers wide: it allowed them to draw the opposition full-back out, to access the space in the channel between him and the centre-back.

In his interview with canofootball.com, Guardiola spoke of 'two or three zones which are undefendable'. While that particular term is perhaps an exaggeration, during their most successful seasons this zone was indeed extremely difficult to defend against City. Successfully accessing it resulted in City being able to directly attack the centre-backs, having bypassed both the midfield *and* one of the full-backs. The high starting positions of City's number 8s close to the channel were an extremely important factor in accessing the space. A book could be written solely about the relationship between the wingers and number 8s in a Guardiola 4-3-3, but here we are going to concentrate on two principle movement patterns, which David Silva and Kevin De Bruyne perfected. The first, was to support the winger to feet, slightly deeper at an angle, to play a

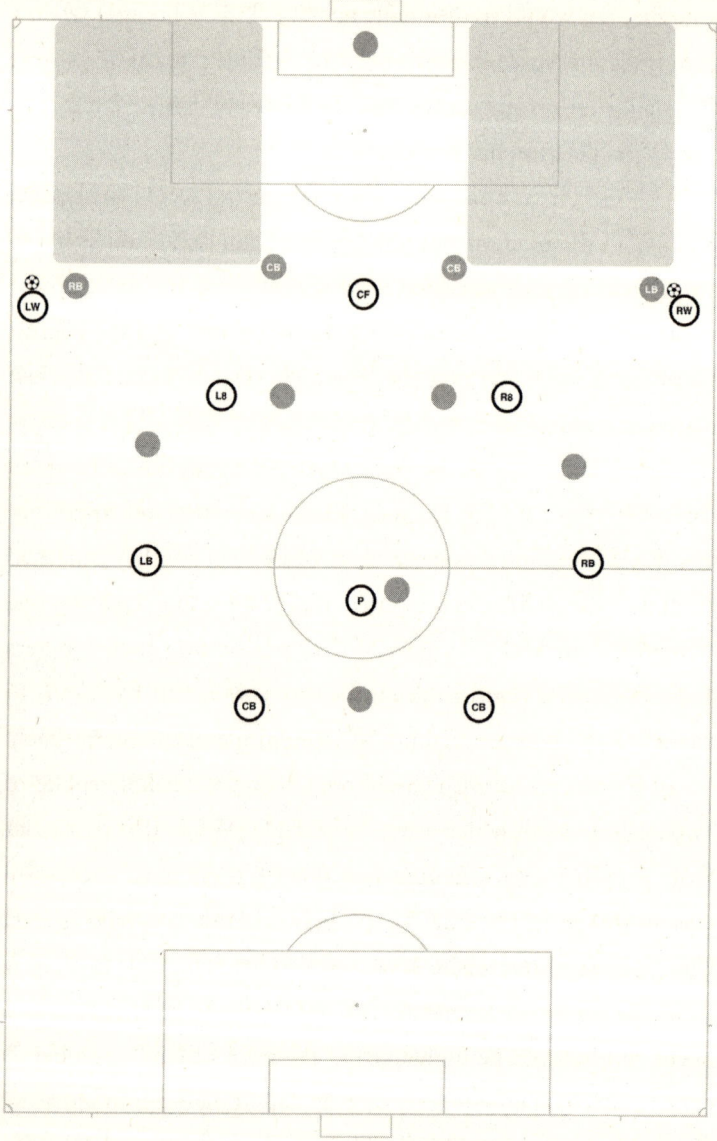

Figure 29. Locations of the channels City targeted between the opposition full-backs and centre-backs when the opposition full-backs moved wide to defend against their wingers

give and go into the space inside the full-back for the winger to run on to (*Figure 30*). The second was for the number 8 to run himself into the space inside and behind the full-back (*Figure 31*).

De Bruyne and Silva's awareness of the location of the space, which movement pattern the situation required and the precise moment to execute the move was incredibly advanced. The first pattern, the give and go, suited a combination with a fast winger, so was more effective when Sterling or Sané played; one of these two almost always played on the left wing. On the right, especially during 2018/19, the left-footed options of Bernardo Silva and Riyad Mahrez were often chosen. Due to their relative lack of pace, they were more likely to cut inside with the ball than run down the outside, so the give and go was less common; instead they would often look to use the second pattern, to slide a pass for De Bruyne into space in the channel behind the full-back. De Bruyne had fantastic athleticism to attack the space, but the key to its success was also timing so Silva, a much slower player, also excelled at this run. But if opposition teams knew that City were going to perform these specific moves, why couldn't they stop them? The first point to make is that due to City's huge amount of controlled possession and the way the system was tailored to supply their front five, they had the opportunity to carry out these moves over and over again, until the opposition lost their concentration and succumbed. The second point is the advantage City's players had of being part of a consistent system of play for a relatively long time, enabling them to perform these moves automatically. The opposition, on the other hand, played against City twice a season, so although they may have worked all week in training on the defensive strategies they needed to stop them, it paled into comparison to City's time practising these specific moves themselves.

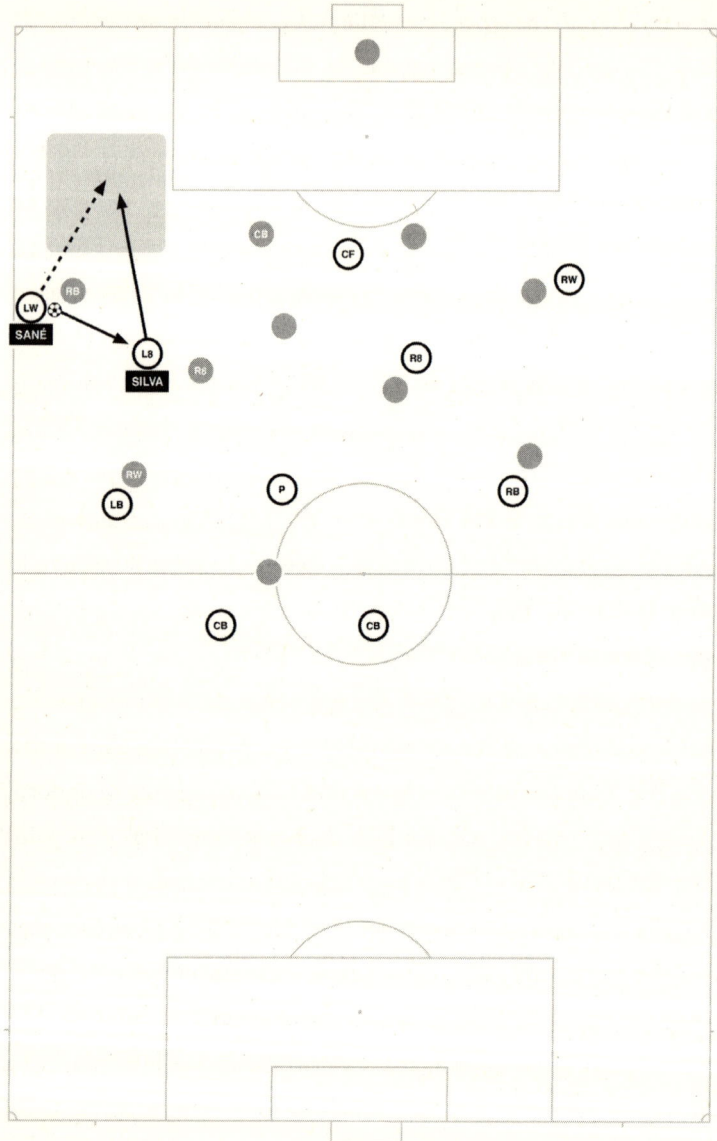

Figure 30. An example of how Sané would draw out the opposition full-back and combine with Silva to play a give and go around the full-back, with City's winger then receiving the return pass in the channel

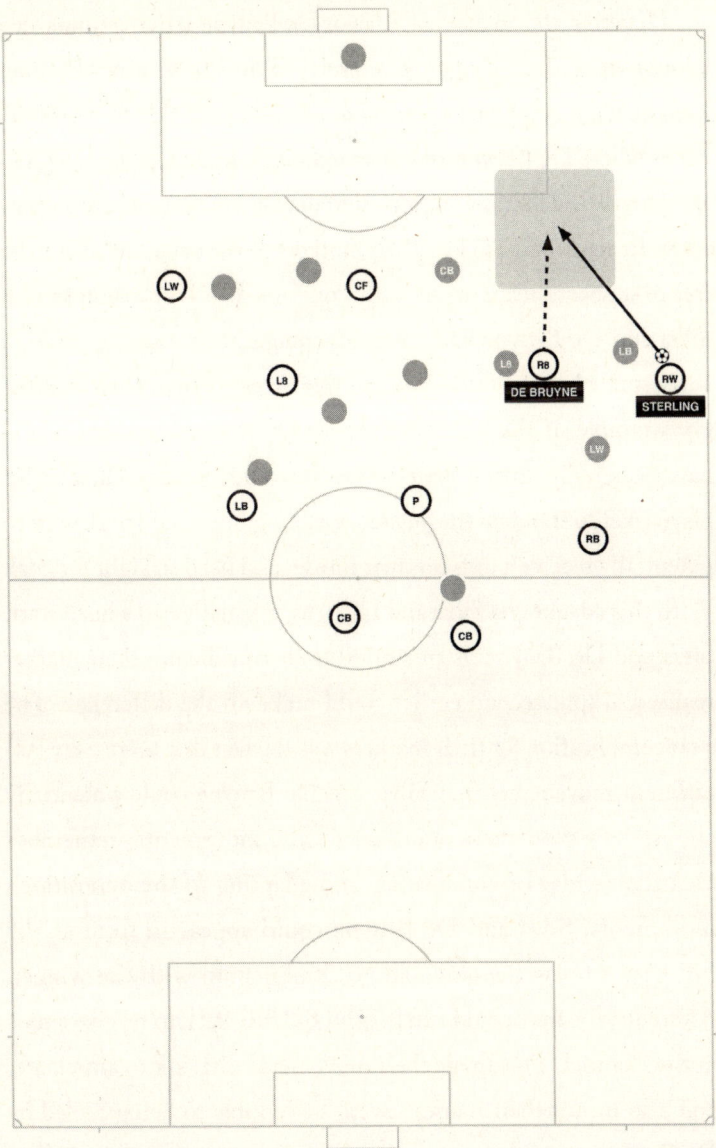

Figure 31. *When the space to play a give and go was limited, or the angle of the pass inside to City's number 8 was blocked off, De Bruyne and Silva would make runs directly into the channel to receive a pass from the winger behind the full-back*

However, the chances of Silva or De Bruyne arriving unmarked in support of their winger were pretty slim; almost every Premier League team employed a central midfielder each side to patrol the zones where De Bruyne and Silva operated. In fact, some took it to an extreme and literally attempted to man-mark them wherever they went. In attempting to lose their markers to the extent needed to be free to support their wingers with a one-touch pass or a support run, Silva and De Bruyne had a key advantage: their starting position was usually horizontally closer to their winger than their marker. For example, if the ball was central, De Bruyne's marker would have been more central than he was. It would have been bizarre for his marker to stand on the outside, enabling Silva and De Bruyne to potentially receive a pass on their inside, and head straight for goal. With this advantage, Silva and De Bruyne usually had a head start. Silva and De Bruyne often started their runs before their marker realised; a split second earlier could make all the difference. The next complication for their markers was the fact that there were two different movements that Silva and De Bruyne could potentially choose based on their opponents' own movements; remember Guardiola's idea of anticipating and adapting to the opposition's movements. Silva and De Bruyne could appear in front of the full-back to play the give and go combination with the winger. Alternatively, they could run behind the full-back to receive a pass in the channel. This made their movements difficult to anticipate, and also meant their markers were susceptible to being fooled by De Bruyne and Silva pretending to make one movement, before changing direction and making the other as soon as their opponent responded to the first one.

In terms of the give and go movement pattern, the final action of a through ball was the same pass that City would ideally have played without firstly having to pass to the winger. For example, against teams who were less compact, teams who left space behind their midfield in an attempt to press higher, or in transition situations before a team could regain their shape, City's wingers were often put through on goal by a pass from their number 8 slotted between centre-back and full-back. The inside runs the wingers made in these situations were similar to those made by Liverpool's wide forwards, with the difference being that the pass was from higher up and played on the ground through a gap, rather than over the top from deep. The majority of the time, however, the opposition forced City to pass wide first and draw the full-back out, before looking for the through ball via a give and go. In effect, they found an alternative way to supply their number 8s with the ball in an advantageous area of the pitch. The action of the give and go happened incredibly quickly. Often it would seem as if the opposition had it covered, with Silva or De Bruyne's designated marker remaining tight, and the move slowing down. But their marker would often switch off, thinking they had everything under control.

The key was often the time between the City players making their movements and the opposition players reacting. De Bruyne and Silva would make a sudden movement to show for the ball, giving them enough space to receive. The instant Sterling or Sané released the ball for the pass, they then made their movement behind the full-back. The penalty won by Sterling against Newcastle in January 2018 showcased the give and go at its best. Zinchenko supplied Sterling with an angled pass, allowing him to receive 'open', facing the inside. Seeing Sterling 'doubled up' upon by two Newcastle players, David Silva appeared on the Newcastle players' inside, and exchanged passes with the City winger, who was on the move inside Newcastle wing-back Javier Manquillo the instant that he released the ball. This enabled Sterling to receive 'goal side' of Manquillo, who brought him down in the box. Sterling and Sané had the advantage that the full-back had to turn before running back towards his own goal, whereas City's wingers could simply accelerate forward.

Perhaps the most advanced version of this give and go occurred when City's winger had received the ball out wide in the final third, with the opposition able to retreat into their own box. In this situation, the proximity to the byline meant there was usually no room for the number 8 to make the channel run, and seemingly no room for the return pass of the give and go. Instead, the number 8 would often drop off, and the winger would pass back to him, before sprinting on the inside of the full-back for the return pass. The details of why this reverse give and go was so advanced and consequently so difficult to defend against will be covered in the chapters concerning City and Liverpool's final third strategies, but as it is a combination between a wide winger and number 8, it is worth mentioning in this chapter. There were several examples of this reverse give and go which directly led to goals, including Leroy Sané's goal in September 2017 against Crystal Palace, when the German passed back to David Silva, before instantly running on the inside of Palace right-back Timothy Fosu-Mensah.

We're now going to analyse the movement of the number 8 into the channel, which often resulted in the classic De Bruyne cross from the byline for the opposite City winger or Agüero to score. The De Bruyne cross remained one of City's major weapons beyond their two record points seasons, arguably even increasing in prevalence and effectiveness. City would create this situation over and over again until De Bruyne could be successfully fed in the channel between centre-back and left-back. Since the change on City's right from Sterling to Bernardo Silva or Riyad Mahrez, the run arguably became even more difficult to control. This may seem strange, as Bernardo and Mahrez are left-footed players who lack real pace, yet they were generally asked to hold their width just the same. In fact, as Guardiola tweaked his system during the 2019/20 season, often trying different patterns on City's left side, their right-side patterns remained similar, almost always involving one of Bernardo or Mahrez holding width, and De Bruyne playing as the right-sided number 8; this was presumably because the Belgian's runs were so effective. So as teams paid more and more attention to his runs, why did changing to a left-footer on the right make De Bruyne's life easier? Neither Bernardo nor Mahrez really wanted to dribble past the outside shoulder of the left-back on to their weaker right foot; instead their strengths consisted of the ability to run at the left-back on his *inside* shoulder and whip in a cross or shoot towards the far corner, using their favoured left foot. This meant that when defending against Bernardo or Mahrez, the left-back and any player who came to support him would focus on closing off the inside route on to his left foot, and actively attempt to encourage him to run down the outside shoulder of the full-back on to his right foot. That is not to say these players wouldn't dribble on the outside shoulder and manage to cross the ball or shoot – Mahrez in particular was under-rated at using his right foot – but for the defender, the odds were that this was a less dangerous option than allowing him to shoot or cross with his left.

However, this is where the situation became a double-edged sword. The problem with showing Mahrez or Bernardo the outside route was that this would open up the passing lane into the channel for De Bruyne's run. When Sterling and De Bruyne were paired together, the left-back knew that the City winger generally wanted to run or pass on his outside shoulder, which meant he could adjust his position to block those options off. On the other hand, when a left-footer played on the right with De Bruyne, the left-back had to adjust his position to defend his inside shoulder where the winger wanted to dribble, *and* his outside shoulder where he could pass to De Bruyne. The other difference between the two left-footed wingers and Sterling was that they were the type of players who had the vision and technical ability to appear to be cutting inside to cross or shoot, before at the last second changing their body position and slipping the ball on the outside shoulder of the left-back to De Bruyne; the City number 8 only needed a yard of space to cross first time.

The De Bruyne run became so well highlighted that something interesting began to happen; it started to affect the way some left-backs defended. They knew that as soon as they closed down the winger, De Bruyne would make the run into the space in the channel behind them. So, instead of rushing out to close the winger down, left-backs began to stay narrow to wait for cover behind them. In addition, when facing Mahrez or Bernardo, the left-back often showed less urgency to close them down, as if they were less of a threat, possibly due to their lack of pace in comparison to Sterling. However, rather than function as a solution to the De Bruyne run by staying narrower to block the space for him to run into, arguably by doing this left-backs actually made the situation easier for De Bruyne. As Bernardo or Mahrez advanced inside with the ball, the left-back usually then had to come out to close him down to an extent anyway, often finding himself in a situation where he was caught between closing the winger down and protecting the space on his inside. As he had to face the ball, he didn't know precisely

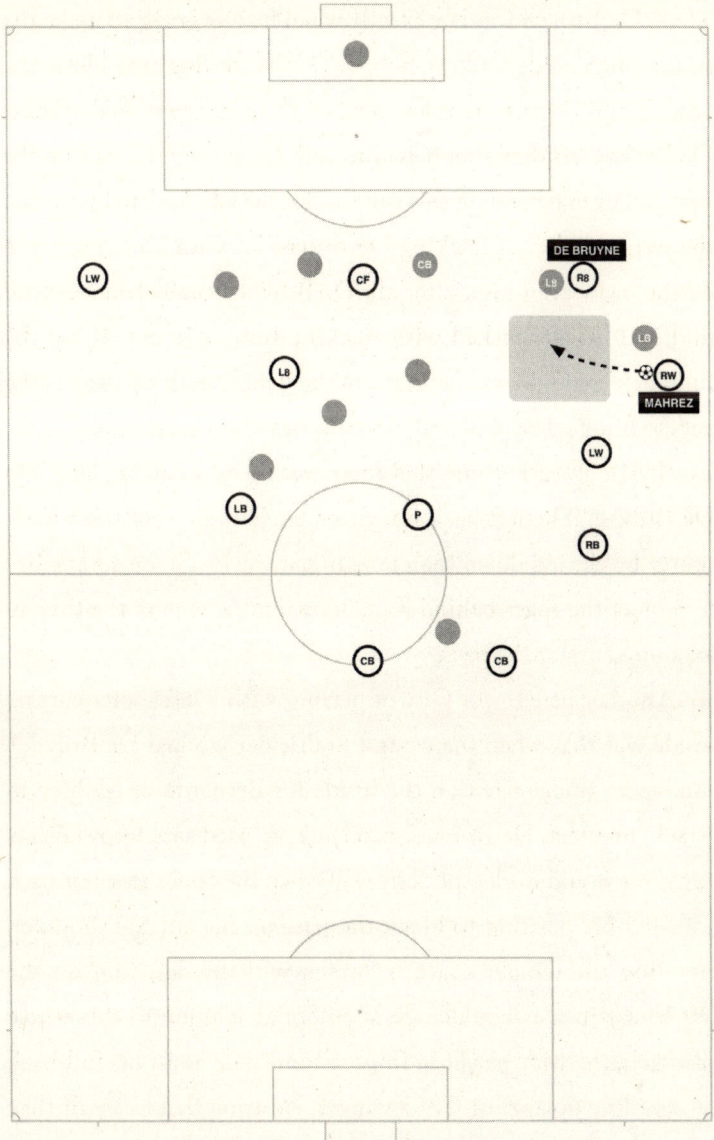

Figure 32. When a left-footer, such as Mahrez or Bernardo Silva, was playing on City's right, De Bruyne's run was often a decoy to take away the opposition left-back's cover from either the opposition's left wide midfielder or left number 8, for City's winger to cut into the space inside the opposition left-back on his stronger left foot

where De Bruyne was nor exactly when he was going to make the run, so he couldn't adjust his position accordingly to block the passing lane. Bernardo or Mahrez, on the other hand, were facing De Bruyne, so they simply had to wait for the run to execute the pass. A key to defending this run was for the left-back to know that the responsibility of tracking De Bruyne lay with his team-mates on the inside, not him; after all, De Bruyne usually had a central midfield marker tasked with tracking him. The best thing the full-back could do was get tight to the winger early as soon as the pass to him had been played, keep his head down, and either make a tackle or at least ensure that there was no easy passing lane into De Bruyne. The left-back was more likely to prevent the pass at source by closing down than remain narrow in a doomed attempt to protect the space behind him, allowing the winger the time to look up and play the pass.

Another benefit for City of playing with a left-footer cutting inside was that when the central midfielder tracked De Bruyne's run, space was created on the inside for Bernardo or Mahrez to attack; in effect, De Bruyne's run could be used as a decoy (*Figure 32*). This would work especially well when the opposition left-back adjusted his position to block the pass on his outside shoulder, enabling the winger space to attack with his left foot on the left-back's inside shoulder. As a potential solution to this whole situation, the wide player in front of him could assist his full-back by doubling up against City's winger, ensuring that as a pair they could block the passing lane on the full-back's outside shoulder to De Bruyne, at the same time as preventing the winger from cutting inside on his left foot. The tighter the left-back got early, the more he could delay and allow time for his wide player to get back and help. Ideally the wide player wouldn't be dragged back to

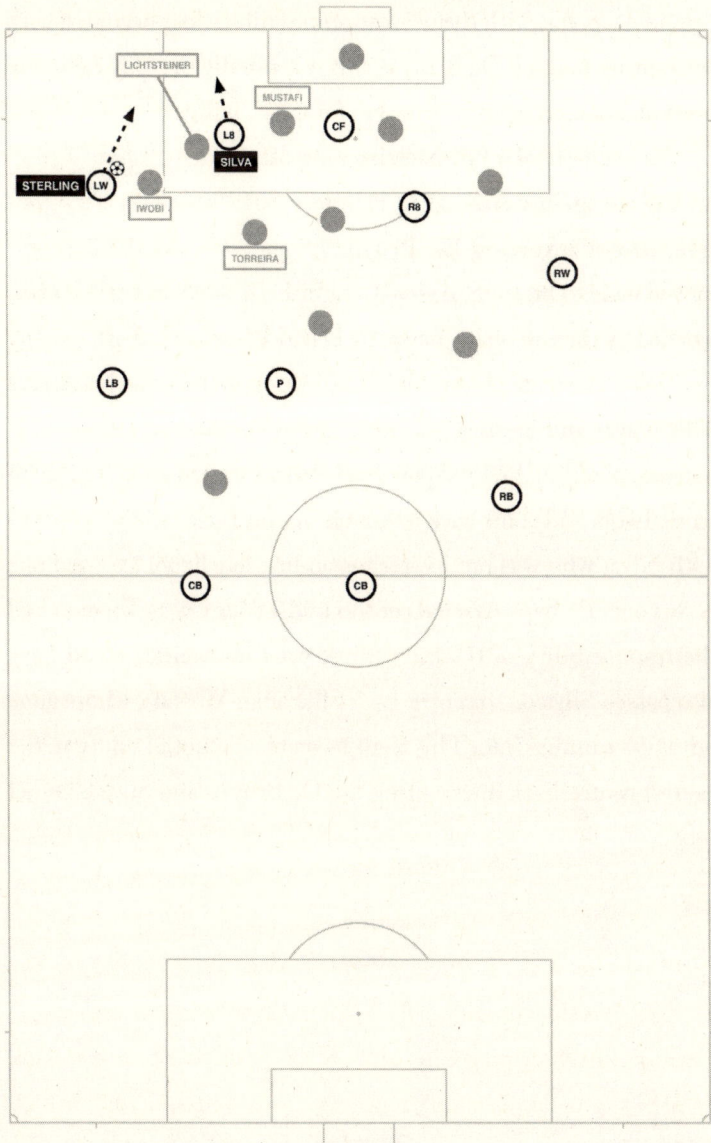

Figure 33. *For this goal in February 2019, Arsenal right-back Stephan Lichtsteiner backed off from Sterling to cover David Silva's run inside him, leaving wide player Alex Iwobi to be beaten one versus one by Sterling, who then crossed for Agüero to score. Arsenal central midfielder Lucas Torreira was too high to track Silva, but centre-back Shkrodan Mustafi could have covered Silva's run, enabling Lichtsteiner to assist Iwobi against Sterling*

defend deep, but with the nearest central midfielder occupied with attempting to track De Bruyne, this was usually the only option to prevent a one versus one situation for City's winger.

An example of a full-back backing off, contributing to a goal, took place against Arsenal in February 2019, albeit on City's left side, so not involving De Bruyne (*Figure 33*). As the ball was moved wide to Sterling, Arsenal's right-back Stephan Lichtsteiner, worried by the run on his inside by David Silva, backed off, passing Sterling on to wide player Alex Iwobi. A one versus one between a wide player and Sterling was never going to result in a favourable outcome; Sterling breezed past Iwobi before crossing for Agüero to score. Iwobi had come back to double up, yet Lichtsteiner's concern with Silva, who was not his responsibility, left Iwobi exposed one versus one. Perhaps Arsenal central midfielder Lucas Torreira had the responsibility of tracking Silva, yet Lichtsteiner could have also passed Silva on to centre-back Shkrodan Mustafi, whose zone Silva was running into. This leads us on to a potential solution: the nearest centre-back intercepting the De Bruyne and Silva channel runs.

Chapter 8

A modern solution to a modern attacking problem

WE'VE DISCUSSED a key factor for the opposition when City's winger received the ball: the left-back concentrating on getting tight to the winger early to apply pressure on the ball and keep the winger's head down, rather than worrying about the number 8's movement behind him. We've also proposed the importance of the wide player doubling up when possible to prevent a one versus one situation. And of course, we've mentioned that almost every team tasked a central midfielder with tracking the City number 8's run, especially De Bruyne. However, some teams tended to use another solution to this situation, which perhaps appeared risky, but could be effective at nullifying the threat of De Bruyne. This was for the left sided centre-back to come across and intercept the pass to him, or at least get close enough to prevent him from crossing. Or, even better, to fill the space early to prevent the pass being played in the first place.

In English football, centre-backs did not traditionally tend to defend outside the width of the penalty area because teams usually played 4-4-2, with two out-and-out wingers and two forwards. The strategy was for the wingers to remain wide and create a yard of space on the outside before crossing the ball into the box. Therefore, if crosses were going to be raining in on a regular basis and with two forwards to defend against inside the box, it was perceived as essential for the two centre-backs to remain in their central positions to defend. However, in the modern game there are fewer teams who play with two forwards, and there are even fewer forwards who are specialists in the air. More importantly, the principal tactic of simply crossing the ball from wide is less frequent, at least at the top level. Burnley are one exception, but how many other teams in today's Premier League play like Burnley? Teams do of course still cross the ball, but many now tend to keep possession until they can cross the ball from a position where they have a higher percentage chance of the cross being successful. This usually involves delivering from a narrower position than the touchline, where the cross is more of a pass which picks a player out, than a low-percentage punt into the area. With many teams now using smaller forwards in comparison to the centre-backs they face, lower crosses which don't involve an aerial duel have become more fashionable. From these crossing positions nearer the penalty area, centre-backs have a really difficult task, even if the two of them are in good positions within the width of the goal, as the time they have to adjust is reduced between the ball being struck and it entering their zone, due to the shorter distance between the origin and destination of the cross. Equally, from a low cross nearer the penalty area, the centre-backs' height advantage over the forward(s) is irrelevant.

All this means that when the ball is moved wide, the relevance of the centre-back nearest to the ball dropping back into the penalty area to defend a cross has reduced. Instead, limiting the space between the full-back and centre-back in order to prevent teams from crossing from this more more dangerous zone on the inside of the full-back has gained relevance. Arguably it was better to use the nearest centre-back to help prevent the ball being crossed from such a dangerous position in the first place, by moving across to deal with De Bruyne, when he looked to make a run into the right channel (*Figure 34*). There were two reasons why using the nearest centre-back could be preferable: firstly, from the inside pass from the winger to De Bruyne, the ball and the centre-back were usually moving towards each other, whereas De Bruyne himself had to catch up with the ball. Secondly, the centre-back's angle of approach was 'down the line' of the potential cross, which meant De Bruyne would not be able to deliver the ball first time as long as the centre-back got close enough when he received the ball, as doing so would result in a blocked cross. Delaying a first-time cross bought time for more players to recover into the box.

De Bruyne's central midfield marker didn't have the same advantages the centre-back had. If teams relied solely on a central midfielder tracking De Bruyne's runs between left-back and centre-back, the chances were that he would get caught out and beaten to the ball at some point, when you consider the high number of times City performed this movement pattern in games. The central midfielder had to attempt to track, but the centre-back also needed to be in a position to cover. To avoid being caught out, every time De Bruyne made the run his central midfield marker would have to get to the ball either first or at the instant that De Bruyne looked to strike the ball, as he wasn't approaching from an angle which prevented a first-time cross. Any lapse in concentration from the central midfielder and his centre-backs were sitting ducks in the

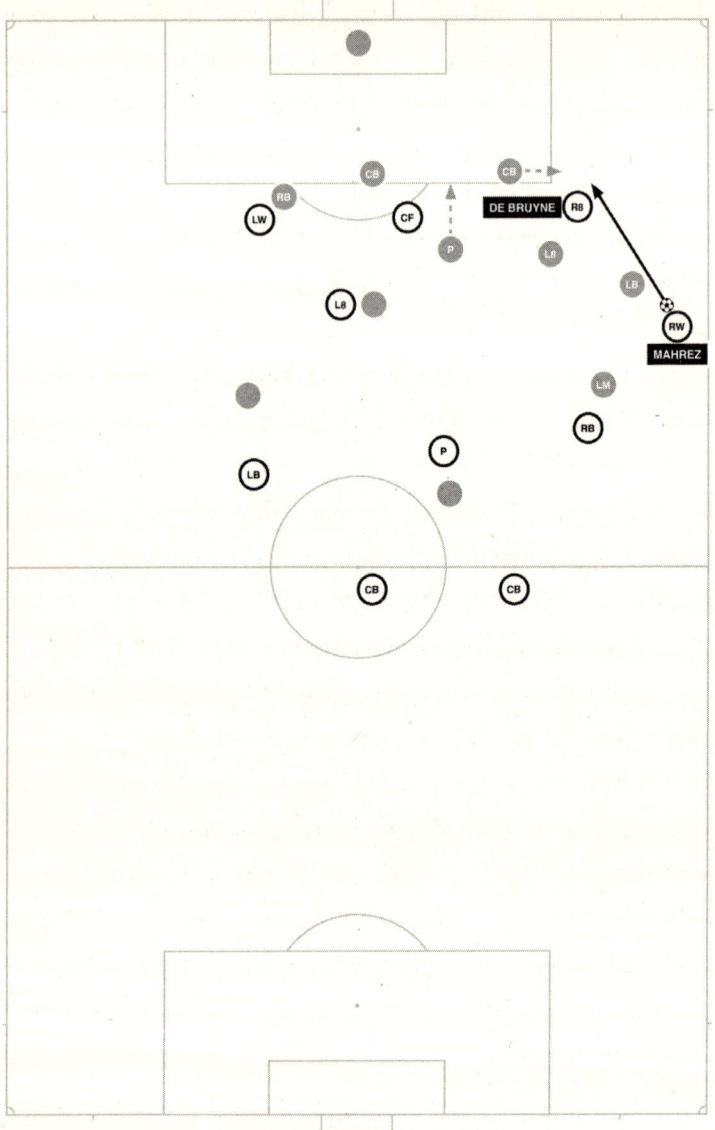

Figure 34. *An example of a potential solution which didn't rely on the central midfielder successfully tracking De Bruyne 100 per cent of the time. Instead, the nearest opposition centre-back could come across and block De Bruyne's space to run into. The centre-back had the advantage of moving towards the ball, and at an angle which enabled him to block a first-time cross. If the opposition were playing with a deep pivot, he could fill in the space between the two centre-backs, should the first centre-back have been bypassed*

middle for a first-time cross from a short distance, to one of City's numerous players attacking the box. Dealing with this problem with a mixture of man-for-man (the central midfielder) and zonal marking (the centre-back) was arguably the best solution.

The thinking behind this strategy was that De Bruyne effectively became a second forward with the run he made; if a team was setting up to deal with a two-forward system, it would be the centre-back's job to deal with the forward's channel run on his side. However, this solution was not easy; it needed practice on the training ground, clear communication between players, and intelligent players who could see the movement pattern happening early enough to move themselves into position. When deciding whether to come across, the centre-back had to consider if he could get there in time to affect the situation by stopping De Bruyne reaching the ball and crossing. If the answer was yes, it was probably the right decision to cover his run and try to prevent the cross from happening. However, if the answer was no, the centre-back would probably be better staying centrally to deal with the cross and protect the goal.

If a team were to use their left centre-back to nullify De Bruyne in a back four, they would likely need to make little adjustments. If the centre-back was going to leave the width of the goal in order to be in a position to cover De Bruyne when the pass was played, it was crucial that the left-back applied pressure to City's winger, preventing him from advancing towards the penalty area and being able to lift his head and place the ball beyond the opposition centre-back who came across to cover De Bruyne. The likes of Bernardo and Mahrez had the vision to assess the situation and place the ball into the gap between the centre-backs for City's forward or left-sided number 8. While Silva wasn't known for his heading ability, his run into the space was often enough to move the remaining centre-back away from Agüero, leaving him unmarked. If he was able to react quickly enough, the opposition's right-back may be able to move narrower to cover Agüero, but the chance of this happening in time to have an impact was low, and it would also have meant City's left-winger was free at the back post, a zone where Sterling and Sané scored many goals. It's important to point out that Guardiola and his support staff watched carefully how teams defended, so they had a good idea of how teams aimed to cover City's movement patterns, enabling them to make small tactical adjustments to counteract the opposition's solutions. With this in mind, teams who used their ball-side centre-back in a back four to get across and cover De Bruyne had to be very careful; the way in which their midfield adapted to the situation was key.

With this particular defensive strategy, it was helpful to play with three central midfielders, in a 4-1-4-1 formation. Although here we are explaining how a back four could nullify City, there were certain scenarios where it was difficult to avoid dropping into a back five, simply because City played with five front players. The defensive movements took place as follows: as the opposition's left centre-back moved across to track De Bruyne, and their midfield pivot moved to fill the gap which began to open between the two centre-backs. He would be, in effect, a spare man, as Silva would have been the responsibility of the right-sided number 8, and De Bruyne the left-sided number 8. By zonally filling the space between the centre-backs, there would be no gap for Silva or Agüero to exploit. The opposition team would therefore have transitioned into a back five to defend against City's front five, in the specific scenario of defending their box when De Bruyne made his trademark run.

Of course, rather than transitioning into a back five, playing an actual back five with three central defenders was helpful in defending against City's front five; five defenders were able to spread out across the width of the pitch and cover the five players to a greater extent than four. This meant the left wing-back would already be closer to City's right-winger, potentially enabling him to intercept the pass out to the winger in the first place, or at least to be tighter earlier to prevent the winger from lifting his head and playing the pass inside. In a back five, the left centre-back would also have been further over towards the wide area, so he would have had less distance to cover in order to occupy the zone into which De Bruyne made his run. Finally, in a back-five system, even with the left centre-back removed from the box there were two remaining centre-backs to defend against any cross that did come in. As these favourable situations demonstrate, there were some sound arguments for playing a back five against City; later we will cover how City themselves adapted tactically against this system.

Finally, let's explain what De Bruyne did when he couldn't make the run into the channel, either because the centre-back had come across to plug the gap, because the full-back, with help from his wide player doubling up, had managed to block the passing lane into him, or because his central midfield marker managed to successfully track him. Unfortunately for the opposition, the danger didn't end there. De Bruyne would often check his run to create himself a yard of space on the edge of the box, giving the winger an option to lay the ball back to him. His marker, expecting a cross from City's winger or the channel run from De Bruyne, would often retreat deeper, encouraged by the fact De Bruyne was not perceived to be in such a dangerous position, having been prevented from running into the channel. From just outside the area, De

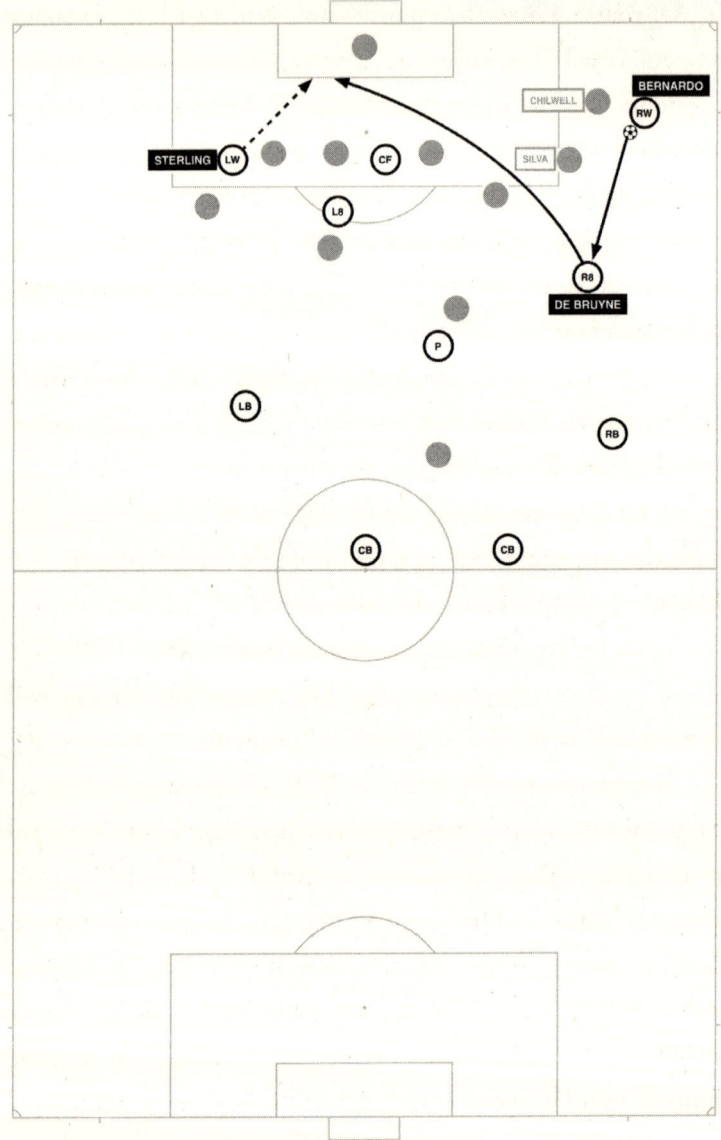

Figure 35. For this goal scored against Leicester in February 2018, central midfielder Adrien Silva dropped deep to block the space for De Bruyne to run into the channel. Instead, the City number 8 held his position deeper to receive a backwards pass, before whipping a first-time cross behind the Leicester defensive line for Sterling to score

Bruyne would unleash a whipped cross, often first time, into the space between the defensive line and goalkeeper. Most of the time he wouldn't even look, simply expecting City's centre-forward, left-sided number 8, and left-winger to make the box; De Bruyne is a world-class crosser of the ball, possessing devastating pace, whip and accuracy in his delivery. Later we will analyse why this type of cross was so difficult to defend. The fact he had the ability to deliver first time without looking meant he only needed to arrive a yard or two ahead of his designated marker.

A classic Kevin De Bruyne assist occurred in February 2018 against Leicester (*Figure 35*). Right-winger Bernardo Silva ran at left-back Ben Chilwell, and central midfielder Adrien Silva, De Bruyne's opposite number, dropped deep to plug the space for De Bruyne's channel run. Instead, the Belgian held his position deeper, waited for Bernardo to cut the ball back to him, before whipping an inch-perfect first-time cross for Sterling to tap into the net. As the level of detail in this chapter shows, preventing – or reducing the effectiveness of – the combination play between City's wingers and number 8s was an extremely complicated yet vital aspect of keeping City's chance creation to a minimum.

Chapter 9

Liverpool's full-backs as wing-backs

WHEREAS CITY tended to position both full-backs deep and narrow, Liverpool's full-backs regularly moved high and wide to provide an attacking threat. The statistics emphasise their attacking contributions: Robertson and Alexander-Arnold were ranked numbers one and two among Premier League full-backs playing at least 25 games for open-play assists, expected assists and chances created (all per 90 minutes) during the combined 2018/19 and 2019/20 seasons. The reason the full-backs primarily provided Liverpool's width was of course that Salah and Mané's predominant positions were inside and high, either on the outside shoulder of the opposition full-backs looking for a diagonal pass on the inside, or on the inside shoulder, *between* centre-back and full-back, from where they could make a run into the channel.

However, it was not set in stone that Mané and Salah needed to spend the entire game in these ultra-narrow positions. At times, for example, especially with Alexander-Arnold tending to play deeper than Robertson, Salah would drift wide, into a similar position to City's right-winger. From there, he did exactly what City's winger did – attacked one versus one against the full-back, or passed into the channel for Liverpool's high right-sided number 8 to make the same run De Bruyne did for City. When Alex Oxlade-Chamberlain was selected to play as a number 8 for Liverpool this pattern occurred more regularly, as his electric pace suited this type of run. However, it was the exception not the rule. In the case of Mané, although he would also occasionally move wide, his attributes – for example his pace to attack space, and his goalscoring ability – were more effectively used inside.

The central midfielder-full-back rotation

Although their attacking intent was clear, it would be wrong to say that both full-backs were regularly very high at the same time. Usually, one or both of the full-backs' starting positions was fairly conservative, as they were also required to be potential options to help construct the attack from deeper. This tended to be Alexander-Arnold, with Robertson pushing on higher, although still not quite like a winger; a better description of Robertson's positioning would be that of a wing-back. Like Alexander-Arnold, Robertson's positioning enabled him to drop deeper when Liverpool needed him to assist with build-up play, but also move high to provide width further up the pitch.

The tendency of Robertson to play as the higher of the two is reflected in the statistics: Robertson created more open-play chances and registered more open-play assists, both overall, and per 90 minutes, than Alexander-Arnold. In addition, Robertson had a greater percentage involvement in Liverpool's open-play moves leading to shots, and received a larger percentage of Liverpool's final-third passes, especially in 2019/20 (*Graph 4*). One of the main reasons Robertson was able to start higher than Alexander-Arnold

Robertson had relatively more involvement in the final third than Alexander-Arnold

Robertson received more of the team's passes in the final third and was more involved in moves leading to shots from open play in 19/20.

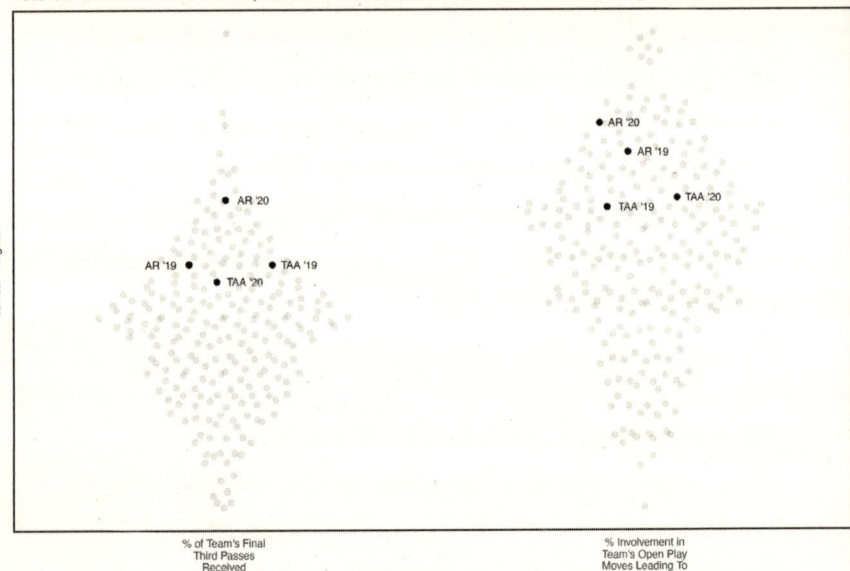

Note: Statistics are on a per–90 basis unless specified. Data are from full–back or wing–back starts only.
Each point represents a Premier League full–back in a season between 16/17 and 19/20 with minimum 10 starts, ranked from lowest up to highest for each statistic.
Data source: Stats Perform

Graph 4.

without Liverpool forming too expansive a shape was the positioning of the number 8s. Whereas on Liverpool's right their number 8 tended to be positioned higher, in the right pocket, Liverpool's left-sided number 8, usually Wijnaldum, tended to drop deeper, as a second pivot, and at times so deep that he formed a back three, in the triangular 1-2 shape we have already discussed in detail. This deep position of Wijnaldum gave Robertson the security to move higher. Of course, Alexander-Arnold was also able to move higher. With Wijnaldum sitting deep, Liverpool's pivot, usually Fabinho, was able to shift across to cover for Alexander-Arnold if necessary.

The tactic of a central midfielder dropping deep and wide to allow a full-back to push on is common in modern football. The main function of this structured rotation is to form a triangle with an option deep and narrow (the central midfielder), an option wide (the full-back), and an option high and narrow (the wide player), adhering to the principle that one must fill each space. Now we are going to analyse in more detail how Liverpool performed this structured rotation in order to cause maximum problems for the opposition. Firstly, let's define the word rotation in football terms, and outline why teams benefit from rotating. A rotation in its simplest form is a player moving into a space previously filled by a team-mate. The term *structured* rotation can be used when it involves a clear pre-planned movement where each player fills one of the available spaces. Another type of rotation is where two players swap positions with each other, filling each other's original position; in a later chapter, we will outline how at times both City and Liverpool's number 8s and wide players interchanged positions, with the wide player becoming the number 8, and the number 8 the wide player.

The distinction between so-called structured rotations, and scenarios where players move where they want on the pitch, is important. The downside of unstructured movements is that they can result in a team becoming 'out of shape' when attacking. Remember the story Thierry Henry told about being substituted for moving over to the other side of the pitch from his left-wing position. The view is that players must be positioned correctly at all times in order to attack with the optimal numbers of players, positioned in the necessary spaces, so they can work together to give the best chance to hurt the opposition.

While the structure must be maintained, rotating the players who form the structure is seen as beneficial. When teams attack using possession-based build-up but without rotation, the game tends to follow a theme. The defending team allows the attacking team's defenders possession, knowing they don't want to play long forward passes, resulting in the ball being passed from side to side without penetrating the opposition, usually between the back four (or five). The midfield pivot(s) may be able to receive, but they are then closed down quickly to prevent them from turning. Without rotation by the in-possession team, the task for the out-of-possession team is made fairly simple: the scenarios they face are consistent, so their individual roles are clear, and they know where their opposite numbers are positioned to receive the ball so are able to either prevent them from receiving, or close them down quickly enough to force them to pass the ball backwards. In a 4-3-3 where the players don't rotate, the opposition usually simply match the three midfielders up with their own midfielders, and uses their wide player and full-back against the opposition wide player and full-back. Everything is very predictable; without rotation, creating chances relies on individual players winning a duel against their marker, either by taking the ball past them, or making an untracked run.

In the case of Liverpool, on their left side the rotation worked as follows (*Figure 36*): Wijnaldum's deep position enabled Robertson to move higher, which meant Mané didn't need to play wide. In turn, Mané's narrow position meant Wijnaldum didn't need to play high. The personnel on Liverpool's left side suited the positions they found themselves in. We have already discussed the reasons for Mané playing narrow, from where he could make runs in behind. Robertson has some of the attributes of a winger, in terms of his pace and crossing ability. The only slight question mark is why the deeper role tended to be played by Wijnaldum instead of Liverpool's other number 8 options. Jordan Henderson, for example, was usually used as an advanced right-sided number 8, not the deeper role performed by Wijnaldum, who was a competent passer but hardly a top-quality deep-lying playmaker; arguably to a lesser extent than Henderson, anyway. In fact, earlier in his career Wijnaldum was often used as

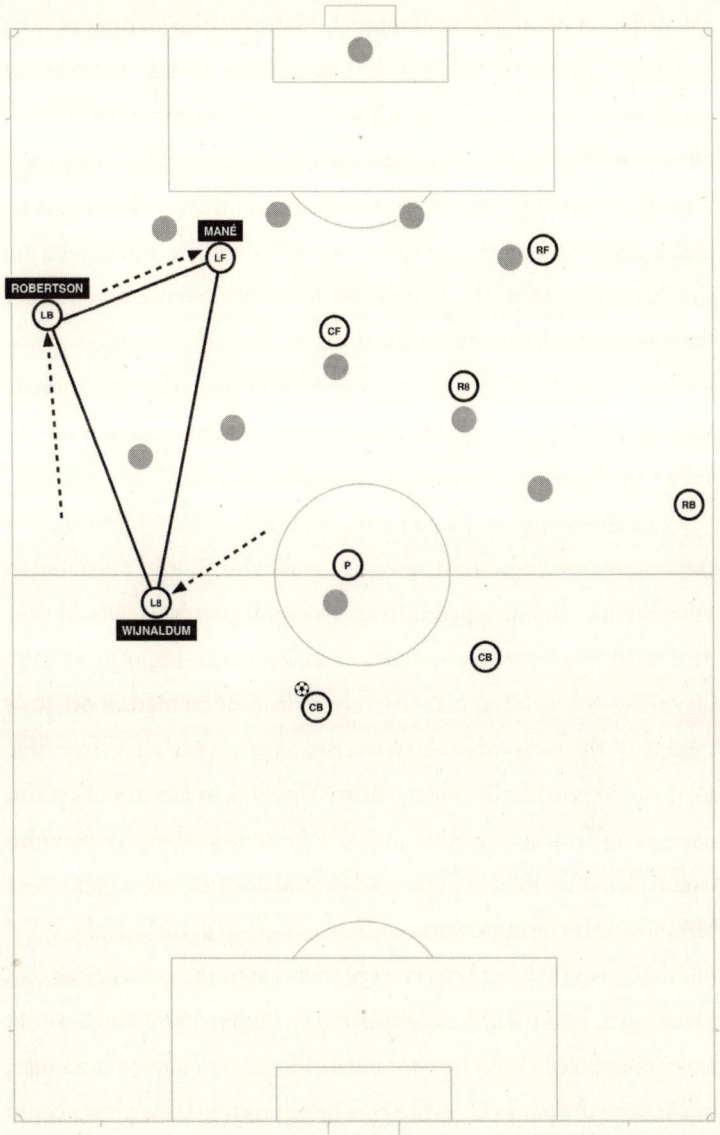

Figure 36. The common rotation on Liverpool's left. Mané moved inside, Robertson moved high and wide, and Wijnaldum moved towards Robertson's original position

a wide player or attacking number 8. However, this in itself may be one of the reasons why he was deemed suitable for a deeper role: his ability to carry the ball forward into space and commit an opposition player, and then take the ball past them if necessary. Wijnaldum was actually remarkably reliable in possession, both with his decision-making and his ability to protect the ball physically. In fact, during the 2019/20 season, the Dutchman lost possession less frequently than any other Liverpool outfield player. This is a common theme for teams whose full-backs and central midfielders rotate; they do so to enable their central midfielders space to receive and use their ability on the ball to help build the attack.

The rotation on Liverpool's left side asked questions of the opposition. The first question was who should close down Wijnaldum, who dropped into an awkward position. Should they deal with him man-for-man or zonally? If the opposition were playing 4-4-2/4-4-1-1, his relatively wide position made it difficult for one of the forwards to move across, and even if they were able to, it would potentially free up either Van Dijk or Liverpool's pivot, depending on who the other forward concentrated on. Wijnaldum would be too far for one of the two central midfielders to go to close him down. If the opposition were playing 4-1-4-1, the right-sided number 8 would be able to start higher due to the presence of two more central midfielders, but moving so high to close down would leave a big hole behind him for either Firmino to move across into, or Mané to drop into (*Figure 37*). The opposition wide player could compensate to some extent by tucking in narrowly to block any potential pass into the pocket, but this would then give Robertson extra space out wide.

A third option in both systems, but to a greater extent in a 4-1-4-1, would be for the wide player himself to close down

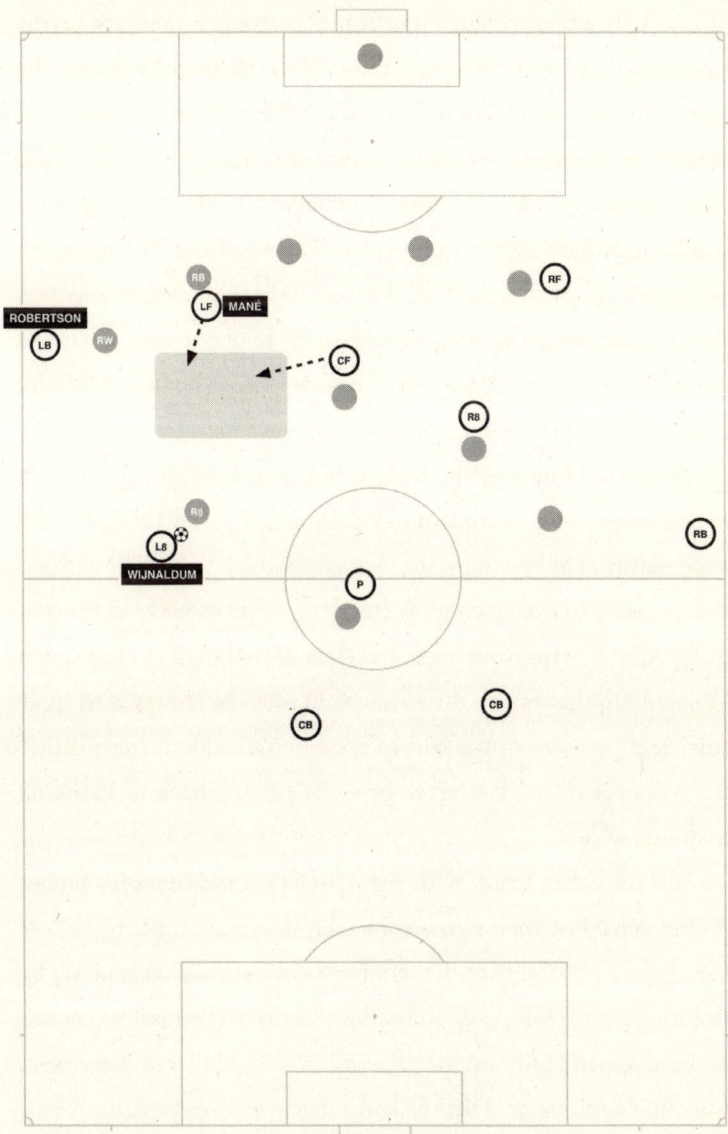

Figure 37. *Example of man-for-man defending of the Liverpool rotation. The opposition right number 8 moves high to close down Wijnaldum, the right-sided wide midfielder tracks Robertson, and the right-back stays narrow with Mané, who has space to drop into in the pocket due to the opposition central midfielder moving higher. Essentially, to deal with Liverpool's rotation the opposition players have rotated positions themselves*

Wijnaldum, either moving away from Robertson to do so, or having remained high in the first place rather than dropping back with the Liverpool left-back (*Figure 38*). This option may have made sense because Wijnaldum would have moved towards the zone of the wide player anyway, and his angle of approach when closing down would potentially enable him to block the pass from Wijnaldum to Robertson. However, much of the time Wijnaldum was too narrow for this, meaning that the opposition wide player would have to move a long way inside to close down. As long as he was successful in his task of preventing the pass to Robertson, there would be no problem. However, the higher Robertson moved, the greater the distance between him and Wijnaldum. This meant that if the wide player could be bypassed, for example by Van Dijk, without the necessity to even pass to Wijnaldum, or if the wide player first dropped back with Robertson, but then moved high to close down Wijnaldum, the vertical distance would often be too great to apply sufficient pressure to the ball to prevent Wijnaldum from lifting the ball over the wide player's head, or passing back to Van Dijk to do likewise.

On the other hand, with the opposition wide player's higher position enabling their number 8 to stay deeper, at times there may have been a possibility of the number 8 covering the wide player by sprinting out to close down Robertson; Liverpool themselves pressed in this manner. However, the pace and crossing ability of Robertson, combined with the fact that he had a tendency to cross early, meant that this could not be a solution throughout 90 minutes; it would be a recipe for disaster giving Liverpool's full-backs that much space. But what about the opposition full-back? Could he sprint out and close down Robertson? This would depend on how high the Liverpool left-back was; unless he was almost in line with the full-back, this

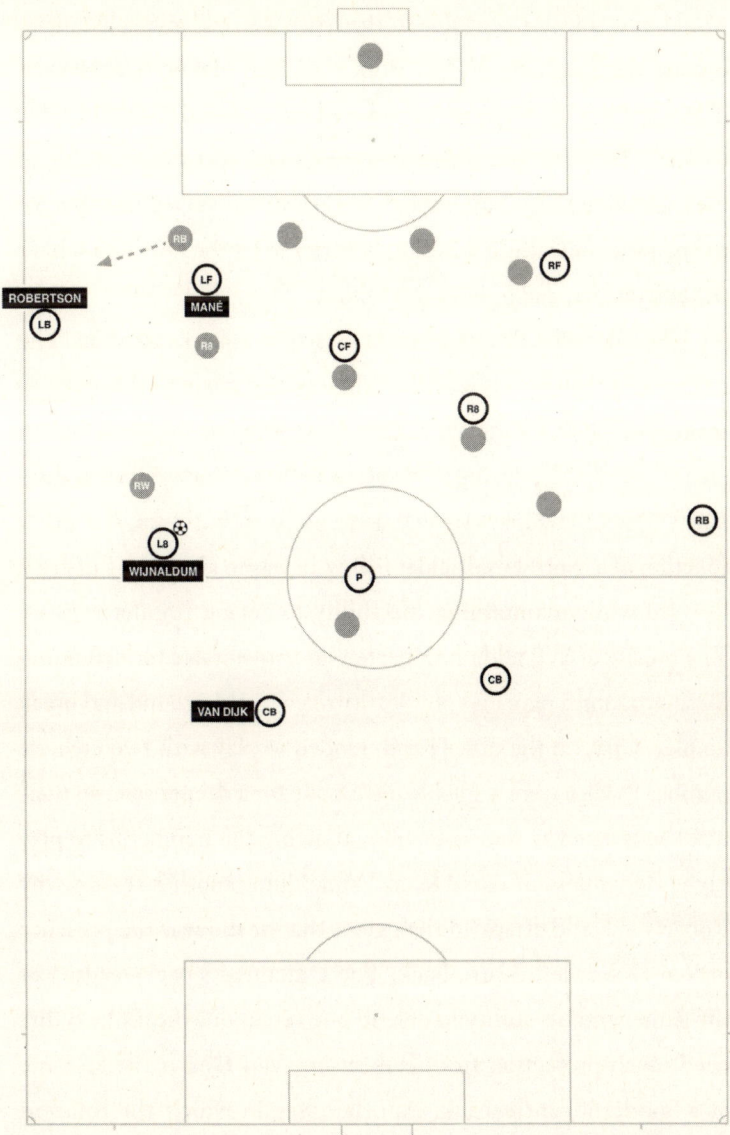

Figure 38. *Example of zonal defending of the Liverpool rotation. The central midfielder, right-sided wide midfielder and right-back all remain in their zones rather than following their original 'man'. If the ball is passed to Robertson, for example following a pass back to Van Dijk, the right-back moves wide to close him down*

would be a risky strategy due to the space it would give to Mané in behind the full-back. When Robertson was higher up, however, it was a viable strategy, which we will cover in more detail in due course. The better pressing teams were in certain scenarios able to use their wide player or number 8 to close down Wijnaldum, but for the majority of teams it was simply better to let the Dutchman have the ball deeper, and to hold their shape.

The dilemmas described were caused by a simple rotation. The strength of Liverpool was that they varied their positioning to make it difficult for the opposition to stick to one simple defensive plan. For example, during some phases of play, Robertson was deep and Wijnaldum high. As well as to assist in build-up, the other function of a central midfielder filling in was to allow the full-back forward while maintaining the ability to defend counter-attacks. The profile of Wijnaldum in particular was suitable for defending these situations; pace and physicality to cover the ground and break up play. City, on the other hand, tended to play with two creative number 8s who were arguably unsuitable for a deeper role, so their full-backs acted as the protection, allowing the number 8s to play high. Regardless of cover from Wijnaldum, another reason why Robertson could attack to the extent that he did was the presence of Van Dijk at left centre-back. The Dutchman's pace, reading of the game, and his ability to defend one versus one meant he didn't need much protection from Robertson; Van Dijk is the epitome of a 'modern' centre-back. Another way in which the rotation helped against defending counter-attacks was the high position of Liverpool's full-back itself. If the opposition wide players dropped back with Robertson or Alexander-Arnold, they would be so far from Liverpool's goal that there would be a great distance to counter-attack before reaching Liverpool's goal.

The relationship between Robertson and Mané

Robertson and Mané interacted very effectively on Liverpool's left side to create space for each other high up the pitch. There were several ways in which these two players worked off each other's positions and movements, depending on how Robertson was dealt with by the opposition. Robertson and Mané had an incredible relationship, but the scenario described is one faced against the majority of Premier League opponents: a high and wide full-back and a narrow wide player. Robertson was either tracked by the wide player, or zonally dealt with by both the full-back *and* wide player.

Let's begin by analysing the movements that occurred when Robertson's high position was dealt with by the opposition wide player dropping back to mark him. In this scenario, the wide player would be wider than his own full-back, and if Robertson had moved very high, he may even have been all the way back, parallel to his own full-back. The thinking here was that if the wide player was close to him and vertically level, Robertson would not be given the necessary time to run with the ball or cross. Preventing early crosses from Liverpool's full-backs was extremely important, because they would often deliver before the centre-backs could recover into the space in front of their goalkeeper. However, the negative was that unless there was central midfield cover in front of Mané, the Liverpool player on the ball had a pass into Mané's feet available, as there would be only partial protection, or no protection at all from the wide player in front. Although in this scenario Mané would have been marked from behind by the full-back, he often displayed the necessary strength to hold the full-back off and either turn and run with the ball, or find a team-mate. On Liverpool's right, Salah would also show deceptive strength and ability with his back to goal; watch, for example, his goal in Liverpool's 4-1

Champions League win over Genk in October 2019, or his strike against Napoli in December 2018.

As well as passing to Mané's feet in front of the full-back, Liverpool had a movement pattern to use the man-marking scenario caused by asking the wide player to drop back *against* the team performing it, in order to access the space in behind the full-back. Man-marking creates one versus one situations and individual responsibility – the full-back was responsible for Mané and the wide player for Robertson – there was no helping each other out. We have already discussed how, because he was responsible for Robertson, the wide player could not protect his full-back by blocking the passing lane to Mané. By the same token, the full-back could not help the wide player out with Robertson, because it would mean leaving Mané free. The second problem was that because the wide player had to drop deep and wide, perhaps even parallel to his full-back, a gap was created between the two of them; in effect the wide player became a wing-back in a back five (*Figure 39*). This meant there was a potential passing lane between the two players, for Robertson to move in behind the opposition wide player to receive goal side of both wide player and full-back, essentially bypassing both opposition players vertically. To exacerbate the problem for the opposition, as Robertson made his forward run, Mané would often move in the opposite direction, dropping short to show for a pass in the pocket. Assuming the opposition full-back followed Mané in an attempt to prevent him from receiving unchallenged, this meant the wide player had sole responsible for Robertson; the full-back was too high to help out.

Without the full-back on his inside, the wide player had a difficult task in his artificial 'wing-back' role. Many wide players did not possess the necessary defensive qualities to successfully

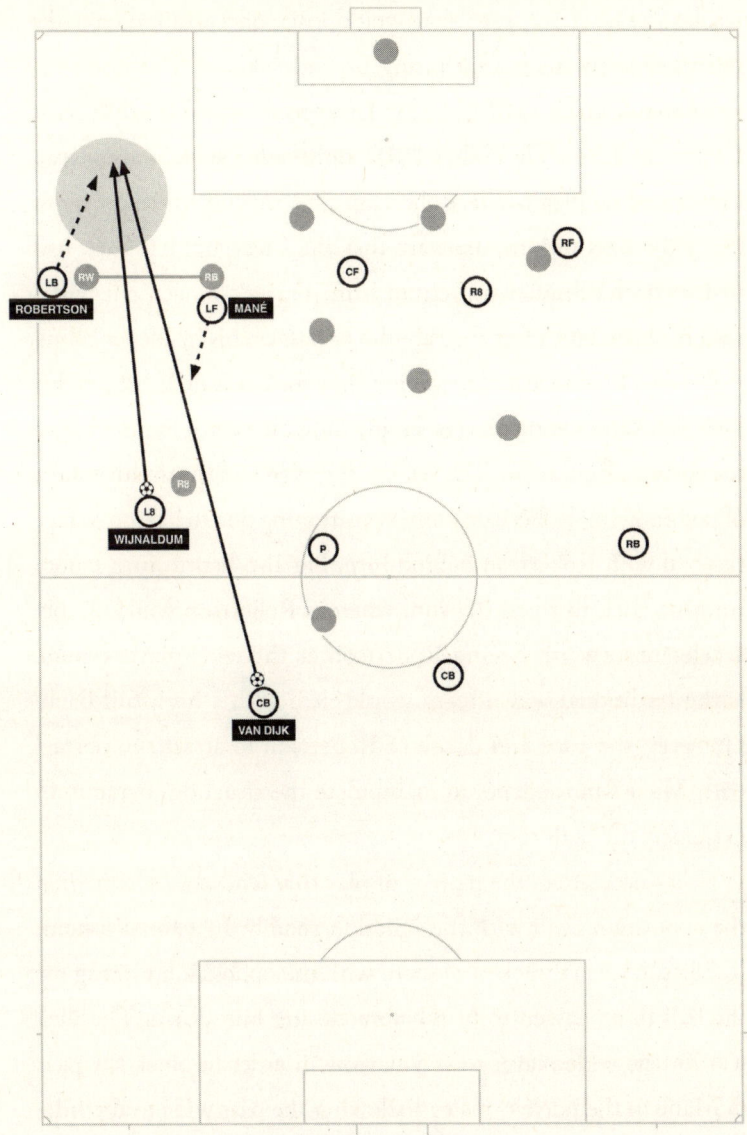

Figure 39. *By tracking Robertson man-for-man, the opposition wide player has to drop into the defensive line, essentially becoming a wing-back in a back five. When this occurred, Mané would make a movement towards the ball, taking the right-back with him and opening up space for a pass to be played in behind for Robertson*

track the Robertson run; they would lose concentration or make mistakes with their positioning or body shapes. For example, for Steve Cook's own goal for Liverpool's third goal against Bournemouth in December 2018, right-sided wide player Ryan Fraser had no idea where Robertson was, moving wider to try to block the pass to him, unaware that the Liverpool left-back had in fact darted higher in behind him. Fraser's movement wider simply opened up a line for Fabinho to pass on his inside, enabling Robertson to receive and cross first time for Cook to divert into his own net. Other wide players simply didn't have the required pace to stay with Robertson. The wide player also had the disadvantage of not knowing Robertson's exact positioning due to having to face the ball with Robertson behind him. He also had to turn before running back to track the run, whereas Robertson could simply accelerate forward. Seeing Robertson as the wide player's 'man' is the traditional way a team would deal with a high full-back. However, the pace and desire of Robertson to attack, combined with Mané's movements to manipulate the situation, made it an extremely difficult task.

Let's now assess the pattern of play that tended to occur when the opposition dealt with the situation zonally. In a zonal system, Robertson wasn't tracked as such, with the opposition waiting for the ball to be passed to him before closing him down. The idea was for the wide player to stay narrow in order to block the pass to Mané in the pocket, instead allowing the pass wide to the full-back, before either the full-back or wide player closed him down. The main advantage of this system was that by the wide player blocking the passing lane to Mané in front of the full-back, the full-back was able to hold his position vertically, and remain in a position to assist with Robertson if needed. The responsibility for

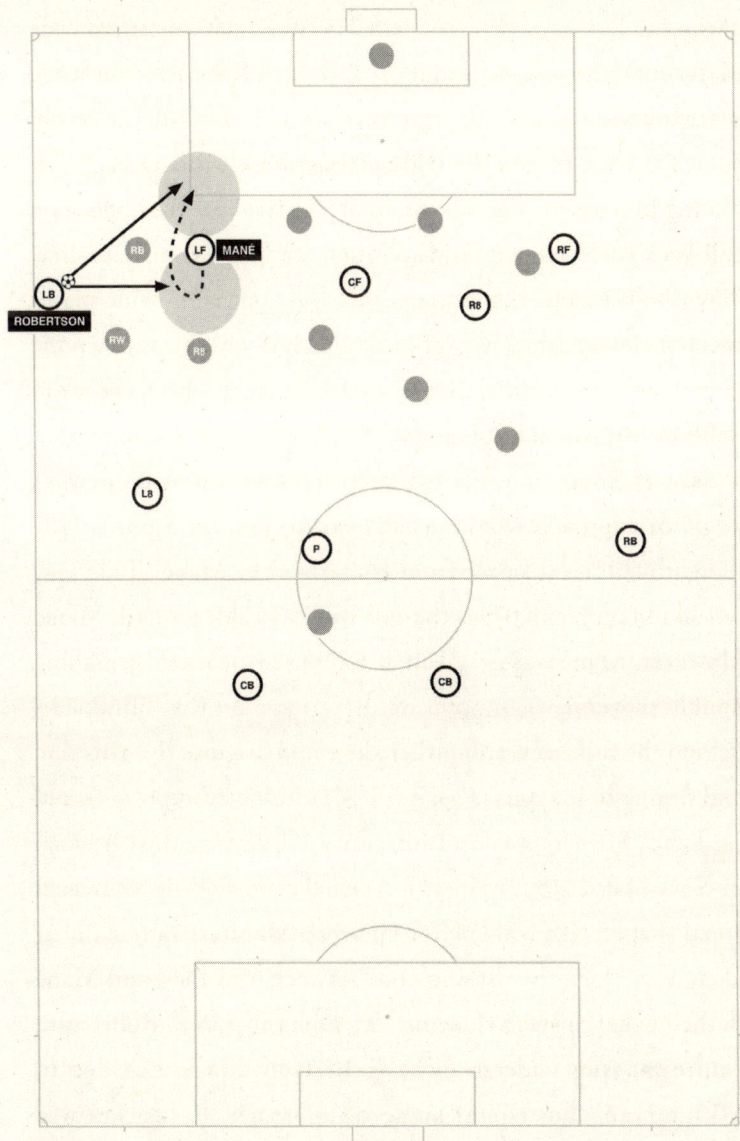

Figure 40. *When Robertson received wide, from his position behind the opposition right-back, Mané would move either into the space in front or behind the right-back, depending on the right-back's position. Often Mané would make a double movement, showing for the ball in one direction, before running in the other direction*

closing Robertson down was shared between the opposition wide player and full-back, depending on how high Robertson was when receiving the ball. If Robertson was more or less parallel or deeper than the wide player, the wide player himself was tasked with closing him down. The advantage of this was that the opposition full-back could remain in his position, and not leave Mané free. The disadvantage, though, was that the opposition wide player was not closing down Robertson at an angle which was down the line of a potential cross, should the Liverpool left-back choose to deliver early, which he often did.

Or, if Robertson was too deep to cross, the wide player's angle of approach would usually fail to prevent a potentially dangerous forward pass from Robertson to Mané. This may not sound problematic, as the full-back was able to mark Mané. However, Mané was excellent at fooling his marker by making double movements in opposite directions, on the 'blind side' behind the full-back, from where he could disguise the direction and timing of his runs (*Figure 40*). A fantastic example occurred for James Milner's goal in Liverpool's 1-1 draw against Arsenal in November 2018 (*Figure 41*). Arsenal were holding a compact zonal shape, with wide player Henrikh Mkhitaryan remaining narrow to block the passing lane between Van Dijk and Mané in the pocket, instead showing Van Dijk the pass to Robertson, before moving wide to close Robertson down. But due to Mkhitaryan's horizontal angle of approach, Robertson was free to pass forward, and crucially Arsenal right-back Héctor Bellerín was unsure in which direction Mané would show for the ball. The Liverpool wide forward made a brilliant double movement, dragging Bellerín out, then at the moment when the right-back turned to face the ball, dipping in behind him,

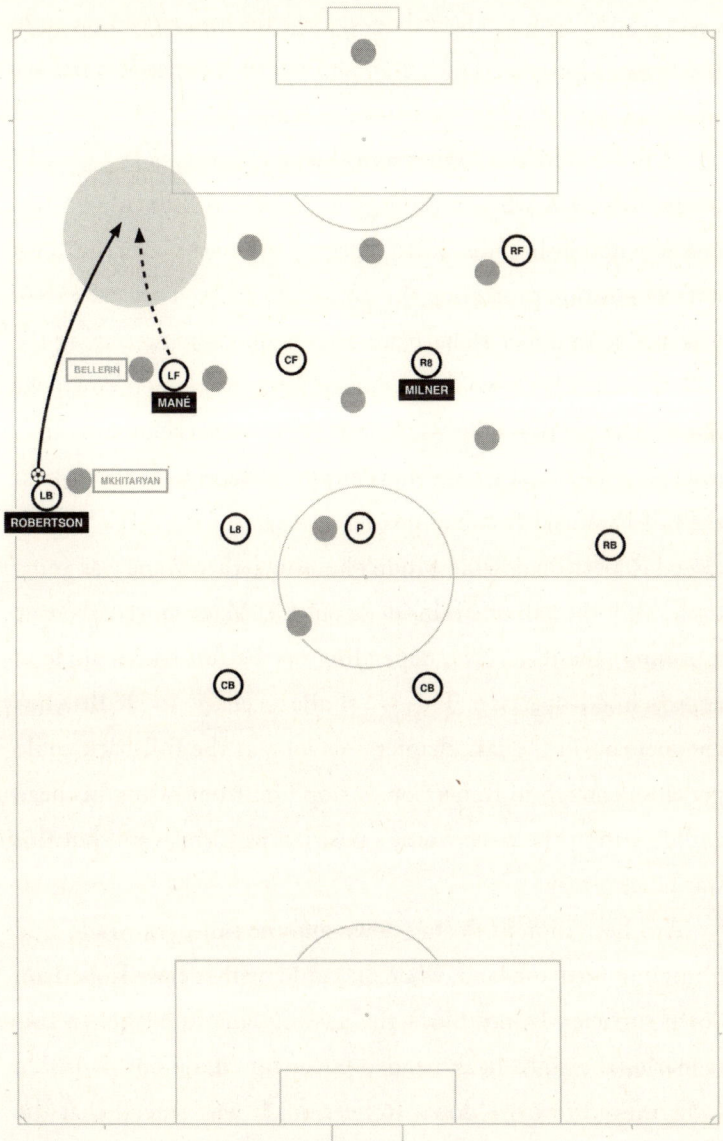

Figure 41. The situation for a goal scored by James Milner against Arsenal in November 2018. Robertson received wide, with Arsenal wide midfielder Henrikh Mkhitaryan unable to block Robertson's forward pass with his angle of approach from the inside. Mané, from his position behind Arsenal right-back Héctor Bellerín, first made a movement for a pass in front of Bellerín, before instead darting into the space behind him, as Bellerín anticipated the pass in front

giving Robertson a relatively easy pass for him to run on to in the space. This was Mané's standard move; Robertson could see Mané's movement but the full-back couldn't.

If Robertson was higher and therefore more or less parallel to the full-back when receiving, it was the full-back who was tasked with closing him down, because the wide player, from his narrow position protecting the pocket, to an even greater extent was unable to affect Robertson's first action when receiving the ball. The full-back would be approaching Robertson down the line of his next pass or cross, so usually had more chance to affect it. However, once again the movements of Mané made the task for the full-back as difficult as possible. When the full-back himself closed Robertson down, he didn't know whether Mané was going to show for the ball on his inside or outside; Mané moved to create a passing lane to receive, depending on the full-back's angle of approach to Robertson. This is a similar scenario to De Bruyne's channel run in the last chapter – as long as the full-back could get close enough to Robertson to stop him from lifting his head and executing the pass, Mané's position was irrelevant, but this was no easy task.

Any hesitation in closing down and the full-back would find himself in no man's land, where he could neither close Robertson down sufficiently, nor block the passing lane to Mané. In this scenario, the right-back needed cover for Mané on his inside as he moved to close down Robertson. It was crucial that the opposition's right-sided central midfielder moved over to block the pocket on the full-back's inside shoulder, and for the right-sided centre-back to move across to block any pass on his outside shoulder. The further the centre-back moved over, the more he could act as a deterrent to the pass back inside. This was a similar solution to the one proposed to track the De Bruyne run; it required the centre-back to cover wider to prevent the attack at source, rather than simply remaining centrally to deal with a potential cross.

Against Liverpool this solution was risky, even if the centre-back did manage to move across in time, simply because Mané was so quick. As mentioned in the last chapter, the centre-back had to possess a certain amount of agility, speed and one versus one defensive qualities to deal with De Bruyne. However, in this scenario against Liverpool, he wasn't defending against a player with De Bruyne's profile, but a specialist wide forward, who had attacking attributes which a centre-back may not have been able to stifle. Although woefully defended, Liverpool's third goal against Salzburg in October 2019 was a good example of the rotation on their left side causing problems. Salzburg's wide player was more concerned with Wijnaldum than Robertson, allowing Van Dijk to chip the ball over his head to the Liverpool left-back. The Salzburg right-back, unsure whether to stay with Mané or close down, hesitantly moved towards Robertson, allowing an easy pass down his outside for Mané, with Salzburg's right centre-back unsure whether to move across to Mané or stay central. The lack of pressure on Mané allowed him to cross for Firmino, and Salah scored the rebound from the goalkeeper's save.

When teams defended Robertson zonally, the Liverpool left-back did his best to make things as difficult as possible, often positioning himself so he wasn't parallel to either opposition player, potentially creating confusion for the opposition full-back and wide player in terms of which one of them should move wide to close him down. Any hesitation, and Robertson would be able to cross or advance with the ball untracked. This occurred when

Liverpool equalised against Manchester United in October 2019. By the time the goal was scored, United were playing with wing-backs in a 5-4-1, which meant that Aaron Wan-Bissaka, United's right wing-back, had a wide player, Andreas Pereira, covering in front of him. On the pass wide to Robertson, Pereira and Wan-Bissaka both looked at each other, with the latter then making a late attempt to close down, but failing to prevent Robertson's cross, which eventually found its way to Adam Lallana, who tapped in at the back post.

There was another scenario in which Liverpool's wide forwards and full-backs interacted to create space for each other, more specifically when the ball was switched from towards the opposite side (*Figure 42*). The movement was as follows: as the player on the ball looked up to assess his options, Liverpool's wide forward on the opposite side made his classic diagonal run between full-back and centre-back. At the same time, the Liverpool full-back made a run on the overlap, into the space vacated by the opposition's full-back moving inside to track the wide forward's run, which was in fact a decoy. Instead of passing to the wide forward, the ball was switched to Liverpool's full-back. This was a similar movement pattern to City's number 8 making a run between full-back and centre-back to 'pin him in' in order to free up space for their winger out wide; the main difference for Liverpool was that it involved different players in the system. Similar to City, the principle was along the lines of: if Liverpool were going to play wide, they were going to make sure the opposition was as narrow as possible first, to create the maximum space and time for the receiving full-back.

Many teams who want their full-backs to overlap use this movement pattern. However, with Liverpool, the decoy run of the

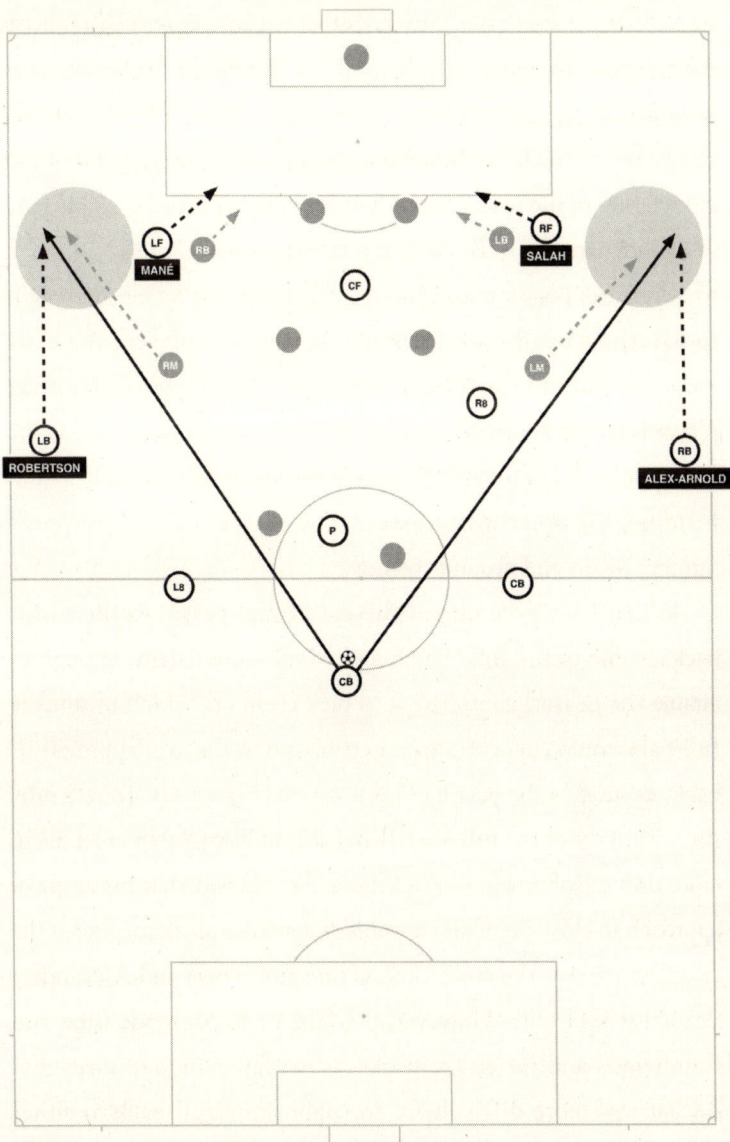

Figure 42. Internal runs of Salah and Mané would often act as a decoy to force the opposition's full-backs inside for the ball to instead be played on the outside to Liverpool's full-backs. This meant the reliance was on the opposition's wide players to track Alexander-Arnold and Robertson

wide forward was especially effective because it was so realistic for the pass to be actually played for the Salah or Mané, as it occurred so regularly. Therefore, the opposition full-back had no choice but to track Salah or Mané inside until it was clear that the destination of the pass was on their outside, because the inside pass was more dangerous. By then, it was often too late for the full-back to adjust his position and intercept the ball, or be close enough to Liverpool's full-back to close him down to prevent the early cross. The advantage of the full-back crossing rather than a wide player is that it allows for an extra player to attack the cross, as the Liverpool's wide forward who made the decoy run was able to join Firmino, the other wide forward, and maybe one of Liverpool's number 8s, in and around the box.

When Liverpool played these diagonal passes to their full-backs, some of the time Salah and Mané were narrow enough to enable the nearest centre-back to pick them up, which meant the full-back could concentrate on getting out to the overlapping full-back, as soon as the pass had been struck (*Figure 43*). To reiterate, the advantage of the full-back being able to leave Salah or Mané to close down Robertson or Alexander-Arnold was that his angle of approach to close them down would potentially block the line of the cross, which was the most likely action Robertson and Alexander-Arnold would take. However, if Mané or Salah made their run from wider, and the centre-back was not far enough towards that side, it was more difficult for the opposition full-back to either pass Mané or Salah on, or adjust his position once the ball was on its way, in order to get out to Alexander-Arnold or Robertson in time. In this scenario, the wide player in front needed to help him out, which was often the strategy regardless, rather than only an emergency.

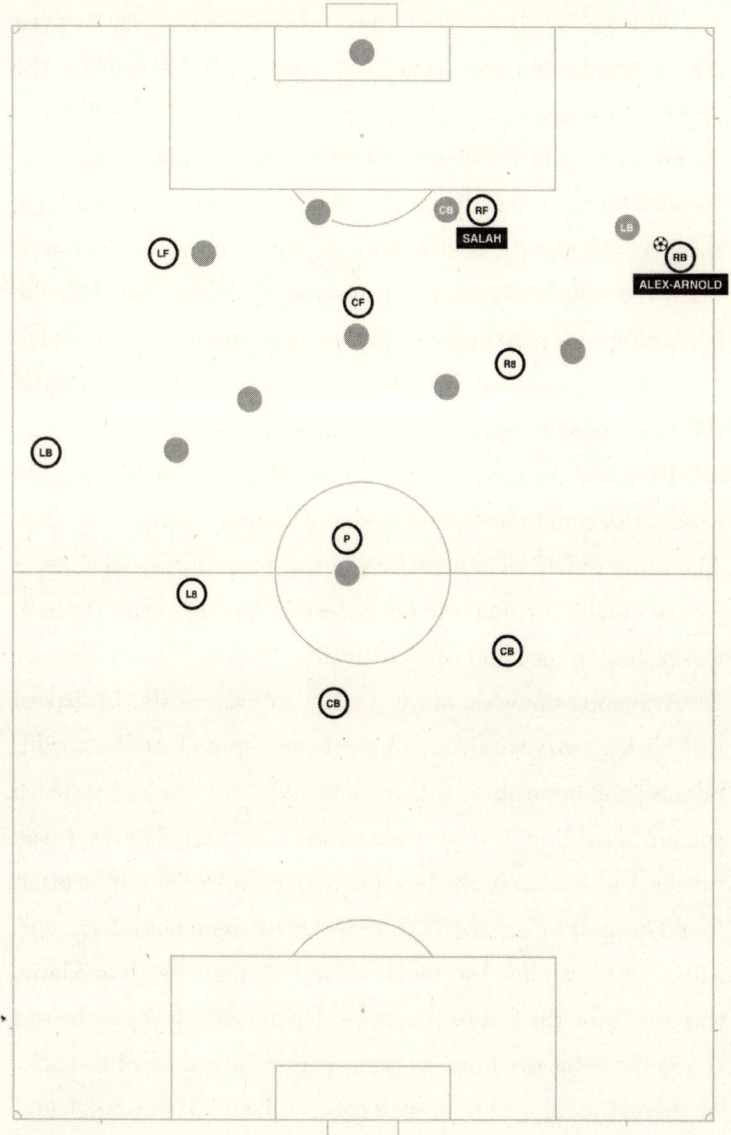

Liverpool's full-backs as wing-backs

Figure 43. Where possible, once the pass was on its way and the destination of the pass was clear, the opposition's full-back could pass Salah on to the nearest centre-back and move wide to close down Alexander-Arnold

We have already analysed why from the switch of play between Alexander-Arnold and Robertson it was very difficult for the opposition wide player to be in a position to track Robertson; as the switch of play was struck from the right touchline, if the wide player were to drop early with Robertson, he would leave a huge space inside, and the midfield would not be compact. However, when the switch of play was from a more central position, the opposition wide player could afford to be positioned slightly wider, as the whole team would have already been more central, and therefore more compact. This meant that when the opposition's full-back was dragged inside to track Mané or Salah's run, the wide player could track Robertson or Alexander-Arnold's overlap. The same problems existed for the full-back in this scenario: a lack of suitable attributes to track the run, having to face the ball, and having to turn and run backwards.

Arguably, the wide player failing to prevent the Liverpool full-back's cross would not have been the end of the world, because the opposition full-back would not have had to leave the box, enabling him to defend the cross itself. However, the full-back's position in the box was frequently irrelevant; he often found himself in 'no- man's land' where he could not intercept it. Most crosses would clear his head, and his man, Salah or Mané, was usually on the full-back's inside, having already made the run across the defensive line. As crosses from Liverpool's full-backs were usually whipped in at such pace, and with Mané, Salah and Firmino often joined by one of Liverpool's number 8s in the box, it was very difficult for the opposition's centre-backs to pick up both the flight of the ball *and* organise themselves to mark the significant number of Liverpool players who attacked the ball; preventing the cross was really important.

There was one final scenario in which the opposition wide player tracking the Liverpool full-back was non-negotiable; when Robertson or Alexander-Arnold moved into the box towards the back post to get on the end of a cross from the opposite side, perhaps even from their fellow full-back. This could occur when Liverpool needed to throw players forward to equalise or win later on in games, and was perhaps encouraged by Klopp against teams who sat so deep that their counter-attack threat was minimal, and extra Liverpool players were needed higher up the pitch. In this scenario, the opposition full-back simply had to be extra narrow, as the Liverpool wide forward on their side would be in the box, sometimes even level with the goalkeeper. The golden rule for a full-back is usually that if a goal is to be scored, it must be scored on their outside rather than inside shoulder. This meant that the opposition full-back was not always able to be in a position to prevent a shot at goal should the ball be crossed over his head. Or, on occasion, the opposition full-back would over-cover, when actually their centre-backs didn't need them to be so narrow.

Against Aston Villa in November 2019, Robertson scored a crucial late equaliser at the back post. Villa right-back Ahmed Elmohamady was narrow covering Alex Oxlade-Chamberlain, but the ball was crossed over his head for Robertson to arrive just ahead of wide player Anwar El Ghazi to head home. Villa had spent 86 minutes defending valiantly against Liverpool's regular patterns, before conceding a headed goal to Liverpool's left-back, an unlikely threat! Liverpool scored a similar goal against City themselves in January 2018 (*Figure 44*). With right-sided winger Raheem Sterling nowhere to be seen, Alexander-Arnold picked out Robertson with a pass/cross over the head of City right-back Danilo, who was tied up with Wijnaldum inside, for the Liverpool

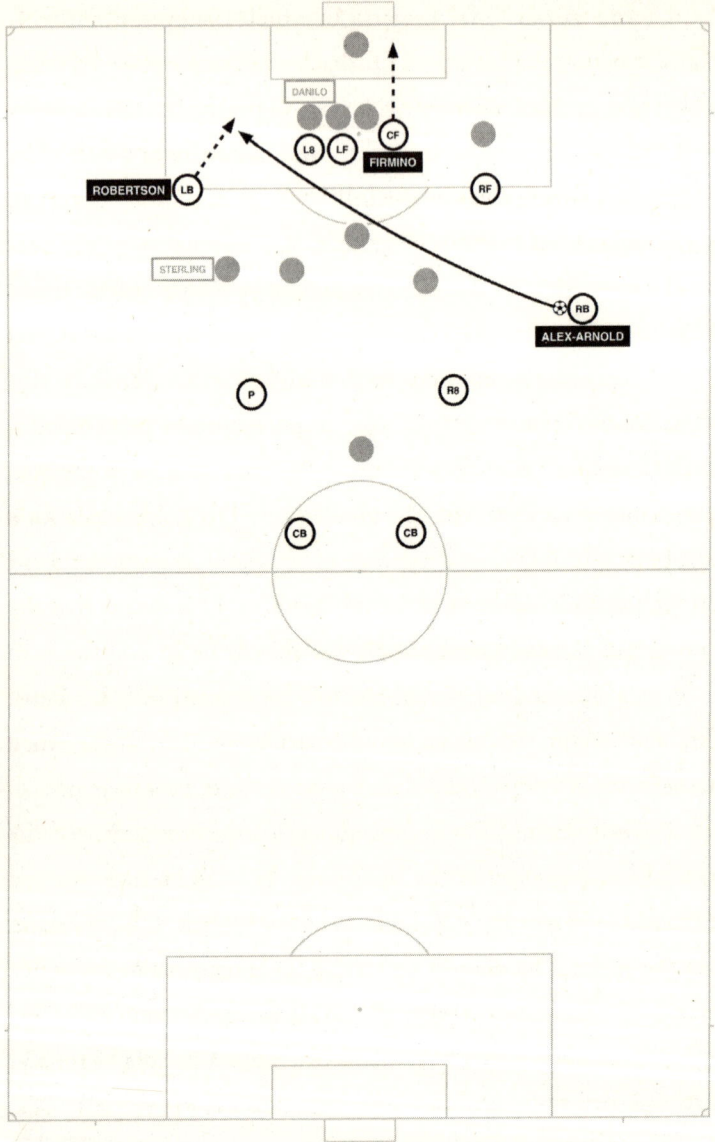

Figure 44. *The situation which occurred for a goal scored by Firmino against Man City in January 2019. With right-back Danilo occupied inside by the presence of three Liverpool players in the box, Robertson made a run into the space on Danilo's outside. Sterling, who was watching the ball, failed to see Robertson, enabling the Liverpool left-back to receive the pass from Alexander-Arnold and find Firmino in the middle*

left-back to square for Firmino to score. Sterling would probably have argued it was not his task to track so deep into his own area, and that the problem was Danilo simply failing to adjust to the flight of the ball to head clear. However, with City 1-0 up after 64 minutes in a crucial game, perhaps Sterling should have adapted to the situation and tracked the run.

There were no easy answers for how to prevent Robertson and Alexander-Arnold from overlapping and feeding passes into Mané and Salah behind the opposition full-back, or delivering dangerous crosses. Teams attempted to track them man-for-man, zonally, or a bit of both. Some teams had one plan for Robertson and another for Alexander-Arnold. Some, for example, would play a full-back as a right-sided wide player so he could track Robertson man-for-man. Overlapping full-backs are by no means uncommon in modern football, but the overlaps of Liverpool's full-backs were extra problematic for the opposition, as the dangerous narrow positions and runs of Mané and Salah made it so difficult for the opposition's full-backs to share the burden of dealing with Robertson and Alexander-Arnold by moving wide to close them down. This factor, combined with the intensity of their forward runs and the quality of their crosses, made them a formidable pair. The attacking threat of their full-backs enabled Liverpool to exploit the wide areas as yet another one of their attacking weapons, especially when faced with compact opposition defensive blocks.

Although the two teams used different positions for different functions, as with City, it was necessary for opposition teams to balance being compact centrally, and not over-covering so that Robertson and Alexander-Arnold were given too much space to do damage in wide areas. This is where City and Liverpool's usual strategy of placing eight players in central areas, and only one wide each side, was so effective. The numbers centrally meant the opposition would have to concentrate their efforts in the middle, but this meant that when the ball was moved wide, they struggled to effectively defend these zones.

Chapter 10

Full-back underlaps

THE MAJORITY of the time, the movement patterns by City's wingers and number 8s outlined above meant the full-backs' jobs in possession were done, enabling them to concentrate on planning for a potential turnover of possession. However, in some scenarios the full-back on the side of the ball was required to make an attacking run in order to help City break the opposition down. Perhaps City's winger and number 8 had been successfully prevented from combining, which almost certainly meant the opposition wide player had moved very deep to help out his full-back. Often that run was an underlap, a term which refers to a run on the inside of a team-mate positioned wide. We are going to use City as the example for this movement pattern as their full-backs tended to be in positions to underlap more regularly, due to the fact their wingers spent more time out wide than Liverpool's wide forwards. However, Klopp's side also scored goals from their full-backs underlapping. When Divock Origi, for example, played on their left, he had a tendency to stay wider, with Robertson making underlaps on his inside.

An underlap is a movement which has increased in prevalence over the past few years, in line with the strategy of doubling up on a wide player also becoming more common. You may hear of coaches or pundits saying full-backs should 'leave the wide player one versus one' by remaining deeper. By this they mean that if the full-back moves forward, he may drag the opposition wide player back with him, killing the one versus one situation. The belief is that the wide player would only drop back to defend should the full-back run forward. It is true that some teams ask their wide players to track the full-back only when he goes forward rather than automatically getting back and helping out regardless. But this is usually because they ask a central midfielder to double up with the full-back instead. It is therefore rare that a dangerous winger is ever left one versus one on purpose. When defending against City, with the one versus one ability of their wingers, it was certainly not an advisable strategy to leave the full-back in this situation, so it would rarely occur. Equally, the nearest central midfielder often struggled to assist the full-back because he was occupied with tracking City's number 8. So, as almost every opposition team's wide player would attempt to drop back and double up, any City full-back joining in the attack was only likely to positively impact the situation for their own winger – if not to receive the ball, then to provide a decoy to take away one of the two players defending against the winger.

Essentially, the underlap attacked the same space as the De Bruyne run described earlier: the space between the full-back and centre-back, when the full-back had moved wide to defend against the winger. If City's number 8 couldn't access it, perhaps their full-back could; City's full-backs often made these runs when the number 8 their side was not in a position to support the winger (*Figure 45*). However, on many occasions, City's number 8 had made his classic channel run, but it had been well covered by an opposition central midfielder, preventing the pass. Essentially a three versus three situation occurred out wide (the full-back and wide player for both teams, plus the City number 8, and the opposition central midfielder. While there was no numerical disadvantage for the opposition, the fact that the opposition wide player was likely to have doubled up on City's winger meant that City's full-back was potentially free to make the underlap undetected on the inside; this run is arguably more difficult to detect and track than an overlap. The key to full-backs' effective underlaps is their narrow starting position. If they start too wide their run will be more easily seen by the opposition wide player and full-back. But if the starting position is narrow, the run usually comes from behind the opposition wide player, making it more difficult to detect.

These runs could be very effective, especially from a full-back with Kyle Walker's electric pace. Because the run was often undetected by the opposition wide player, the amount of space between the opposition players defending wide (i.e. the full-back, wide player and potentially the number 8) and the players on the inside was often key to either preventing the underlap from occurring in the first place or intercepting the pass. This meant the nearest remaining players in the defensive and midfield lines – the centre-back and second central midfielder – needed to be far enough across. However, the confusion for the opposition was often that the player most likely to cover this space – i.e. the nearest central midfielder – had been removed from a position from where he could do so, having had to track City's number 8. City had effectively moved two players – the opposition's full-back

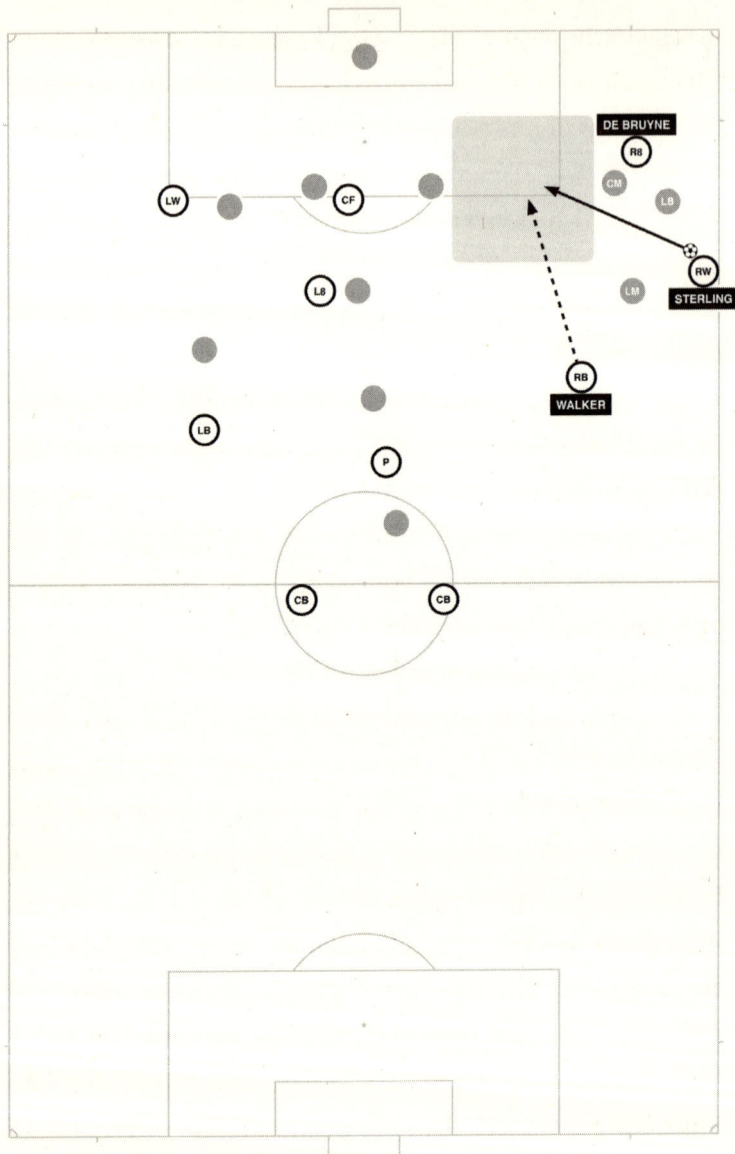

Figure 45. An example of a situation which often lead to City's full-back making an underlap. With Sterling doubled up on and the opposition's central midfielder forced wide to track De Bruyne, space often opened up in the inside channel for, in this case, Walker to exploit, often undetected by the three opposition players defending wide

and one of the central midfielders – out of the inside channel. This was often when the full-back would make his underlap. When the full-back joined in, dealing with City in wide areas was essentially a case of defending three versus three out wide, while maintaining short distances between these three players and the nearest players on the inside. Again, the nearest centre-back needed to be across to the extent that he could cover behind these three players to intercept the pass or run, should the full-back's run be undetected. Getting this right enabled teams to lock City out wide, covering all their attacking strategies, meaning they had to move the ball backwards and attempt to attack the other side.

Chapter 11

The concept of 'free 8s'

WE HAVE described how width was fundamental for City, whose wingers remained wide both in order to exploit the opposition full-backs in one versus one situations, and to stretch teams with the aim of opening up space in the inside channel. In the case of Liverpool, we have discussed how having a player high and wide was not always essential due to Mané and Salah providing an option to play directly over the top of the opposition's defensive line. However, much of the time Liverpool's full-backs provided width high up by making attacking runs on the outside of the wide forwards, in order to play incisive passes back inside, or whip in dangerous crosses.

Now we're going to look at how both teams created width without needing their wide player or full-back to be positioned high and wide, which involved a non-traditional movement from their number 8. Kevin De Bruyne has referred to his role as a 'free 8', which probably relates to the fact that he wasn't limited to just one zone of the pitch, e.g. the pocket on the right-hand side. On occasion he would drop deeper, allowing Walker to push on, but more often De Bruyne's freedom would see him move wide himself,

Manchester City celebrate their 2017/18 title win on the way to winning a record 100 Premier League points.

Raheem Sterling and Leroy Sané were used effectively as wide wingers in City's record points winning seasons.

Fabian Delph was successfully converted into a left-back by Pep Guardiola.

Kyle Walker's conservative role when City attacked enabled him to use his pace to defend against opposition counter-attacks.

The inside positions of City's full-backs in possession allowed Kevin De Bruyne and David Silva to go and express themselves higher up the pitch.

City's players celebrate following a trademark De Bruyne cross for Sterling to score against Leicester in February 2018.

Goalkeeper Ederson was a key signing ahead of the 2017/18 season.

After losing out on the title despite winning 97 points in 2018/19, the following season Liverpool finally got their hands on the Premier League trophy.

Roberto Firmino dropped deep as a 'false 9' to create space for Sadio Mané and Mo Salah in behind.

Virgil Van Dijk's range of passing was a key supply to Liverpool's dangerous front players.

Sadio Mané rounds goalkeeper Manuel Neuer to score against Bayern Munich in March 2019 having made a trademark run inside from a Van Dijk long pass.

Liverpool's full-backs Trent Alexander-Arnold and Andy Robertson were big attacking threats, but they also played an increased role in building the attack, especially during 2019/20.

Roberto Firmino scores against Manchester City in January 2019 following a pass from one Liverpool full-back to the other.

Jordan Henderson scores against Tottenham in October 2019 having arrived at the back post as part of his role as a 'free 8'.

on the outside of the winger. The pattern involved a rehearsed, co-ordinated movement, requiring the winger to adjust his position at the same time as the number 8 moved wide, but not usually into the pocket, instead remaining parallel with the opposition's defensive line, in a similar zone to Mané or Salah's regular position for Liverpool. As the opposition full-back was pushed inside by the winger's movement, City's number 8 attacked the space this created on the outside. The structure was maintained: a player wide and a player inside. This movement wasn't limited to De Bruyne; David Silva also had licence to rotate positions with Sané. When Bernardo Silva played, he was regularly encouraged to make the movement wide when playing as a number 8, as it suited his attributes; he was used to playing as a right-winger.

For Liverpool, it was usually their right-sided number 8 who tended to play as a 'free 8', moving high and wide. The reason for this tendency was that right-back Alexander-Arnold's starting position was a little deeper than left-back Robertson, so there was more of a requirement for a 'free 8' moving wide in front of him to provide width higher up. The player chosen to perform the role for Liverpool needed to possess suitable attributes, such as the mobility to make the run, and the ability to deliver crosses to a reasonable standard. The likes of Jordan Henderson, James Milner and Alex Oxlade-Chamberlain performed the 'free 8' role on various occasions; all three of these players had played as wide players at some point earlier in their careers. During the 2019/20 season, Henderson in particular perfected the movement pattern. Unlike for City, for Liverpool it was less of a rotation, as Salah was usually already positioned narrowly – there was less of a need for him to make a substantial movement to create the space for Henderson, as the gap already existed to a certain extent (*Figure 46*).

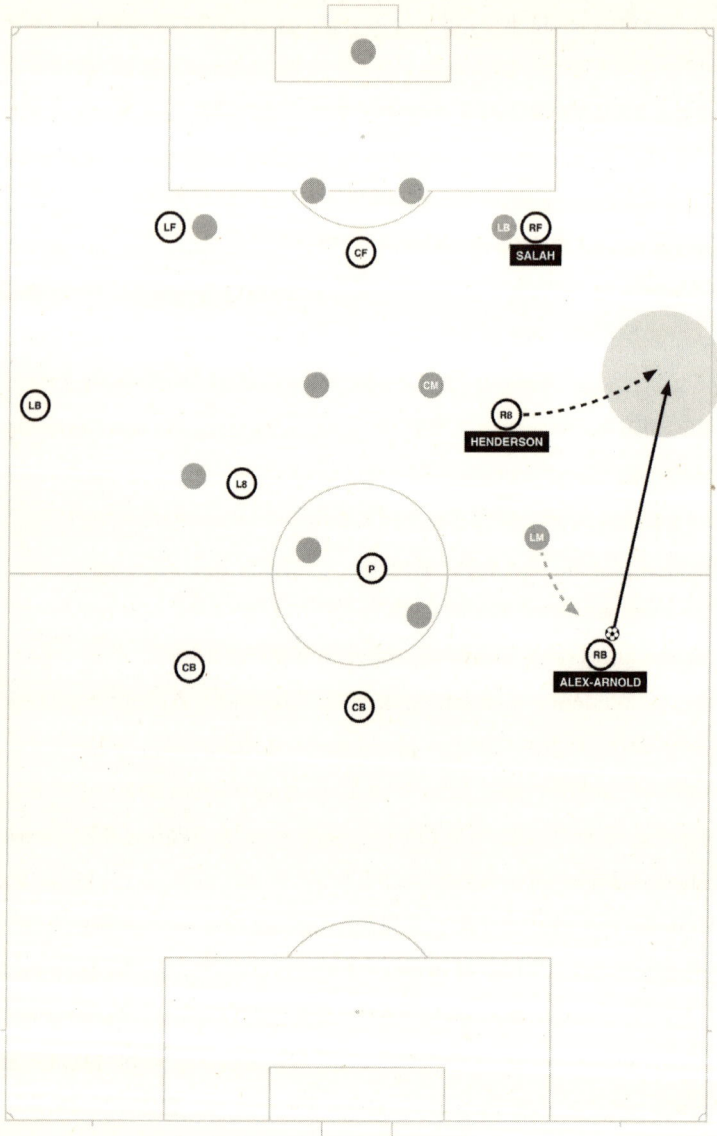

Figure 46. An example of a situation where Henderson would move wide to receive. A gap was created when the opposition's left-sided wide midfielder moved high to close down Alexander-Arnold, whilst Salah's regular high, narrow position pushed the opposition left-back deeper and inside. A dilemma was created for the opposition in terms of who should close Henderson down, the left-back, central midfielder or left wide midfielder?

For both City and Liverpool, the theory behind this strategy was similar to the attacking concepts we have already analysed: if they were going to use the wide areas, the positions of their wide forwards/wingers would ensure that the opposition was as narrow as possible first, so there would be more space for the number 8 moving wide. Against Liverpool, the opposition full-back had to be narrow already due to Salah's positioning and the position of the ball. The movement would occur in several different scenarios. When attacking higher up the pitch it would often be in the form of an overlap, following a dribble inside from City's winger or Liverpool's wide forward. An example of this occurred for City's third goal in the Champions League quarter-final second leg against Tottenham in April 2019 (*Figure 47*). Bernardo Silva dribbled inside taking left-back Danny Rose with him, leaving space for De Bruyne to arrive on the overlap, escaping the attentions of his marker Victor Wanyama, before crossing first time for Sterling to score at the back post. As the opposition central midfielder was required to mark the number 8 on the inside and in front, in order to prevent a pass to his feet or on his inside, he consequently had a difficult task in tracking the number 8's run to the outside.

Rather than overlap, often the number 8 would move all the way to the touchline to receive. The clever part of using the number 8 rather than the full-back to move into the wide area high up the pitch was that there was no natural solution for the opposition, which was the case when the full-back moved higher to provide width; in this scenario the likelihood was that the opposition wide player would track him. The number 8 making the run instead also had the advantage of enabling the full-back to remain behind the ball to defend the counter-attack. While the nearest opposition central midfielder had no doubt been assigned the task of tracking

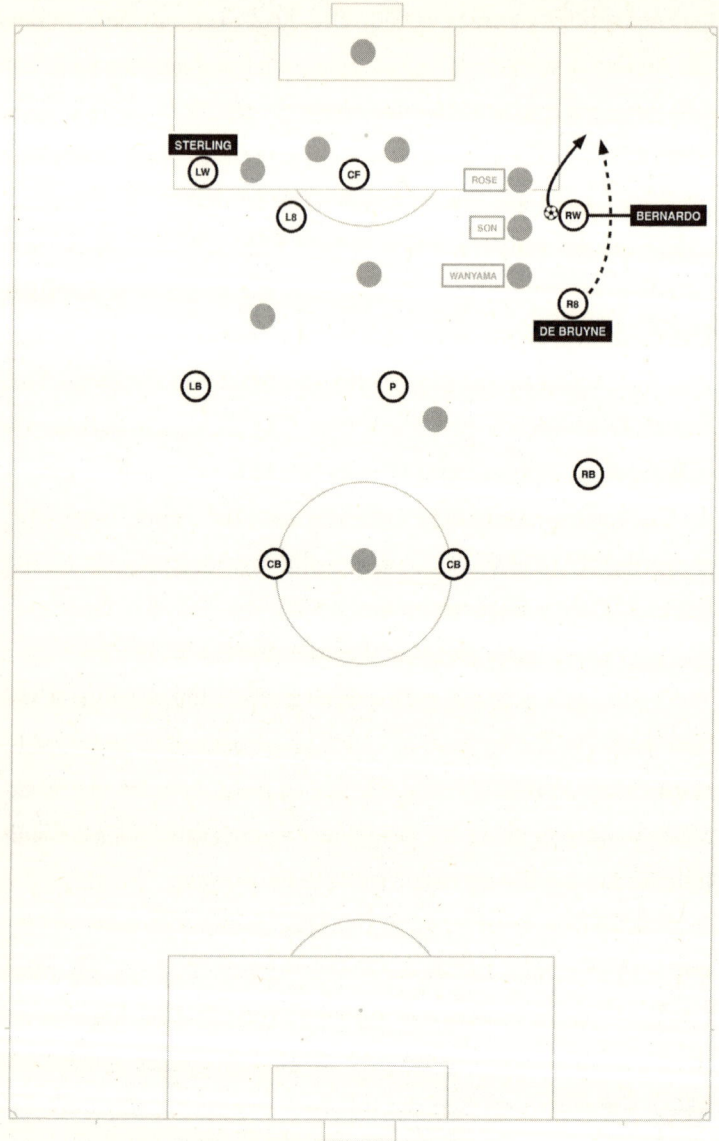

Figure 47. *For this goal against Tottenham in April 2019, City winger Bernardo Silva dribbled inside, taking left-back Danny Rose inside with him, before slipping a pass down the outside to the overlapping De Bruyne, whose marker Victor Wanyama seemed to pass De Bruyne on to left-back Rose, or wide midfielder Son Heung-Min, who slipped over. De Bruyne was free to receive before crossing for Sterling to score*

the number 8's forward runs, did that extend to tracking him to near the touchline, so far from the centre? Was the number 8 enough of a danger out wide so far from goal to vacate the centre to close down? Should the opposition full-back leave City or Liverpool's wide player to go out to close down the number 8, as technically the wide area was his zone to defend? Or, as the full-back could be considered as 'occupied' by the City or Liverpool wide player, should the opposition wide player treat the number 8 in his wide position as if he were the City or Liverpool full-back who had gone forward? And if so, should the opposition wide player leave the full-back spare and drop back to close down the 8?

These questions highlight the problem teams had when preparing for games against City and Liverpool. Guardiola's and Klopp's players knew their own movement patterns inside out having worked on them for months or even years. Opposition teams on the other hand had just a few days of training sessions and video analysis meetings to prepare their players. How much information was too much information for the players? How many of the different scenarios could the players take in without becoming confused as to what was expected of them in a given situation? This particular movement pattern may have only happened a handful of times in a game, yet it could have been the difference between conceding a goal and not conceding. Or between losing 3-0 and 4-0!

For City, as well as disorganising the opposition, this strategy was a way of getting their key influencers on the ball against teams who were ultra-compact centrally, especially teams who defended without orthodox wide players in an attempt to block off the centre. City scored a goal involving the movement of a 'free 8' against Southampton in December 2018. Southampton's plan was to place their wide players centrally in an attempt to prevent City's full-backs creating overloads in central midfield, but this left a big space in front of their full-backs for City's number 8s to move into. Bernardo Silva obliged, moving wide to collect a pass from Vincent Kompany, before exchanging passes with Riyad Mahrez, and picking out fellow number 8 David Silva in the box to score.

For both City and Liverpool, the strategy was also useful against teams who had a tendency to man-mark the number 8s, as it either allowed them to receive passes where their marker wouldn't follow them, or if they were followed wide, it left a hole in the centre for another City or Liverpool player to take advantage of. For example, for Liverpool the number 8's run wide would often serve as a decoy, dragging his marker with him and opening up space on the inside for Alexander-Arnold to fire a pass into a team-mate, usually Firmino or Salah. You would often see Henderson, when playing as a number 8, check the position of Salah and Firmino before making an unselfish run wide to clear his man out of the way. James Milner was also very clever with his use of this particular movement. Against West Ham in August 2018, Milner played an important role as a 'free 8' in the build-up to Liverpool's first goal which was scored by Salah. Alexander-Arnold received a pass deep, and was closed down by West Ham's wide player. Higher up, Salah's narrow position was pinning back West Ham's left-back, creating a large gap between the two West Ham players. Milner made a run from the inside towards the touchline, into the space between the two West Ham players, taking West Ham's ball-side pivot, Declan Rice, with him, opening up a big gap between Rice and the other pivot, Mark Noble. Naby Keïta, Liverpool's other number 8, moved into the gap and was found by Alexander-Arnold. Keïta then turned and fed Andy Robertson, who crossed first time for Salah to tap in. The goal would not have occurred without the unusual 'free 8' movement of Milner in the build-up.

The regularity of Liverpool's right-sided 8 overlapping Salah was particularly confusing for the opposition left-sided wide player, because he was likely to have been instructed to focus his attentions on Trent Alexander-Arnold. This meant that as he closed the Liverpool right-back down, there was a huge space out wide for Henderson to move into and receive. Equally, with Salah remaining narrow, the wide player closing down Alexander-Arnold would likely show Alexander-Arnold the outside route, with the aim of preventing him from passing inside to Salah or to Henderson himself; the wide player would presume the Liverpool number 8 would show for the ball inside, between the lines. This played into Henderson's hands, as unbeknown to the opposition wide player, he would make the run into the space behind him, a gap which was usually of a significant size due to Salah pushing the opposition left-back deep and inside. Considering the complex situation this created for the opposition, it's a really well thought-out tactic. In effect, the two opposition players designated to defend out wide were split, enabling City or Liverpool's number 8 to exploit the resulting space.

Henderson sometimes remained out wide for an entire phase of play. For example, he may have made a run out wide as Liverpool attacked that side, but as the ball was moved back to the centre, instead of moving back into his natural position, he would often stay high and wide and attack the box from there. In Liverpool's victory over Tottenham in October 2019 (*Figure 48*), Henderson scored a goal arriving at the back post on the outside of Tottenham's left-back, who was unaware of his presence. Who was supposed to pick him up? Tottenham's wide player, Son Heung-Min, had

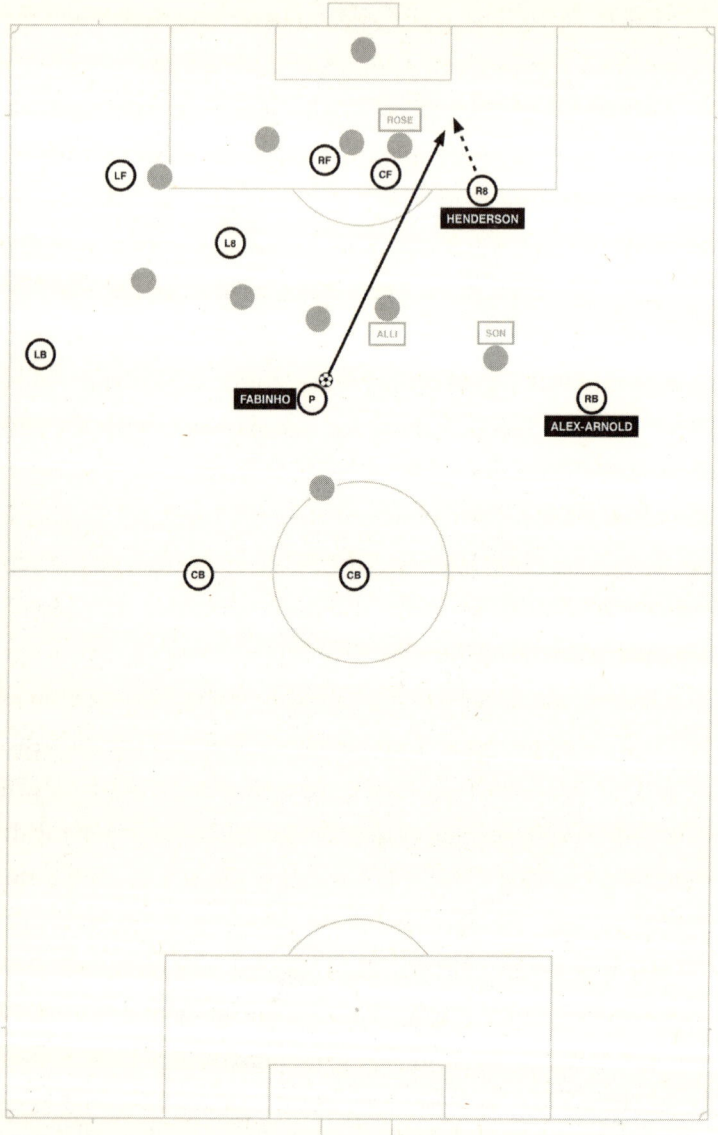

Figure 48. The situation which occurred for Henderson's goal against Tottenham in October 2019. Having remained wide on the right, Henderson had in effect become the overlapping right-back, yet Tottenham wide midfielder Son was focused on the actual right-back, Alexander-Arnold, who remained deep. Dele Alli, Henderson's opposite number, was too central to track Henderson as his positional reference was the location of the ball. Left-back Rose was occupied by the Liverpool players on his inside, which left Henderson free to make an untracked run and to receive a pass from Fabinho

not tracked Henderson as he would probably have done should Alexander-Arnold have been the player to make the forward run. Meanwhile, left-back Danny Rose was occupied with Salah inside. In addition, Tottenham's number 8, Dele Alli, was in a central position, following the principles of mirroring the location of the ball and protecting the centre of the pitch as the priority. The only real solution would have been for Son to treat Henderson as if he were an advanced full-back, rather than worrying about Alexander-Arnold, who was in a deeper, less dangerous position. But with this being a fairly novel tactic, and the fact that it was just one of Liverpool's many variations, Son wasn't able to think quickly enough to provide a solution.

Intriguingly, when Liverpool's number 8 remained wide on the right despite the ball moving back centrally, the movement pattern Liverpool often used was identical to when it was their full-back who was high, as described in the chapter on Liverpool's attacking full-backs. Salah would make a diagonal run between left-back and centre-back, taking the left-back narrow with him. But the run was often a decoy, and instead the ball was switched to Liverpool's number 8, allowing him the time and space to control the ball and advance. The number 8 would in effect become the full-back, yet the opposition wide player often didn't treat him like a full-back, as in the Tottenham example described above. This is because he would still see the actual Liverpool full-back, who remained deep, as his man to deal with.

Another example occurred for Mané's headed goal from a Henderson cross against City in November 2019. From a throw-in, Henderson moved on the outside of Salah, before receiving a pass from Firmino. City's left-back Angeliño did not close him down, instead leaving him to İlkay Gündoğan, who moved wide to

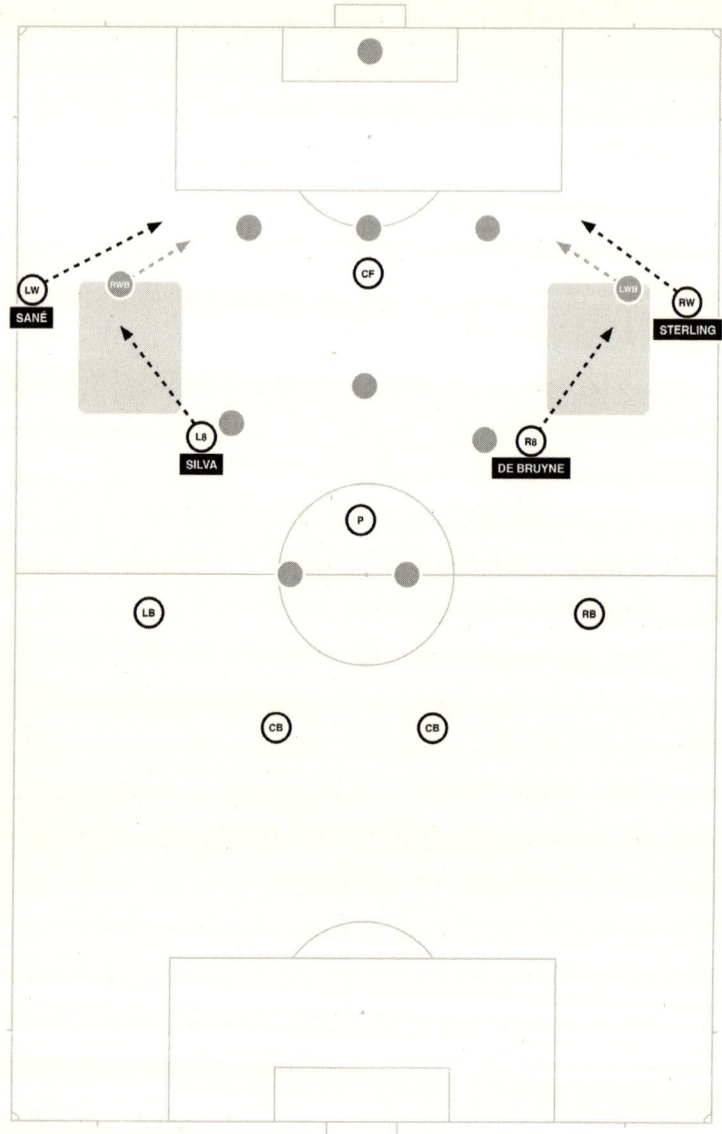

Figure 49. *Against 5-3-2, both City and Liverpool would often ask their number 8 to move wide on the outside of the opposition central midfielders. City would create even more space in front of the wing-backs by their wingers making inside runs*

close down, as technically Henderson was his opposite number. In the confusion, neither City player did enough to prevent the cross. Sometimes, Liverpool took the role of the 'free 8' to an extreme. For example, there were games where James Milner was asked to play as a traditional number 8 out of possession, but in possession to spend all his time out wide, as if he were a wing-back. Trent Alexander-Arnold was also asked to perform this dual role on a couple of occasions.

There is one formation which the idea of 'free 8s' moving wide is particularly effective against: a 5-3-2. Against this system there is always space in the areas in front of the wing-back, as there is only one player naturally disposed to defend wide areas: the wing-back himself. Instead of principally using their own full-backs to move forwards and create two versus one situations against the opposition wing-backs, City and Liverpool often asked one or both full-backs to remain deeper, instead encouraging their number 8s to move into the space between their full-back and winger to receive, on the outside of the opposition midfield three. City and Liverpool's wide players would push back the opposition wing-back with an internal run, giving their number 8s space to receive (*Figure 49*).

City scored a goal using this strategy against Manchester United's 5-3-2 in April 2019. Sterling made an internal run to push left wing-back Luke Shaw and left centre-back Victor Lindelöf deeper and inside, with number 8 Bernardo Silva moving into the newly vacated space on the outside to receive, before firing past David de Gea to give City the lead. As long as a suitable player was used as a 'free 8', this was an innovative tactic which asked tough questions of the opposition. As it was an unusual pattern, and one of many variations in City and Liverpool's armoury, it was difficult for the opposition to have a clear plan to prevent its effectiveness.

Chapter 12

City's and Liverpool's 'final ball'

SO FAR we have focused on how City and Liverpool progressed from build-up play to the attacking third, analysing the patterns they used to enable their attacking players to receive in the best conditions possible. Now we are going to assess how they created a shooting opportunity in two scenarios: 1) The last action at the end of an attack. 2) Having been thwarted down one side, switching the ball to the other side.

Reducing the randomness from crosses

As is the case with many football tactics, placing every type of cross in the same category is far too simplistic. A slow, high cross from the touchline with just two men attacking the box is very different to a whipped cross in behind the retreating centre-backs with three or four players arriving at the perfect time to attack the ball. For a cross to be successful – or in other words for it to result in a shot at goal – the players attacking the ball must time their run at the right moment, into the exact position that the ball is being crossed to, despite neither the crosser knowing exactly where the player attacking the cross will make his run, nor the player attacking the cross knowing the exact destination of the delivery. In addition, for it to be successful, the attackers must beat the defenders to the ball. With these factors there is a certain amount of randomness, which City and Liverpool aimed to reduce as much as possible to increase their chances of success.

Much was made of City's high volume of crosses in Guardiola's fourth season (they averaged 19 open-play crosses per game compared to 13 in 2017/18), with the suggestion that his side crossed the ball too often instead of using their regular patterns. This criticism usually followed a game they failed to win. Following City's incredibly successful record points seasons, more and more opposition teams chose to defend very deep. Guardiola has made the admission that when opposition teams simply defended in their own third with nine or ten players, there was little space to do anything other than cross the ball, and get as many players in the box as possible in the hope that one of them managed to beat a defender to the ball. This was especially the case when losing or drawing late on in games, which occurred more often in his fourth season, and partially explains City's increased crossing volume. Crossing when the opposition were camped deep in their penalty area was clearly not ideal for the players Guardiola had; City lacked tall players in their front five.

On the other hand, during their record seasons, City were a team who crossed the ball in selected scenarios, and in specific ways, which rendered the lack of height Guardiola's players possessed unimportant. The main principle was to ensure their crosses avoided aerial duels, removing the importance of the height advantage of the opposition defenders over their front five. Liverpool, also disadvantaged in terms of the height of their players attacking the box, would to some extent also look to cross in situations where they could avoid aerial duels. However, Klopp's team were not so limited in terms of the exact scenarios when they looked to cross the ball; the quality of the delivery, the movement of their front players, and the number of players who attacked between the width of the goal meant they could score even when the situation required being on the right side of the randomness which results from crossing. This has parallels with the general difference in philosophy between Guardiola and Klopp; Guardiola wanted everything his team did to be controlled, whereas Klopp didn't mind some randomness as long as his players did the right things to maximise their chances of success.

Beginning with City, let's examine the two types of cross they scored many of their goals from, having immediately entered the final third (*Figure 50*): 1) A smashed cross from the byline between the defensive line and goalkeeper. 2) A cut-back from the byline in front of the centre-backs. These actions usually occurred in the scenario where City's winger had beaten his full-back on the outside, or when their number 8 had made the classic channel run on the inside of the full-back. Neither of these crosses usually involved an aerial duel, which meant there was no advantage to the defending team in terms of height. If City were able to access their front five quickly and attack the opposition defence before the rest of their team could recover, there usually wasn't much of a numerical advantage in the box for the opposition either, as there would have been if the opposition team had been able to recover into their box early. This was one of the merits of playing with five players so high up the pitch; the crosser potentially had four other players to pick out. The runs that City's front five made when attacking the box were patterned, so although the crosser didn't necessarily know the exact location of where he needed to deliver

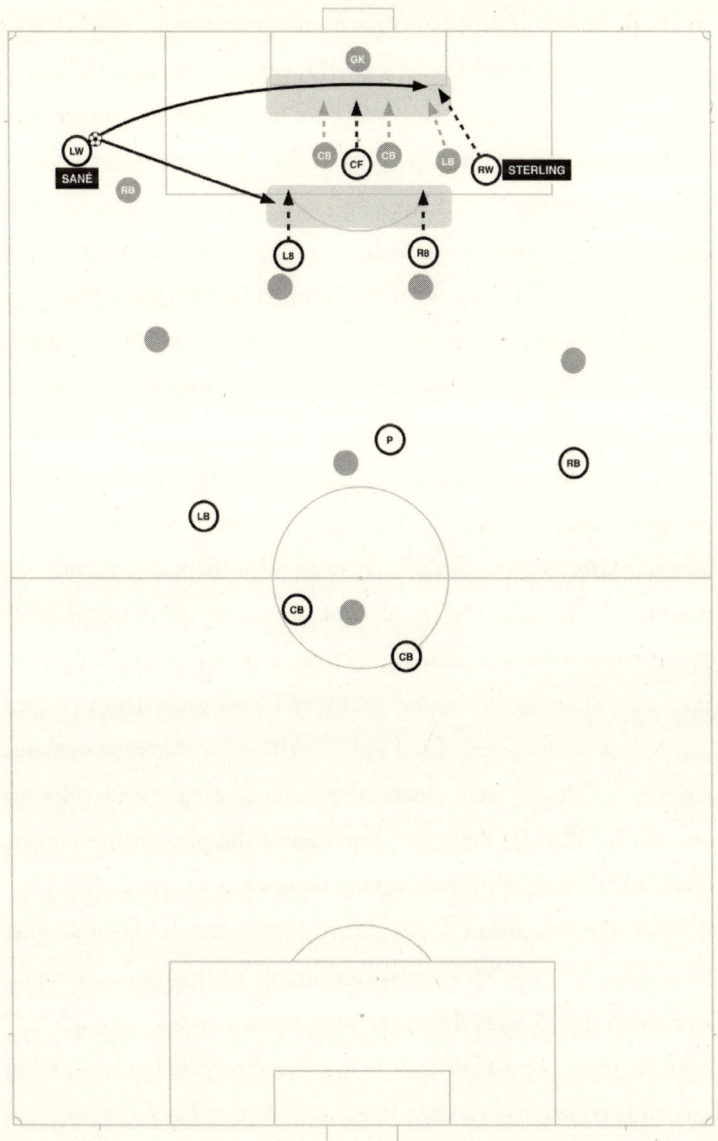

Figure 50. Having beaten the opposition full-back, City's wingers attempted to either smash an early cross between the defensive line and goalkeeper, or to cut the ball back for their number 8s between the defensive and midfield lines. City's winger would often cross for the other winger to score at the back post

the ball, he could cross into particular zones into which City's players were expected to arrive. All these factors enabled City to reduce the randomness, converting the cross into more of a pass.

The first type of cross involved the ball being delivered into the available space between the centre-backs and goalkeeper, crucially before the opposition defensive line could drop back and fill it. This was the classic De Bruyne cross, whipped in with incredible pace behind the defenders. In a 7-2 win over Stoke in October 2017, De Bruyne registered two assists with very similar early crosses in behind Stoke's defence, firstly for Gabriel Jesus, and secondly, Leroy Sané, to reach before their markers. In fact, the latter assist for Sané could be labelled a through pass more than a cross – but this was City's aim with their crossing – for them to be more like passes. Of course, there are multiple examples of when the cross didn't require the outstanding technical ability of De Bruyne to take advantage of the space; many of City's goals from crosses involved a fairly simple final ball. Both centre-forward options, Agüero and Jesus, were clever; they would often start level with or even behind the defensive line before the pass to the winger preceding the cross occurred, giving themselves a vertical advantage to reach the ball ahead of the centre-backs. Jesus's tap-in against Wolves in January 2019 is a nice example of this. Jesus, starting level with the Wolves defensive line, reacted to the through ball from Aymeric Laporte to Sané before the Wolves defenders, giving him the necessary advantage to get to the cross first.

In addition to the centre-forward, City's winger on the opposite side to the cross's origin always made the back post. As the ball was delivered early with the aim of missing out the opposition centre-backs, a race to get to it first was created between the opposition full-back and City's winger; the duel became about speed rather than height, giving the City man the edge. During 2017/18 and 2018/19 Sané laid on eight very similar assists for fellow winger Sterling. Both players were simply too quick for their full-backs; the ball would be slipped through for Sané who would make a square pass/cross to the back post for Sterling to arrive ahead of the opposition left-back to score. With many of City's goals from an early cross, the defensive line often could have done more to fill the space between themselves and the goalkeeper earlier; often their reaction was too slow. The higher the defensive line however, the more difficult it was to recover into the space; early crosses between the defence and goalkeeper following a pass in behind the full-back were perhaps one of the main reasons that discouraged teams from defending higher up the pitch against City. The goalkeeper could facilitate the situation by being ready to move off his line and intercept the cross; when the ball was being delivered from near the byline, there was no reason why the goalkeeper could not take up an aggressive starting position, an extra couple of yards off his line.

If the opposition defenders successfully filled the space between themselves and their goalkeeper, City used their second type of cross: a cut-back in front of the retreating centre-backs, usually for one of their number 8s to shoot. Like many of City's tactics, this stood out not so much for its novelty but for how robotically they carried it out. If City's winger managed to beat the full-back on the outside without assistance from a number 8, then both number 8s were free to make runs into the penalty area. Alternatively, their number 8 *was* the player cutting the ball back for the other number 8. The latter occurred for City's first goal at Southampton in December 2018. Having made the classic number 8 run into the channel behind Southampton's left-back, Bernardo Silva received a pass from Riyad Mahrez. As Agüero and Sterling made their runs between the defensive line and goalkeeper, causing the defensive line to retreat, Bernardo instead cut the ball back into the resulting space in front of them for David Silva to score from near the penalty spot.

Ideally, the opposition possessed diligent, defensively minded central midfielders who sprinted back to fill the space in front of the centre-backs; many teams used specific zones their central midfielders were supposed to take up when defending a cross. However, there were always occasions when the midfielders could not react quickly enough to fill the space in time, leaving the centre-backs to deal with potential crosses both in front and behind them. It was essential that the centre-backs kept their bodies side on when retreating towards their goal, as this enabled them to adjust in either direction depending on where the ball was crossed to; behind or in front. Some teams may have even designated the centre-back nearest to the ball to move deeper to protect the space nearer the goal, blocking the space behind the centre-backs. This left the other centre-back slightly higher, ready to anticipate and intercept a cut-back in front.

The speed at which these moves occurred made it incredibly difficult for the opposition to react and adjust; just as City filled the spaces in the box to enable the crosser to deliver into a zone and expect a runner to arrive, the opposition had to do the same; ensure that a player filled each space to cover all eventualities. Every opposition team knew that City regularly scored goals from a low cross into the space between centre-back and goalkeeper, or from a cut-back, but despite this they were often unable to prevent these type of goals. One reason for this was that City had so much of the ball that they were able to try these moves over and over again in games. It took just one lapse of concentration as the opposition players tired, or one poor split-second decision, and the ball was in the back of the net.

Liverpool, on the other hand, used a higher volume of crosses, but with less attempt to control the randomness. In order to assess to what extent a team looks to cross the ball, it is important to go beyond simply analysing the total number of crosses, as some teams enter the final third more often than others, so have more opportunity to cross. One way is to divide the number of passes a team attempts in the final third by the numbers of crosses. Using this metric, Liverpool's record points-winning team delivered a cross every nine final-third passes, indicating a greater tendency than City, whose record breakers delivered every 14 passes. Apart from their tendency to cross more often, another obvious difference was that the majority of crosses that Liverpool delivered came from their full-backs (during their two record seasons, Alexander-Arnold and Robertson averaged over ten open-play crosses per game between them, the highest combined full-back total in the Premier League, and a greater number than the total crosses of the whole Norwich team in 2019/20 combined).

Left-back Robertson could be considered an excellent crosser of the ball, but right-back Alexander-Arnold is arguably the best in the Premier League at this particular skill. Considering the incredible pace and trajectory he put on his crosses, he was also remarkably accurate. In this context accuracy doesn't necessarily mean picking out a specific player, but instead his ability to deliver between the width of the goal, naturally the most dangerous zone. Liverpool's two full-backs had the highest assists and expected assists (xA) among Premier League full-backs from crosses during the 2018/19 and 2019/20 seasons. It is interesting to consider how Guardiola would use Alexander-Arnold in his City team. Would he be given the licence to cross whenever he wanted, or told to deliver only in certain favourable scenarios? Intriguingly, when Benjamin Mendy was selected to play for City, he was given more licence to go forward than any of City's other full-backs; consequently he produced a high volume of crosses, although mainly following the principle of delivering early into the space between the centre-backs and goalkeeper. Does that mean that if Alexander-Arnold played for City, he would be used similarly, in a role which involved moving higher up the pitch than that of Kyle Walker? As Alexander-Arnold also possesses the attributes to play as a second pivot or third centre-back in possession, perhaps he would be used alternatively in different games. Or, maybe City's structure would be altered to enable him to perform both a deeper and more advanced role in the same game, to take advantage of both his passing and crossing, as was the case with Liverpool's system.

Let's analyse a scenario where in a similar vein to City, arguably Liverpool's crosses could be considered as passes to a greater extent. Like many of City's crosses, on occasion the ball was delivered from the byline by an overlapping full-back; Robertson in particular used his incredible energy to constantly make these runs. However, Liverpool would also often deliver crosses in behind the opposition defensive line from deeper, without needing to access the channel and get to the byline (*Figure 51*). The principle was the same: to cross the ball into the space before the opposition defensive line could fill it, avoiding an aerial duel for their front players. Whereas for City it was the speed of their attack which enabled them to cross before the opposition defenders had recovered, for Liverpool it was the fact they were often prepared to cross earlier in the attack. The opposition's defensive line would take their position off the ball's location, ensuring they were high enough to reduce the distance

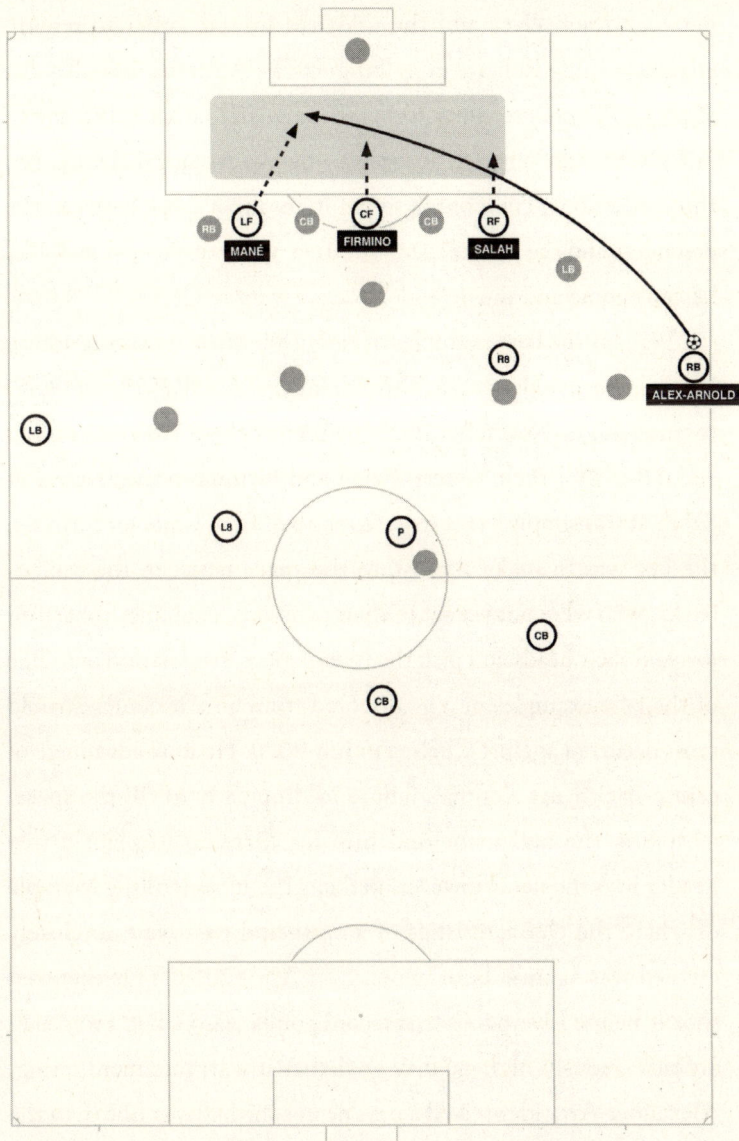

Figure 51. *Liverpool's full-backs often crossed between the defensive line and goalkeeper from deep, for their front three to attack, before the defenders could recover into the space*

between themselves and the midfield line, in order to remain compact. Andy Robertson, talking to The Athletic, describes the strategy: 'There are times to hit the area and either make one of our players run on to it or force a mistake from a defender. On those occasions, I'm looking to put in into that space between the defenders and the goalkeeper – the area where the keeper feels like he can't come and the defender doesn't want to clear it.'

Perhaps the best examples of early Robertson crosses resulting in goals occurred against Tottenham in March 2019, and City themselves, in November 2019. neither of these crosses involved aerial duels for their scorers, Salah and Firmino respectively. For Salah, it was simply a race to get to the ball first, while for Firmino, the key was to make a run into the space between the centre-backs, who were not yet set in their positions, enabling Robertson to avoid their heads and pick the Liverpool centre-forward out. One of the best examples of a goal scored from an Alexander-Arnold cross occurred against Chelsea in July 2020. He took advantage of centre-back Kurt Zouma's failure to drop early to fill the space, whipping the ball in behind him for Firmino to plant a free header into the net. However, perhaps the most striking example of where the characteristics of a cross and pass were so closely aligned was against Bournemouth in April 2018. This occurred shortly before Liverpool's first record points season, but it was such an outrageously high-quality goal that it warrants mentioning. Alexander-Arnold received a pass nearer the halfway line than the Bournemouth penalty area, and with a technique reminiscent of David Beckham, whipped an early ball behind the Bournemouth defence for Salah to loop an improbable header over the goalkeeper.

Firmino would often have trouble in beating the centre-backs to the ball in the space behind them, as his starting position was often too deep. However, for Mané and Salah the scenario was favourable in terms of reaching the cross first, as they were already in high, inside positions. For example, when the ball was with Alexander-Arnold on the right, Mané was already narrow on the opposite side, making his run into the box shorter, and giving him the potential to attack a cross within the width of the goal fairly easily. In these scenarios, the opposition full-backs had a responsibility to close the gap between themselves and their nearest centre-back to ensure that Mané or Salah could not arrive in between the two of them to score. However, full-backs often struggled to do this when the ball had been switched from their side to the opposite side, before being crossed centrally. Having defended out wide their side, full-backs were often too slow to recover to the inside of Mané and Salah, not anticipating that a cross may come in so early from the other side.

A great example of this was the goal Liverpool scored against City themselves in November 2019, which involved the classic switch of play from Alexander-Arnold to Robertson. Following the switch of play from his side, City's left-back Angeliño, instead of immediately tucking in more centrally, allowed Salah on his inside, with Robertson crossing from the other side into the space behind centre-back Fernandinho for the Liverpool wide forward to finish. As usual when discussing Mané and Salah's narrow positions, the centre-backs could help out, as they were required to zonally defend between the width of their goal when the ball was crossed regardless of the opposition. However, due to the fact that in this scenario there was space behind the defensive line, Liverpool's full-backs had the technique to use the space bend the ball around the centre-backs and back for Liverpool's wide forward to meet it behind them; sometimes the centre-backs could do little to affect the cross.

Now let's analyse Liverpool's crosses from higher up, when the opposition were more set in their defensive positions. Here there was no advanced tactic; their chances of scoring were increased by the quality and pace of the delivery, the significant number of players they were able to attack the box with, and the movement of their players to attack available space. The system itself ensured Liverpool regularly had a significant number of players attacking the box. One advantage of giving the full-back, or in Liverpool's case, sometimes a number 8, licence to move forward and overlap the wide forwards and cross the ball was the fact it enabled the ball-side wide forward to be in the box for a cross. For example, when Alexander-Arnold moved forward on Salah's outside, the Egyptian was in a position for a cross or cut-back. Salah's position, usually on the inside of the left-back, often had the effect of dragging the defence across towards Liverpool's right, potentially leaving more space towards the back of the goal, perhaps for Mané to arrive in front of the opposition right-back. Alternatively, on occasion a centre-back moved towards Liverpool's ball-side wide forward, but the other one failed to filter across accordingly, allowing Firmino to exploit the space between the two of them. Finally, at times the opposition right-back had to move extra narrow in order to close the gap between himself and the right-sided centre-back, leaving space behind him to cross for Mané to have a free header.

Playing with a narrow front three enabled Liverpool to have three players ideally positioned to exploit any gaps in the defensive line, with the quality of the delivery helping them to be picked out without an aerial duel with an opposition centre-back. The timing of Mané and Salah's runs was of the level of a natural centre-forward; they would often position themselves behind their marker, before darting across the front of them as the cross was delivered.

On occasion, a fourth player would arrive to further overload the box. For example, Andy Robertson occasionally arrived behind the opposition right-back at the back post, filling the space which the right-back vacated to deal when tracking Mané. More often, one of Liverpool's number 8s made the box. Wijnaldum, when given freedom to play higher, occasionally popped up with goals, as his two goals from crosses in the famous 4-0 Champions League semi-final second leg demolition of Barcelona in May 2019 demonstrated.

No matter exactly how Liverpool played their system on a given day, one of their number 8s was regularly high enough up the pitch to make the box when Liverpool crossed the ball. Of course, Liverpool didn't always score directly from crosses, but often from corners forced by a delivery into the box; Klopp's team scored the highest number of goals from corners during their record seasons. Against teams who defended in a low block, the volume and quality of their full-backs' delivery, combined with the movement and numbers they got in the box, made crossing an important weapon, and yet another way they were able to attack a team in order to score a goal.

Exposing the defensive principle of 'squeezing the box'

We're now going to analyse the scenarios that occurred when City and Liverpool had exhausted all their movement patterns one side, usually because the opposition had shifted across sufficiently, achieving an optimal balance between defending centrally and out wide. When this occurred, City and Liverpool were not able to deliver their desired final pass or cross into the box in the first phase of the attack. Of course, both teams possessed players who were capable of creating a moment of individual brilliance to unlock a deep defence. However, we're going to focus on what City and Liverpool did tactically in these scenarios by analysing two strategies, which although slightly different in outcome, were designed to exploit the same defensive principle: the opposition defensive line 'squeezing the box' – or in other words, pushing up – following a City or Liverpool backwards pass. When this occurred, City and Liverpool would often do one of two things: 1) Cross the ball into the newly created space behind the defensive line. 2) Target the space behind the opposition full-back on the opposite side, available due to the defensive line's position towards the side of the ball's original location.

Let's begin with the first strategy, a cross as the defensive line attempted to push up following a backwards pass. The location of the cross was vertically outside the opposition penalty area, but horizontally level with it. The idea was similar to many of the crosses already described; to deliver the ball into the space between the defensive line and goalkeeper, avoiding an aerial duel. De Bruyne's crosses from this position were particularly dangerous, but the close proximity to the box means that really any player's crosses from this zone are likely to cause problems. City's full-backs also often received the ball in this zone before crossing effectively, with their narrow, deeper positions making them an option for a backwards pass.

City's full-backs were often left completely spare, as the opposition's wide player was often dragged very deep to help his full-back out against City's winger. Trent Alexander-Arnold also regularly found himself crossing from a similar position and in a similar scenario for Liverpool; Henderson or Salah attacked the defensive line higher up, occupying the opposition wide player, enabling the Liverpool right-back to wander forward and whip the ball in behind the defensive line. The high quality of the delivery meant that the defensive line only had to push up a few yards for the necessary space to be created behind them. For example, for City's first goal against Leicester in February 2018, Leicester's centre-backs moved only a couple of yards from the edge of their own six-yard box, allowing De Bruyne, from a backwards pass from winger Bernardo Silva, to deliver for Sterling to score.

Crossing distances were short from this location, so crosses often had the characteristics of a chipped pass. Another reason that explains why the strategy of crossing from this zone was successful follows a similar theme as many of City and Liverpool's attacking strategies: it was designed with the defensive principles of the opposition in mind. Following a backwards pass, defensive lines were coached to push up to close the space in front of them. Some teams were very aggressive with their defensive line, determined to push up whenever they could. Pushing the defensive line up had two functions: 1) To force City or Liverpool's attacking players further away from their goal in an attempt to stay onside. 2) To catch their attackers offside if they remained nearer the goal. However, as City and Liverpool found themselves in these positions so regularly against deep opposition teams, their front players were well-rehearsed at ensuring they were ready for the opposition defensive line to push up, enabling them to take advantage of the space behind them.

This occurred for a goal from an Alexander-Arnold cross against Watford in February 2019 (*Figure 52*). Watford, who came with a plan to discourage crosses by holding or pushing up outside their penalty area as often as possible, did not account for the Liverpool front players adjusting their positions to remain onside, before making a run in the opposite direction to the defenders

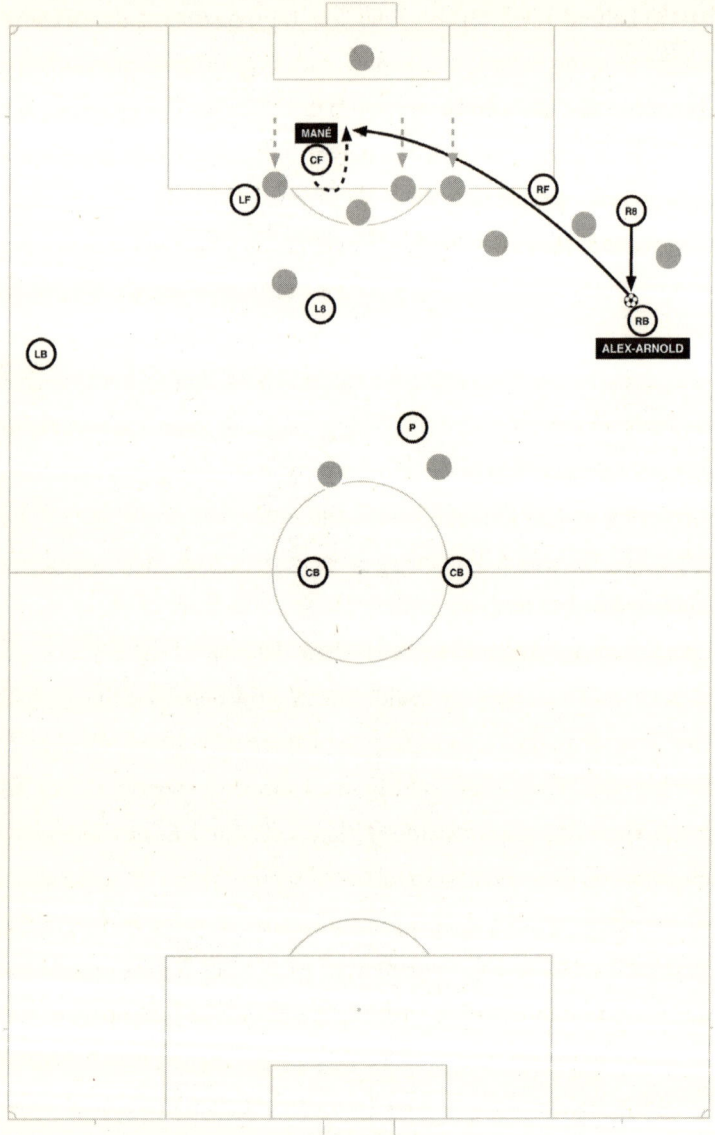

Figure 52. *The situation for a goal scored against Watford in February 2019. Watford came with a plan to push up out of the box whenever they could. From a backwards pass the defensive line pushed up, but Mané adjusted his position accordingly to stay onside, before making a run towards goal to get on the end of Alexander-Arnold's cross*

at the moment the ball was struck. For Liverpool's second goal, Wijnaldum's backwards pass to Alexander-Arnold encouraged the defensive line to move up a few yards. Mané took two steps backwards to remain onside as the defenders stepped forward, before darting in behind them to meet the Liverpool right-back's first-time cross and score his second goal of the half. The key for the opposition was the whole defensive line moving up together. If one opposition defender remained deeper than the others, City and Liverpool's attackers could take their position off the deepest player and remain onside. Liverpool in particular excelled in a different scenario when the opposition were especially keen to clear the box; following a corner. When the ball was headed clear, they were well-versed in delivering the ball back in as the defensive line pushed out, for late runners to attack the cross. There are many examples of Liverpool goals scored from the second phase of a corner, as the defensive line pushed up. One of the best was the first goal in the 4-0 win over Leicester in December 2019, when Alexander-Arnold whipped a cross over the squeezing Leicester players for Firmino to head past Kasper Schmeichel.

Let's now analyse the second scenario, which occurred when City and Liverpool passed the ball back centrally, removing the possibility of a cross, but opening up the possibility of a switch of play in behind the opposition full-back on the opposite side. Against very well-organised teams, sometimes City and Liverpool had to move the ball all the way back to their centre-backs before being able to switch play, which gave the opposition time to shift across themselves and plug the gaps both centrally and in the opposite wide area. However, in an ideal scenario, their midfield pivot became available to receive and switch the play. We mentioned in the chapter on City and Liverpool's build-up play that these two teams used a shape where their midfield pivot didn't usually need to drop deep in line with their centre-backs. Instead, in City's case one of the full-backs, or in Liverpool's case one of their number 8s, dropped deep to help progress the ball around the opposition's front players. One advantage of this was that it allowed the pivot to influence the game higher up the pitch, where his passing qualities could have more of an impact, in scenarios such as the one we are now describing.

Whereas extremely well-marshalled when City and Liverpool were building up, when they attacked a wide area, their midfield pivot often found himself free to receive. As City and Liverpool's front players made runs into, or level with, the penalty area, they dragged opposition midfielders with them, away from the pivot. There was often a grey area for the opposition midway in their own half where City and Liverpool's pivots regularly found themselves free. The opposition defenders and midfielders had so much else to concentrate on in deeper areas, and the forward(s) tended to pass on the responsibility to the rest of the team; often the forward(s) considered the pivot to be too deep for him to close him down. This could especially be the case when a team was playing with just one forward, who if he dropped too deep, would leave nobody up the pitch as an 'out ball' when his team won the ball back. From this position, the pivot was able to carry out one of City and Liverpool's strategies we've already highlighted, but this time from higher up the pitch; the diagonal ball to one of the wingers/wide forwards on the opposite side, often into the box (*Figure 53*). As this pass was played from higher up the pitch, if it was well executed it was likely to result in a direct opportunity to score a goal.

For City, perhaps the best example of a goal directly resulting from this tactic was scored against West Ham in November 2018.

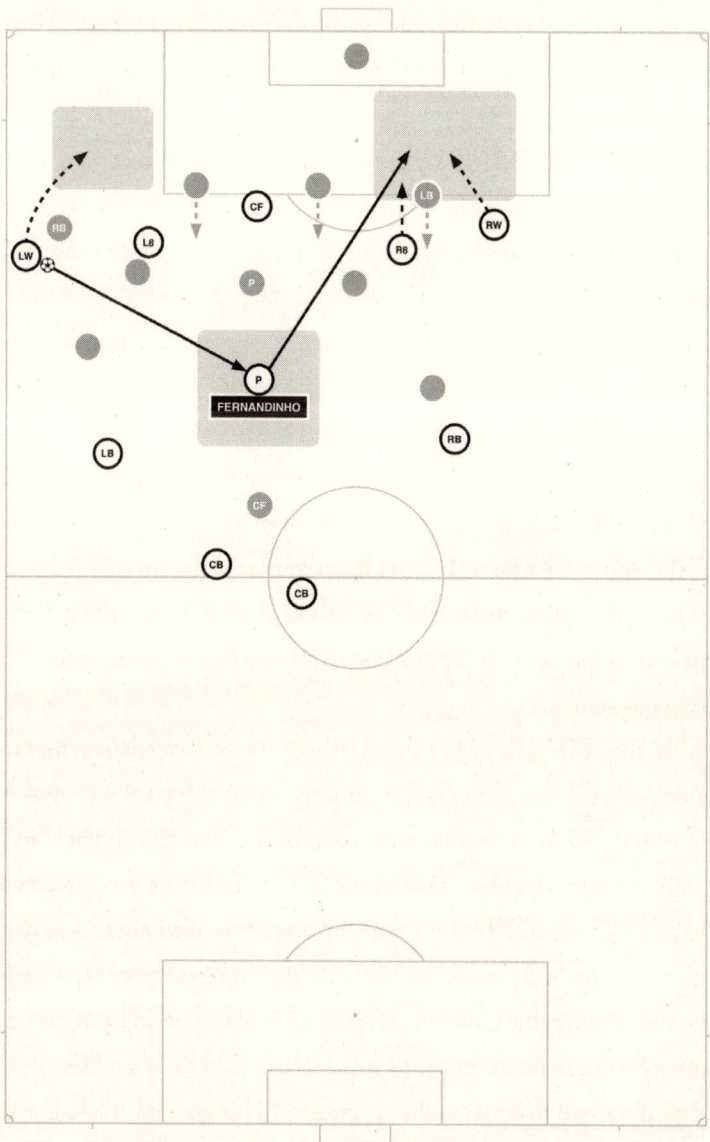

Figure 53. *The ball would be passed back to City's pivot, who was in an awkward space for the opposition to close him down; he was too deep for the midfield line, but too high for the forward line. From there, Fernandinho would look for diagonal passes in behind the defensive line as they moved up, for either City's wingers or number 8s*

Fernandinho, City's pivot, received a backwards pass from David Silva, in between the West Ham forwards, who were too high, and the central midfielders, who were too deep. Fernandinho looked to his right and floated a pass over the head of West Ham left-back Arthur Masuaku for Sterling to square for Sané to score. For Liverpool, Fabinho assisted Mané in a similar manner in the win over Manchester United in December 2018. A backwards pass from Firmino caused the United defensive line to push up to the edge of the box, with Fabinho taking the opportunity to chip a diagonal pass to meet Mané's perfectly timed run across and in behind the defensive line. In the case of Liverpool, we have already analysed the main characteristics of this situation in detail, as it was similar to the situation where their wide forwards made internal runs in behind when Liverpool had the ball in deeper areas, albeit with the added factor of the opposition defensive line pushing up as the pass was struck.

If the full-back didn't ensure the City or Liverpool winger/wide forward was beyond him exactly when the pass was struck he would play him onside, with no time for him to run back and affect the resulting shot. Due to the fact the full-back was forced to make a split-second decision, occasionally he decided not to push up following the backwards pass, instead remaining deep and tracking the run, playing the City or Liverpool wide player onside, but giving him a chance to intercept the pass or at least affect the shot. However, as we discussed in detail in the chapter on Mané and Salah's diagonal runs in behind, remaining deeper than the centre-backs usually removed the centre-backs' possibility to drop back and intercept, as the City or Liverpool wide player was able to start higher and remain onside, so consequently the pass could be played further behind the centre-backs, where they couldn't reach the ball.

Key to defending this situation was applying pressure on the player with the ball; this is one of the main cues for defences to begin to push up in the first place as the ball moves backwards. The best outcome was for the pressure to prevent the pass at source but if not, at least result in the defensive line having an idea of when the pass was going to be played – i.e. when the pressure was applied – enabling them to hold their line higher before dropping at the optimal moment. However, applying the necessary pressure required a clear strategy of who was supposed to close down City and Liverpool's pivot in these areas. Should one of the central midfielders push up having been dragged towards their own box? Or should a forward or number 10 have tracked the pivot all the way almost into his own third? Much of the time teams had to improvise, and simply use their nearest man.

Two advanced versions of the give and go

When analysing the combination play between City's wingers and number 8s, we outlined how their wingers would draw out the opposition full-back before playing a pass inside to the number 8, and then immediately make a run on the inside shoulder of the full-back. City played these give and go moves very regularly, but they also had an incredibly advanced version in their armoury. This 'reverse' give and go involved incorporating two tactics into one move: 1) Drawing out the full-back, as City did with the regular give and go. 2) Making the pass inside a backwards one, so that the defensive line would push up and space would open up behind them. This followed a similar rationale to the strategies described in the previous section on City's final ball, but with the distinction that City exploited the same side that they had originally attacked. Whereas the regular give and go involved an exchange of very short passes, the reverse give and go involved slightly longer passes, with the second pass executed from a deeper and more central position. This meant that in order to face the ball the opposition centre-backs would have to turn completely away from City's winger, giving them no chance of seeing the run, even if they were expecting it. For the regular give and go, the return pass was always along the ground, threaded through the space between the centre-back and full-back. On the other hand, for the reverse give and go, the pass was chipped over the defensive line, enabling both the pass and run to be more central.

City scored an outstanding goal using the reverse give and go against Arsenal in February 2019 (*Figure 54*). Fernandinho switched the ball to Sterling on the left wing, where he was faced with Arsenal right-back Stephan Lichtsteiner closing him down, with wide midfielder Alex Iwobi ready to double up, and Lucas Torreira covering David Silva's space in the pocket. İlkay Gündoğan was available deeper and more central, so Sterling passed back to him and immediately made a diagonal run across the defensive line. None of Arsenal's defenders saw Sterling's run, as they had turned to face the ball. In addition, the backwards pass caused them to push up a few yards, increasing the space into which a pass could be played. Gündoğan executed a sublime first-time pass to meet Sterling's run, with City's winger immediately finding Agüero, who put the finishing touches to the move. It was a goal of the highest quality.

City scored a similar goal against Crystal Palace in September 2017. Sané passed inside and backwards to Silva, who lofted the return pass over the head of Palace right-back Timothy Fosu-Mensah, for the City winger to score. Full-backs have a bad habit of thinking their job is done having defended out wide; after sprinting

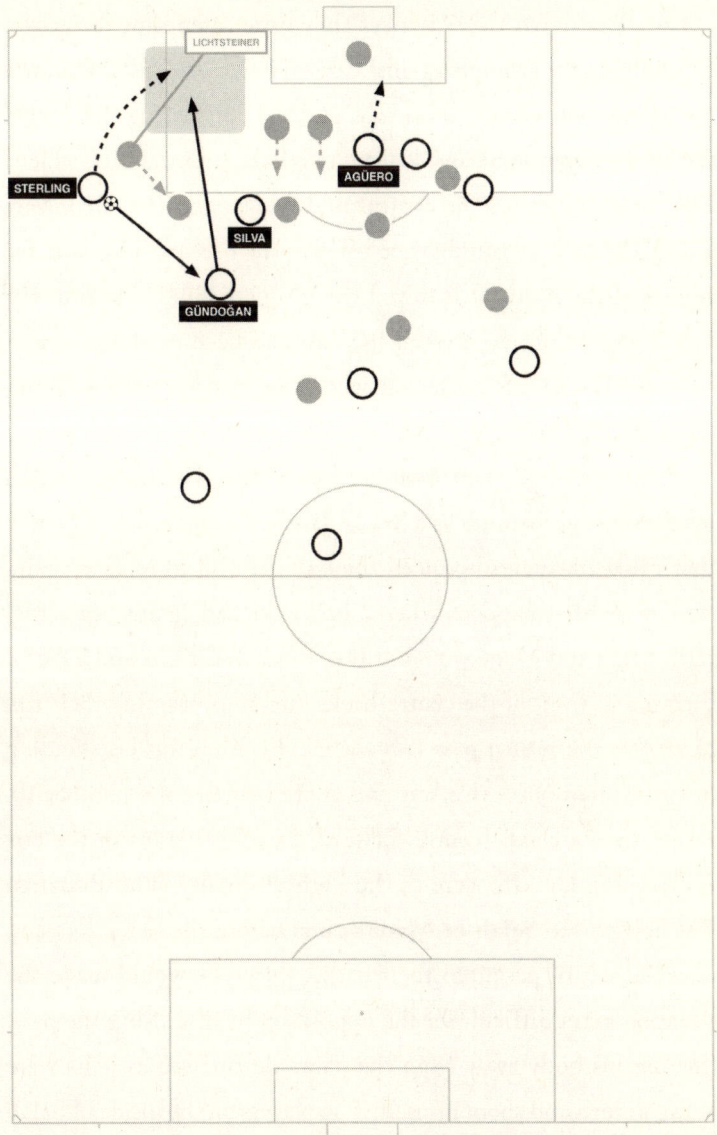

Figure 54. Goal scored against Arsenal in February 2018 from a 'reverse' give and go. Sterling passed back to Gündoğan, and then immediately made a run on the inside of right-back Stephan Lichtsteiner, who turned to face the ball. The defensive line pushed up from the backwards pass, opening up the space for Gündoğan to lift a perfect pass into Sterling, who squared for Agüero to score

out to close down City's winger they were often slow to recover centrally. In the example against Crystal Palace, Fosu-Mensah saw Sané's run but reacted too slowly, perhaps not sensing the danger due to the cover on his inside from two Palace central midfielders. But the problem for the central midfielders was that they were facing the ball, so couldn't see the run themselves. This was the genius of the move; it involved the ultimate blind-side run. For City's opposition, even when the ball had been passed centrally, they still weren't safe on the side which they had just put significant effort into defending.

Liverpool had their own version of the give and go which involved using Firmino as a 'wall', labelled as such as it appeared that his team-mates bounced the ball off him to receive again, similar to what happens when a ball is kicked against an actual wall. Salah and Mané would dribble towards the box and look for Firmino in front of the centre-backs, before continuing their run to receive the return pass (*Figure 55*). Firmino was outstanding in these situations – this was one of the benefits of a number 10, rather than a classic centre-forward, as a focal point in the box – Firmino's lay-offs were of the highest quality. The Brazilian was able to see Salah or Mané's runs before the defenders and play the return pass into their paths. Often he would make the situation extra difficult for the opposition by disguising the pass, turning his body away from the pass's destination as if he were going to turn and shoot himself. The players on the inside of Salah or Mané, such as the centre-backs and central midfielders were drawn to Firmino, diverting attention away from the Liverpool wide forward's inside run. Mané scored a goal from this move against Salzburg in October 2019. Having already beaten the Salzburg right-back, the right-sided centre-back began to move

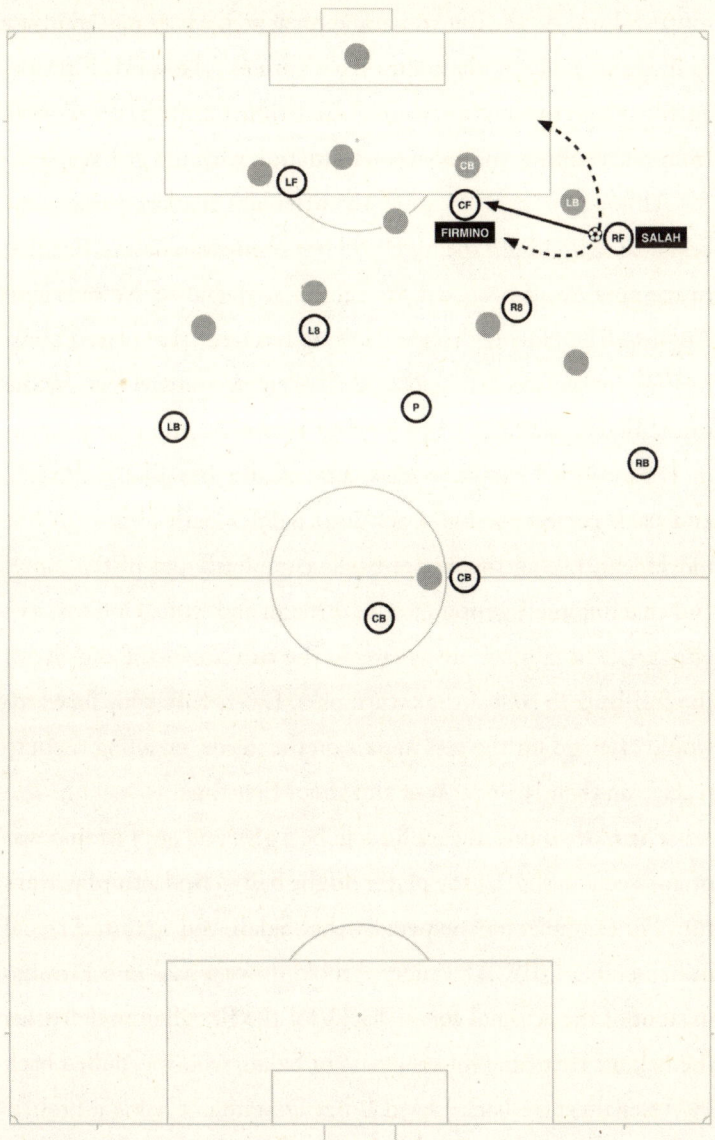

Figure 55. *When receiving wider, Salah and Mané would often pass the ball to Firmino in front of the centre-backs before looking immediately for the return pass on the inside of the full-back*

towards him. As the centre-back approached, Mané passed inside to Firmino, drawing the centre-back's attention towards Firmino, enabling him to collect Firmino's first-time return pass and score from his resulting one versus one situation with the goalkeeper.

Although it involved a slightly different situation, perhaps the best goal to highlight the high skill level and awareness of Firmino in the final third occurred for Salah's goal against Newcastle in August 2019. Having dropped deep to receive, Salah played a pass to Firmino between two Newcastle central midfielders, before immediately making a run beyond them. As the centre-backs moved towards Firmino to make a tackle, the Brazilian controlled and back-heeled the ball back into Salah's path almost in one movement, taking the centre-backs completely out of the move, and enabling the Egyptian to run through and score. Unlike City's wingers, who almost always made the run down the outside of the full-back to collect the return pass, Liverpool's wide forwards would often go for the return pass on the inside, enabling them to receive on their stronger foot and shoot first time.

The move didn't always have to be a give and go; Firmino was often used as a wall by the player on the ball to find a third player's run. For example, for the penalty that Salah won against Arsenal in September 2019, Alexander-Arnold drove a pass into Firmino in front of the Arsenal centre-backs for the Brazilian to deftly lay the ball off first time into the pass of Salah, who was pulled back by Arsenal centre-back David Luiz. Despite not being a prolific goalscorer, Firmino was arguably the unsung hero of Liverpool's record points team. In the next chapter, we are going to analyse his role, and make comparisons to Sergio Agüero, City's own centre-forward.

Chapter 13

Firmino and Agüero – modern centre-forwards

TRADITIONALLY A centre-forward's main task is to be in the box to score goals, not to be involved in creating the chance in the first place. However, in the view of some modern managers, Guardiola and Klopp being two of them, every player must contribute to the system in terms of how it functions in both defence and attack; City and Liverpool's centre-forwards had requirements in terms of their positioning and movements as their teams transitioned from building up to attacking play higher up the pitch.

Let's begin by assessing the role of City's centre-forward. Despite excelling as a goalscorer, Sergio Agüero had to alter his game to fit into Guardiola's system. Perhaps the main adjustment to his game in possession was the requirement for him to drop in front of the centre-backs, in order to provide a third option for City to pass between the lines, in addition to the options provided by the two number 8s. This was where a traditional number 10 would operate, in a space which we have previously stated is difficult to access in modern football, as the opposition teams prioritised defending compactly in central areas. As City didn't play with a traditional number 10, their centre-forward was their main access to that space. This made sense – referring back to the five vertical lanes of the pitch, it was City's centre-forward who was positioned in the middle lane. As he progressed under Guardiola, Agüero became a master at timing his runs deep and involving himself in moves leading to chance creation; Agüero's per cent share of City's chances created in open play while on the pitch increased from 9.5 per cent in the season preceding Guardiola's arrival to 10.9 per cent during his first season, and increased to 15.8 per cent in 2017/18, reflecting Agüero's increased contribution to City's attacking play. Agüero's per cent share of City's assists also increased during the aforementioned seasons.

When a centre-forward is asked to drop deep he is often labelled a 'false 9', a role famously performed by Lionel Messi during Guardiola's time at Barcelona. Some football observers label a player a false 9 if the player selected to play through the middle's 'natural' position is a winger or attacking midfielder, not a forward. Guardiola has on occasions, for example, used Raheem Sterling in the centre-forward position, resulting in the natural winger being labelled a false 9. However, Sterling's role when asked to play through the middle arguably wasn't much different from the role of Agüero in City's system.

So was Agüero a false 9, or simply a centre-forward who dropped deep to receive? Arguably he was the latter, for two reasons. Firstly, Agüero's starting position was high. This was one of the keys to him successfully receiving a pass unchallenged, as he tended to start behind the centre-backs in positions where they couldn't see him, before timing his run deep at the exact moment when the ball was ready to be passed. David Silva used a similar tactic when he was being tightly marked as a number 8 – he took his marker deep almost into his own defensive line, remaining behind him so he couldn't easily be seen – before checking back and showing for the ball in the pocket.

The second reason is that Agüero didn't end up dropping any further than he needed to for the role required of him; his task was to appear between the lines and lay the ball off or turn and run with it. This meant he was still high enough to get himself into the box, helping him to maintain his prolific goalscoring record. So arguably Agüero wasn't a false 9 nor a traditional centre-forward who stayed high to stretch the play or play up against the centre-backs – his role could perhaps be termed a 9 and a half – part number nine, part number ten – as essentially he performed both roles. Two of the tasks of City's centre-forward were the same as those of a false 9 – to receive unmarked behind the midfield, or to drag out a centre-back to open up space in behind. But a third function, to effectively play as a fourth midfielder, positioned deep to start with, wasn't the case with Agüero. On the odd occasion, Guardiola used the likes of Bernardo Silva or De Bruyne as genuine false 9s who had licence to start deeper and remain deeper for whole phases of play, but the majority of the time Agüero, or the alternative forward, Gabriel Jesus, were centre-forwards who dropped short.

Liverpool's Roberto Firmino, on the other hand, was a genuine false 9. Unlike Agüero, Firmino didn't tend to start behind the centre-backs, looking to drop late undetected to receive the ball. Instead, he *wanted* the centre-backs to see him, as he was often a decoy runner to create space for Mané and Salah in behind. We have already analysed this situation in detail in a previous chapter. However, the relationship also worked the opposite way around;

Mané or Salah were often the decoy runners for Firmino to receive himself. The Liverpool wide forwards' high, narrow positions occupied the opposition defensive line, making the defenders wary of stepping too high. Salah or Mané would often make a run in behind at the same time that Firmino dropped, enabling Liverpool's false 9 to receive and turn (*Figure 56*). In fact, by the time of Liverpool's first record points-winning season, 2018/19, many centre-backs were under instructions to pass Firmino on and hold their positions deeper to protect the space behind them.

Although an exaggeration because it occurred following a turnover of possession with the opposition not set in their opposition shape, perhaps the clearest example of a goal involving Firmino as a false 9 occurred against Burnley in August 2019. As soon as Liverpool won back possession, Salah and Mané made movements in behind, sending the Burnley central defenders backwards, and consequently creating an enormous gap for Firmino to receive behind and between Burnley's two central midfielders. From there, he was able to supply Salah with a forward pass, before continuing his run untracked to the edge of the box, where he received a return pass and fired into the net.

Rather than disguise his position from the centre-backs, it was arguably the midfielders from whom Firmino wanted to disguise his position. As a true false 9, Firmino appeared to have licence to go wherever space appeared, taking up positions of varying widths and depths to receive possession, depending on the opposition's set-up and strategy, as a 'free' player. With one of Liverpool's number 8s usually dropping deep, and the other one often moving wide, Firmino was often a vital link player between the players building up and the front players, in the centre of the pitch. He was constantly checking the positions of his opponents and team-

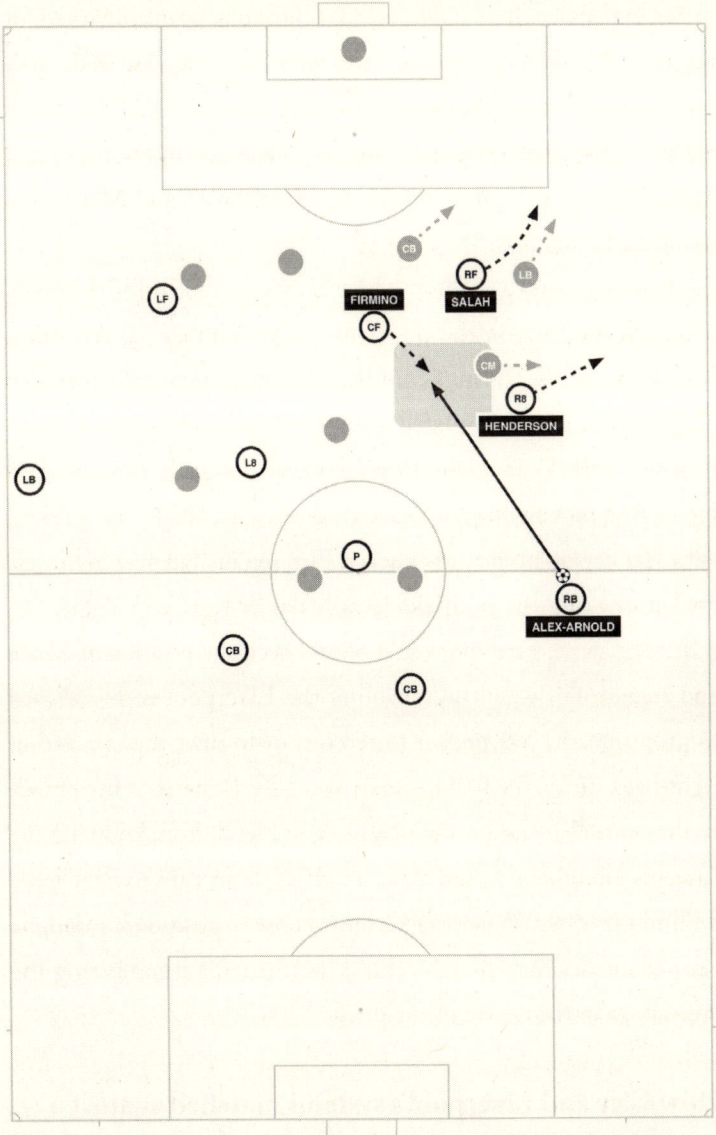

Figure 56. *Examples of the movements Liverpool would make to clear space between the lines for Firmino to receive. Henderson would often drag his marker away from the centre, while Salah would run in behind to force the defensive line back*

mates to decide where it was best for him to appear unmarked, or where he should move to in order to take his marker out of the way and create space for a team-mate. To reiterate, he could drop deep without Liverpool missing his presence higher up due to Salah and Mané's positions high and inside; in effect Salah and Mané were two centre-forwards.

With Firmino as a false 9, Liverpool's specific midfield shape varied depending on the positions of the number 8s. At times, with both number 8s high and Fabinho deep, Firmino's presence between the lines completed a midfield diamond shape. Often, however, with Wijnaldum dropping deep alongside Fabinho, and Henderson moving high, it formed more of a 2-2 shape. Sometimes, with Henderson in the right pocket, Firmino drifted over to the left pocket, making the midfield rectangular or square in shape. On other occasions, Firmino would often check the position of Mané and remain fairly central, enabling the Liverpool wide forward to drop into the left pocket to receive, or to drag the opposition right-back under the ball to create space for Robertson in behind. In the centre Firmino could play close to Henderson, knowing the Liverpool number 8 would make unselfish decoy runs to clear space for him to receive. Wherever Firmino chose to position himself, he became an auxiliary fourth central midfielder, outnumbering the opposition in the centre of the pitch.

How City and Liverpool's systems matched against a double pivot, four-man midfield

As a classic false 9, Firmino had licence to go where he wanted *regardless* of the opposition formation. On the other hand, City's centre-forward's movements varied *depending* on the opposition's set-up. There was one scenario where City's centre-forward was very clearly encouraged to drop off to receive: when the opposition used a double pivot system, for example in a 4-4-2, 4-4-1-1 or 5-4-1 out-of-possession shape. Many teams chose to defend with a double pivot against City as it appeared to match them up well in midfield, because it ensured there were always two deeper midfielders to shadow City's two number 8s. In addition, in a 4-4-2 or 4-4-1-1, there were two forwards (or a number ten and a forward) to put pressure on City's pivot and centre-backs. Against the double pivot system there were three possible spaces for City to break the lines: between the wide midfielders and pivots on each side, and between the two pivots themselves. Many teams encouraged their two pivots to man-mark City's number 8s; Jose Mourinho, for example, was a strong advocate of assigning a man to be responsible for both David Silva and Kevin De Bruyne almost wherever they went. It was against this strategy that City's centre-forward dropping to receive between the pivots was most effective. Silva and De Bruyne's fairly wide positions created a large gap between their two markers for Agüero to fill (*Figure 57*). The problem for the opposition was created by the disciplined positioning that Guardiola asked of his front five.

We have already described how City's wingers held their wide positions, patiently waiting for the pass to arrive. City's number 8s did the same. For example, if City were building up on their left side, De Bruyne, the right-sided 8, would usually hold his position in the pocket on the right side, rather than move over towards the ball. This meant his marker, the left-sided pivot, either had to leave him free in order to shift over and plug the gap between himself and the other pivot, or stick tight to him on the opposite side to the ball. If he did the latter, he could potentially prevent De Bruyne's supply when the ball changed sides – but in doing so he would leave space for Agüero to exploit between himself and the other pivot.

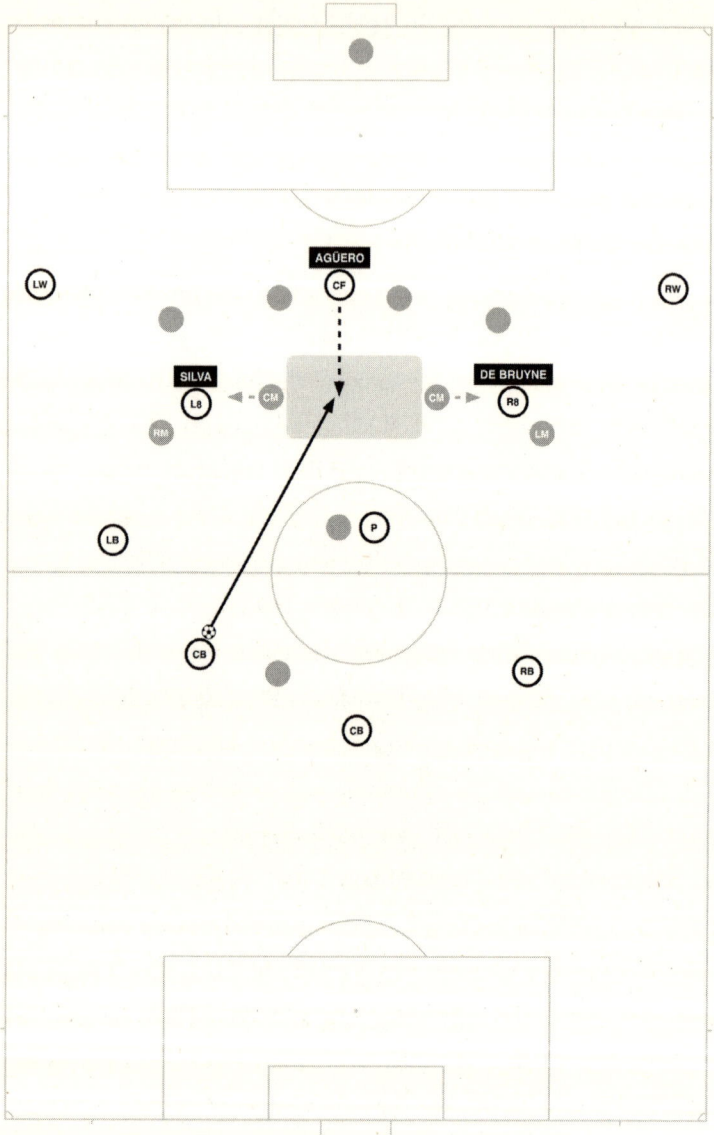

Figure 57. *Silva and De Bruyne's fairly wide positions in the pockets created a large gap between their two central midfield markers for Agüero to drop into to receive, especially if their two markers had a tendency to man-mark the two City number 8s*

With Agüero's movement deep, superiority was created between the lines, with a three versus two against the two pivots.

Against Liverpool, the strategy of man-marking their number 8s in a double pivot was less common. If you were to pause a Liverpool game and assess the position of their number 8s, at times there was a remarkable vertical and horizontal distance between the two of them, with Henderson moving high and/or wide one side, and Wijnaldum deep and/or wide the other. If Liverpool's number 8s were man-marked by the opposition pivots, Firmino would have a field day in between the two of them. For Liverpool's third goal against West Ham in August 2018, scored by Mané, West Ham's pivots were split by Liverpool's number 8s, and Firmino took advantage (*Figure 58*). West Ham's two pivots, Mark Noble and Jack Wilshere, appeared under instructions to track Keïta, Liverpool's left 8, and Milner, the right 8, wherever they went. For the goal, Keïta dropped deep to receive, taking Wilshere with him, before passing to centre-back Joe Gomez. Milner moved wide on the right side to receive in the space created by Salah pinning back left-back Arthur Masuaku. Noble moved across to Liverpool's right to close Milner down, but Wilshere was unable to plug the gap between himself and Noble – having previously closed down Keïta, Noble was unable to recover in time – which enabled Firmino to receive completely free between the two West Ham pivots. The movements of Liverpool's number 8s split West Ham's pivots, creating the gap for Firmino to exploit.

Even on the occasions when Liverpool's number 8s were positioned in more traditional number 8 positions in the pockets like De Bruyne and Silva, Firmino's presence between the two opposition pivots created the same three versus two overload as City's centre-forward did, but on a more regular basis, as Firmino

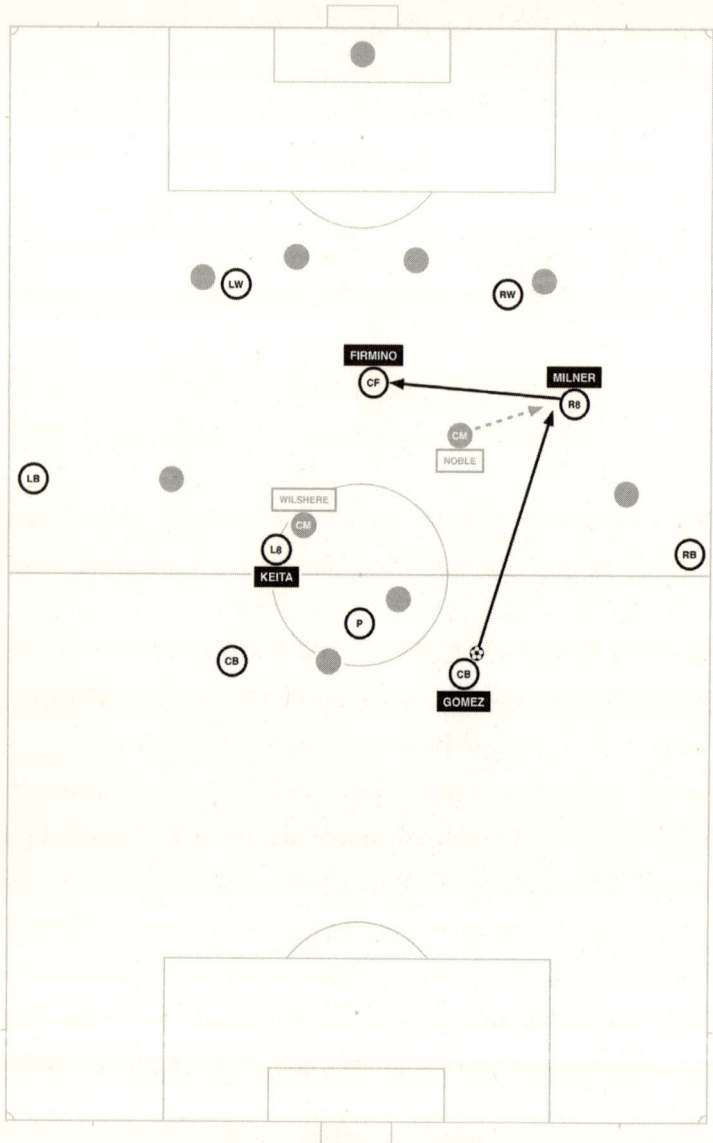

Figure 58. *The situation for Liverpool's third goal against West Ham in August 2018. West Ham's two central midfielders, Mark Noble and Jack Wilshere, showed a tendency to man-mark Liverpool's number 8s, James Milner and Naby Keïta. Wilshere followed Keïta deep, while Noble moved wide to close down Milner. This created a large gap between the two West Ham central midfielders, leaving Firmino completely free to receive between the lines from Milner*

was almost always positioned between the lines. As well as the negative consequence of man-marking Henderson and Wijnaldum, there was little benefit; the creative threats of the likes of Henderson and Wijnaldum were not the same level of De Bruyne and Silva, so simply didn't require the same attention. This didn't mean that one or both number 8s were left spare, but instead that it was more favourable to deal with them zonally, with the opposition right-sided pivot passing Wijnaldum on to a team-mate when he dropped deep, and picking him up when he moved higher.

Instead of Wijnaldum, often the two opposition pivots would concentrate on the two players usually positioned between the lines; Henderson and Firmino. Perhaps the two pivots would fill the space between the lines, and pick up the player who came into their zone. When this occurred, Liverpool would make movements in an attempt to disrupt the opposition's pivots. Whenever Henderson was marked, he made unselfish runs to move his marker out of the way in order to make space for Salah or Firmino between the lines (*Figure 56*). For example, when Alexander-Arnold had the ball towards Liverpool's right, Henderson would make a horizontal movement towards the outside of Salah, taking one of the pivots with him. This may have been enough to create a passing lane into Firmino between the two opposition pivots. However, if the right-sided opposition pivot moved across to pick Firmino up, the Liverpool centre-forward would often make a vertical movement towards the ball, taking his man higher, and instead creating a passing lane into Salah between the two pivots. Should the two pivots manage to prevent the passes to Firmino and Salah by shifting across to Liverpool's right as a pair, Mané would often drop to potentially receive in the left pocket, via a pass from Fabinho or Wijnaldum, before the nearest pivot could move back across to cover the pocket.

Like City, Liverpool created superiority between the lines in the form of multiple players who could appear between or to the side of the pivots, and work off each other's movements to receive. Any hint of man-marking, and one of Liverpool's attacking players would attempt to move their marker out of the way, for a team-mate to receive instead. As will be described shortly, the key to the opposition surviving in a double pivot against City and Liverpool was the narrow position of their wide players to cover the pivots' outside shoulders.

Could the numerical superiority created by Firmino and Agüero dropping between the pivots be negated, however, if one of the centre-backs followed the centre-forward in order to prevent him from receiving or at least turning with the ball? As the centre-forward, he was technically a centre-back's 'man' to mark. Clearly with some of the very deep positions Firmino took up this wouldn't be considered. But what about when he started higher and just dropped off a few yards? As teams played more and more regularly against Klopp's Liverpool, they realised that their centre-backs holding their positions was non-negotiable, at least before they were sure the ball was going to be passed to Firmino. This was the key factor; for Liverpool the run was often a decoy to create space for Salah and Mané in behind. We have already analysed this situation in detail in the chapter concerning Liverpool's diagonal passes in behind. By stepping higher, the centre-back was attempting to prevent something that either wasn't going to happen, or was potentially less dangerous than what happened as a consequence of their actions: the opening up of the space in behind. Once the ball had been struck, and it was obvious that the target of the pass was Firmino, there was greater motive for the centre-back to step in, as long as he could affect the pass by making a tackle or intercepting; with the movement of Salah and Mané in behind, simply forcing Firmino back wasn't enough, if he simply passed back to a team-mate, who immediately passed in behind.

With regards to City, however, the question was different, because unlike Liverpool they were attempting to pass to their centre-forward, not use him as a decoy to pass long in behind. So was it a favourable solution for one centre-back to step in with Agüero? In this situation City would be left without a forward in his natural position, which meant the other centre-back was spare, as City's wingers were usually positioned wide. However, really the question needed answering in reverse: what did City want the opposition to do? 1) Agüero to pick up the ball and turn, but face a team with a back four in place, and pressure from the recovering central midfielders around him? Or, 2) A centre-back to come out in an attempt to prevent Agüero from turning, but in doing so leave just three defenders deeper with sizeable gaps in between them to exploit?

While City could take advantage of the first situation, arguably for them the second situation was even more favourable, as long as their centre-forward could get a pass off, because their whole system was based around trying to move an opposition player out of shape to create space for a team-mate. When a centre-back followed Agüero, City had a specific move (*Figure 59*) to bypass the centre-back. As the ball was passed to Agüero, either Silva or De Bruyne began to make a supporting run to give Agüero a first-time pass. This was a classic example of what is termed a 'third man' run: the third player in the optimal position, the number 8, was closely marked, but could be accessed via a pass from the first player (the player on the ball) to a second player, the centre-forward. Silva and De Bruyne were already on the move from their usual positions

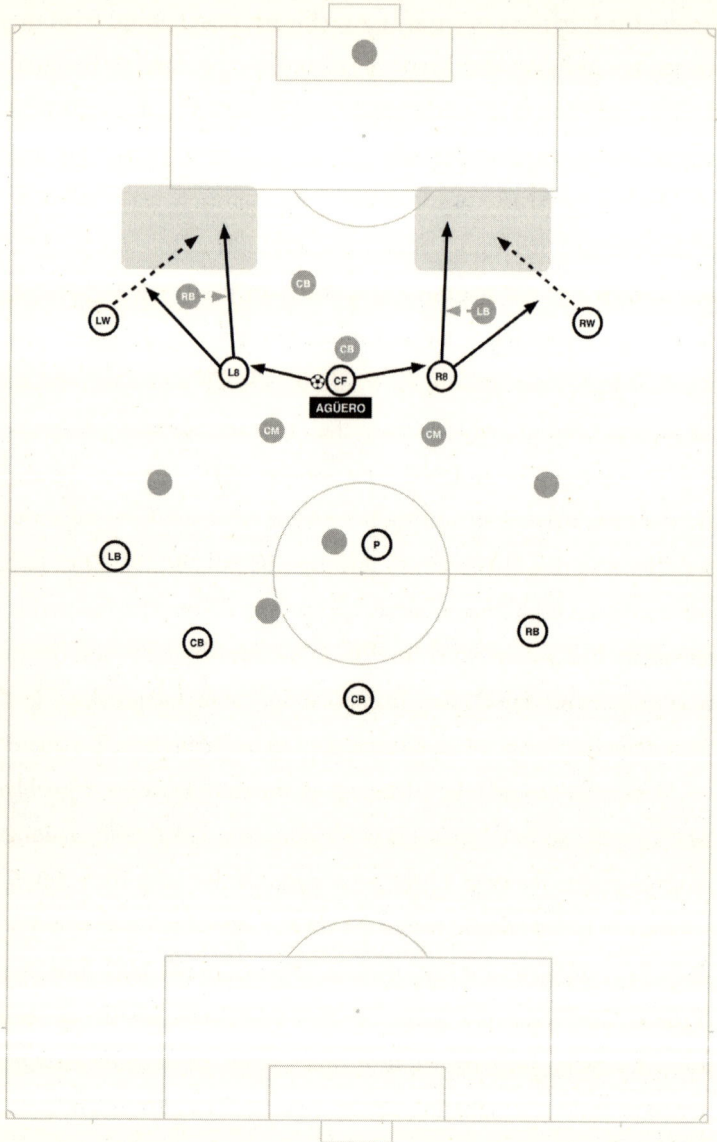

Figure 59. *The situation which would occur should a centre-back follow City's centre-forward deep. Agüero would look for a quick lay-off to one of the number 8s, taking one of the centre-backs out of the move. The number 8 would then look to thread a pass either on the inside or outside of the opposition full-backs to City's wingers, depending on the full-backs' positions*

behind their marker as the pass was played towards Agüero, giving them an advantage over their marker.

In this situation, the opposition still had one centre-back remaining in place behind the ball, but he was stranded centrally, with a huge space either side of him. However, it wasn't the centre-back who had the problem; technically his man was Agüero, who was behind the ball having dropped short, and City's wingers were too wide to run directly into the centre-back's zone. Instead, it was the full-backs who had a problem; the removal of one of the centre-backs from the defensive line opened up space to play a through ball along the ground for one of City's wingers to receive behind the full-back. As long as the run and pass were timed correctly, City could exploit one of the large spaces either side of the deeper centre-back with a pass on the inside of the full-back for the winger to be put through on goal. Competent full-backs would instantly narrow off the second they saw their centre-back step forward with Agüero, ensuring they could cut off the passing lane on the inside of them. But this meant City's winger could then check his run and instead create a passing lane on the outside of the full-back to receive, and take the full-back on for pace.

Some teams, especially those who liked to press from the front, used the defensive strategy of one of the centre-backs stepping forward as the centre-forward dropped as a general rule against any opposition. City themselves defended in this manner, especially against teams who played with one forward. However, most teams don't play a front five with two quick wingers who were able to hold such high starting positions, placing them in a perfect position to exploit the space behind the centre-back as soon as it appeared. To reiterate a point made previously, if a team defended in a mid-block rather than low block, a high defensive line was essential to preventing the pass to Agüero or City's number 8s between the lines. If the space for Agüero to receive was restricted to a minimum, it didn't matter how many players City placed between the lines. However, clearly a high line came with other risks – there was much more space for City to use their strategies in wide areas to get in behind the defensive line – such as the combinations between the wingers and number 8s to access the channel, or the diagonal switch of play to City's winger over the full-back's head.

To recap, we have discussed how Firmino and Agüero exploited the double pivot system when the opposition pivots left space between them. But what about when a double pivot was performed in more of a zonal structure (*Figure 60*)? In this system the centre-backs could remain in their slots to a greater extent, as the midfield pivots moved across the pitch together, attempting to reduce the space between the lines as a pair. Let's describe an example for both teams. As City build up on their left side, the right-sided opposition pivot shifts across the pitch to patrol the pocket where Silva is positioned. Rather than man-marking De Bruyne in the right-hand pocket, the left-sided opposition pivot also shifts across towards City's left side. Or, as Liverpool build up on their right, the opposition's left-sided pivot moves across to cover Henderson, in the right pocket. Rather than mark Wijnaldum, Liverpool's left-sided number 8 (note, Wijnaldum could be positioned deep, or high in the left pocket), the opposition's right-sided pivot also shifts across towards Liverpool's right side. In both these examples, there is no passing lane between the two pivots for Agüero or Firmino to drop into, because the gap is plugged.

Although this strategy provided a solution to the problem of the centre-forward dropping into the space between the two pivots, the consequence was that De Bruyne was now free, in the pocket on

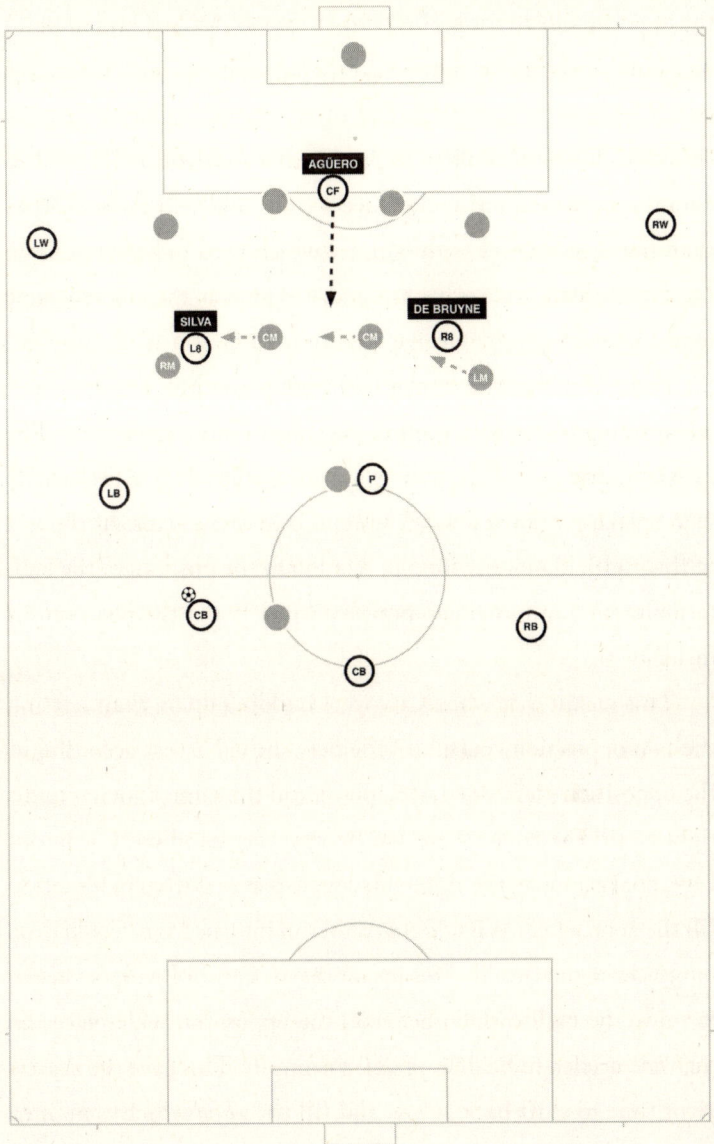

Figure 60. *An example of how the space which City's centre-forward looked to drop into could be filled zonally, by the opposition central midfielder on the opposite side to the ball moving across towards the side of the ball, and the wide midfielder his side shifting across to fill the zone where De Bruyne, in this example, operated*

the opposite side to the ball. Or for Liverpool, Wijnaldum (if high) or Mané were free to move into the opposite pocket. Crucially, this is where the 'zonal' part of the system in theory aided the situation. It's important to highlight that midfield fours tend to contain more diligent wide players than midfield fives. Rather than the classic 4-4-2 with wingers which used to be common in English football, wide players in midfield fours in the modern game tend to have better defensive qualities. In fact, it is not unusual for a central midfielder to play as a wide player in a 4-4-2, at least when facing teams who want to play passes into the pockets. The usual requirement of the wide player in a midfield four, especially when playing against a 4-3-3 system, is to move across as the rest of the midfield moves across in relation to the position of the ball, to maintain a minimal gap between himself and the pivot on his inside.

This meant that when City were building up on their left and the two opposition central midfielders shifted across accordingly, the opposition's left-sided wide player did the same, moving to his right to fill the zone where De Bruyne was standing. Or, in our Liverpool example, the right-sided wide player shifted to his left to fill the zone which Wijnaldum could run into, or Mané could drop into, as he regularly did. This meant that as City or Liverpool began to move the ball to the other side, the opposition wide player on that side needed to hold his position centrally. This gave the nearest pivot time to shift back across and fill the zone which contained De Bruyne, in City's case, or Wijnaldum or Mané in Liverpool's case. The wide player couldn't worry about the pass wide his side; he needed to prioritise preventing the pass on his inside.

If well-rehearsed, zonally protecting the space between the lines could help block the supply to the players in the pockets, without the centre-backs being pulled out of position. However, the main disadvantage of using a compact midfield four against City or Liverpool in order to prioritise preventing them from playing between the lines was that it neglected coverage of the wide areas, where both these teams equally excelled. The main principle in a zonal midfield four is to show the opposition wide at all costs. A wide player in a midfield four who over-covered narrowly to block central passing lanes was unlikely to be wide enough to prevent the supply line between City's full-back and winger (*Figure 61*) – nor to be in an optimal position to get back and assist his full-back against the winger. Equally, against Liverpool, an ultra-narrow wide player in a midfield four was unlikely to be able to stop the Liverpool full-backs from advancing with the ball and whipping in dangerous crosses, nor from passing back inside to Salah and Mané in dangerous positions. In addition, when Trent Alexander-Arnold played deeper, it was more difficult for a wide player in a compact four to close him down in his narrow, deeper position. Finally, it was more challenging for the left-sided pivot to track Henderson when he made a run out wide into the space between Alexander-Arnold and Salah, as he had to do so from a more central starting position.

Against both City and Liverpool, the fact the opposition's wide players needed to move relatively centrally when the ball was on the opposite side of the pitch made the opposition especially susceptible to the switch of play. Against other teams, the principle of always showing the opposition wide was usually very effective. However, against City and Liverpool, it was essential to maintain a balance between being compact enough centrally, yet sufficiently spread to avoid being exploited in wide areas. A five-man midfield usually offered a greater spread without losing compactness, and therefore

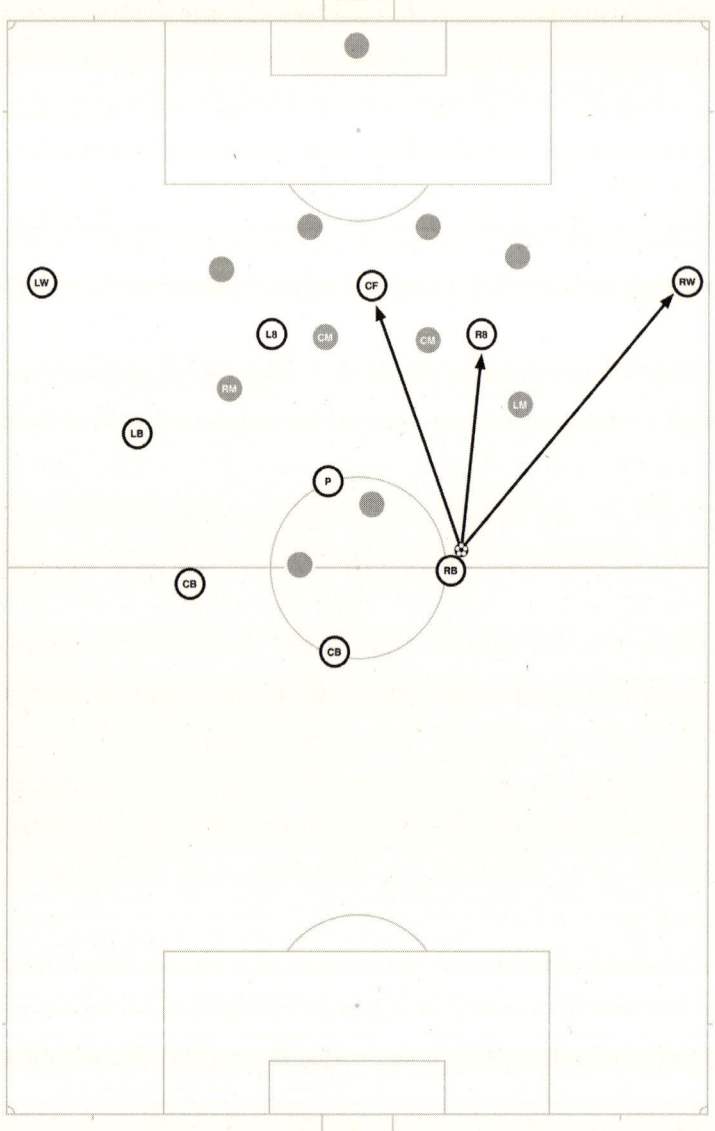

Figure 61. A double-pivot, four-man midfield was usually unable to cover the three passes City looked for each side. If the wide player was very narrow to protect the pocket on his inside, as was usually necessary, City would play around the defensive block by passing wide to their winger

more of a balance between the centre and the wide areas. Arguably this was the case to a greater extent against City. Against Liverpool a balance also needed to be maintained between having enough players deep to deal with their attacks between the lines and in wide areas, but also using a second forward or advanced midfielder to help apply pressure to reduce the volume and effectiveness of the long passes from the back. A system with a double pivot in a midfield four permitted a second forward to apply greater pressure, whereas with a midfield five, this was more difficult. When facing Liverpool there were so many attacking weapons to neutralise that deciding which one was the number one priority was difficult.

Chapter 14

A five-man midfield to prevent supply to City's front five

WE HAVE already addressed many of the strengths and weaknesses of a four- and five-man midfield against Liverpool in previous chapters while analysing specific scenarios and movement patterns, such as Wijnaldum dropping deep to receive, the relationship between Robertson and Mané, and the switch of play between the full-backs. Therefore, in this chapter, we are going to assess the intricacies of a five-man midfield against City. In this context we are referring to a five-man midfield as a 4-1-4-1 (4-5-1), not a 4-2-3-1/4-4-1-1, which contain double pivots. This means we are describing a system with either one or three pivots, depending upon whether the three central midfielders are positioned with the central of the three deeper, and the two outside midfielders further forward, or as a flat three. The wide players can also defend in different ways: either positioned in a parallel line with their nearest central midfielder, or higher up, at an angle.

So how could a five-man midfield assist in reducing the supply to *all* of City's front five, including their wingers? As City played with five players covering the entire width of the pitch, with players both on the inside and outside of the opposition's defensive block, there were five potential forward passes available for the five players City used to build up. For example, if Kyle Walker had the ball towards City's right, his three nearest forward passes were out wide to Sterling, the right-winger, to De Bruyne in the pocket, or to Agüero, who was ready to drop short. Many opposition game plans focused too strongly on preventing a direct pass into City's number 8s, while neglecting the two other ways City accessed these players: via the centre-forward or the wingers. The double pivot system was often insufficient to prevent all three of these passes as it didn't spread wide enough. On the other hand, a five-man midfield, consisting of three central midfielders, enabled the midfield to horizontally cover more of the pitch, without losing compactness. For example, the central pivot could patrol the space in front of the centre-backs where Agüero dropped short to receive, and the two outside number 8s could play slightly wider than in a double pivot system – helping them to stay close to City's number 8s – even when the ball was on the opposite side of the pitch.

This left the wide players to position themselves in the passing lane between City's narrow full-back and wide winger (*Figure 62*), but with the priority of preventing the pass into City's number 8 first, they couldn't be too wide. The wide players may even have been able to provide extra security for the full-back from the diagonal switch of play. It has already been mentioned that the vast majority of teams who played a back four could not avoid dropping into a back five in certain scenarios simply because City had a five versus four. When City switched play to their winger at the same time as their number 8 made a run in between centre-back and full-back, the full-back had no choice but to move extra narrow to

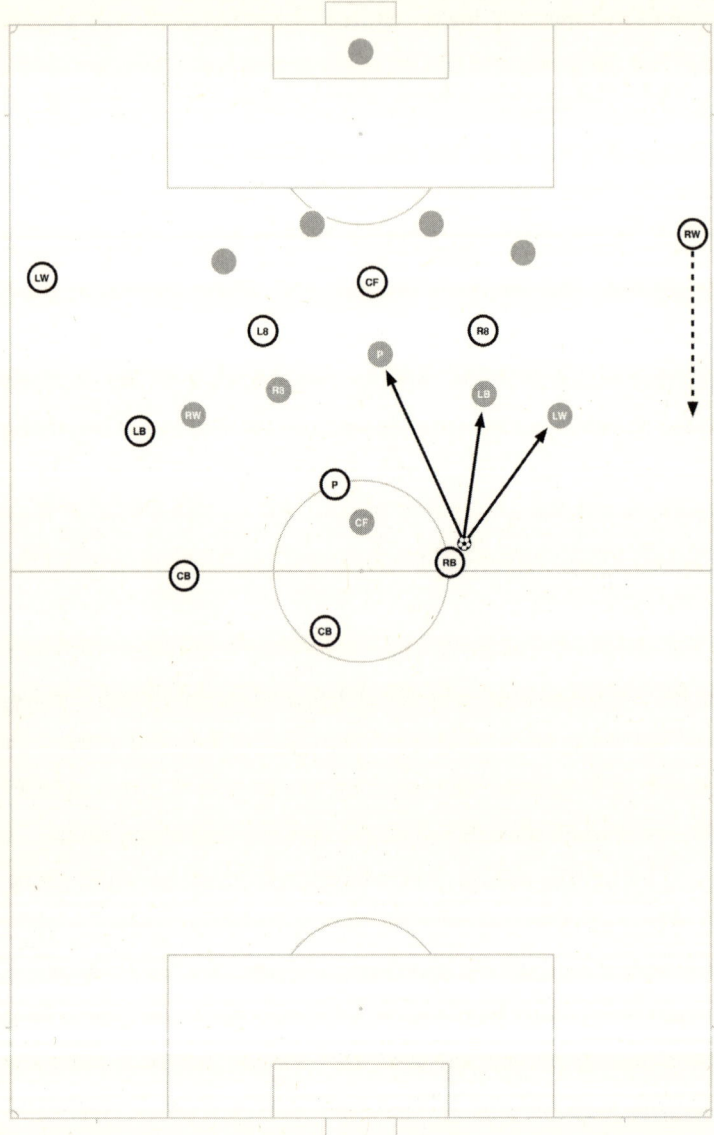

Figure 62. *A five-man midfield could spread wider, potentially blocking not only the passes City wanted to play on the inside of the midfield, but also reduce the supply to City's dangerous wingers by blocking the passing lane to them, or by forcing them to receive deeper*

plug the gap, before they knew for certain the ball would be passed to the winger, not the number 8.

As stated, as with a midfield five the midfield line contained one more player than the defensive line, the opposition's wide player could be wider than in a midfield four, and therefore wider than his own full-back. Therefore, often the distance which the opposition's wide player had to run to close down City's winger was shorter than the full-back's, so perhaps the wide player could intercept the pass and consequently save the full-back a great deal of running. However, arguably this strategy was more for emergency situations when the opposition full-back simply couldn't cover the number 8's run inside them, *and* move wide to defend against City's winger in time, especially nearer the box where the winger could get off an early shot. The negative was that it resulted in the wide player dropping very deep and expending a great deal of energy defending. In addition, wide players generally can't be relied upon to do this job consistently. Another more obvious point is that not many wide players were capable of defending against City's wingers, so it was far better that the full-back covered the City winger whenever possible.

The main problem that a five-man midfield caused was that it only permitted one player to try to disrupt City's build-up play. The question had to be asked: what was a more effective strategy for preventing the supply to City's front five? 1) An extra player to apply pressure to City's build-up and reduce the superiority and control City had between their build-up five – but at the same time one less player as security to block the passes into the front five, and help out deeper when the pass was played forward? Or: 2) One less player to apply pressure during City's build-up, allowing City greater superiority and control to try to find a pass into their front five – but at the same time an extra player deeper to block the passes into the front five, and help out deeper when the ball was played into the front five? Usually in a five-man midfield the forward was tasked primarily with preventing City's pivot from receiving passes, leaving the number 8s to screen passes into City's number 8s, and a spare zonal pivot in front of the centre-backs to prevent the passes to Agüero, without one of the centre-backs having to vacate the defensive line.

Of course, City had strategies to progress the ball without the use of their midfield pivot, when the opposition forward shadowed him. For example, the pivot moved to one side to receive, or the centre-backs used the extra space given to them to dribble forward. As the City centre-back advanced with the ball, he gave the nearest player of the opposition's central midfield three a decision to make: did he leave his position to close down the City centre-back who was now effectively in a midfield position? Or did he hold his position, leaving the centre-back free on the ball, but enabling him to block the City number 8's space behind him? City deployed centre-backs who were very comfortable at travelling with the ball and completing difficult passes between the lines. The difficulty for the opposition central midfielder was that he was facing the ball and therefore could not see the exact positions of the City players behind him. As the distance between the passer and the receiver reduced the further the City centre-back advanced with the ball, the more a slight alteration in position, for example, by the City number 8, could be crucial in creating the angle and passing lane required for him to receive a pass.

Therefore, applying pressure on the ball was arguably an equally efficient method of the opposition number 8 blocking the pass behind him. However, by the opposition's central midfielder moving higher to apply pressure, he may be able to block the direct route to the number 8, but in doing so he would often open up an indirect route. Should the City centre-back have been able to pass to a team-mate, for example the winger or full-back, the opposition number 8 was unlikely to be able to get back in time to block the pass back inside to City's number 8. The central pivot would also usually have been too far away to move across in time to cover behind him, at least to prevent a quick combination between the number 8 and winger that side. Free from his marker in the pocket, there was no need for City's number 8 to run into the channel where he could be picked up by the centre-back moving across. This situation asked the same question posed previously: when was it better to move a midfielder forward to apply pressure to prevent City from finding one of their front five? And when was it better to allow City to advance without pressure, but with all their passes into the front five blocked?

When the opposition didn't attempt to move a central midfielder higher to apply pressure, instead playing with three deep central midfielders (a triple pivot) in a flatter line of three, City had a strategy to confuse the opposition midfielders, involving their centre-forward (*Figure 63*). As outlined, against a double pivot system, Agüero or Jesus's role was to drop *between* the two pivots. However, against a three-man central midfield the space between the two number 8s was blocked by the pivot. Instead, City's number 8 often deceived his marker by moving more centrally, into the middle vertical lane where Agüero would normally appear. As the number 8's marker stepped across to block the pass into the number 8, Agüero appeared in the vertical lane which was previously occupied by the number 8.

An example of this movement pattern occurred for Bernardo Silva's goal against Leicester in December 2018. Leicester, with

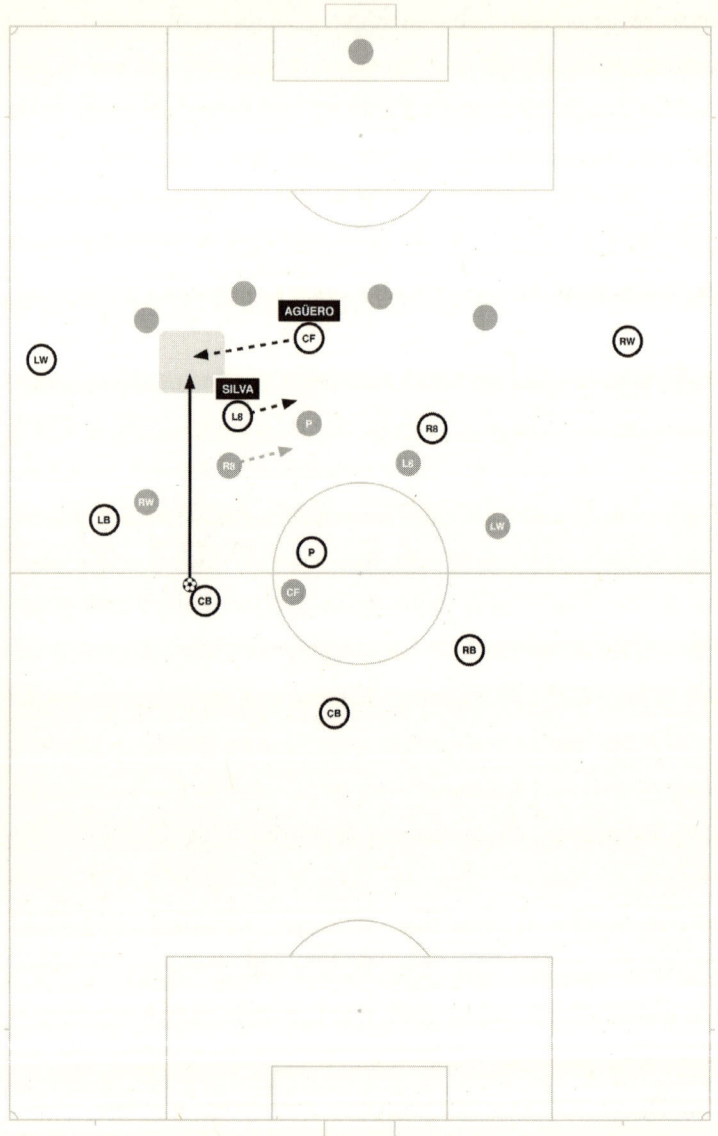

Figure 63. A move City often performed against a five-man midfield. Silva and Agüero would swap positions to confuse their markers, with City's centre-forward receiving in the left pocket where Silva was originally positioned

their three central midfielders, were blocking all three passes between the lines. De Bruyne then crossed over into the middle vertical lane, behind the central pivot, and Agüero appeared in De Bruyne's original position to receive, behind the number 8. Agüero then passed through to Bernardo Silva to score, with both centre-backs having been tempted out of their slots by the positions of Agüero and De Bruyne, as an emergency fix for the situation. The original problem was compounded by City centre-back Aymeric Laporte's freedom to dribble forward through midfield, completely unchallenged, having escaped the attentions of Leicester's centre-forward; the Leicester central midfielder closest to him did not feel he could leave his man, Bernardo Silva, to close down City's centre-back.

Chapter 15

Exposing a single pivot – midfield rectangles and double false 9s

WE HAVE already established that Firmino played the role of a false 9, positioned between the lines rather than as a traditional centre-forward. This meant the opposition centre-backs often had nobody to mark, there were two players positioned in front of them (Firmino and Liverpool's right-sided number 8), yet too deep for the centre-backs to close them down, especially because there were also two players positioned on their outside (Mané and Salah), ready to exploit the space behind them as soon as they stepped forward. This description of Liverpool's front four has parallels with tweaks City occasionally used against a 4-1-4-1, single pivot system, especially when the opposition attempted to press with their number 8s, leaving the pivot more isolated between the lines.

The rationale for the opposition was that the increased pressure higher up would aid prevention of the supply to City's number 8s. To compensate, the opposition pivot would move across to the number 8 on the side of the ball to close down. Against this type of opponent, City sometimes looked to create a rectangle or box shape around the three opposition central midfielders. The idea of using a rectangle midfield shape against an opposition midfield three was not novel to City, but the positions Guardiola selected to form the rectangle was unusual. One of the number 8s would usually drop out of the pocket alongside Fernandinho, taking his marker with him. İlkay Gündoğan was often used for this role, as he was very reliable in possession in deeper areas. City's other number 8, usually De Bruyne, would remain high in the other pocket. This left one more player to form the higher part of the rectangle. Instead of asking their winger to move narrow into the pocket, City encouraged their centre-forward to drop into the pocket to the side of the pivot not occupied by De Bruyne. The 4-3-3 merged into a 4-2-2-2, but the final two were wingers, not forwards.

City sometimes used this system against Liverpool, who pressed in the manner described, with their number 8s higher than their own pivot, leaving City's number 8s behind them. However, perhaps the game where City had greatest success with this tactic was the 6-0 thrashing of Maurizio Sarri's Chelsea in February 2019 (*Figure 64*). In fact, with the free kick City's centre-forward won for the third goal, three of City's four first-half goals could be attributed to Agüero dropping into City's left pocket to complete a midfield rectangle. Chelsea's pivot, Jorginho, not the most mobile of players, was constantly left two versus one against De Bruyne and Agüero between the lines, with number 8s Ross Barkley and N'Golo Kanté asked to vacate space to press higher. Unaware of City's plan for Agüero to drop to into City's left pocket to the right of Jorginho, Chelsea's pivot naturally tended to drift over towards De Bruyne in the right pocket, leaving a huge space for Agüero to exploit. Chelsea right-sided number 8 Kanté was particularly confused with the situation, focusing his attention on Gündoğan,

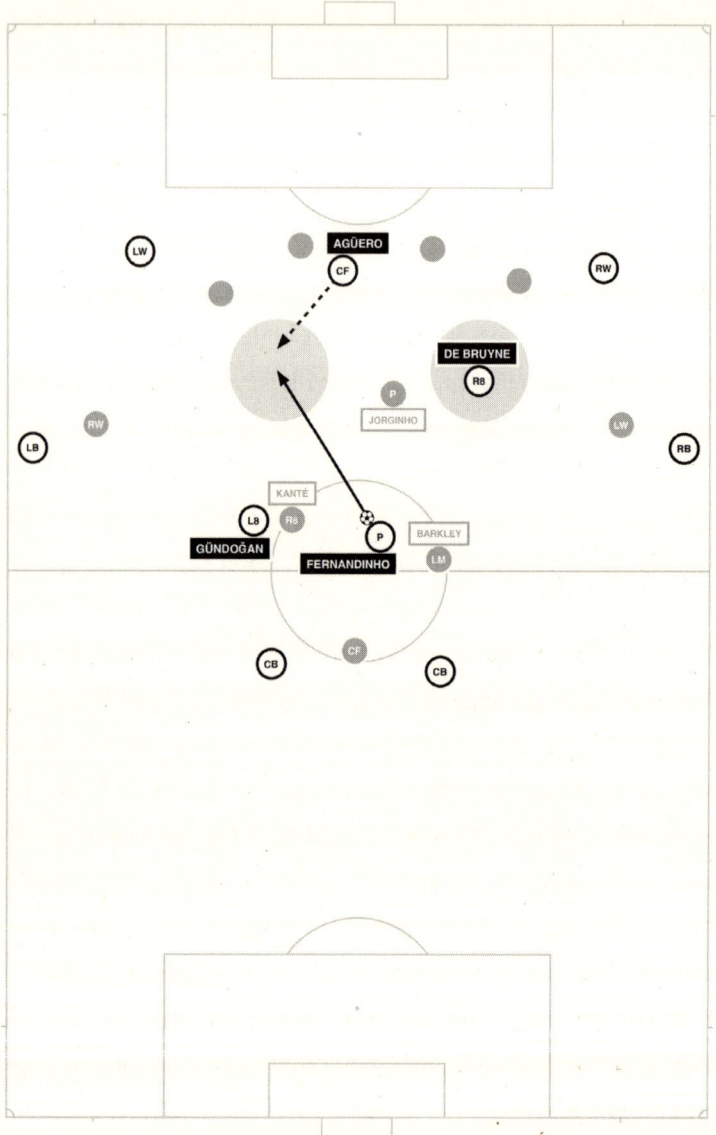

Figure 64. *A pattern performed most notably in City's 6-0 win over Chelsea in February 2019. Kanté was drawn to Gündoğan, and with Jorginho focusing his attentions on De Bruyne, Agüero was free to receive in the pocket behind Kanté*

rather than protecting the space behind him, probably because: 1) He had been instructed to shadow Gündoğan, presuming that City's left-sided number 8 would play higher, as he usually did. 2) He perceived that City's threat between the lines had reduced, as Gündoğan was no longer there, and that City's left-winger would remain wide, so he didn't need to remain deep to protect the space. However, as soon as Kanté vacated, Agüero appeared behind him to receive a pass. This left City with Agüero and their other number 8 either side of Jorginho.

In other games there were alternative variations to form the rectangle. For example, instead of Agüero dropping into the pocket, City's winger could move narrow to become the fourth player in the rectangle, and their full-back could push on. Due to one number 8 moving deep, a build-up five would remain, with the full-back's higher position maintaining the front five instead. The principle of forming a midfield rectangle against a three-man central midfield where the number 8s tended to press high remained, but the players performing each role could be altered.

The specificity of Guardiola asking his centre-forward to drop to one side to complete a midfield rectangle (4-2-2-2) has parallels with an alternative forward-less (false 9) system City occasionally used against a single pivot. The trouble with playing an orthodox false 9 against a single pivot system is that the false 9 finds himself dropping into the space occupied by the opposition pivot; there was less benefit compared to when facing a double pivot. Instead, in recent seasons, Guardiola has occasionally used a system which contained two false 9s, so could be termed a *double* false 9, in order to form the 4-2-2-2. One of their number 8s played in the deeper part of the rectangle to ensure City had two pivots to draw out the two opposition number 8s, and create the space behind them.

Meanwhile, the two false 9s were positioned further forward, either side of the opposition pivot, to complete the rectangle, and the two wingers were the highest players on the pitch, ready to take advantage of the space in behind should one of the centre-backs be drawn out to close down one of the false 9s.

This system was used effectively in City's Champions League Second Round first leg game against Real Madrid in 2019/20, due to the Spanish's side's very aggressive 4-1-4-1 press; Bernardo Silva and De Bruyne played either side of Real Madrid's single pivot, with Gabriel Jesus and Riyad Mahrez high and narrow wingers, similar to Salah and Mané's positions for Liverpool (*Figure 65*). The idea was that when one of Real Madrid's centre-backs moved high to close down Bernardo or De Bruyne between the lines, Jesus and Mahrez would attack the space behind the centre-backs. As there were two false 9s, it wasn't possible for Real Madrid's pivot to easily cover both Bernardo Silva *and* De Bruyne. The system created some incredible freeze-frame images of Real Madrid's centre-backs, confused by having nobody to mark, pushing very high on to one of De Bruyne or Bernardo, or, thinking Jesus was the centre-forward (as the only natural centre-forward on the pitch, this made sense), moving towards City's left to mark him. On another day, City could have exploited the situations much better, with Ederson in particular failing to find Mahrez or Jesus in the huge spaces in behind the Madrid centre-backs.

Just as the single false 9 system is usually only labelled as such with the absence of a natural forward, the double false 9 was only really highlighted when the players selected to play centrally weren't Agüero or Jesus. However, there really wasn't too much difference between the double false 9 system and the hybrid 4-3-3/4-2-2-2 system described in the Chelsea game of City's centre-forward

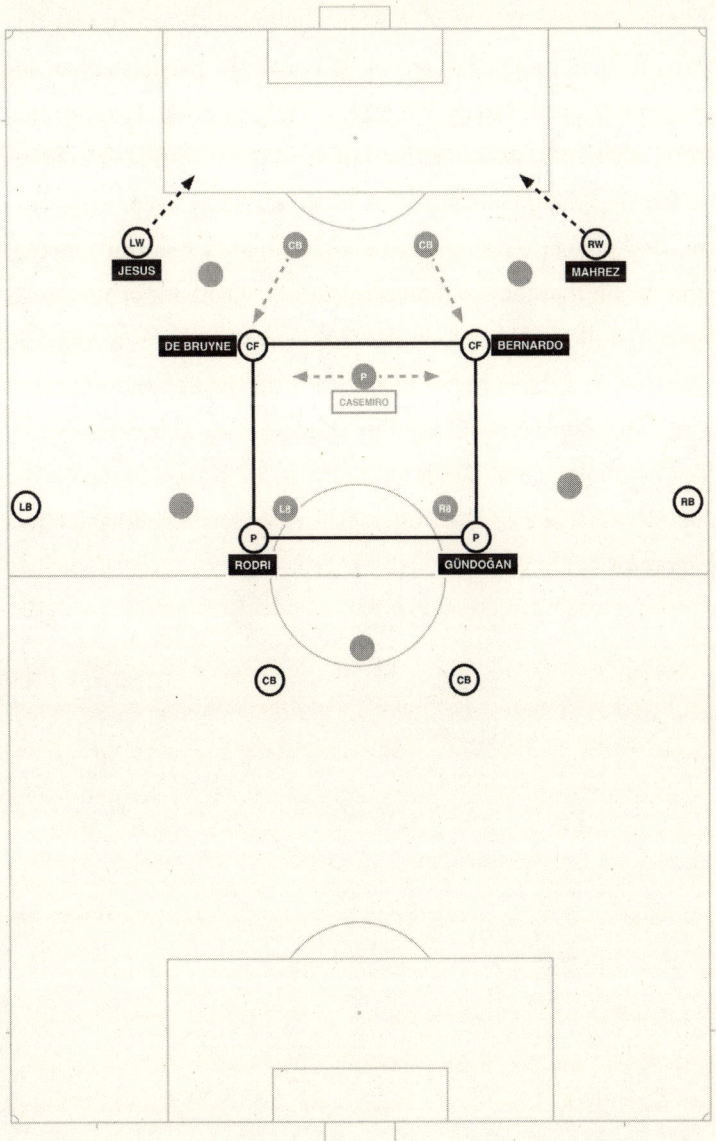

Figure 65. The 'double false 9' system played against Real Madrid in February 2020. Real Madrid pivot Casemiro was left with both De Bruyne and Bernardo Silva to deal with. Faced with nobody to mark, one of Real Madrid's centre-back was often tempted to move high to close down, leaving space in behind for Mahrez and Jesus

dropping to one side of the pivot. The main difference was that when Agüero dropped to receive in one of the pockets either side of the pivot, he did so from a high starting position. On the other hand, when there was no natural forward in the team, both players performing the double false 9 roles were already deep, occupying the two pockets, rather than starting higher before dropping. This meant that they could receive deeper, where the centre-backs couldn't follow them, to create a four versus three overload in midfield, in a shape that was awkward for the opposition to deal with. The alternative positioning of players again highlights that for Guardiola, it was the positioning of the players based on the opposition's defensive system, not the exact formation, which was important.

Chapter 16

Liverpool's alternative shape – 4-2-1-3/4-2-3-1

AS FOR Liverpool, the lopsided version of 4-3-3 they played in possession was arguably similar to a double false 9 (4-2-2-2) system, as it featured two pivots (Fabinho and Wijnaldum), two players between the lines (Firmino and Henderson), and two wide forwards (Mané and Salah). This being said, perhaps Firmino played too centrally for Liverpool's midfield shape to consistently be described as a rectangle, as he would often leave the left pocket free for Mané to drop into. However, Klopp's desire for two players between the lines and two high between the full-backs and centre-backs occupying the opposition defensive line is demonstrated clearly in the other formation he used.

On the odd occasion during the 2019/20 season, and in 2018/19 for 11 games, Klopp used a 4-2-1-3 (this could also be labelled a 4-2-3-1), which often merged into a 4-2-2-2 (or 4-2-4); there were two pivots, two players between the lines (the number 10 plus one of the wide players), and two high (the centre-forward and the other wide player). The similarity in the players' positioning between the lopsided 4-3-3 and the 4-2-1-3 was only apparent in possession; out of possession Liverpool pressed in more of a 4-4-2/4-2-4, rather than a 4-3-3. The only real difference between the lopsided 4-3-3 in possession and the 4-2-1-3 was that the shape was formed by different positions on the pitch, with the 4-2-1-3 for a more attacking four players high up the pitch than in the 4-3-3, as there was one less central midfielder – there was no need to play Fabinho, Wijnaldum *and* Henderson; the extra player could be a number 10.

In the 4-2-1-3, Firmino was the number 10, Salah the centre-forward, Mané the left-sided wide player, and Xherdan Shaqiri often the right-sided wide player. The two players positioned high were Mané and Salah, just like in the regular 4-3-3 system. Despite effectively being the centre-forward, Salah didn't usually play very centrally between the centre-backs, instead taking up his regular 4-3-3 position between left-back and centre-back, in the right channel. Salah was very effective as a centre-forward, especially on the turnover, where his pace enabled him to directly attack the centre-backs. For example, the second and fourth goals in Liverpool's win over Bournemouth in December 2018 demonstrated the threat of Salah from a central position; one goal occurred following a pass in behind for Salah, and for the other he received a pass to feet before turning and running at the centre-backs. Firmino, as a number 10, was in his regular position between the lines. However, instead of one of the central midfielders moving high, which would occur in the 4-3-3, Shaqiri moved narrow off the right to become the second player between the lines.

As in this system there were constantly two deep pivots, rather than one of the numbers 8s dropping to become the second pivot, either pivot could easily move wide between full-back and centre-back to form the back three, with the other maintaining the position of a traditional pivot in front and between the centre-backs. In addition, in 4-2-1-3 the full-backs had greater licence to move high both at the same time, because the protection always existed behind them. For Robertson and Mané, their patterns and movements were very similar to in the 4-3-3, as they formed a triangle with the left-sided pivot on Liverpool's left. A similar triangle was formed on the right, as Shaqiri played in a similar position to the high number 8 in the 4-3-3, with Alexander-Arnold moving high to provide the width, and the pivot that side provided the protection.

When using the 4-2-1-3, Klopp occasionally decided that he wanted the narrow wide player between the lines to come from the the left side, and the high narrow wide player to come from the right (the opposite of where Mané and Shaqiri were usually selected to play). For example, Naby Keïta sometimes played in the pocket as a narrow left-sided wide player in this shape, with Mané switching to the right to play narrow but, crucially, high that side. The front four all had licence to change positions to receive between the lines, making them difficult to pick up. One reason for Klopp using this shape during the 2018/19 season may have been to help new signing Fabinho to adapt to Liverpool's style of play and the Premier League as a whole. In addition, at Monaco, his previous team, Fabinho was accustomed to playing in a double pivot system. Many pundits and managers refer to new arrivals arriving from foreign leagues needing to adapt to the pace and intensity of the Premier League. Therefore, it may have been perceived that having a constant midfield partner alongside him would result in Fabinho having less space to cover out of possession than as the sole pivot in the 4-3-3, where both 8s pressed higher, and would sometimes go forward at the same time. Regardless, Liverpool's alternative shape demonstrated that like for Guardiola, for Klopp it wasn't the label of 4-3-3 or 4-2-1-3 that was important, but the positioning of the players within it; Liverpool's shape and principles were similar in both systems.

Chapter 17

How did a back five match up against City's front five?

IN CONSIDERING the drawbacks of a back-four system, the idea was introduced that playing with a back five provided solutions to some of the problems City created. As City effectively played with a front five, a back five, unlike a back four, wasn't at a numerical disadvantage. It was previously stated that the five City attacking players were spread out across the width of the pitch, with each filling one of the five vertical sections, if the pitch were to be divided accordingly. A back five enabled the opposition team to position a defender in each of these five slots. Another advantage of a back five was that the widest of the defenders, the two wing-backs, had a shorter distance to close down City's wingers than the two full-backs in a back four.

This in theory meant two things: 1) City were less able to switch the ball to their wingers, as the reduced distance between wing-back and winger meant the pass was more likely to be intercepted. 2) When the ball *was* switched to their wingers, the reduced distance enabled the wing-back to move close enough to him to prevent the winger from accelerating with the ball. Two disadvantages of a back five have also been mentioned: 1) If a team didn't usually play with a back five, were they able to change to this system seamlessly with only a few days to prepare for a match against City? 2) A back five may have provided solutions for some of City's strategies against a back four, but City had specific strategies against a back five.

Another negative of using a back five was that the extra defender often gave a false sense of security. Let's explain. A consequence of using a back four against City's front five is that their numerical disadvantage forced the defenders to rely on each other to defend. The full-backs knew they had to protect the centre-backs by tucking in narrowly, as City in effect placed three players (the two number 8s plus the centre-forward) between the full-backs and centre-backs. This created a four versus three situation centrally in the opposition's favour, or a series of two versus one situations, where a player was performing two 'half and half' roles. Specifically, the two centre-backs were up against City's centre-forward, the right-back and the right centre-back against City's left number 8, and the left-back and left centre-back against City's right number 8. To maintain these central overloads the defenders had to accept that City's wingers were available out wide, and that they couldn't be closed down until the ball was on its way to them. Doing so too early would result in losing the defending team's numerical superiority centrally; while the ball was central the priority was defending the centre not the wide area. However, as soon as the ball was on its way to City's winger, the defenders shifted over to create a four versus four, leaving the fifth City player, the winger on the opposition side, spare, but in a position where he would be difficult to access.

How did a back five match up against City's front five?

As the extra player in the defensive line meant the defenders could spread wider in a back five, the wing-backs often forgot the priority of protecting the centre. When the ball was central, the five defenders could create a five versus three centrally, spreading wider than a back four would do, but not *too* wide. If the wing-backs were positioned too wide, although City's wingers were covered, the five versus three advantage centrally became a three versus three, which was a less-favourable scenario than the four versus three advantage centrally in a back four, with the wingers spare. At least in a back four, City's three centrally placed players forced the opposition full-backs to play very narrowly. This meant that most passes were forced down the outside of the back four, keeping all the defenders on the inside of City's winger. However, in a back-five system that was not necessarily the case. The extra security centrally often resulted in the wing-backs almost man-marking City's wingers and anticipating a pass to them, crucially *before* it occurred. On one hand this helped the wing-backs reduce the supply of passes into the feet of City's wingers. However, it had the negative effect of opening up space between the wing-backs and wide centre-backs, crucially before the ball had been passed wide from a more central position.

At this point it would be fair to ask why this mattered. If the wing-back was bypassed, the opposition still had four other defenders in place to defend the goal. However, this was often not the case. The key once again was the interaction between City's wide players and number 8s. Due to the existence three centre-backs in a back five, the high position of City's number 8s placed them in the zone of the wider two centre-backs, often directly in front of them. Simple opposite movements from City's number 8 and winger would open up space on the inside of the wing-backs. Specifically, as City's number

8 showed for a pass, the likelihood in a back five was that the centre-back would see it as his job to close the number 8 down, or at least move forward a few steps in anticipation of a pass. However, as soon as he did so, the opposition wing-back lost the security which had enabled him to defend tight to City's winger, as there was now space for City's winger to make a diagonal run into the area which was previously filled by the centre-back. (*Figure 66*).

A great example of this pattern occurred for Gabriel Jesus's goal against Wolves in January 2019. Wolves' right-sided wide centre-back Ryan Bennett got caught too high, anticipating a pass from Laporte to Gündoğan in the pocket in front of him. At the same time, right wing-back Matt Doherty was too wide and tight to Sané in his desperation to prevent a pass to his feet, not realising the large space on his inside that Bennett had vacated, which enabled Laporte to pass on Doherty's inside. An almost identical example occurred for City's first goal against Bournemouth in December 2018. With Zinchenko on the ball, Bournemouth right wing-back Simon Francis moved wide anticipating a pass to Sané, at the same time as right-sided centre-back Steve Cook moved higher than the rest of the defensive line, bothered by Gündoğan's position in the pocket in front of him. Cook's movement opened up space behind him for Sané, who could see all the way along the defensive line, to make a diagonal inside run. Sané got to the ball ahead of the Bournemouth goalkeeper, touching it square for Bernardo Silva to score. Two more examples occurred for the second and third goals against Schalke in the Champions League second round second leg in March 2019. Schalke's wing-backs were caught too wide and deep in an attempt to affect a potential pass to City's wingers. With no cover on their inside from the centre-backs, Sterling and Sané were found by passes to supply their inside runs into the vacant

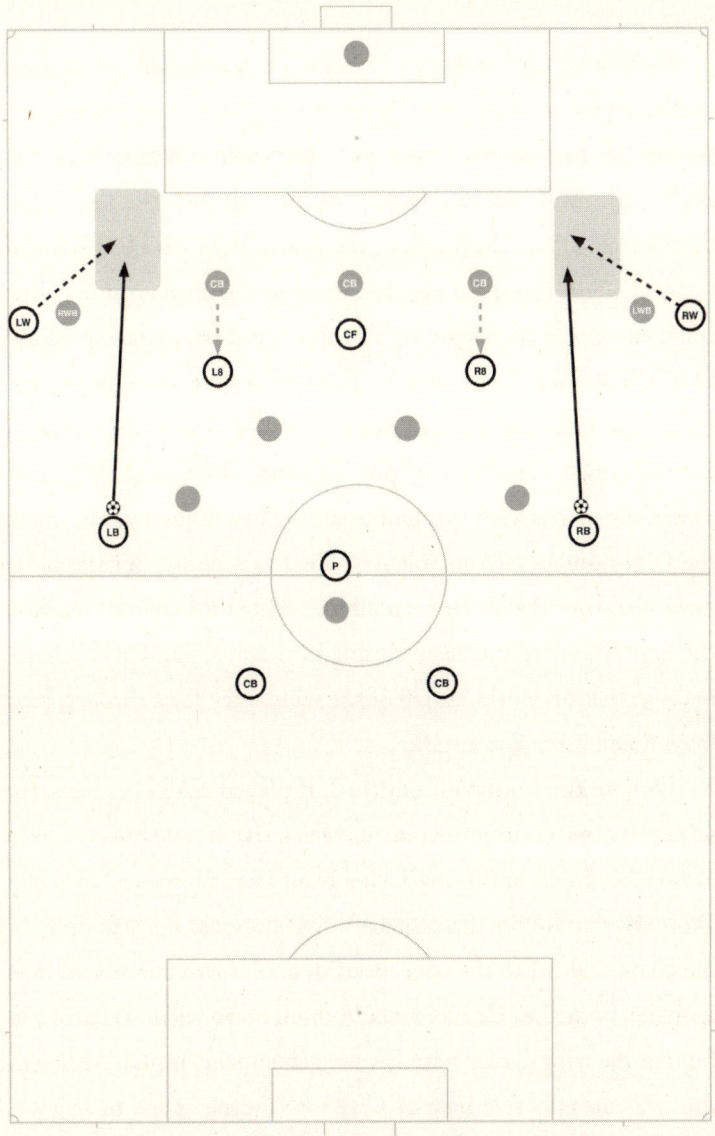

Figure 66. *How City attempted to exploit back-five systems using their regular 4-3-3 shape. If the opposition wing-backs positioned themselves too wide before the ball had been passed wide, City's wingers would make runs into the space behind and inside of them. A large space would often be created on the inside of the wing-backs because the opposition's wide centre-backs were tempted forward to close down City's number 8s in the pockets*

space.

As by looking to intercept in front, the opposition wide centre-back would often find himself vertically higher than City's winger, the winger had the necessary space to attack in behind him. He could stay onside because he was still in line with the rest of the defence, who were deeper than the centre-back who had stepped forward. The other defenders had no reason to push up at the same time; there was no trigger of a backwards pass, or new pressure on the ball, and in fact they may not even have been aware that one of their team-mates had moved forward. The extra man in a defence which a back five adds is one more player to contribute to a breakdown in communication, resulting in a disjointed line. Here the City number 8's run was described as a decoy, but the same move could occur with him actually receiving the ball in the pocket, the opposition's centre-back closing him down, and City's winger making the run on the inside of the wing-back for a through pass from the number 8 himself.

Despite the limitation outlined, if played with the necessary principle of protecting the centre, a back five was an effective way of matching and nullifying City's front five. However, City had alternative strategies against back-five systems. For example, in the chapter entitled 'the concept of free 8s' it was mentioned how against a back five, City's 8s would often move wider to receive in front of the wing-backs, with the wingers moving inside. Although this was an effective way of City's 8 finding space to receive, arguably any system which caused City to come away from their incredibly effective front-five system featuring wide wingers and high number 8s was arguably advantageous.

A 5-3-2 system was especially effective against City (*Figure 67*). Before a game against Sheffield United, who regularly played 5-3-2,

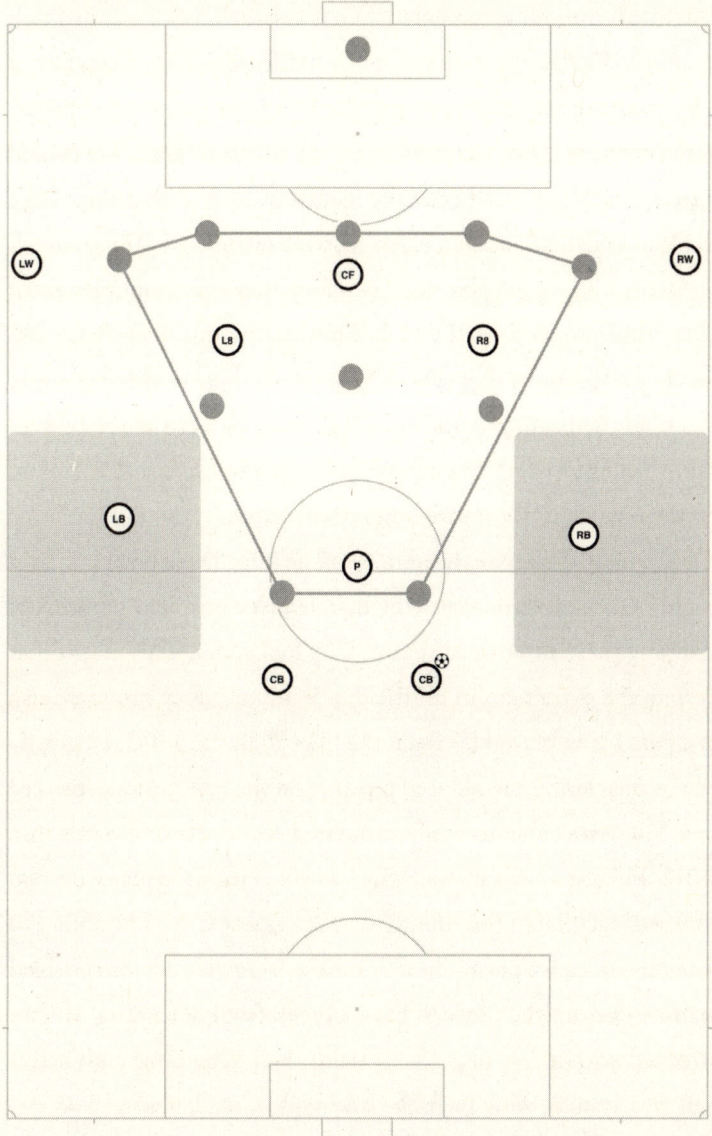

Figure 67. *A 5-3-2 was effective against City's 4-3-3 because it funnelled City into the least dangerous area, in front of the wing-backs. A 5-3-2 also blocked the three passes City attempted to play between the lines, and the high number of players positioned centrally enabled the wing-backs to concentrate on City's wingers*

Guardiola himself commented, 'That system – 5-3-2 – is difficult to attack.' Firstly, the 3-2 shape of the midfield and forwards forced City to attack the space just described, in front of the wing-backs, as the centre was completely blocked off. City were therefore invited into the wide areas, but crucially relatively deep, with a wing-back in place to defend, and an extra centre-back to cover the channel. Secondly, the system possessed two forwards to attempt to prevent City from progressing the ball. Thirdly, the midfield in a 5-3-2 was in a triple pivot shape, which meant all three midfielders were blocking the passing lanes into City's number 8s (when they were central) and forward, forcing the 8s wider to receive, and therefore on the outside of the entire opposition shape.

We have already analysed in detail how the triple pivot midfield could be advantageous over the double pivot midfield in terms of stopping these three inside passes City looked for. This meant that despite the extra man in midfield, a 5-4-1 arguably ran more risk of a pass being played between the lines than the 5-3-2, especially when considering the reduced pressure on the ball the lone forward in a 5-4-1 was able to apply compared to the two forwards in a 5-3-2. Finally, any formation which enabled teams to play with two forwards facilitated the counter-attack against City. The ability to counter-attack isn't just important for scoring goals; it also enabled teams to get up the pitch to have a break from defending. If City attacked with a five plus five system, then defending with a five plus five system, which a back five enabled, made sense.

Chapter 18

Liverpool against a back five – isolating the centre-backs

WHEN FACING back fives, many teams move at least one of their wide players inside in an attempt to creative a one versus one situation against one of the opposition's wide centre-backs. For Liverpool, this was of course where Mané and Salah were consistently positioned regardless of the opposition system. This meant that Liverpool didn't have to make significant alterations to their system against back fives, as arguably their usual positions were very suited to playing against this defensive system. In theory, the one versus ones between Mané and Salah and the wide centre-backs could be converted into two versus ones in favour of the opposition by the wing-backs tucking in very narrowly. This meant that the wide centre-backs were covered by the wing-backs on their outside and the middle centre-back on their inside. However, Mané and Salah were just one of Liverpool's attacking threats; by providing extra security against one threat, the risks of being exposed in another way increased. This was especially the case in the wide areas, where with the wing-backs tucked in too narrowly, and no orthodox wide player in front of them, Liverpool's full-backs could run riot.

The problem was that it was very difficult for a wing-back to get out to Alexander-Arnold or Robertson adequately, *and* protect their wide centre-back against Mané or Salah (*Figure 68*). The wing-back could tuck in centrally and wait for the pass to Liverpool's full-back, before sprinting out. However, Robertson and Alexander-Arnold were superb crossers of the ball, especially the latter, so if the wing-backs were too narrow, it was difficult to get out in time to prevent the cross. The quality of the delivery from Liverpool's full-backs and the way Liverpool attacked the box made allowing Liverpool to put in a large volume of crosses problematic, especially when the full-backs were able to cross the ball early into the space behind the centre-backs.

In previous chapters it was described how Liverpool's wide forward on the side of the ball would often make a run into the space vacated by the wing-back when he moved wide to close down, with the aim of detaching the nearest centre-back to clear space in the box. A great example of this run occurred for a goal scored by Firmino against Tottenham's back five in March 2019. Alexander-Arnold switched play to Robertson, so Kieran Trippier, Tottenham's right wing-back, ran out to close Liverpool's left-back down. As Trippier moved wide, Mané ran into the space Trippier vacated, taking Tottenham's right centre-back Toby Alderweireld with him. Robertson, seeing Mané's run tracked, instead crossed the ball into the space behind Alderweireld. Having been on the other side of the pitch when Alexander-Arnold was in possession, left-sided wide centre-back Jan Vertonghen failed to recover centrally quickly enough following the switch, leaving middle centre-back Davinson Sanchez alone to defend the cross.

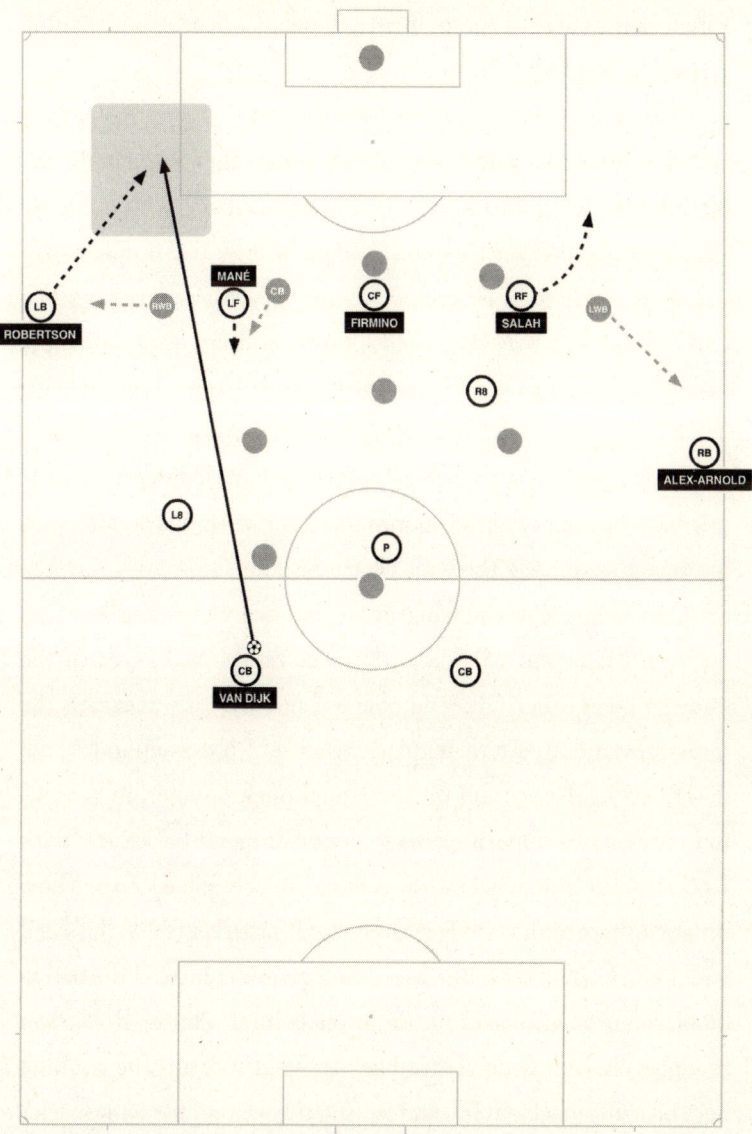

Figure 68. *The problem for the opposition's wing-backs against Liverpool was their ability to deal with Liverpool's full-backs whilst simultaneously being narrow enough to protect their wide centre-backs against Salah and Mané. For example, if Alexander-Arnold was slightly deeper, the opposition's left wing-back would leave space behind him for Salah to run down the side of the centre-back. On Liverpool's left, Mané would take the centre-back towards the ball, leaving space behind him for a pass to be played into for Robertson to run in behind the right wing-back*

Robertson delivered the ball over Sanchez's head, and Firmino arrived to head into the net.

Perhaps to enable themselves to close down Robertson and Alexander-Arnold more quickly when they were high, the opposition's wing-backs may have positioned themselves higher and/or wider. When this occurred, however, the problem was the same as the one described when a back five played against City's front five; the wing-backs, knowing there were four more defenders, were given a false sense of security, spreading too wide in a bid to get tight to City's wingers. With Liverpool, it was their full-backs who drew the wing-backs higher and wider before the full-back himself made a run into the space behind him, for a pass between himself and the wide centre-back.

On the inside of the wing-backs, the one versus one situation between Mané and Salah and the wide centre-backs created the same problem which City's number 8s caused. This was exactly the same movement pattern regularly used by Robertson and Mané described in the section on their relationship, when in a back-four system, an opposition wide player dropped back early with Robertson to form a back five. Against an actual back five, Mané dropped short to show to feet, dragging his marker (the right-sided wide centre-back) with him as a decoy, enabling instead the ball to be played over his head into the space behind him for Robertson to chase. As the wide centre-back stepped forward, he couldn't help his wing-back out by intercepting the pass on the wing-back's inside. Van Dijk in particular would regularly pepper opposition right wing-backs with passes behind them and on their insides for Robertson to chase. This occurred, for example, for Salah's goal against Sheffield United, a side with a well-practiced back-five system, in January 2020. Wide centre-back Chris Basham followed

Mané a few yards higher, leaving right wing-back George Baldock with a huge area to defend behind him. Van Dijk looked to pick out Robertson's run, causing a furiously back-pedaling Baldock to slip at the moment when he looked to intercept the pass, enabling Robertson to find Salah for a simple goal.

To prevent the wing-backs from easily closing them down, Robertson and Alexander-Arnold weren't always positioned so high that they were parallel with the wing-backs; often they received deeper, where they were more difficult to get to. In back-five systems, a wide player either didn't exist (in a 5-3-2 or 5-2-3), or they were forced to cover very narrowly (in a 5-4-1) when the ball was on the other side of the pitch. This meant that when Robertson or Alexander-Arnold received deeper, the wing-backs had to consider vacating the defensive line vertically to close them down. However, doing so meant that the wing-back's angle of approach to close down was often vertical *and* horizontal, opening up a passing lane to find Mané or Salah in the newly vacated space down the side of the wide centre-backs. In this situation, the fact there was an extra defender in a back five compared to a back four was irrelevant, because the spare defender, i.e. the middle centre-back, could not do anything to prevent the one versus one, as the run from Mané or Salah was away from the centre, where the middle centre-back was positioned. A one versus one between Mané or Salah and a centre-back was usually a significant mismatch.

The false 9 role played by Firmino was effective against a back five as the opposition's middle centre-back, as a spare player with nobody to mark, had a tendency to want to step into midfield to close him down, both before *and* after the pass was played forward, due to the security of having four other defenders. As soon as this happened, the opposition transformed into a back four where the two wide centre-backs were split far apart, creating ample space for Mané and Salah to run into. Albeit involving different players, and in their 4-2-1-3 shape not 4-3-3, this exact move occurred for a goal against Wolves in December 2019. Salah, playing as the centre-forward, dropped off, tempting Wolves' middle centre-back Conor Coady to follow him. This left Liverpool's wide forwards, Adam Lallana and Mané, two versus two against the Wolves wide centre-backs, with space to run into behind Coady. Van Dijk produced his usual high-quality long pass over the top, for Lallana to receive and score. Unless the system was an ultra-defensive 5-4-1, where the 'wide players' played very deep and the team was essentially camped in their own box, a back five arguably wasn't suited to nullifying Liverpool's main two threats: the inside positions of Mané and Salah, and the passing and crossing of Robertson and Alexander-Arnold.

Chapter 19

Goalkeepers starting attacks

WITHOUT DOUBT, playing out from the goalkeeper was a fundamental strategy of Guardiola's record points-winning City, while by the time of Liverpool's record points season, Klopp's sides had made big improvements in their ability to use their goalkeeper like an extra outfield player. However, it would be a myth to say that City and Liverpool were determined to play short passes from the back when the opposition high-pressed. But neither did City nor Liverpool do what many other teams do when faced with a high press: push all their players up for their goalkeeper to kick long over the halfway line for both sets of players, positioned closely together, to compete for the first and second ball.

Alternatively, City and Liverpool usually did something in between. They would always *set up* to play out, but instead of always passing short, they would often play a longer pass which bypassed the press, but crucially while the opposition was still in their open, high-pressing shape. Goalkeeper restarts where the opposition pressed high presented a fantastic opportunity to attack the opposition defence without facing ten outfield players in a compact shape in their own half.

Ederson – the most important signing of the Guardiola era

The title of this section may seem strange, as this is the first time Ederson, City's goalkeeper, has really been mentioned. This is principally because he saw relatively little of the ball. There were many reasons for this, such as City's high percentage of ball possession, their clever positioning to progress the ball without needing to pass back to the goalkeeper, or simply how deep City's opponents tended to defend, enabling City to have possession far from their own goal. However, one of the main reasons that Ederson didn't have many touches was that when he did have the ball at his feet, his distribution was so good that it reduced the tendency of the opposition to press.

When Guardiola arrived at City, one of his first actions was to bring in Chilean Claudio Bravo from Barcelona to replace multiple title-winning goalkeeper Joe Hart. The new manager's justification was that he needed his goalkeeper to be excellent with his feet, perceiving that Hart did not possess the necessary ability to receive and distribute to his new manager's high standards. At the time many people were critical of the decision, and unfortunately for Bravo and Guardiola, as the season 2016/17 season progressed, the criticism grew stronger. There was nothing wrong with the decision to dispose of Hart – Guardiola had been recruited to implement his own style of play, and the goalkeeper he inherited clearly wasn't to the standard required to do so. Instead, the mistake Guardiola made was his choice of replacement.

There is no doubt that any team looking to play out from the back needs a goalkeeper who possesses the necessary ability with his feet, an attribute for which the demand has increased dramatically during the last few years. This can't, however, come at the cost of the main function of a goalkeeper: to save shots he should save, or for City's goalkeeper, to exceed expectations with his shot-stopping compared to the average Premier League goalkeeper.

As his confidence dropped, by early 2017 Bravo almost completely lost this ability, eventually being replaced in the team by understudy Willy Caballero. City's good work in possession was often being undone by their opponents seemingly only needing to hit the target once or twice to score. Of course, Bravo wasn't alone in making mistakes – City's defence also committed errors leading to goals – but with Bravo in goal, City were being punished for almost every defensive error. Out of the 44 goalkeepers who started at least 20 Premier League games between the beginning of the 2016/17 season and the end of 2019/20, Bravo had the lowest save percentage, at just 56.4 per cent. He also had the second worst record for xG Prevented per 90, a statistic which compares how many goals a goalkeeper prevents with how many a goalkeeper would be 'expected' to save, based on the difficulty of the shots he has faced. On *Monday Night Football* in January 2017, Jamie Carragher commented, 'Manchester City have now got to be looking for another goalkeeper for next season, or bring Joe Hart back, because if Pep Guardiola wants to win the Champions League or the league, which is why he's been brought in, he won't win it with Bravo.' But crucially, could Guardiola find a goalkeeper as good as Bravo with his feet? The answer was a resounding yes; in Ederson, who arrived from Benfica, he found one with an even better ability. Ederson proved an outstanding signing, as he possessed every quality a modern goalkeeper needs. Later his form would dip, but during City's two record points seasons he was arguably the best goalkeeper in the Premier League.

We're going to focus on the in-possession aspects which made Ederson such a vital addition. We have previously discussed how the specific positioning of City's players in their 4-3-3 made them extremely difficult to stop once they had controlled possession. Because of this, the majority of opposition teams used a mid-to-low block, attempting to restrict City's space nearer their own goal rather than press them high up. However, throughout Guardiola's first season, and in the early stages of Ederson's time at City, many teams would look to high press City from their own goal kicks. These situations were like set plays. As long as teams could set up how they had planned before City had the ball back in play, the opposition had an element of control; a set pattern with how to defend, based on the ball being with City's goalkeeper.

During Guardiola's first season City had mixed success playing out from the back, leaving many pundits questioning the value of them doing so. There was an impression that it wasn't possible to win the Premier League by playing such a 'pure' style of football. Playing out from the back is a risk-reward tactic. The reward is that due to the other team having to press in a relatively 'open' rather than compact shape, if the team in possession manages to play through or bypass the opposition press, it is likely to end in a favourable situation for their forward players, who can attack the unprotected opposition defenders. But how big is the risk of conceding a goal compared to the reward of scoring? One mistake deep in the in-possession team's own half and the opposition can potentially score relatively simply. For the opposition, high pressing is also risk-reward. If the in-possession team beats or bypasses the press, the out-of-possession team are arguably more likely to concede a clear-cut chance than if instead they had simply retreated to the halfway line and formed a compact shape there. But if they win the ball back high up the pitch, their reward is their increased likelihood of creating a goalscoring opportunity.

Although City played out from the goalkeeper as a means of attempting to score directly in the same phase of play, this wasn't the only reason. The other function was to increase their amount of controlled possession, instead of potentially giving the ball back to the opposition by kicking long. This was an element missed by some pundits. If City were able to play through or bypass the press a few times, the opposition would then drop off and let City have the ball, deciding that the risk of pressing was greater than the reward.

City wanted as much controlled possession as possible because it increased their opportunity to create chances using their pre-planned movement patterns. If every time they were pressed they waved their defenders up and kicked long with all the players from both teams close together, they were unlikely to have much success; their forwards were small, and they would have been relying on a 'second ball' game, where they had no advantage over the opposition. In other words, City would have had limited control over how they created chances from these situations, leading to a probable reduction in volume and quality of chances created. This meant that the opposition's justification for high pressing City from their own goal kicks was the reverse; not only to attempt to win the ball high up to score a goal, but also to prevent City from gaining controlled possession, enabling them to form their dangerous attacking patterns.

During Guardiola's first season City were searching for control when the ball was with Bravo. It wasn't that Bravo was poor with his feet, he was very competent; but Ederson was another level, a game-changer. He had the composure to lift his head under pressure, the vision to assess the best option, and outstanding technical ability to execute to perfection several different types of passes. However, there was one particular type of distribution which Ederson could perform but Bravo could not, which was the catalyst for the achievement of more control from their own goalkeeper restarts: Ederson's ability to expose the opposition press by passing in behind the opposition defence.

To explain why this pass is so important, it is necessary to analyse the principles, both of playing out from the back, and defending with a high press. Even though a pressing team could be considered to be in an 'open' shape; that is, the distances between their players are greater than usual, both horizontally and vertically, the aim is still to remain as compact as possible. In order to press successfully against City, the starting positions of the defending team's first line of the press needed to be high, usually as far as the edge of the City penalty area. To ensure relative compactness, some of the defending team's second line of the press would also have to step forward, or City would simply bypass the first line by passing to players placed between the first and second lines. Finally, to ensure compactness between the second line and third (last) line, the third line would have to step forward, usually up to, or close to, the halfway line.

If the last line were too deep, City would bypass the second line by passing to players placed in the space between the second and third lines. Both Bravo and Ederson were capable of finding players between the second and third lines with correctly weighted, chipped passes, or even sometimes passes along the ground. However, by the third line moving forward, the opposition could make the area City had to play in as small as possible. This is a key principle of a high press; the smaller the space City could use, the more difficult it would be for their players to either lose their markers to receive, or overload the opposition in a particular area. If the opposition's strategy was to make the pitch as small as possible, City's aim was to make it as large as possible.

City's shape from goalkeeper restarts contradicted their set-up in general play, which is why this topic has been left until now to analyse. In order to stretch the opposition as far as possible, City's full-backs were positioned higher and wider relative to the position of the ball than in general play. In addition, at least one of their number 8s was either deep, or at least deep enough to be in a position from where he could drop deep when required. Finally, City's wingers and centre-forward were positioned high, behind the opposition defenders, as from a goal kick they could not be offside.

With the spread positioning of their players to make the pitch as large as possible, City created maximum difficulty for the opposition to remain compact vertically and horizontally, while simultaneously covering every pass Ederson could execute. The key factor with the change of goalkeeper was that Ederson possessed a greater range of passing, allowing City to stretch the opposition further vertically by positioning their front players higher, yet crucially still within range. Whereas Bravo was not able to kick much further than the halfway line (*Figure 69*), Ederson was able to kick deep inside the opposition half (*Figure 70)*, even to the edge of the opposition penalty area on some of the shorter Premier League pitches. With City's front players behind them, the opposition defenders had a decision to make. Did they drop deeper ensuring that Ederson couldn't kick the ball over their heads, but in doing so leave space between themselves and the second line of the press? Alternatively, did they remain high, reducing the space in front of them, but risking Ederson playing one of City's front three through on goal with a pass over their heads?

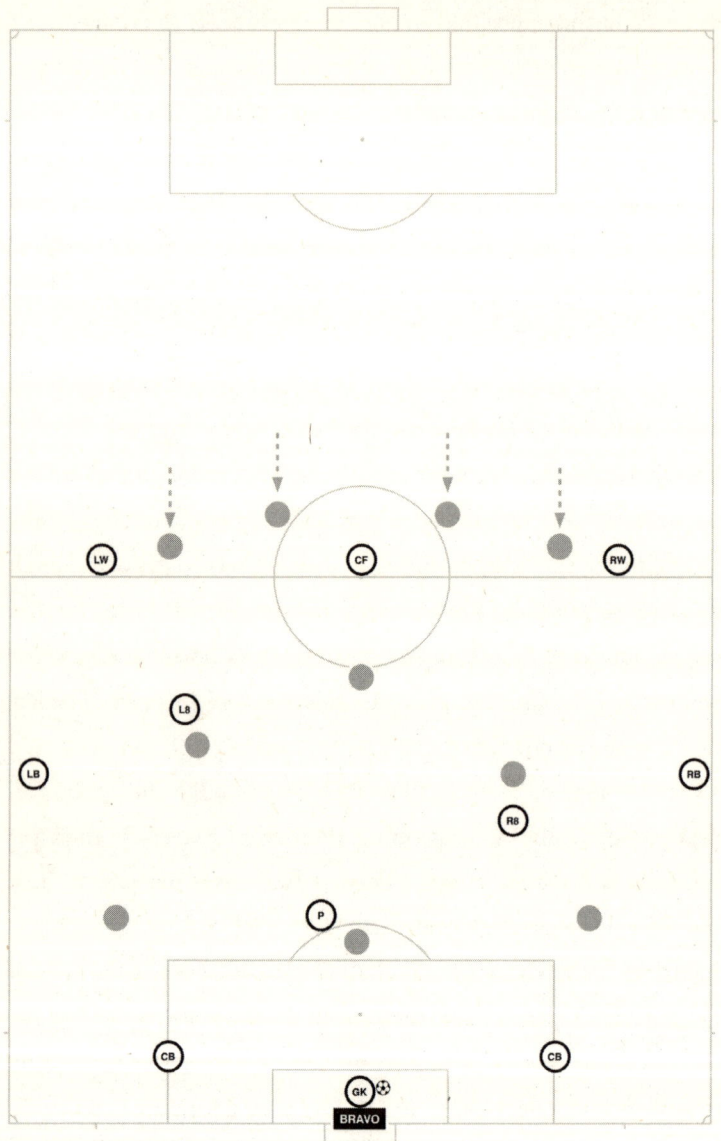

Figure 69. With Bravo in goal the opposition defensive line was able to push right up, restricting the space for City to play out, as there was no threat of Bravo kicking in behind them

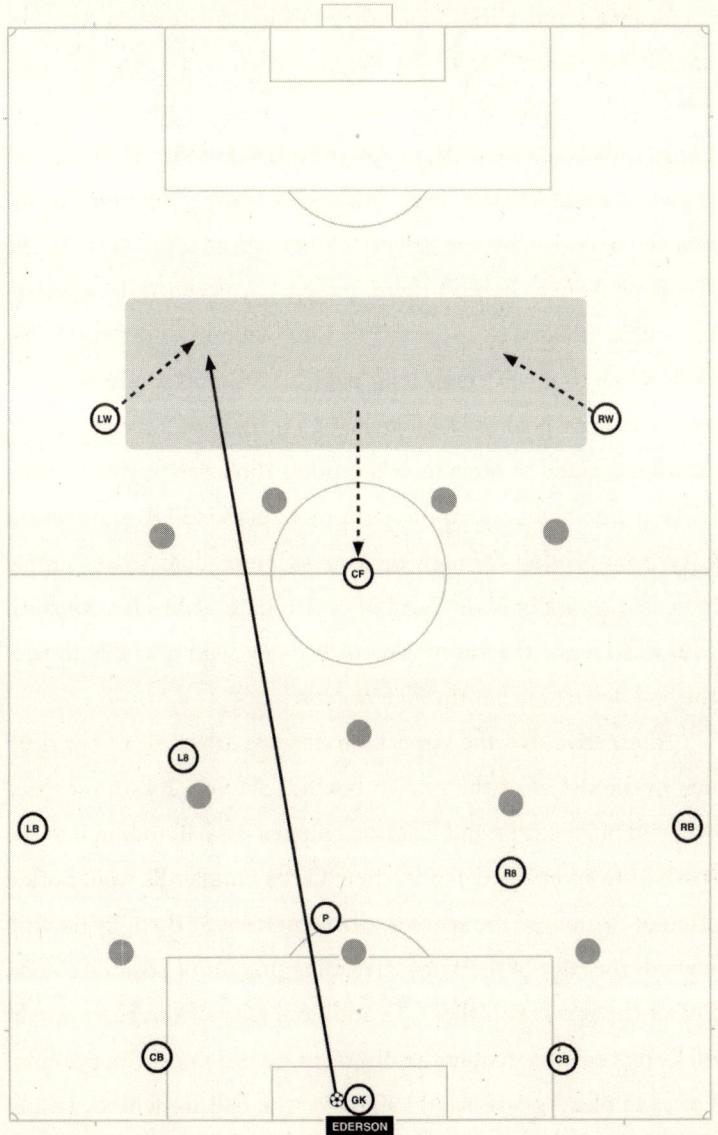

Figure 70. With Ederson in goal, if the defensive line pushed up high, City's goalkeeper was able to kick the ball over the top of them for one of their front three to receive

Ederson and City's front three simply adapted to how the opposition defended. If the defence remained high, Ederson attempted to find one of the front three with a pass over the top. For example, against City in August 2018, Huddersfield were so keen to prevent Ederson from finding a team-mate in his own half that the majority of their defensive line neglected to deal with the threat of Agüero behind them, giving City's centre-forward an incredible amount of space to run into behind the defensive line to latch on to an Ederson long pass. Another example occurred for City's first goal in the Carabao Cup Final of February 2018. Arsenal decided to leave their defenders three versus three on the halfway line in an attempt to push more players high and prevent City from playing through their press. Instead, Ederson simply launched a pass over the head of centre-back Shkrodan Mustafi, who was caught the wrong side of Agüero, who was able to take the ball down and run through to score.

Alternatively, if the opposition defence dropped off too deep due to the threat of the pass in behind, one of City's front three dropped off centrally and Ederson chipped the ball to him into the space in front of the defensive line. City's number 8s would often attempt to enlarge the space available in front of them by moving towards the edge of their own area, dragging the opposition second line of the press with them. In addition, City's front three would make movements in opposite directions to disjoint the opposition. For example, Agüero would show for the ball in behind, taking a defender with him, creating space for Sterling or Sané to drop deeper to receive a pass. Both the number 8s dropping deeper, and the front three stretching the defensive line, helped City score their second goal at Everton in March 2018 (*Figure 71*). As Everton put on a very aggressive high press, De Bruyne and Silva took their

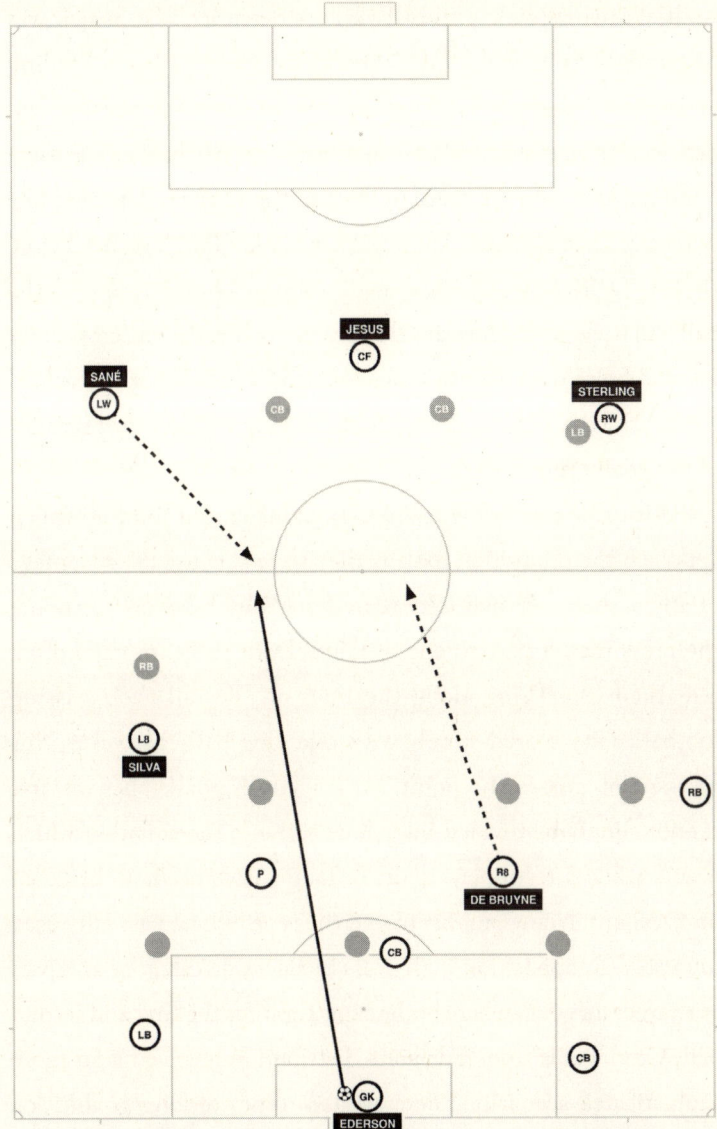

Figure 71. *The situation which occurred for City's goal against Everton from City's own goal kick in March 2018. City's front three pushed Everton's defensive line deep, while Silva and De Bruyne cleared the space between the defensive and midfield lines for Sané to drop into to receive. Ederson chipped a pass to Sané, and De Bruyne sprinted past his marker to receive off his teammate, before crossing for Jesus to score*

midfield markers away from Everton's defensive line, which was forced back by the very high starting positions of Jesus, Sterling and Sané. A huge gap was created between Everton's midfield and defence. As Jesus pushed Everton centre-back Michael Keane back, Sané sprinted into the space in front of the Everton defensive line to receive from Ederson. Sané beat his marker Phil Jagielka, before finding De Bruyne, who had made a support run to receive as the ball had been passed forward from Ederson. De Bruyne crossed for Jesus to score with a close-range header. Everton's high press had been ruthlessly exploited, with City scoring within a few seconds of the goalkeeper restart.

With Ederson in the team, City didn't appear to mind which approach the opposition took as they were able to take advantage of any scenario. When City scored goals by Ederson bypassing the press with a pass to one of City's front three, pundits often remarked something along the lines of, 'For all their passing football, City scored simply with one long ball.' However, this assessment misses the point. Passing from goalkeeper restarts cannot simply be divided into short or long; the situation which occurs when a team plays short or long passes needs to be taken into account. Many pundits placed the type of long pass City used to expose an opposition high press in the same category as a pass to a target forward, where both teams fight for the first and second ball. City's goals from Ederson's distribution involved a far more sophisticated scenario. There are two types of long goal kicks: 1) When the goalkeeper has waved his team up to form a more compact shape when the kick is played, resulting in all the players clustering together. 2) When the ball is passed forward with both teams in an 'open' shape, with the possession team set up for the option of playing short, and the opposing team set up to stop them.

The second scenario, which City used, relied less on randomness, as the pass was less likely to involve an aerial duel and therefore more likely to be completed. There was, however, still some element of randomness or 'second ball' reliance. If from the pass over the top, the opposition's centre-back managed to drop back and head the ball, there was a second ball to be won. Equally, if one of City's front three dropped short to receive a chipped pass but one of the centre-backs managed to read the pass and beat him to the ball, the ball was likely to be headed deep into City's half. Due to these potential outcomes, as soon as they knew the ball was going long, City's players reacted accordingly by sprinting forward. If they didn't win the second ball, they would themselves be caught in an open shape, and risk conceding a goalscoring chance. Like in the example for the goal against Everton, at least one of their number 8s would sprint into a position to win the second ball high up, or receive a lay-off from one of City's front three who had dropped short to receive, with the other midfielders and centre-backs pushing up to cover the space behind him, and the City full-backs moving towards the inside. This was one of the few scenarios where City actively relied on their players winning second balls, but they made sure that they maximised their chances to be successful.

Alisson and Van Dijk – Liverpool's own game-changers

There are parallels between City's acquisition of Ederson and Liverpool's purchase of fellow Brazilian Alisson, signed ahead of the 2018/19 season; Alisson undoubtedly helped Liverpool progress from being a very good team to one capable of winning 99 Premier League points. Firstly, Alisson was an improvement on the previous goalkeeping options available to Klopp, Loris Karius and Simon Mignolet, at the most important task of keeping the ball out of the net – Alisson consistently achieved better save percentage and xG Prevented statistics than his two predecessors. Klopp was perhaps reluctant to accept that Karius, a goalkeeper who he personally signed, was nowhere near the required standard of Premier League champions, with Liverpool's manager regularly defending his acquisition during the 2017/18 season. Perhaps the tipping point was Karius's performance in the Champions League Final defeat of that same season when the German was at fault for two of Real Madrid's goals.

Secondly, like Ederson, Alisson was also more comfortable with the ball at his feet than the previous occupants of the Anfield club's number one shirt. This enabled Liverpool to use him like an extra outfield player, with the centre-backs knowing they could receive from and pass back to their goalkeeper with confidence. The move for the first Premier League goal Liverpool scored following Alisson's arrival began by their goalkeeper calmly passing to Joe Gomez under pressure from West Ham forward Marko Arnautović. Later the same season, the crucial second in Liverpool's 3-1 win over Manchester United in December 2018 also occurred from a short goal kick. Alisson passed to Fabinho on the edge of Liverpool's own box, who had to return the ball to his goalkeeper having been immediately closed down from behind. Despite pressure from two Manchester United players, Alisson refused to simply clear the ball, instead finding Andy Robertson, who played his way out, enabling Liverpool to progress the ball into United's half, where Xherdan Shaqiri eventually put the finishing touch to the move.

Perhaps it could be said that Alisson was *too* keen to play out under pressure than to play a longer pass; arguably he wasn't as competent with his feet as Ederson. For example, in just his fourth Premier League game, in September 2018, the Liverpool goalkeeper was tackled by Leicester striker Kelechi Iheanacho, who squared for Rachid Ghezzal to score, with Alisson having taken an unnecessary risk with his team 2-0 up away from home. Without a doubt, Liverpool's goalkeeper did not possess the same range as Ederson to pass in behind the opposition defensive line. This in theory enabled opposition teams to push their defensive lines higher, restricting Liverpool's space to play out. This meant that to expose teams whose defensive lines pushed right up as they pressed from the front, Liverpool had to access the space in behind by Alisson passing first to an outfield player, for whom a pass in behind was more within range, because an outfield player could strike the pass from marginally higher up the pitch.

However, Liverpool still needed a goalkeeper with Alisson's technical ability to pass the outfield player the ball in the first place. Sometimes this involved one fairly simple pass, but on other occasions, Alisson needed to be the link who passed from side to side until one of the outfield players had the time and space to play forward. Of course, the other hugely significant signing that Liverpool made was Virgil van Dijk, who has arguably been the best centre-back in the Premier League since arriving at Anfield from Southampton in January 2018. As well as his excelling at his main task of defending, Van Dijk helped Liverpool play out from the back by demonstrating excellent composure under pressure, and an outstanding passing range.

Liverpool improved their pass completion percentage of the first pass from a goal kick every season under Klopp, up to and including their title-winning season of 2019/20. As a short pass from a goal kick is always more likely to be completed than a longer pass, this essentially meant they were able to pass short more often. Arguably this was both a direct and indirect function of Klopp's side improving every year in these situations. The direct function was that due to their goalkeeper and centre-backs being better on the ball than previously, a short goal kick became to a greater extent reward than risk, so they would choose to play short more often. The indirect function was that like with City after Ederson's arrival, as Liverpool improved at playing out, teams pressed less in these situations, as for the opposition, the risk became greater than the reward. There was a third reason to explain the significant increase in Liverpool's per cent pass completion from goal kicks, specifically the improvement from 2018/19 to 2019/20: the change in goal kick rule to permit outfield players to receive passes in their own penalty area enabled Liverpool to alter their strategy. For the Premier League as a whole, the average pass completion percentage from goal kicks jumped from 53 per cent to 60 per cent between these seasons. Liverpool's increase was even greater, from 74 per cent to 84 per cent, giving Klopp's side the highest pass completion figure from goal kicks in the Premier League in 2019/20.

Coinciding with the change in goal kick rule was an alteration in Liverpool's set-up. Previously, Liverpool tended to set up to play out using just their goalkeeper, the two centre-backs and their pivot. With most opposition teams placing three players high to press, Liverpool often didn't have the required numerical superiority to progress the ball. In addition, the rule that an outfield player had to receive the ball outside the penalty area often meant that the first pass to the centre-back would often immediately put the receiving player under pressure, resulting in him having to return the ball to the goalkeeper. From this backwards pass, an opposition player was often be able to close down Alisson to the point where he would have to either clear the ball under pressure, or take a big risk with a short pass.

In addition, as Alisson wasn't able to kick the ball behind the opposition defensive line, the line could squeeze up fairly high to close the space between themselves and the second line of the press, and therefore restrict the opportunity for Alisson to chip the ball to a Liverpool player between the lines. Alisson's 'out ball' was therefore a chipped pass into their full-backs. Liverpool's goalkeeper was more than capable of completing this pass, but it was a difficult one; if the opposition anticipated it, the result would often result be an aerial duel, which wasn't a situation of strength for either Alexander-Arnold or Robertson. If not an aerial duel, the opposition player would often at least be close enough to prevent Liverpool's full-back from playing his next pass. Liverpool's goal kicks were, after all, a pre-planned set piece for the opposition.

From the beginning of the 2019/20 season, Liverpool increased their numerical superiority from goal kicks. Just like in general play, one of their number 8s, usually Wijnaldum, dropped deeper to give another option alongside the pivot. In addition, one or sometimes both of Liverpool's full-backs dropped into their own third to become potential options to receive passes. Higher up, this left Firmino in the left pocket, Liverpool's right-sided number 8 in the right pocket, and Salah and Mané high and narrow. The shape was usually a 2-2-2-2 through the centre of the pitch, with the full-backs wide, altering their vertical positions to become an option on the outside of the opposition press. The main reason why it was advantageous to drop at least one of their full-backs deeper was the new-found opportunity for Liverpool's centre-backs to receive more centrally, inside their own penalty area, which occurred due to the change in goal kick rule. With the previous rule, the Liverpool centre-backs had to position themselves much wider, outside of the penalty area where they were blocking the space which the full-backs could drop into.

With Liverpool's centre-backs more central, the opposition's two forwards were also more central, giving Liverpool's full-backs more room to receive to the side. Prior to the change in goal kick rule Liverpool had often attempted to create this situation artificially. One of their centre-backs would move centrally, taking up a position alongside the pivot, with the full-back then dropping into the space created by the opposition forward moving extra centrally to track him. Alternatively, if the opposition pressed with three players, the increased vertical and horizontal distance between the centre-backs and full-backs made it more difficult for the outer player of the three, i.e. the opposition wide player, to press the centre-back and prevent the ball being chipped over his head, by either the centre-back or goalkeeper. Regardless of whether the opposition pressed with three or two players, the addition of the second pivot deep occupied to a greater extent the pressing opposition players more narrowly, giving Liverpool's full-backs more space out wide.

With the change in goal kick rule and set-up, Liverpool's ability to play *beyond* the press improved in two ways. Firstly, by the deeper receiving positions of Liverpool's full-backs (*Figure 72*). Their situation mirrored the scenario when receiving deep in open play; they were often free to open out and play forward, either into the channel for Salah or Mané, or back inside. Often, Liverpool's pivot would be free, as the opposition forward(s) would usually mark him by screening in front of him, so as soon as the angle was changed with the pass to Liverpool's full-back, the pivot was accessible behind the forward(s). Alternatively, Liverpool's full-backs could potentially pass between the lines, to Firmino in

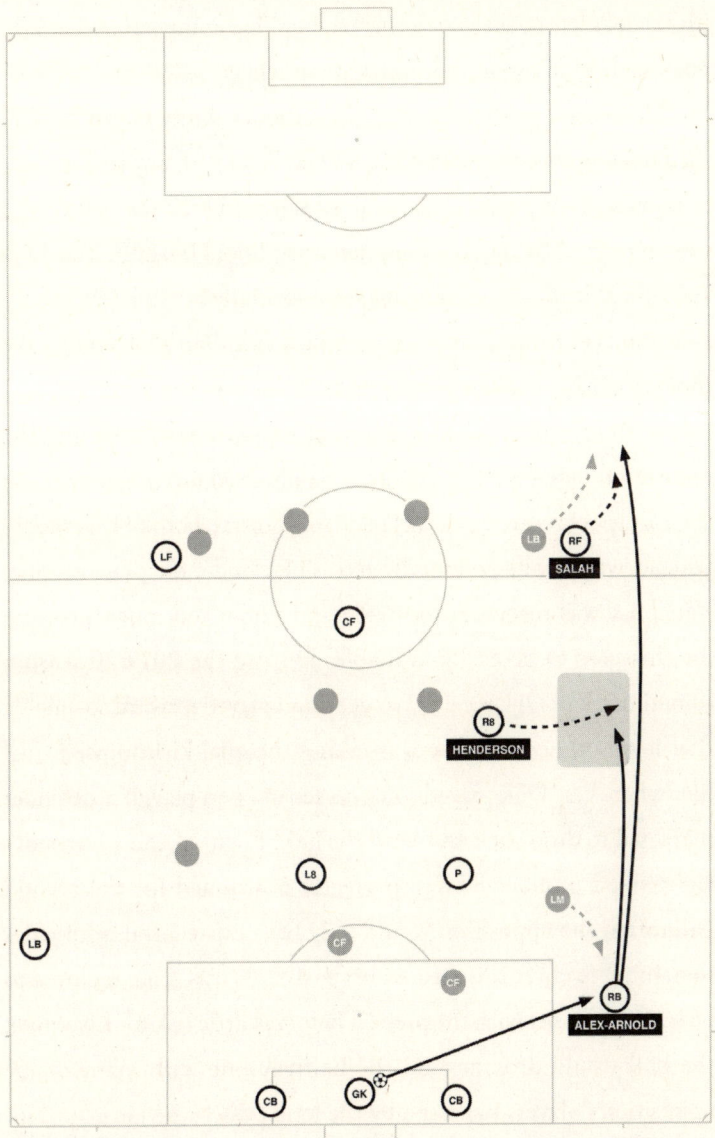

Figure 72. *With the change in goal kick rule enabling Liverpool's centre-backs to position themselves in their own penalty area, there was room for Liverpool's full-backs to drop to receive in positions which were difficult for the opposition wide players to close them down. Just like in open play, a large gap often occurred between the opposition left-sided wide player and left-back, which was exploited by Henderson*

Liverpool's left pocket, or to their right-sided number 8 in the right pocket, depending on the side of the pitch.

The second method by which Liverpool's ability to play beyond the press improved concerned Van Dijk. As stated, unlike Ederson, Alisson did not possess the required range to kick the ball all the way in behind the opposition's defensive line. However, Van Dijk was now able to take on this role; he essentially became Liverpool's Ederson. With the change in goal kick rule Van Dijk could take the ball off his goalkeeper just outside his own six-yard box, and before an opponent could reach him, smash a pass in behind the opposition defensive line to either Salah or Mané (*Figure 73*). As the Liverpool centre-back was relatively central, both of Liverpool's wide forwards were potentially accessible. Under the previous rule, Van Dijk was receiving too wide and under too much pressure for this pass to be easily available. During the 2019/20 season, sometimes Van Dijk received so deep and played forward so quickly that it was almost as if he was taking the goal kick himself. Just like when Van Dijk played long passes in open play, if a defender managed to drop back and head the ball, Firmino and Liverpool's right-sided number 8 were perfectly positioned for the second ball; often the opposition would only have one central midfielder remaining to cover this area, as his partner(s) was often required to be higher to assist with the press. There was little risk for Liverpool; the ball would drop around the halfway line with many of the opposition's players bypassed by the long pass.

Short build-up from the goalkeeper

Firstly, let's define an important principle for City and Liverpool when playing out from the back: players must take up their positions as quickly as possible, and the goalkeeper must get the

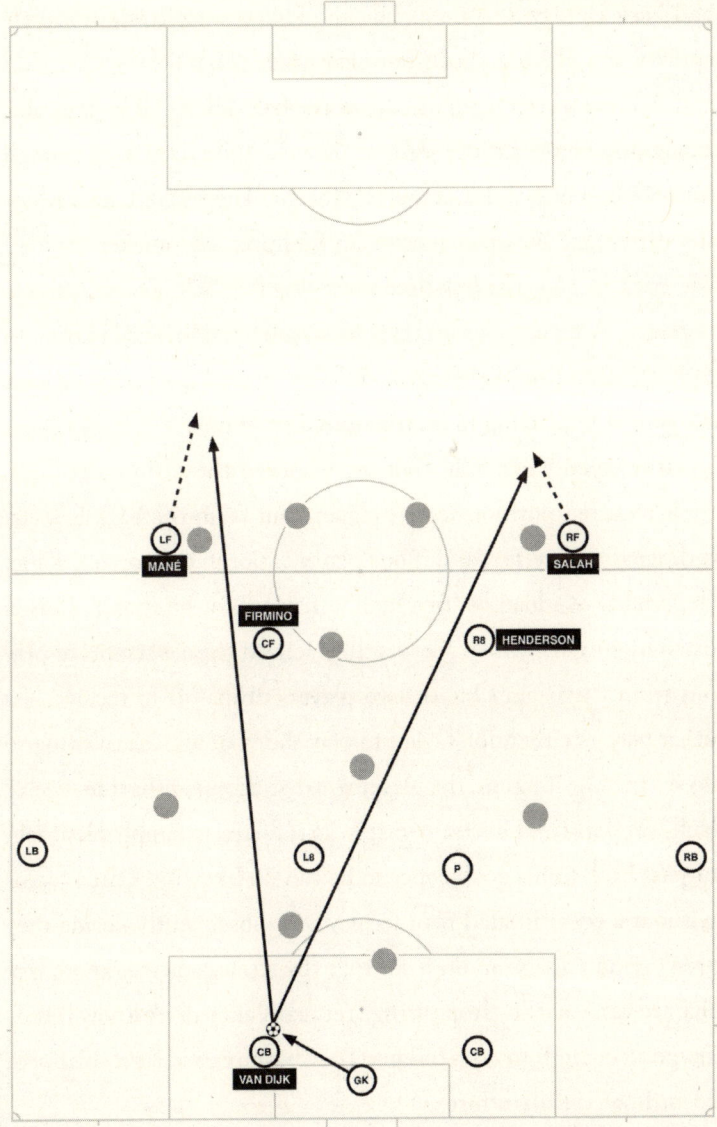

Figure 73. *Liverpool's usual goal kick set-up. With the change in goal kick rule, Van Dijk could receive short from Alisson relatively unchallenged before bypassing the opposition's press with a pass in behind their defensive line for Salah or Mané. Henderson and Firmino were usually positioned between the lines ready for the second ball*

ball back in play as soon as he can. This principle doesn't solely apply when playing short, but also when playing long; Ederson and Alisson would regularly throw the ball down and look to play a long pass before the opposition's defence could drop deep enough to cover it. These quick actions by the goalkeeper were sometimes the difference between success and failure; the quicker the ball was back in play, the less time there was for the opposition to re-organise. A team relies on their forward(s) and/or wide players to form the first line of the press, yet these players are often the least diligent at recovering to their required positions.

It is equally essential that the whole of the team moves into their required positions early; playing out from the back is a co-ordinated team effort and if one player is not in the correct shape, the crucial overload or 'free man' often cannot be found. This is often highlighted when a less well-practiced team attempts to play out from the back. One or two players drops off to receive, yet other players either don't want to play short, or aren't expecting to do so. In this situation, the player who has dropped short to receive lacks support from his team-mates, so is forced to simply play long, or pass back to his goalkeeper so he can do likewise. Often teams without a co-ordinated plan to play out subsequently decide they aren't good enough to do it, or that the strategy brings more risk than reward, so they stop trying. Yet really they don't know if they are good enough to do it because they haven't used a pre-planned, co-ordinated team effort.

The strategies and movement patterns City and Liverpool implemented from goalkeeper restarts also took place whenever their goalkeeper had the ball at his feet, for example from back passes, as the two scenarios were similar. The first aspect to note is that the centre-backs of both teams were 'split', positioned more or less parallel to each other, and the full-backs were usually wide, forming a more traditional back four in possession shape. This is in contrast to one of the centre-backs moving more central, as one often did when building up higher up the pitch. The main reason for the difference was the involvement of the goalkeeper as an 11th outfield player, or deep, third centre-back. When City and Liverpool were building up near the halfway line, passing back to their goalkeeper would enable the opposition to push up high and defend much further from their own goal.

It is, however, worth noting however that whenever City or Liverpool were being pressed to the extent that there was no time to form their in-possession shape (for example, following an opposition clearance where their centre-backs were forced to run back and chase a pass over top), their goalkeepers would move to the edge of their penalty area or even higher to receive the ball and restart the in-possession sequence, in order to prevent City or Liverpool from having to restart the attack from so deep. In some games, Ederson in particular was used well out of his penalty area almost as an extra outfield player, or third centre-back. Intriguingly, after the COVID-19-enforced break during the 2019/20 season, Ederson seemed to have been encouraged to move very far out of his goal as the 'pivot' to help circulate the ball between City's centre-backs, a tactic which ended when Southampton's Che Adams chipped him to score into an empty net following a loss of possession as mentioned in the chapter on City's build-up play.

For both City and Liverpool, the key to reducing their risk of giving the ball away while attempting to progress the ball through the opposition press was to create numerical superiority in their own third of the pitch. Exactly how many players they needed deep depended on exactly how many players the opposition committed to their press; the greater number of players they committed, the greater necessity there was for more City and Liverpool players to drop in support. In addition, exactly where the players positioned themselves depended on exactly how the opposition pressed. City and Liverpool always had an overload when playing out from the back because their goalkeeper could participate whereas the opposition's goalkeeper could not, making the situation 11 versus ten. Against the vast majority of teams, City and Liverpool had a further overload deep in their own half due to the high positioning of their front three, in City's case, or in Liverpool's case the presence high up the pitch of Mané and Salah (with Firmino slightly deeper). Most of the time, this kept the opposition back four/five deep to retain an overload over City and Liverpool's front players, as the opposition didn't want to leave their defenders one versus one.

As from a goal kick the ball is central and therefore the opposition is unaware which side it is going to be passed (Ederson and Alisson would place the ball in the middle of the six-yard box giving them equal opportunity to pass to either side), the width of the pitch needed to be covered by the opposition to the extent that should City or Liverpool pass the ball to their full-backs, a player was close enough either side to close them down. However, the wider the opposition positioned a player each side, the more space there was centrally. Some teams attempted to achieve the optimal balance by asking one or both of their full-backs/wing-backs to perform a dual role of starting deep and narrow, but ready to be able to press City or Liverpool's full-backs as soon as the ball was passed to their side. Alternatively, a team could keep all their defenders deep and instead ask one of their central midfielders to perform the dual role, starting to the right and left of centre before moving across horizontally when the ball was passed to City or Liverpool's full-back their side. However, exactly where City and Liverpool's full-backs positioned themselves vertically depended on which opposition player was tasked with pressing them; they would alter their positions to make it as difficult as possible for them to be closed down before they could play a pass.

So, if City and Liverpool's goalkeeper could participate, and in most cases the defensive team had to maintain numerical superiority against City and Liverpool's front players by keeping their defenders back, there was usually an overload around their own penalty area. City and Liverpool's exact set-ups to play out depended on the intricacies of the opposition press. However, it is possible to analyse general patterns which tended to occur depending on whether the opposition first line of the press consisted of two or three players.

Playing out against a two-man first line of the press

Let's first assess what occurred against a two-man first line of the press, often used by teams who played a 4-4-2/4-4-1-1 formation. The two pressing players were usually the two forwards, with the wide players positioned deeper, as part of the second line of the press. For City, against a two-man first line of the press, just like when building up around the halfway line, four players (the goalkeeper, the two centre-backs and the pivot) were usually all they required, because it gave them a four versus two overload. Ederson was subsequently given the choice of passing to either centre-back or City's midfield pivot, depending on which passes the opposition chose to cover. As the opposition's priority was usually preventing the pass to City's pivot, one of the opposition's two forwards always had to be close to him. This meant the other forward would choose a centre-back to cover, and the other centre-back would be spare.

If Ederson wasn't involved, it may have been possible for the two players to work together and close down at angles where they were able to stop the centre-back on the ball from safely passing to either of his team-mates. However, with Ederson available to help transfer the ball between the centre-backs or to the pivot, it was very difficult for the two to stop all four. Ederson would often play a give and go with one centre-back to move the two forwards, before passing to the other centre-back to dribble out the other side. If the two forwards spread wide to be close to the two City centre-backs, Ederson could simply pass between them to the pivot; City's goalkeeper was incredibly composed when playing this type of pass.

The numerical superiority of these four City players in a diamond shape enabled them to move the ball between each other to bypass a two-man press by either dribbling out with the ball or making an unopposed forward pass (*Figure 74*). This four versus two overload created by using the goalkeeper is a fairly standard method of playing out versus two forwards, but City were masters at it. Perhaps the difference between City and other teams was the importance of the small details. There was a big emphasis on 'attacking' the forwards by dribbling towards them and drawing them to one side, opening space for a team-mate centrally or on the other side. In addition, City were well-rehearsed in passing to the stronger foot of the receiving player, and passing in front of him so he could immediately look forward. Furthermore, the player receiving would do so with an 'open' body shape, enabling him to turn and play forward more efficiently.

Liverpool also often used a four versus two overload against a two-man first line of the press, using Alisson as the pivot to pass the ball from centre-back to centre-back or to the pivot. However, as already stated, with the change in goal kick rule they often

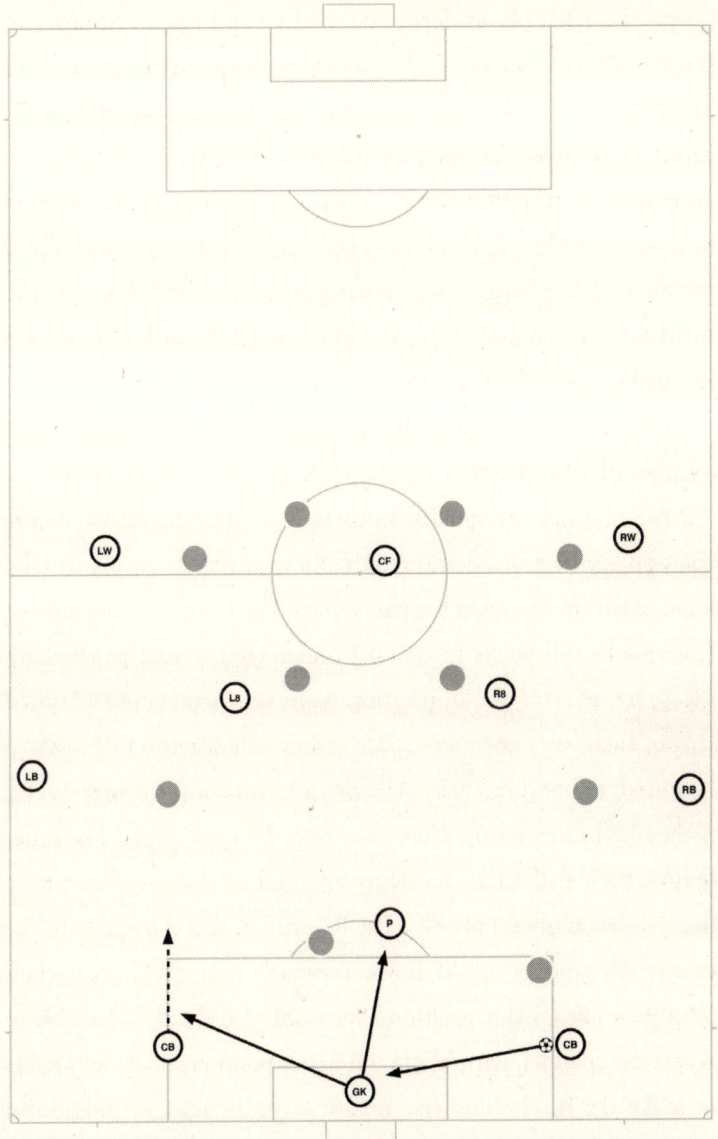

Figure 74. *Ederson was used as a pivot to move the ball from side to side until one of the centre-backs was able to bring the ball forward, or the two opposition forwards split too wide, leaving the pivot free between them*

dropped a fifth player deep, one of their full-backs, in order to progress the ball more quickly. This strategy was especially effective against a two-man first line of the press because the pressure on the centre-backs from the two forwards was applied from the *inside*, at an angle which prevented the pass to the pivot and deep number 8. Consequently, the forward would force the centre-back to play to the *outside*, giving him a passing lane to the full-back. If the full-back was too high, he would immediately be closed down and trapped out wide by the opposition wide player.

However, by being positioned deeper, the full-back was in a more difficult position for the wide player to close him down. Alisson often passed quickly to Liverpool's deep full-back, before the opposition team could regain their shape, as teams usually focused first on stopping the pass centrally to the pivot; this enabled Liverpool's full-backs to pull off undetected to receive the ball. However, even if the opposition were set in their pre-planned shape, there was adequate space either side for the full-back to be found, either directly by Alisson or by one of the centre-backs, if they had received the first pass from the goalkeeper. For other teams, their full-backs receiving the ball so deep may not have been so favourable. However, for Liverpool, and especially in the case of Alexander-Arnold, it was a scenario they could use to their advantage. From this position Liverpool's full-backs were able to access the channel, with Mané and Salah positioned narrowly ready to make the run behind the opposition full-backs, or provide an option to feet, pinning the opposition full-back with their back to goal. Alexander-Arnold, of course, could execute any pass from this position, often switching play to Robertson, or drilling a pass between the lines for Firmino; it was favourable for Liverpool to get their right-back on the ball early in the attack.

Although passing into the channel was seen as favourable, Liverpool often did manage to progress the ball via their full-backs without having to resort to a long pass (*Figure 72*). They did this when the opposition wide player closed down their full-back when in his deep position, which resulted in a big vertical gap being created between the opposition wide player and his own full-back. As soon as the opposition wide player began to close down the full-back, Liverpool's ball-side number 8 sprinted from a central position into the space out wide between opposition wide player and full-back. The number 8's starting position could be either deep in front of the back four, or a high in the pocket. This meant that if the opposition wide player closed down while showing Liverpool's full-back the outside route, there was an option for a fairly simple pass down the line. The wide player would likely show the outside because Liverpool's two pivots were potentially accessible with a pass back inside. The role of Mané and Salah was to pin the opposition full-back deep to create a larger gap, and to maintain the space between opposition full-back and wide player by ensuring that he wasn't tempted to close down Liverpool's number 8 himself.

Like when Liverpool used this tactic in open play (analysed in the chapter concerning the concept of free 8s), the nearest opposition central midfielder had a decision to make: did he remain central enabling Liverpool's number 8 to have the ball out wide? Or did he go with him, leaving space centrally for Liverpool's front players to exploit. Sometimes Liverpool took this strategy to the extreme, with one of their number 8s moving early into the space out wide, before the goal kick had even been taken. The quick decision-making forced on the opposition was often decisive in enabling Liverpool to draw the opposition out before attacking the space vacated with their front three. City would sometimes also use the tactic of their full-back dropping to receive before passing on his outside for one of their number 8s to make a run from the centre into the space behind the opposition wide player.

However, City's full-backs didn't begin deep as an option for the goalkeeper; instead they wanted to give the centre-backs, pivot and goalkeeper the chance to progress the ball themselves; the full-backs were only used as a secondary plan. To achieve this, the space needed to be as large as possible for these four players to operate in and use their overload to progress the ball – one of the ways to do this was for their full-backs to force the opposition's wide players back. Unlike Liverpool, City were not attempting to use their centre-backs centrally to force the two forwards very narrow to create space for their full-backs on the outside of the forwards; instead they used their centre-backs wider in an attempt to stretch the forwards as much as possible so they could progress the ball using the gaps created. Of course, we are analysing City's goal kicks from a period before the change in goal kick rule, so the situations were slightly different; following the change in goal kick rule, City's goal kick set-up was also adapted to the new situation.

Playing out against a three-man first line of the press

Due to the four versus two overload created by possessing a goalkeeper who was comfortable in possession, any team serious about pressing City and Liverpool really needed to commit three players to the first line of the press, either before the ball was back in play to help prevent the first pass, or to press once that first pass had been made. There were several ways this three-man first line of the press could be formed. We're going to use the common example of a centre-forward marking City or Liverpool's pivot(s) and the two wide players high, between City and Liverpool's centre-backs and full-backs, but also narrow enough to threaten a pass played either side of the centre-forward. This left three central midfielders deeper, either parallel to each other as a flat three, or in a 1-2 shape. A three-man first line of the press aimed to prevent a passing lane between centre-back and full-back, subsequently trapping City and Liverpool with their centre-backs. To achieve this, the City and Liverpool full-backs were left spare, but difficult to access. Note, Liverpool's full-backs could not move very deep to receive to the same extent that they could against a two-man first line, as the opposition had an extra player to cover the zone which they looked to drop into. Therefore, when City and Liverpool faced a three-man first line of the press, the key to bypassing it was finding a way to access the full-backs in their high, wide positions. The advantage of finding their full-backs was that they were 'free men', because their markers, the wide players, were higher and more central than them.

Unlike against a two-man first line of the press, when facing a three-man first line, City and Liverpool's centre-backs were usually pressed from their outside, and offered the inside route. To find the full-back the ball could be passed aerially, over the head of the opposition wide player, by either the centre-back or goalkeeper. The change in the goal kick rule made this aerial pass from the centre-back to the full-back because the centre-backs could increase the distance between themselves and the opposition wide players by receiving inside the area, closer to the goalkeeper. This gave more time and space to pass over the wide player's head.

However, City or Liverpool finding their full-back was not the end of the world for the opposition, who had a line of three central midfielders behind their front three, with the outside midfielder each side usually tasked with sprinting out to close down City or Liverpool's full-back should the wide player be bypassed.

Alternatively, if City or Liverpool's full-backs were higher, the opposition's own full-backs were sometimes able to reach the full-backs in time to intercept the pass or at least to prevent them from playing forward, potentially trapping City and Liverpool out wide. In addition, an aerial pass to a full-back is fairly difficult and risky; there was a reasonable chance of an interception, or in a bid to minimise this risk, the pass being over-hit, going out of play for a throw in.

When a City or Liverpool centre-back received the ball off the goalkeeper, their full-back that side made things difficult for the opposition by varying his position, either moving higher or lower. Firstly, to open up a passing lane along the ground from the centre-back, a line originally blocked by the wide player, who would have to continuously check his shoulder to see where the full-back was positioned. Secondly, to create a larger distance between the full-back and the player the opposition had designated to close him down – their outside central midfielder or full-back – in order to make the pass less risky in terms of a potential interception.

However, both teams used a strategy which enabled their centre-backs to pass the ball along the ground, while also giving their full-back more time once he received the ball, *before* he was closed down. To execute this strategy, one of City's number 8s started deep alongside their pivot just outside City's penalty area. Liverpool, of course, usually positioned a number 8, usually Wijnaldum, alongside the pivot anyway. This gave City and Liverpool a five versus three overload. If the opposition's wide players were too wide, the space either side of their centre-forward was usually large enough for either City or Liverpool's deep number 8 or pivot to receive a pass from the goalkeeper or centre-back; the centre-forward was not easily able to mark both of these players. With this one pass, the three-man first line of the press was taken out of the attack, as they found themselves higher than the ball. The City or Liverpool player who had received the pass subsequently had the time to turn and play forward with plenty of options ahead of him, as three opposition players had been bypassed.

Often City and Liverpool used an effective variation of this strategy, which freed their full-back up to an even greater extent, by drawing out a fourth opposition player, specifically the outside central midfielder who was positioned closest to the City or Liverpool full-back. One of the City or Liverpool number 8s started high before dropping deep to provide the passing option, (*Figure 75*), rather than originally positioning himself on the edge of the area. Let's use City as the example, as they had a greater tendency to perform this movement pattern. For the opposition's wide player to block the pass from City's centre-back to full-back, he had to approach the centre-back from the outside, in a fairly wide position. This meant that instead of the outside, City's centre-back had a passing lane on the inside. Against centre-forwards who were less switched-on defensively, the pivot was able to move over and receive. However, much of the time the pass to the pivot was not available as he was being marked by the centre-forward. Instead, City's ball-side number 8 sprinted towards the ball. He had a marker following him, the nearest central midfielder in the three-man second line of the press, but the City number 8 only had to move far enough ahead of his marker to play a first-time pass into City's full-back, who was completely free, because the opposition wide player had pressed City's centre-back, and the outside central midfielder City's number 8.

For some teams, this move may have been high risk as it involved a pass near their own penalty area to a player being closed

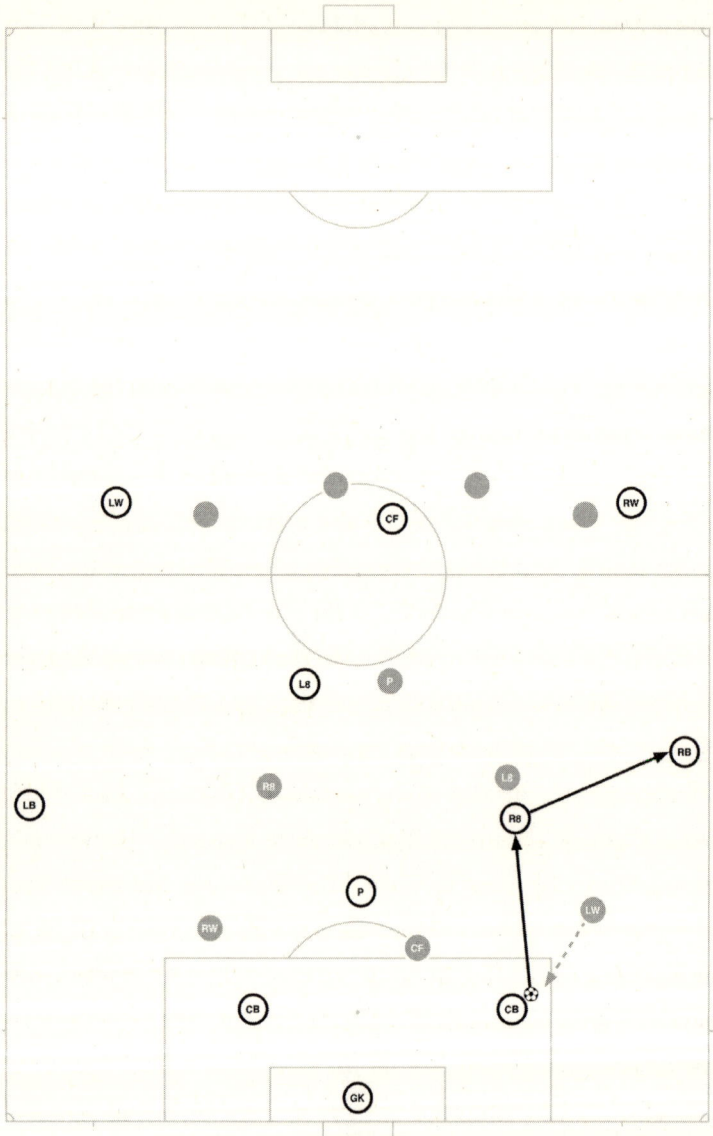

Figure 75. If the opposition wide player pressed the City or Liverpool centre-back, City or Liverpool's full-back would be left spare but without an available passing lane to find him. In this scenario City or Liverpool's nearest number 8 would move towards the ball to receive and play a first-time pass to the full-back, bypassing both the opposition wide player and the number 8's own marker

down from behind; if the number 8 couldn't play a first-time pass to the full-back he had a problem, as he was receiving facing his own goal, under pressure, without easy passing options. However, it was actually a very simple movement pattern which if performed higher up the pitch in a less pressured situation would probably fail very rarely for most competent possession-based teams. With the confidence possessed by City's players and by the repetition in training of the exact movements required, they were able to perform these kind of patterns deep in their own half without too many signs of nerves.

This specific move perhaps demonstrates better than any other the principles needed to successfully play out from the back. Firstly, every player must be in the correct position from where they can provide support runs and passing options for the player on the ball when needed, and especially to enable first-time passes; a player can only play a first-time pass if he knows where his next pass is prior to receiving. Secondly, the in-possession team must sprint to provide these passing options, to match the opposition who sprint when applying pressure. Thirdly, simply having numerical superiority isn't enough, because the opposition players work together to block a path to the 'free man'. The in-possession team needs to be creative, passing to a marked player in order to change the angle and create a passing lane to the free man.

Despite City performing the movement pattern just described more regularly, perhaps Liverpool's goal against Leicester in October 2019 best demonstrates the pattern, with James Milner combining brilliantly with Andy Robertson to play through and around the Leicester press (*Figures 76 and 77*). Leicester pressed as a front three, with wide player Harvey Barnes shutting down

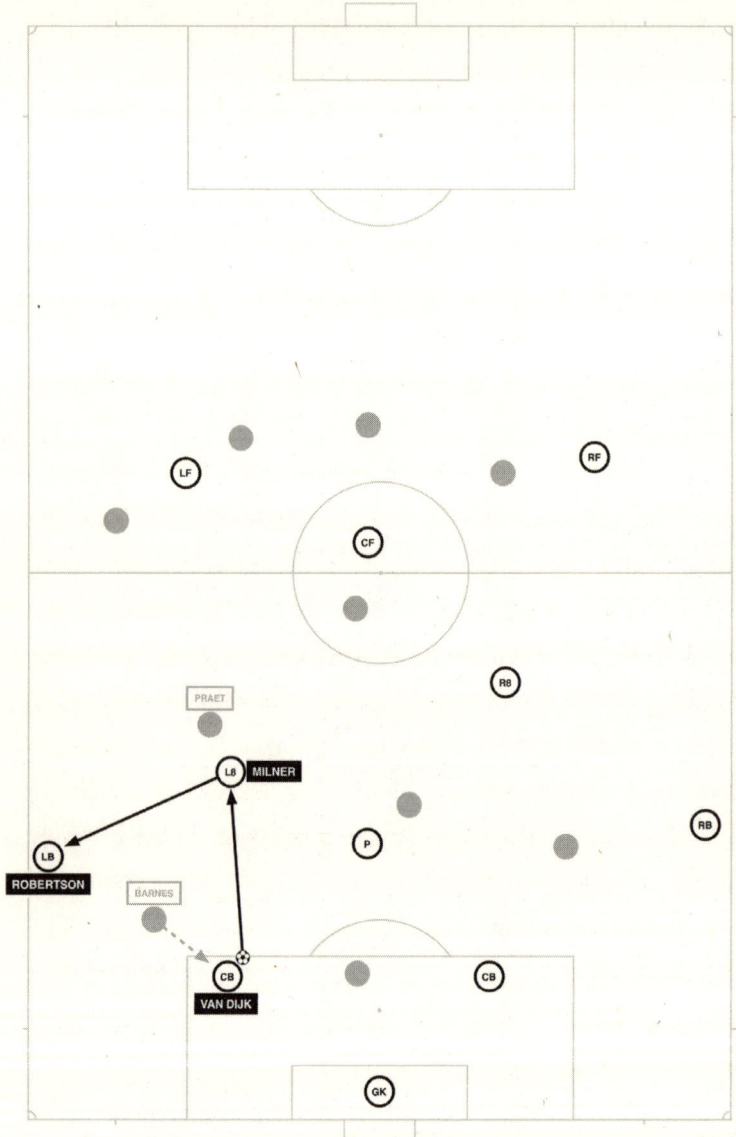

Figure 76. *How Liverpool escaped Leicester's press for Mané's goal against Leicester in October 2019. Leicester winger Harvey Barnes pressed Van Dijk on the line between the centre-back and Robertson, so Milner dropped to receive from Van Dijk, and with his marker Dennis Praet tight, Milner played a first-time pass to Robertson, bypassing Barnes*

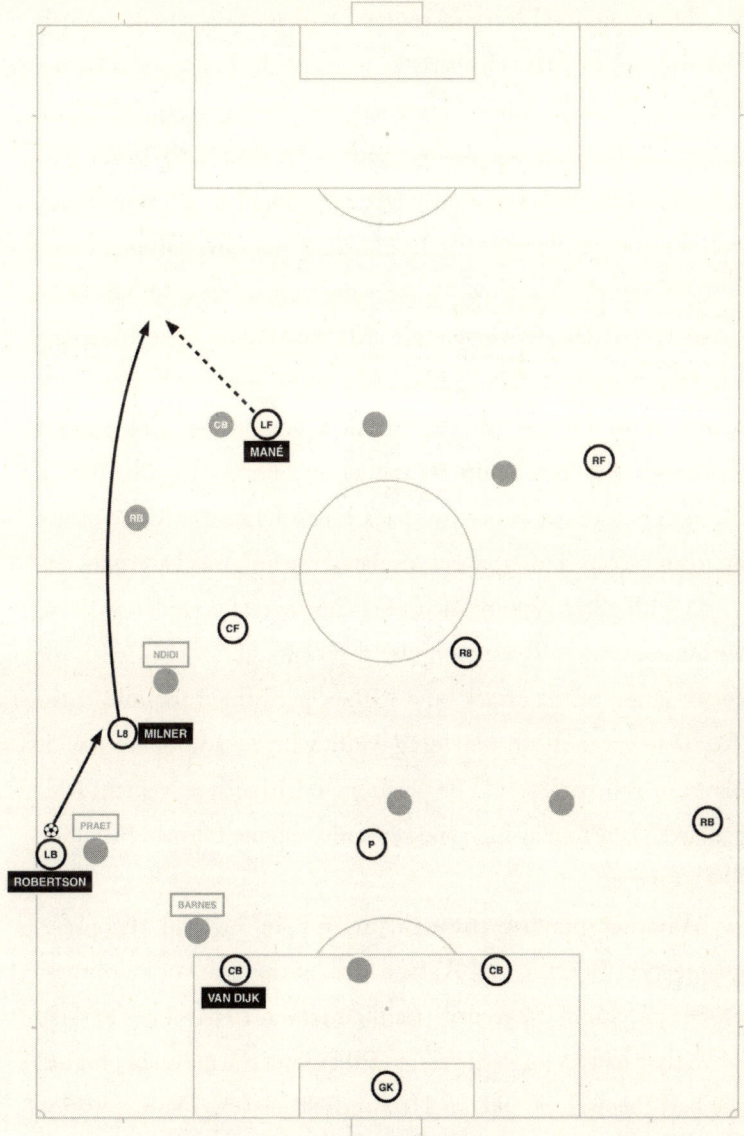

Figure 77. *The second part of Mané's goal against Leicester. With Barnes bypassed, Milner's marker Praet closed down Robertson, leaving Milner free. Before Leicester's pivot Wilfred Ndidi could reach him, Milner received from Robertson and whipped an inch-perfect left-footed pass in behind Jonny Evans to put Mané through on goal*

Van Dijk from the Liverpool centre-back's outside, simultaneously blocking off the pass to Robertson, who was the free man, as Barnes was his opposite number. Liverpool's left-sided number 8, Milner, dropped a few yards deeper to receive and execute a first-time pass under pressure from Leicester's right-sided number 8, Dennis Praet, to Robertson on Barnes's inside. Having pressurised Milner, Praet, sprinted out to close down Robertson, which freed up Milner to make a secondary movement towards the touchline on Robertson and Praet's outside, taking advantage of the angle of Praet's press, which showed Robertson the outside route. Milner took a touch with his right foot before whipping an outstanding left-footed through ball in behind centre-back Jonny Evans for Mané to run on to and score. This goal encapsulated the progress Liverpool had made with their system, incorporating several complex patterns within one move. Robertson was deep enough to assist with the construction of the attack, and Milner performed the role of the 'free 8' to great effect, providing width where traditionally a wide player or full-back would be positioned. Milner's movement wide enabled Mané to play high and centrally, and use his pace in behind like a forward.

Whether playing through, around or beyond the press, goalkeepers Ederson and Alisson were at the heart of all of these moves, providing the security for their players to pass back to them when they had no forward pass, to either reset the move, or progress the ball themselves, like an 11th outfield player. The acquisition of these two goalkeepers, as well as Virgil van Dijk, in Liverpool's case, vastly improved the control with which these two teams were able to play out from the back, while simultaneously exposing teams who attempted to press them high. Consequently, City and Liverpool were able to swing the risk-reward of playing out from

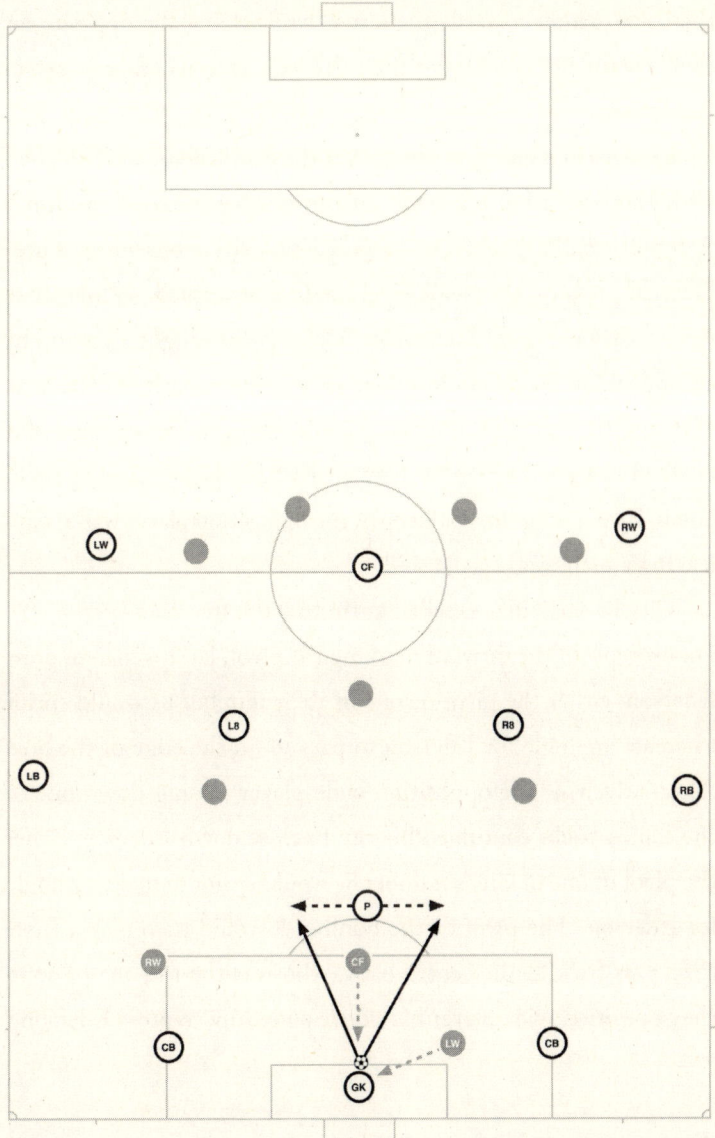

Figure 78. *If an opposition player closed down Ederson, City's pivot would sprint to create an angle for Ederson to pass around the player who closed him down*

the back further towards the latter, while doing the opposite for their opponents in terms of their decision as to whether or not to high press.

Perhaps one question remains: if the goalkeepers were so good with their distribution, why not press the goalkeeper himself? After all, goalkeeper restarts were set-play situations where a pre-planned press on the goalkeeper could be executed. While there were occasions where Ederson or Alisson were caught off guard by an opposition player closing them down, the majority of the time City and Liverpool's numerical superiority deep in their own half enabled the goalkeepers to play around the player closing them down. By pressing the goalkeeper, the opposition player was always leaving a man free.

City in particular excelled at finding the free man (*Figure 78*). For example, if the forward marking the pivot, left his man to press Ederson, either the pivot or one of their number 8s would sprint to create an angle for Ederson to pass to on the edge of the box. Alternatively, if the opposition wide player closing down one of the centre-backs continued his run to close down Ederson, either the pivot or one of City's number 8s would sprint to make an angle for Ederson. The pivot or the number 8 would then play a first-time pass back to the centre-back, who was the free man due to the opposition wide player his side leaving him to press Ederson.

Chapter 20

Why did City and Liverpool high press?

ARGUABLY PEP Guardiola's Barcelona and Jürgen Klopp's Borussia Dortmund are the two teams which have contributed most to the promotion of the modern trend that is pressing; these two managers are synonymous with the concept. However, without more specific information, the word *press* is really no different to the term *closing down*, which is far from a new idea. Every team closes down their opponents, just not necessarily to the same extent in the same part of the pitch. More specifically, teams who close down higher up the pitch are labelled 'pressing teams', or more accurately, high-pressing teams. However, it is important to go further than this and break down a high press into two situations. The first is when the opposition has controlled possession and the high-pressing team could be said to be in their defensive shape, waiting for a trigger to press. Teams press from general triggers which don't change between games, such as a backwards or square pass, or when an opponent has a loose touch. Alternatively, teams may use specific pressing triggers in different games, such as to target a particular opposition player when he receives possession, or to press when their opponents move the ball into a particular area of the pitch. These types of high press are pre-planned in detail.

The second scenario where teams high press occurs following a loss of possession, usually termed a *counter-press*. This is probably the type of press which people are referring to to a greater extent when describing Guardiola and Klopp as managers who use a pressing style. The function of the counter-press is to be able to win the ball back as quickly and as near to the opponent's goal as possible, as far away from the pressing team's own goal as they can. A counter-press may have a general plan – for example the players nearest the ball have the job of pressing the player on the ball, and the players further back must 'squeeze' the space between the lines to prevent a forward pass. However, with the counter-pressing team having just attacked, they are unlikely to be in exact pre-planned positions, at least to the extent that they would be when pressing the opposition from their out-of-possession defensive shape, in the first scenario described. As we progress, we will assess how both City and Liverpool organised the chaotic situation of a counter-press so that it was as consistent as possible.

Before we describe in detail how City and Liverpool differed in their 4-3-3 press, let's examine why some teams high press, but others do not. On a basic level, the reason for any type of high press is no different to any other football tactic: the manager sees it as the best means to either prevent the opposition from creating goalscoring opportunities, and/or for his own team to increase their own volume/quality of goalscoring opportunities. From the defensive point of view, this could be directly, with a successful high press seen as preventing the opposition from progressing to near their own goal. Or, indirectly, in terms of enabling a team to dominate possession, giving the opposition, in theory, less time in possession to create goalscoring opportunities. From an attacking point of view pressing could be *directly* favourable, to win the ball back close to the opposition's goal with few opposition defenders in place. Or, it could be *indirectly* favourable, by the same token of dominating possession; more possession in theory equals more time with the ball to create goalscoring opportunities. City and Liverpool benefited from all these functions. Arguably, the direct attacking benefit applied to a greater extent to Liverpool, with Klopp viewing the press as 'the best playmaker'. For City, the element of control was likely to have been the most highly desired function.

So why doesn't every team high press? One reason may be that their manager feels that a more conservative style of defending is more likely to prevent the opposition from creating chances, as pressing can be a risky strategy if unsuccessful, resulting in increased space for the opposition's attackers, and reduced protection for the pressing team's defence. In addition, it may be that a team's players are not suited to a high-pressing style, as it requires a high physical output and a substantial mental effort. Other teams may vary how high they press between games due to the perceived ability of the opposition at playing out, or in other words, the extent to which high pressing would be risk or reward. In contrast, just like City and Liverpool's in-possession shape and strategies, there was a real consistency to their high pressing throughout a season, regardless of their opponents. This was arguably the most impressive aspect; high pressing requires considerable effort from the whole team but especially from the players who 'set' the press by making the first movements to close down. These players are the forwards, wide players and/or number 8s, who traditionally would be seen as less

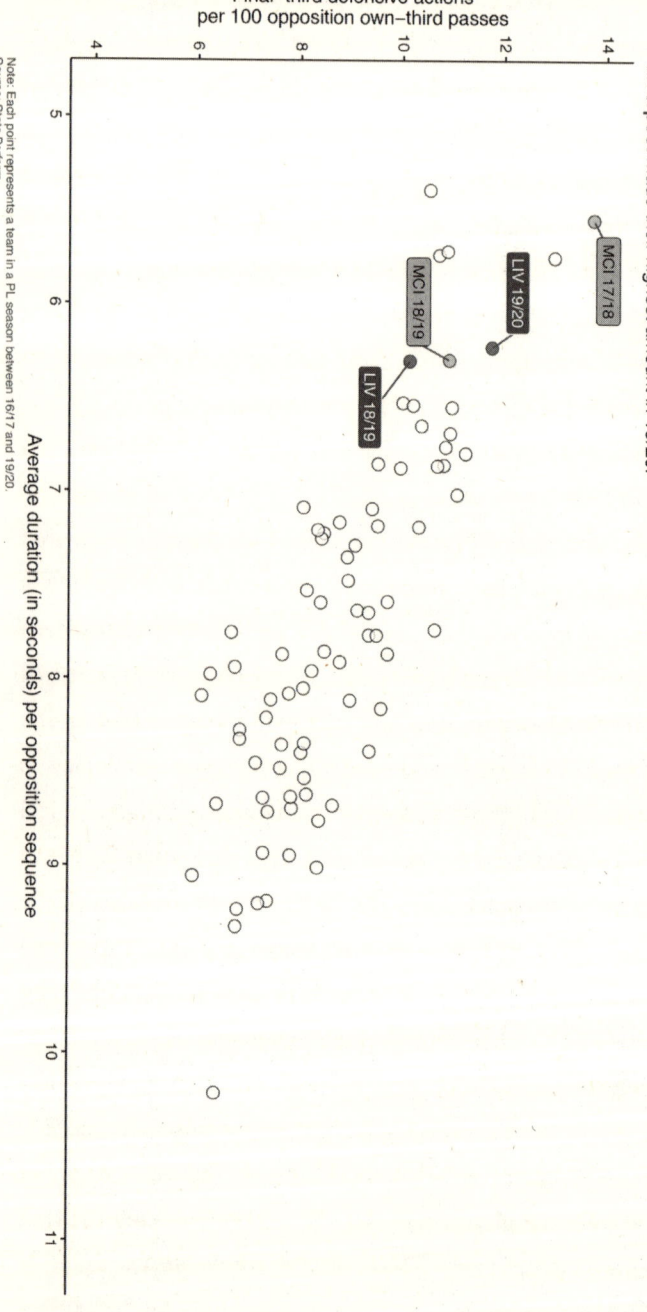

Both teams made a lot of final–third defensive actions and limited opponents' time on the ball

Manchester City made their highest amount of (possession–adjusted) final–third defensive actions in 17/18;
Liverpool made their highest amount in 19/20.

Final–third defensive actions
per 100 opposition own–third passes

Average duration (in seconds) per opposition sequence

Note: Each point represents a team in a PL season between 16/17 and 19/20.
Source: Stats Perform

MCI 17/18

LIV 19/20

MCI 18/19

LIV 18/19

Graph 5.

328

reliable in terms of their out-of-possession work, both in terms of work ethic and defensive understanding. The ability to convince these types of players to perform these high-energy actions out of possession every week over the course of a whole season, or in City and Liverpool's case, multiple seasons (*Graph 5*), is a strong indicator that a manager who has the support of his players.

In order to implement a high-pressing style across a whole season or even era at a club, a manager has to convince the whole squad that it is fundamental to their success. But this alone is not enough; the will to press is important, but knowing when and how to high press is equally essential. The players need to carry the correct pressing patterns automatically – a slight delayed reaction or poor decision can make all the difference in terms of whether the press is successful or not. If executed incorrectly, the rewards start to reduce and the risks increase. In this respect it is no different from playing out from the back; if it goes wrong, is the overall strategy to blame, or the fact it wasn't carried out optimally? Either way, the fault lies with the manager, as it is his job to ensure his players press as automatically and optimally as possible.

Some people may argue that a team must possess players with the required athleticism and aggression to perform a consistent press. Arguably with Liverpool this is the case – Klopp selected players in key positions who are capable of pressing with intensity. The number 8s he chose, for example, were players who had the necessary physical profile to press. But this is also in Klopp's favour; he recruited the correct players to suit his playing style. With City, on the other hand, it is difficult to argue that Guardiola inherited a host of attacking players who were outstanding athletically, nor has he since recruited midfielders and attackers known for their physical profile, or at least not at the expense of a player's ability in possession. Sergio Agüero's improvement in his closing down out of possession demonstrates how Guardiola got the maximum out of players not known for their athleticism or work rate. In addition, although David Silva was always able to cover the necessary ground to press, he was known for being a creative, technical player, not an athletic, aggressive presser of the ball, yet his pressing under Guardiola was very effective.

We're now going to examine how City and Liverpool compared in terms of their high-pressing strategies, in the different *pressing from a shape* and *counter-press* scenarios. We'll begin with how these two teams high pressed when the opposition had sufficient controlled possession to give them enough time to form their *in-possession* shape, and City and Liverpool had enough time to form their *out-of-possession* shape. Both teams, at least during their record seasons, played 4-3-3 out of possession, yet they differed in terms of the exact pressing patterns within this formation.

Before we analyse specifics, let's make clear the principles of a high press which applied to both City and Liverpool. The principle of defensive compactness, both horizontally and vertically, is the same regardless of whether a team is high pressing or sitting deep in a mid or low block. In other words, when a team is carrying out a high press, they are still aiming to be as compact as possible, in order to limit the space the opposition can use to play through the press. While City and Liverpool obtained horizontal compactness in different ways, essentially they attempted to achieve vertical compactness in a similar manner. Put simply, a team cannot successfully high press without their defensive line being prepared to move high. This meant the defensive line moved up as the pressure applied by the front players forced the ball to be passed backwards; the distance between the defensive line and the front players applying pressure was maintained. Most of the time City and Liverpool were aiming for their defensive line to be around the halfway line; any deeper, and the gaps between lines became too big. Any higher, and the opposition's front players could position themselves goal side of their defensive line and still be onside from a long pass in behind the defence. Note, the position of the defensive line around the halfway line only applied when pressing from a shape; when counter-pressing City and Liverpool's defensive lines would often move fairly deep into the opposition half, as usually the vast majority of the opposition team would be much deeper.

The back fours were asked to defend very aggressively; in this context that meant that if the ball was passed into the space between themselves and the midfield line, the nearest defender was expected to move forward and win the ball. This 'front foot' style of defending, combined with the high starting position of the defensive line, made it very difficult for opposition teams to bypass the press and retain possession by passing to their front players to hold the ball up, buying time for team-mates to move forward in support.

However, the high defensive line which City and Liverpool played left ample space in behind them. Many teams' principle attacking strategy was to use this space in behind to bypass the press, but it was far from simple to do so. Firstly, the opposition player on the ball was under pressure, so he had only a small window of opportunity to lift his head, see a run, and execute a pass. Secondly, there had to be a run in behind at the exact moment the player on the ball lifted his head, or the player on the ball would either run offside or not be seen at all. Thirdly, City and Liverpool's defenders were usually positioned side on, enabling them to easily turn and drop as soon as the run and pass was made. Fourth, City and Liverpool's defenders were on the whole fairly quick, so the majority of opposition forwards were unlikely to have a significant advantage in terms of pace to reach the ball before the defenders. Finally, City and Liverpool's goalkeepers were instructed to take up very high starting positions, so even when an opposition forward managed to beat the defenders to the ball, the goalkeeper was usually there to intercept the pass.

Of course, both teams conceded goals where their high defensive lines were exposed – but the greater number of goals they scored and prevented which were influenced by playing a high line to support the press, made the occasional goal conceded worth it. City centre-back John Stones explains how their high press worked: 'We squeeze the pitch so the ball goes back and then we squeeze two or three metres. It sounds so small but it makes a massive effect and knock-on effect for the midfield and strikers. It closes the gaps in between the lines and it forces the other team long as it gives them less space to play in. The keeper plays higher now if the ball goes over the top but if you watch our body position as we're squeezing, it's always on the side so we're ready to go both ways.'

Even though City and Liverpool's defenders were made to defend on fewer occasions than defenders in other teams due to their greater dominance of the ball, when they did have to defend, they were asked to perform a much more difficult task. Being asked to maintain an aggressive defensive line is a difficult skill; on an individual level, it requires consistently good timing in terms of getting to the ball in front of the forward(s) when they drop deep, while also knowing when to drop off, and when to hold the line. It also requires decisive decision-making and confidence in those decisions; hesitation can be disastrous. On a team level, the back four must communicate and take their positions off their team-mates' movements. When City or Liverpool's defenders did get things wrong (or the opposition got things right), they were then left exposed to a greater extent than teams who defended deeper, and who were therefore protected by the lack of space behind them. However, the defensive records of these two teams demonstrate that, overall, high pressing was an excellent strategy for preventing opposition teams from creating goalscoring opportunities.

Mané and Salah pressing the centre-backs from the outside

With Liverpool there is little requirement for us to distinguish between goal kicks and general play, as their set-up and principles were very similar in the two situations. Before analysing how they set up, it's important to note an aspect which arguably set Klopp's Liverpool apart from many other teams; their body language in anticipation of the press was exceptional. For example, when the opposition goalkeeper was in possession, Liverpool's players, to a man, gave the impression that if the ball was passed to their nearest opposition player, they were ready to sprint to close down. This aggressive body language discouraged many teams to attempt to play out against Liverpool, or it at least had the effect of making the receiving player nervous, as he knew he would be immediately pressurised.

Intensity is incredibly important when pressing, but the way in which Klopp organised his players was arguably equally vital. Little that occurred was random; each player knew when to start the press, and exactly how to press. Key to this organisation was the starting positions of the players. It is important to reiterate that the Liverpool back four was positioned high in order to keep the distances as small as possible between themselves and the first line of their press. This resulted in less space for the opposition to use to play through the press and expose Liverpool. Ensuring a vertically compact shape when pressing enabled each line of the Liverpool press to continue to apply pressure if the opposition managed to progress the ball forward. For example, if they progressed beyond the first line of the press, the second line applied pressure, and if they moved past the second line, the third line applied pressure. Liverpool's three lines from front to back consisted of the back four, the midfield three, and the front three (*Figure 79*).

Liverpool were not unique in using their front three in a 4-3-3 to press high; we analysed in the previous chapter how some teams attempted to press City and Liverpool as a front three. However, we were referring specifically to situations where the goalkeeper had the ball. It is rarer, however, for a team to press high as a front three in deeper areas, or at least with the consistency which Liverpool managed. One reason for this is that to press as a front three, the wide players cannot drop back with the opposition full-backs before the ball has been passed to them. To many pundits, if the opposition full-back makes a forward run which contributes to a goal, the opposition wide player is to blame for 'failing to track the runner'. Wide players who don't follow the opposition full-backs back are often said to 'cheat', yet often they are simply adhering to a zonal rather than man-for-man out-of-possession system. Liverpool used a zonal system where their wide forwards did not need to drop back with the full-back; instead, their job was to apply pressure higher up in order to prevent the ball from being passed to the full-back in the first place. Note, we are describing the situation which occurred when Liverpool were applying pressure as the opposition were building up. In other scenarios, such as when the ball was in Liverpool's own half on the opposite side of the

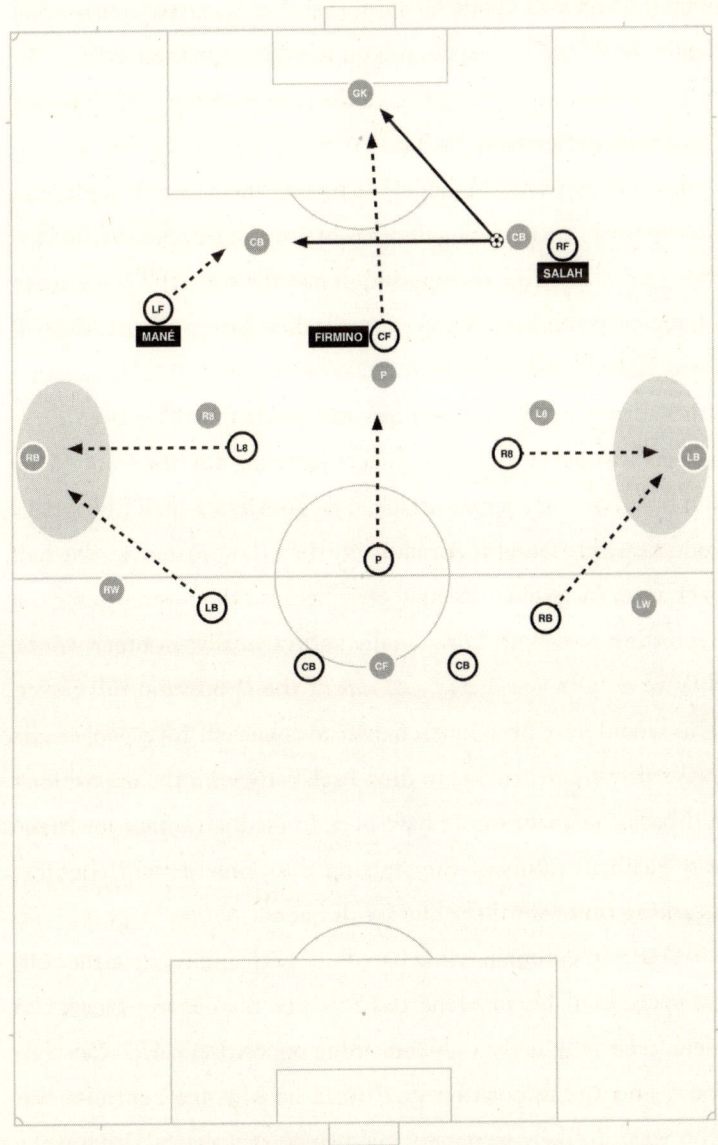

Figure 79. *Salah and Mané pressed the opposition centre-backs from the centre-backs' outsides, leaving the full-backs spare, while Firmino took care of the pivot, and a backpass to the goalkeeper. If the opposition managed to bypass Salah or Mané and find a full-back, either Liverpool's nearest number 8 or full-back would sprint out to trap the opposition wide*

pitch to Liverpool's wide forward, there was some requirement for Salah and Mané to keep an eye on the full-back their side, as the rest of the team moved over towards the side of the ball's location.

There were two main advantages to the strategy of keeping their wide forwards higher. 1) It meant Salah and Mané didn't have to waste energy doing unnecessary running back towards their own goal every time the opposition had the ball. 2) They were in a fantastic position to counter-attack when Liverpool won the ball back. In fact, this second advantage may have indirectly caused a third advantage; the opposition's full-backs may have been more conservative with their movements knowing the threat of Mané and Salah on the counter-attack. The positions which Liverpool's wide forwards found themselves in when their team won the ball back were incredibly advantageous because they were nearer the opposition goal both horizontally and vertically; in other words, they were both *inside and goal side* of the opposition full-backs. This would have been much harder to achieve if Liverpool's wide forwards were instructed to drop back early with the opposition's full-backs, as there would have been limited advantage for Mané and Salah in terms of the starting positions of their counter-attacking runs over those of the full-backs.

Due to their outstanding pace both with and without the ball, the space available to Mané and Salah on the counter-attack was ideal, especially as the only remaining opposition players between them and the opposition goal were usually the centre-backs, who were unlikely to possess the necessary speed to contain the Liverpool wide forwards. In fact, often a diagonal pass into the space behind the opposition centre-backs on transition would see Mané or Salah put straight through on goal, simply due to the mismatch in speed. This occurred, for example, against Brighton in July 2020. Liverpool won the ball back through a combination of Henderson and Keïta after centre-back Adam Webster had attempted to dribble through midfield. Instead of dropping deep and/or wide to track left-back Dan Burn, Salah had remained in his position between Burn and his nearest centre-back, enabling himself to be immediately found on the inside of Burn. The pass from Firmino to Salah was poor, enabling Burn to recover, but Henderson moved forward to pick up the resulting loose ball and score from the edge of the box.

So how were Liverpool able to keep Mané and Salah higher, leaving the opposition full-backs free to attack higher up? The first reason concerns the wide forwards' roles in preventing the opposition from progressing the ball forward with control. The task expected of Mané and Salah when the ball was, for example, with the nearest centre-back, was designed in relation to the positions and angles that a traditional back four, or even five, takes up in possession. The centre-backs are 'split' as the deepest players, while the full-backs are wider higher, at an angle to the centre-backs.

This angle was key to exactly how Mané and Salah were asked to press. Firstly, by starting high and narrow, they were usually close enough to their nearest centre-back to apply pressure should he receive the ball. Ultimately, this was one of their triggers to close down rather than hold their position; could they get close enough between the ball leaving the foot of one centre-back, and the other centre-back receiving, to apply pressure and subsequently force him to clear the ball, or to rush his pass, pass to a team-mate who was already marked, or pass back to the goalkeeper. Sometimes, Mané and Salah held their positions, knowing they could not influence the centre-back receiving the ball sufficiently to justify pressing. To make Mané and Salah's tasks more difficult, it was important that the opposition's centre-backs didn't split too wide, placing themselves near the zones where Mané and Salah were ready to press. Positioning themselves more centrally meant they increased the horizontal distance which Mané and Salah needed to press. Often, it was also beneficial for the receiving centre-back to drop off slightly, to increase the vertical distance between himself and Liverpool's wide forward, again to make pressing more difficult.

However, the majority of the time opposition centre-backs didn't take these steps sufficiently, which meant Mané and Salah could get close enough to them to apply pressure. On occasions they were close enough to threaten to intercept and ultimately prevent the pass being played in the first place, a threat increased further by Mané and Salah's body language, which demonstrated their readiness to press. The opposition's full-back was the free man, but in a traditional back-four or back-five shape, he simply couldn't be accessed with a pass on the ground, as Mané and Salah closed down on the line of the pass between centre-back and full-back. They were pressing from the *outside*, in order to trap the opposition on the *inside*, where Liverpool possessed superior numbers.

Just before they began their run to close down, Mané and Salah would often check their shoulder to establish the exact location of the opposition full-back, in order to determine the precise angle at which they needed to press. As the full-back adjusted his position in an attempt to provide his centre-back with another angle, you would often see Mané and Salah adjust their angle of approach, taking the cue off the opposition centre-backs altering their body shape when on the ball, which they did in order to prepare to play the pass. Depending on how quickly the Liverpool wide forwards pressed, an aerial pass to the full-back was potentially available. However, this was a risk, not only because it was a more difficult pass, but also due to the centre-back having to turn towards the pressure to play the pass; as the centre-back had to face the direction of the ball's origin, he didn't know how close Mané or Salah were to him, meaning he ran the risk of being tackled as he turned. Of course, in this scenario, any interception was likely to result in Mané and Salah running straight through on goal, so risks weren't taken too often by the opposition centre-backs. Again, this aerial pass was made easier if the centre-backs positioned themselves deeper and more centrally, to increase both the horizontal and vertical distance between themselves and Liverpool's wide forwards; this would help the centre-backs to lift a pass over the heads of Mané or Salah to find their full-backs.

Arguably, a right-footed player playing at left centre-back (or a left-footed player playing at right centre-back), was advantageous against Liverpool's press, going against the norm; naturally, where possible, right-footed players play on the right and left-footed players on the left. This strategy makes sense against the more common press which comes from the inside to show the centre-back the outside route, in an attempt to force the in-possession team wide. However, Salah's angle of approach, for example, showed a left-footed opposition centre-back playing on the left side the inside route, on to his weaker left foot, by blocking off the pass to the outside. If the left-sided centre-back was right-footed, however, Salah would be showing him on to his stronger right foot with his press; to play to his nearest full-back, a right-footed centre-back playing on the left only had to partially turn. In addition, when turning he could keep his body between Salah and the ball, reducing his risk of being tackled.

The other advantage was that a right-footed centre-back playing on the left could more easily pass to the right-back on the far side. This would have created more of a problem for Liverpool in the specific scenario where, for example, Mané had pressed the right centre-back, forcing him to pass squarely to the left centre-back, triggering Salah's press. In this scenario Mané would have been a few yards more central than his pre-press starting position, opening up a greater space between him and the right-back on his outside. Due to some teams selecting two right-footed centre-backs, they would often end up with the scenario of a right-footer playing as the left centre-back. A left-footed centre-back playing on the right, however, was a very rare occurrence.

Another strategy teams began to use against Liverpool was to position one of their full-backs deeper and more central, rather than in the traditional higher and wider position of a full-back in a back four. The reasoning behind this was that it made it more difficult for Mané and Salah to block the passing lane between centre-back and full-back, because it created more of a horizontal passing angle between the two opposition players; Mané and Salah were not able to press down the line of the pass. If Liverpool's wide forwards moved higher in an attempt to position themselves in the passing lane, it would mean the gap between them and the nearest Liverpool number 8 would become too large, potentially opening up an easy passing lane into an opposition player in this space, for example the wide player. This would be a far more favourable pass for the opposition, so it would be pointless for Mané and Salah to allow this pass by preventing a far less dangerous one. The key to this being a favourable strategy for the opposition was the plan for when the full-back received the ball in such a narrow position. If he had no available pass, he was effectively trapped fairly near his own goal, as Mané and Salah would immediately close him down. When using this strategy, opposition teams would therefore often position their wide player on the side of the ball wider and deeper than usual in order to open up an angle for their full-back to play around Mané and Salah, on their outside.

This was a similar idea to City positioning Walker inside in a third centre-back role, with their winger providing width to enable a pass on the outside of the opposition shape. However, it was not necessarily an easy strategy against Liverpool's press, as it still relied on the full-back having enough time to open out and play a pass, and for the opposition wide player to retain the ball under pressure from Liverpool's full-back. Nonetheless, it was a method which teams began to use more regularly as they attempted to find solutions to enable them to bypass Liverpool's press.

Napoli, who beat Liverpool in consecutive Champions League seasons, designed a good system to stunt Liverpool's press. In Napoli's 2-0 win in September 2019, Carlo Ancelotti used a version of a 4-4-2 in which he positioned his players to make it as difficult as possible for Liverpool to press (*Figure 80*). On Napoli's right, right-back Giovanni Di Lorenzo moved inside to form a back three as just described, and wide midfielder José Callejón moved wide. This removed Mane's usual ability to press the line between centre-back and right-back, and also meant it was difficult for him to close down Di Lorenzo while preventing the pass wide to Callejón. On Napoli's left side, left-back Mário Rui moved high and wide to provide the option for Salah to be bypassed with a pass over his head, with right-footed left centre-back Kalidou Koulibaly careful not to position himself too closely to Salah, in order to make his pressing task more difficult. We will refer to this system in more detail in the next section.

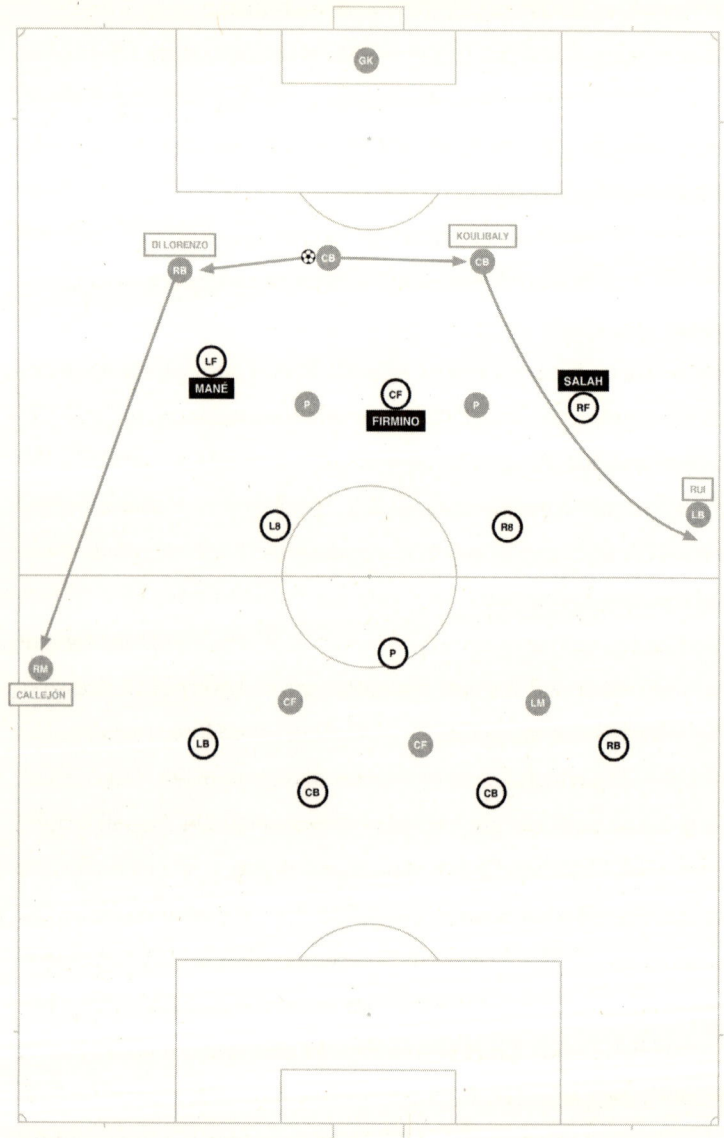

Figure 80. *Version of 4-4-2 played by Carlo Ancelotti's Napoli in a 2-0 win over Liverpool in September 2019, which enabled them to bypass Salah and Mané in two different ways. Napoli's right-back, Di Lorenzo, moved inside to prevent Mané from blocking the passing lane to him, and enabling a passing lane straight to wide player José Callejón, who held his width. On the other side, the right-footed centre-back Kalidou Koulibaly played close to his centre-back partner to increase the distance between himself and Salah, aiding the lofted pass over Salah's head to left-back Rui*

The roles of Firmino and the number 8s

Now we have established the role of Mané and Salah in pressing from the outside to the inside, leaving the opposition full-backs free while attempting to block the pass to them, let's return to the question of how they were able to do this. If a Liverpool game was paused when the opposition was in possession, Liverpool's shape often appeared to be a 4-4-2 diamond, with centre-forward Firmino slightly withdrawn in comparison to Mané and Salah. This is interesting because it meant that as with his role in possession, Firmino, despite being his label as Liverpool's centre-forward, did not initially concern himself with the centre-backs. Alternatively, when Mané or Salah pressed the centre-backs, Firmino's main tasks were the opposition's deepest midfielder(s), and the goalkeeper. At times, for example, from a backwards pass from a midfielder or full-back to a centre-back, when Firmino was confident he could get close enough he would often press the receiving centre-back, but his initial responsibility was usually to block or press the pass to a central midfielder. Firmino's deep position wasn't rare for teams who play more of a conservative version of 4-3-3, a 4-1-4-1, out of possession, but it was unusual for a team who high press in a 4-3-3 for the centre-forward not to close down the centre-backs as his principle task. Firmino's slightly deeper role had the function of enabling Liverpool's second line of the press, their two number 8s and pivot, to start deeper themselves, compensating for the Liverpool wide forwards being high. Because of this, Liverpool's two number 8s were usually positioned roughly parallel with the opposition's full-backs, allowing them to sprint out and close them down as soon as the ball was on its way. The two number 8s were able to position themselves fairly wide due to the presence of Liverpool's pivot in between them. It is important to highlight the similar profiles of Liverpool's number 8 options: the likes of Jordan Henderson, Georginio Wijnaldum, James Milner, Alex Oxlade-Chamberlain and Naby Keïta, all possessed the required energy and mentality to sprint out to close down the opposition's full-backs and either win the ball off them, or trap them wide.

When their number 8 sprinted out to close down the opposition full-back, Liverpool's pivot and far-side number 8 shifted across to plug the space on the pressing number 8's inside. The cover that Liverpool's number 8s gave for Mané and Salah enabled the Liverpool wide forwards to press high without worrying about the opposition full-backs behind them. This didn't mean, however, that from their narrow positions, Mané and Salah wouldn't at times sprint out wide to close the opposition full-back down. If the full-back was roughly parallel to them and they hadn't been able to block the passing lane to him, closing down the full-back was their job. On other occasions, opposition full-backs (or wing-backs) moved very high into positions where it was difficult for the Liverpool number 8 to reach them to close them down. Alternatively, perhaps the full-back received a pass from a switch of play, with Liverpool's central midfielders over towards the other side of the pitch. In these scenarios, Liverpool's full-back sprinted out to them, with the nearest centre-back shifting across behind them to close the space the full-back vacated, and to pick up any opposition players who ran into the channel. Later we will discuss how Liverpool were sometimes exposed by defending in this manner. However, for now, let's recap how Liverpool dealt with the opposition's full-backs – the outside player in each of the three pressing lines was responsible for closing them down depending on how deep or high they were – they were dealt with zonally.

Let's now analyse the two different scenarios which Liverpool faced and the implications they had for Firmino and Liverpool's central midfielders. The opposition would either build up with *one* or *two* pivots, plus their two centre-backs. Against one pivot, Firmino's job was fairly simple; he positioned himself in front of him, preventing the pivot from receiving a pass from the goalkeeper or centre-backs. Here's a specific example. When the opposition's right centre-back received the ball and was being forced inside by pressure from Mané, who had cut off the pass into the right-back, his only passing options were back to the goalkeeper, or to his other centre-back, who would then be closed down by Salah and be faced with the same scenario.

In this example, Liverpool showed the opposition centre-backs the inside route where Liverpool had the numerical superiority of Firmino plus the three central midfielders. Firmino would prevent the pass to the pivot, and Liverpool's two number 8s and pivot covered the potential passes to the two number 8s positioned higher. The lack of options usually forced the centre-back to play back to his goalkeeper. From this pass, Firmino would often release from the opposition pivot to close him down. He could do this due to the narrow positions of Mané and Salah, who were close enough to the opposition centre-backs to prevent the goalkeeper passing short. This meant the opposition pivot, who was potentially free from Firmino, could not be found via the centre-backs, nor straight from the goalkeeper, at least without taking a big risk, as Firmino's angle of approach from the pivot to the goalkeeper blocked the passing lane. The goalkeeper could chip the ball over Mané or Salah's head to his full-back, but under pressure from Firmino this was a difficult skill. Liverpool of course had a solution if this occurred; their number 8s, having not had to push high to close down, were deep enough and wide enough to sprint out to the receiving full-back.

Against the better possession teams who played with one pivot, Liverpool required another solution to deal with him, should he evade Firmino, or when Firmino had released to press one of the centre-backs following a backwards pass. In this scenario, Liverpool's own pivot, usually Fabinho, often pushed up on to the opposition's pivot, either to close him down, or prevent the pass into him in the first place (*Figure 81*). He was able to do this because when an opposition played with a single pivot, for example in a 4-1-4-1 system, Fabinho was technically a spare man, with no direct opponent to mark. This strategy kept the number 8s deep and wider, meaning they didn't have to leave the opposition's number 8s to press the pivot, nor move too far inside so that they couldn't sprint out to the opposition full-back should the opposition manage to pass to him.

The tactic of the pivot pushing up to close down the opposition pivot would often occur in games where a 4-1-4-1 system faced another 4-1-4-1 system. In fact, some teams would do this against Liverpool themselves, as it released their centre-forward to close down the centre-backs, rather than simply sit in front of Fabinho out of possession. It was perhaps seen as more advantageous than one of the number 8s crossing over, exposing the pocket behind them; instead, the pivot was pressing the opposition pivot on his line. Whenever Liverpool played Chelsea, with both teams playing 4-3-3 (4-1-4-1), pivots Fabinho and Jorginho would often end up closing each other down. Generally when facing Liverpool it wasn't a favourable tactic, as Firmino operated in the space behind the pivot. However, Liverpool very rarely faced a team who played with a false 9, so their pivot was free to move higher

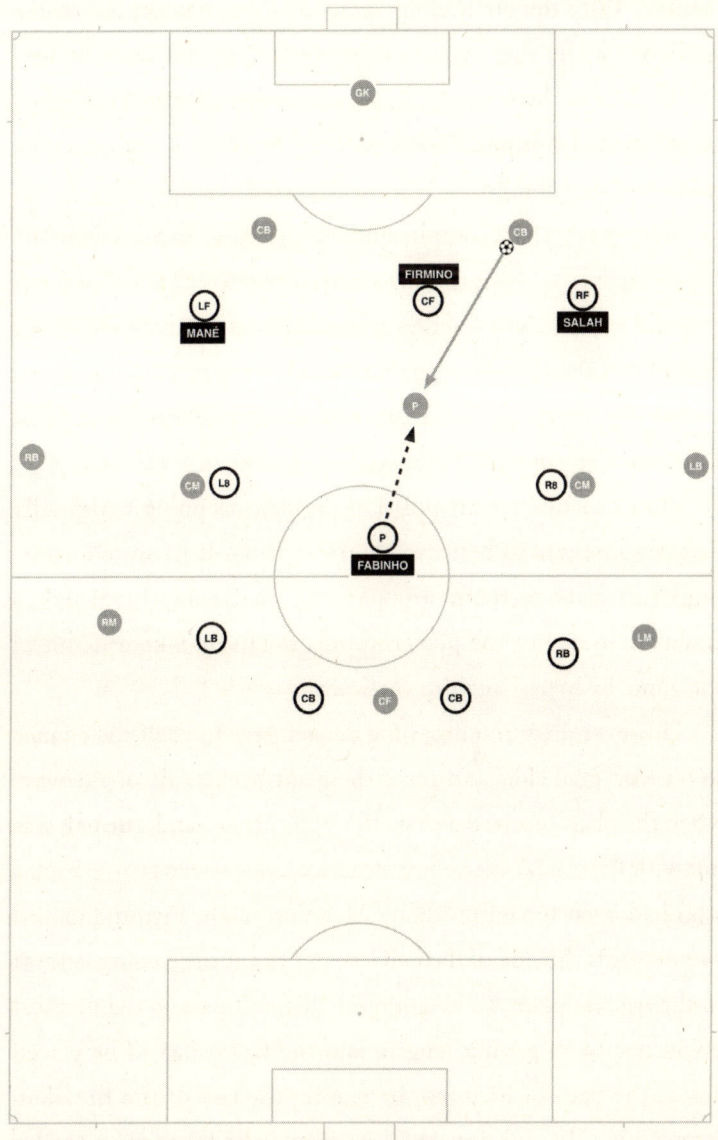

Figure 81. When Liverpool played against a 4-3-3/4-1-4-1, Fabinho would often close down the opposition's pivot, rather than one of Liverpool's number 8s crossing over to close down. Fabinho had no player to mark, and the opposition pivot was on his line, so one pivot pressing the other pivot made sense

at times. With the sufficient pressure on the ball which Liverpool applied, usually there was no passing lane to the space behind Fabinho, or if there was, it was a very difficult pass to execute. In addition, Liverpool's constant high line further reduced the space behind Fabinho.

A slightly more complicated situation occurred when the opposition played with two pivots, as displayed (*Figure 82*), as not only did it create a five versus three situation against Liverpool's first line of the press (the goalkeeper, two centre-backs, and two pivots), but more specifically it created a two versus one against Firmino. For example, from a goal kick, against a double pivot Firmino had to alter his position slightly, dropping marginally deeper so he was in between the two pivots. If he were to start higher in front of them, any pass the goalkeeper managed to complete to one of the pivots would effectively take him out of the game by bypassing him vertically.

However, Firmino dropping deeper gave himself the chance to recover 'goal side' and force the pivot backwards or sideways when the pivot received a pass. If, on the other hand, the ball was not with the goalkeeper but instead with one of the centre-backs, who had been forced inside by Mané or Salah, Firmino moved over towards the side of the ball in order to cut the passing lane off to the nearest pivot, leaving a more difficult pass to the furthest pivot, due to its greater length, and the fact it had to be played across the path of Firmino, increasing the risk of the Brazilian intercepting. In addition, the Liverpool wide forward on the far side was usually close enough to close down the second opposition pivot, as he was positioned near to, or within, his zone. The concentration and energy levels of Firmino were extremely high to the extent that he appeared to take care of two pivots at the

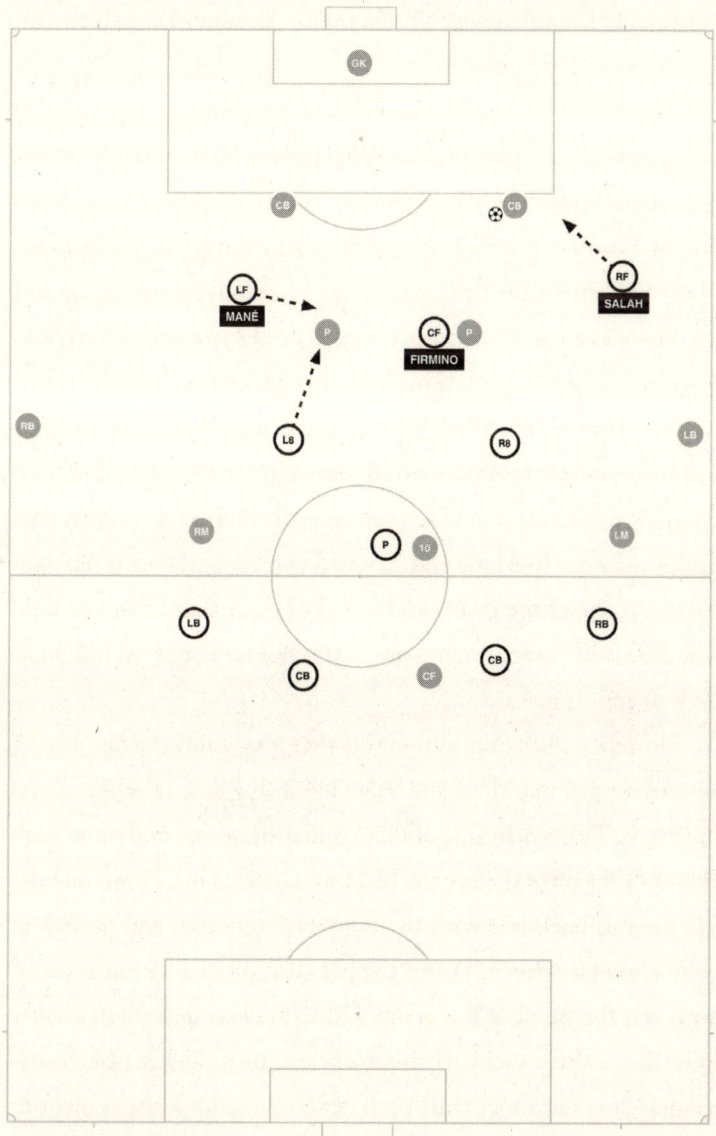

Figure 82. *If an opposition pivot escaped Firmino, Liverpool's nearest number 8 would sprint to close him down from behind, or the nearest wide forward would move inside to do likewise*

same time; the vast majority of Premier League centre-forwards do not possess the necessary attributes to do this.

There were of course occasions when competent possession teams were able to pass to one of their pivots by avoiding Firmino. Napoli, in the example given previously, employed two pivots either side of Firmino to give their centre-backs more passing options. Many opposition teams saw this two versus one situation against Liverpool's centre-forward as a means of of bypassing Liverpool's press by one of their pivots immediately passing wide to their full-backs, taking Mané or Salah out of the game; remember that City and Liverpool themselves used this strategy when playing out from the back against teams who pressed with their wide players in a similar manner to Mané and Salah. Therefore, when the ball was passed to one of the pivots and it was obvious that Firmino could not close him down, the nearest Liverpool number 8 would move high to apply pressure.

However, the complication was that it was also the number 8's job to cover behind Mané and Salah by closing down the opposition full-back. This is why one of them didn't simply go and stand high on one of the pivots before the ball was passed to him; it would have left the full-back free with the number 8 too high and narrow to go to close him down. When the pass was on its way to the pivot, however, the number 8 was often able to close down sufficiently to either make a tackle or interception, or to at least block the passing lane out to the full-back, forcing the opposition pivot to pass backwards.

To help prevent the pass out to the full-back, as soon as the ball had bypassed them vertically, Mané and Salah began to drop, in an attempt to close the gap between themselves and the opposition full-back. An example of Liverpool adapting to a pass which evaded Firmino occurred against Brighton in the recently mentioned game in July 2020. Brighton had the clear plan of using two pivots either side of Firmino. Goalkeeper Mat Ryan managed to find one of them, Davy Pröpper, effectively taking Liverpool's front three of Salah, Firmino and Oxlade-Chamberlain out of the move. However, behind them, number 8 Naby Keïta had his positioning spot on; he was wide and deep enough to close down Brighton's right-back should Ryan have chipped a pass to him. This meant that Ryan attempted to pass to Pröpper instead, but as soon as the ball was on its way, Keïta pressed with incredible intensity, forcing Pröpper into a nervous first touch. As the ball travelled, Oxlade-Chamberlain dropped a crucial couple of yards, which meant that there was a risk of Pröpper's pass to his right-back being intercepted. As Pröpper hesitated to assess the situation, Keïta took the ball off him, finding Salah who scored. Keïta was a player who, at least up to the time of writing, has not fully justified his large transfer fee with his general impact at Liverpool, but there was no doubting his incredible tenacity to press the ball in front of him.

Well-rehearsed opposition teams attempted to reduce the time for Liverpool's number 8 to close down by their pivots playing first-time passes; the pass could almost be played blind, as the pivot knew that the full-back would be completely free due to Mané and Salah's high positions (*Figure 83*). Get this movement pattern right and with two passes both Liverpool's wide forward and number 8 on one side were taken out of the game. This was a more favourable situation than if the opposition passed directly to their full-back, for example with a chipped pass from a centre-back, as in this situation the Liverpool number 8 would still be in place to close down.

However, it was a risk-reward situation; if Liverpool's number 8 managed to tackle or intercept, Liverpool could potentially win the

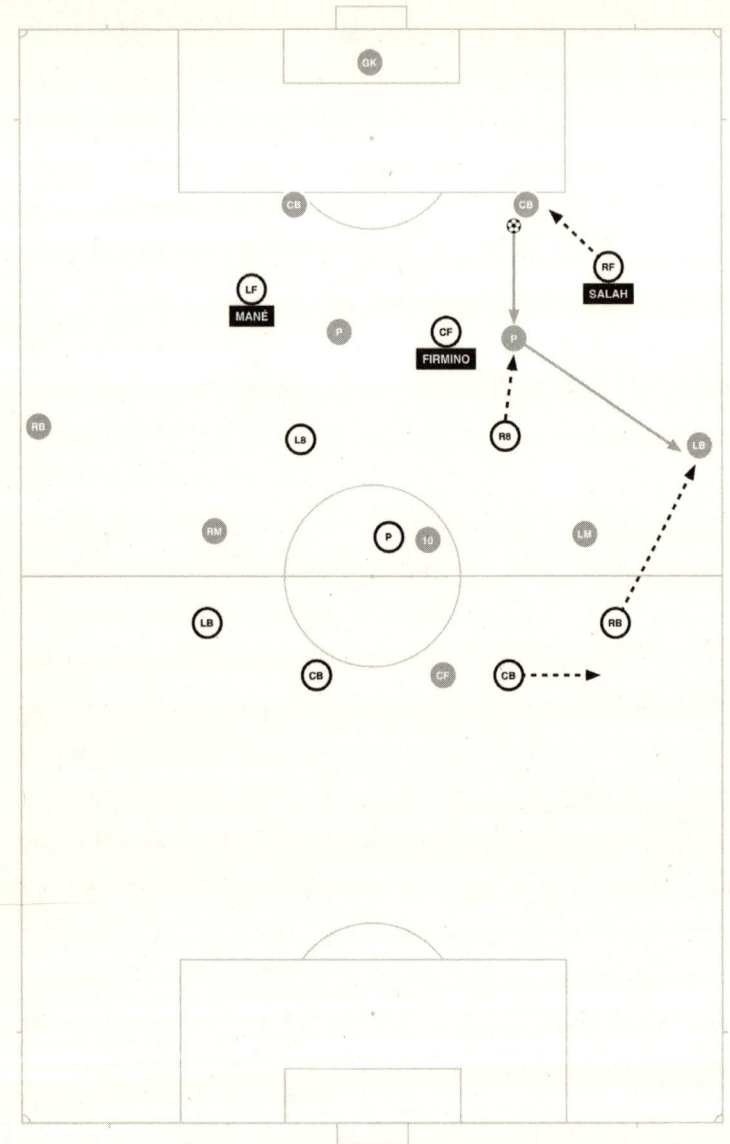

Figure 83. *Some teams would use a first-time pass from one of their two pivots to bypass Salah and Mané's press. Playing with two pivots made it more difficult for Firmino to cover both passes. When this occurred Liverpool's full-back would often move higher to close down, with the nearest centre-back covering the channel*

ball back close to the opposition's goal. The physical profile of their number 8s and the mentality they demonstrated to press enabled the numbers 8s to almost do two jobs at the same time. It was not uncommon to see one of Liverpool's number 8s sprint high to close down one of the opposition pivots, before then recovering to sprint out and close the full-back down. To some football observers, when a team presses they either win the ball back or get exposed. However, when a press has been bypassed, the pressing team can still sprint back to recover their shape and prevent a chance being created. Klopp's Liverpool typified this attitude; if the second line of the press had been beaten, they simply worked even harder to recover and win the ball back.

Despite their incredible work rate, there were times when Liverpool's wide forwards and number 8s were bypassed and the pressure needed to come from somewhere else. In this situation Liverpool's full-back would sprint out to close down the opposition full-back. At times this was very effective, especially with the intensity at which Andy Robertson, in particular, would close down. However, it could also be risky. Sometimes, for example, when Liverpool's number 8 had been forced high and narrow to close down, the full-back had to sprint a great distance to close down. In these scenarios, when the opposition full-back remained in a fairly unthreatening position, it was better for Liverpool's full-back to simply hold his position. Liverpool's ball-side centre-back was tasked with shifting across to fill the space in the channel behind the full-back. Van Dijk, in particular, usually did this fairly well, although often more due to his mobility to get across late just in time than because he filled the space early.

However, often Liverpool's centre-back moving across created a problem centrally. If Liverpool's full-back wasn't able to win the ball or trap his opposite number wide, enabling the full-back to to play back inside, Liverpool's defensive line often became disjointed and exposed. When Van Dijk, for example, moved across to cover the channel, often his partner didn't shift across with him, leaving a huge gap between the centre-backs. Or, perhaps his partner did come across, but Alexander-Arnold didn't follow suit, leaving a big gap between right centre-back and right full-back.

During Liverpool's record points seasons, Alexander-Arnold was still improving his ability to defend as part of the defensive unit; early on in his career he was regularly exposed by runs on his inside having failed to narrow off sufficiently to plug the space between himself and the right centre-back. However, much of the time, Liverpool's press was hugely effective in winning the ball back high up, both as a means of creating chances on the counter-attack, and preventing opposition teams from attacking near their goal. Essentially there were two parts to their strategy: 1) To force opposition centre-backs to pass into a central area, where Liverpool had the numbers and energy to win the ball back. 2) When the opposition passed to the full-back out wide, to trap them near the touchline. Liverpool were masters of all the components of pressing: mentality, intensity and organisation.

City – pressing to force outside

Unlike Liverpool, from goal kicks City's set-up usually did differ from their set-up during open play. From goal kicks, City's press was similar to Liverpool's: the three players they positioned high on the edge of the opposition's penalty area were their two wingers and centre-forward. These three players were tasked with threatening the passes from the goalkeeper to either of the opposition's two centre-backs, and their midfield pivot, so that they wouldn't be played. This was a fairly standard part of their 4-3-3 set-up; the idea was that these three players were sufficient to force the majority of goalkeepers to kick long. Not many teams played short when faced with this situation because the rewards for playing out from the back against City didn't usually outweigh the risks. Most opposing teams did not possess the ability of City's players in possession, especially in the goalkeeping department. Nor did they have such well-rehearsed patterns as City.

Those teams who could compete with City in these departments still had to weigh up the chances of creating a goalscoring opportunity from a move which started with their goalkeeper. Remember, one of City's reasons for playing out from the back was the reward of catching the opposition team in an 'open shape', instead of the usual compact, mid-to-low block they were likely to face for the majority of the game. The opposition, however, were unlikely to need to break City down in a mid to low block, meaning there were other opportunities to expose City's more adventurous out-of-possession strategy, which didn't involve starting an attack from their own goalkeeper, in a situation where one mistake could present players of the quality of Agüero or Sterling with a clear-cut goalscoring chance.

However, the better in-possession teams of the Premier League did still attempt to play a short goal kick. In these scenarios, the way City's front three pressed took a similar form to Liverpool's general press. When an opposition goalkeeper passed short to a centre-back, City's winger that side was tasked with closing him down. His angle of approach was designed to cut off the pass into the opposition's full-back, forcing him to play back inside. This was because the opposition's full-back would have been free, as his marker was City's winger himself. However, City possessed significant numbers centrally, with their centre-forward plus two number 8s. This left the centre-back with the sole option of a pass back to his own goalkeeper, at which point City's centre-forward released to close him down. In this situation many opposition goalkeepers would simply clear the ball, resulting in a successful outcome for City. If despite City's press the opposition were able to pass beyond their front three, the next two lines of the press were activated. City's two number 8s were positioned behind, ready to push in on any of the opposition's central midfielders who attempted to receive in their zones.

Alternatively, the opposition may have passed to their full-backs. This is where City's set-up was more interesting (*Figure 84*). One of the problems encountered when high-pressing a team from their own goal kicks is that the pressing team doesn't know which side the ball is going to be passed. This means that when the ball is in a central position, the pressing team cannot shift over too far to one side until the ball is passed that side, because in doing so they would leave too much space on the opposite side. This means that should a team task their full-backs with sprinting out to close down the opposition's full-backs – which many high-pressing teams do – in a back four the full-backs have to press from a fairly narrow and deep starting position, otherwise the team could be exposed centrally. Alternatively, as we have already analysed with Liverpool, in a 4-3-3 where the wide players press high, teams will often spread their central midfield three out in a fairly flat shape, with the outside central midfielders tasked with closing down the opposition's full-backs should the distance be too great for their own full-backs to close down. However, this option wasn't usually favoured by City, who positioned their two number 8s high in front of the pivot, ready to press any passes to the opposition's central

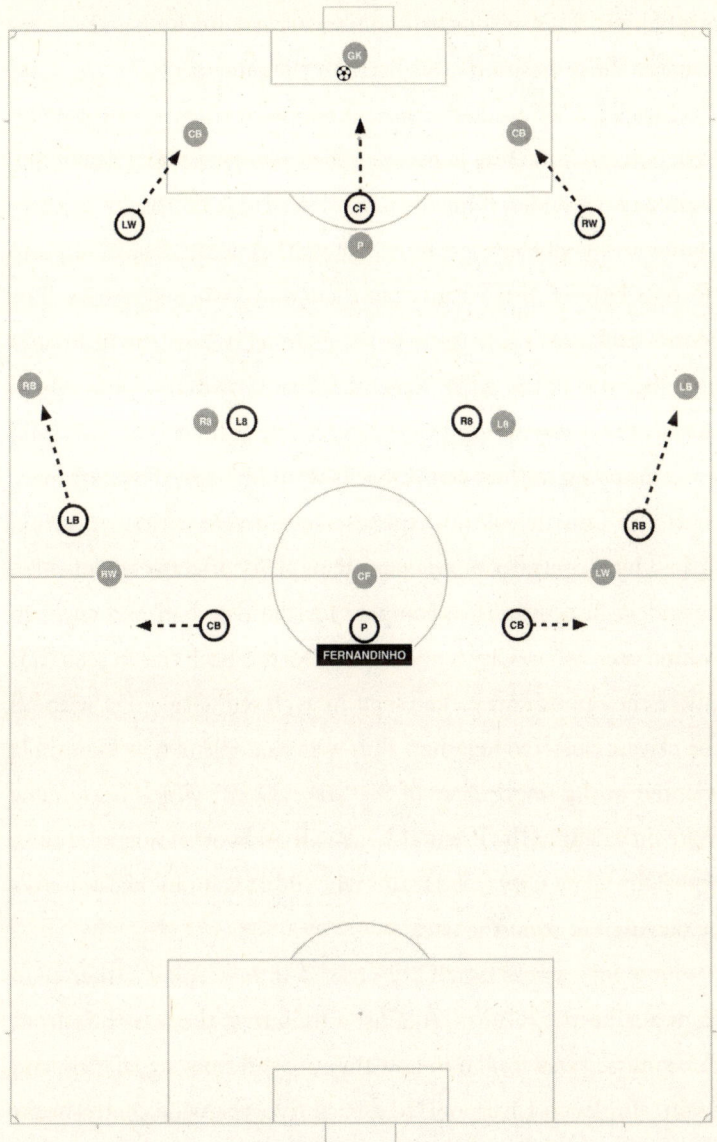

Figure 84. *City's set-up from opposition goal kicks. Notably, Fernandinho would often drop in between the two centre-backs, enabling them to spread wider, which in turn enabled City's full-backs to push higher and wider, on to the opposition's own full-backs. This set-up enabled City to adequately cover both sides of the pitch*

midfielders. This meant their number 8s were too high and narrow to cover the opposition's full-backs at the same time.

Instead, City formed a back three, with their midfield pivot, Fernandinho, dropping in between their two centre-backs, enabling them to split wider. This in turn allowed the full-backs to move higher and wider into positions where they were close enough to the opposition full-backs to close them down when necessary. The centre-backs were able to cover the channel behind the full-backs on either side of the pitch; remember that City didn't know which side the ball was going to be played, so without their midfield pivot dropping in their centre-backs would be forced to start more centrally. This defensive shape also meant that if the opposition kicked long centrally in an open shape, City effectively had three defenders in positions to compete for the first ball and cover in behind each other. City tended to also form a back five in scenarios where the opposition kicked long in a 'closed' shape, i.e. with all the players clustered together. This is an example of how Guardiola adapted to the importance of the 'second ball', which is arguably more prevalent in the Premier League than in other major leagues, especially when City faced teams who didn't want to take any risks by playing out from the back.

Now let's assess how City pressed in open play, rather than from goalkeeper restarts. Against a back five, the way their front three pressed was similar to how they pressed from a goal kick, and again, similar to Liverpool. In a back five, the wide centre-backs are spread quite wide, enabling the wing-backs to move high. This means that the wide centre-backs were effectively positioned in the zones of City's wingers, enabling the wingers to close down the centre-backs while blocking the pass into the wing-backs. This was often also the case should a team build up as a three, with either the centre-backs splitting wider or perhaps a central midfielder dropping to the side of the centre-backs; City's wingers would press the player on their line, forming a front three with their centre-forward to press. However, against a back four which didn't form a back three to build up, during Guardiola's first three seasons City's press took on a different form and had different principles. Instead of pressing teams from the *outside* in order to trap them on the *inside*, the majority of time City set up to press teams from the *inside* to trap them on the *outside*, out wide (*Figure 85*).

Let's assess how they pressed in two different scenarios, starting with a pass from centre-back to centre-back. The principle task of Agüero was to close down one of the centre-backs, bending his run to cut off the passing lane between the receiving centre-back and the other centre-back. By this simple action, City knew the opposition had to play down the side of the pitch of the receiving centre-back. This was crucial to what City were able to do next; it meant the whole team could shift across to that side with the knowledge that they would not be exposed by a pass to the other side. Behind Agüero, City's wingers and number 8s were ready to press the ball if a pass was played to the player in their zone. For example, if the opposition was playing with two central midfield pivots and a number 10, City's two number 8s would be positioned ready to press a pass to one of the two pivots, with City's own pivot taking care of the opposition's number 10.

Meanwhile, City's winger on the side of the ball would be positioned in line with, or often even deeper than, their two number 8s. His task was to remain narrow, blocking the passing lane into the pocket behind him. For example, one of the opposition's wide players or forwards may have dropped into, or already be positioned in, the pocket on the side of the ball. This was a completely different

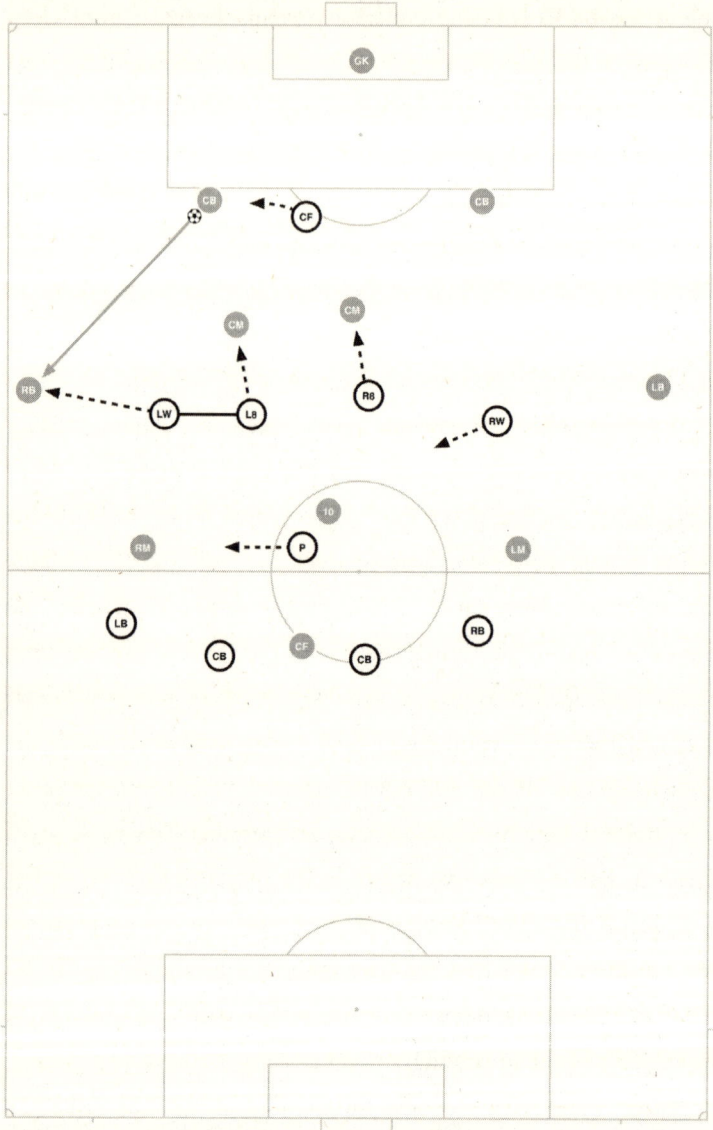

Figure 85. *City's centre-forward pressed on the line between the two centre-backs, keeping the opposition playing one side, which enabled the whole team to move towards the side of the ball. City's ball-side wide player would stay narrow to block the pass into the pocket on his inside, inviting the pass to the full-back, before sprinting out to trap the full-back out wide, with the rest of the team shifting across behind him*

role than that of Liverpool's wide forwards; rather than blocking the pass between centre-back and full-back, by being narrow City's winger was actively encouraging it. The blocking of the pocket by City's winger, combined with the two number 8s marking the opposition's pivots tightly, and Agüero preventing the centre-back from passing to his partner, usually forced the opposition centre-back to pass to their full-back. This was the trigger for City's winger to release, bending his run to force the opposition full-back to play down the line, rather than back inside. As the two passes were executed, first from centre-back to centre-back, and then from centre-back to full-back, City's defensive line and midfield pivot would move across the pitch. They could do this with confidence due to the actions of Agüero and City's winger in ensuring that the opposition had to play down that side. City's winger holding his position, rather than moving wide too early in anticipation of the pass to the full-back, played an important role in forcing the opposition wide before they could attempt to pass into the pocket, giving City's pivot the opportunity to move further across. The shift of the defensive line enabled City to intercept a pass into the channel, and their midfield pivot was in a position to intercept any pass played in front of City's defence.

The second scenario occurred when Agüero had closed a centre-back down, for example, from a backwards pass from one of the opposition midfield pivots to a centre-back – or from a backwards pass from a full-back to a centre-back – but from a deeper starting position, meaning that his angle of approach didn't enable him to block the pass between the two centre-backs. In this scenario, City's number 8 on the side of the pitch of the receiving centre-back released to close him down, with his angle of approach ensuring that he blocked off the pass to the midfield pivot he had left free by closing down. The other opposition pivot was being taken care of by City's other number 8, so there wasn't a simple pass back inside available to the receiving centre-back.

The same pattern played out behind the press as in the previous scenario, with City's winger remaining narrow to cover the pocket, giving time for City's pivot to move across behind him. As was the case in the previous scenario, the opposition centre-back's easiest option was to pass to the full-back, at which point City's winger released to close him down while showing him the outside route. Again, the defensive line moved across to 'shut off' the channel. As soon as City knew that the ball was going to be passed from centre-back to full-back, and therefore remain on the same side of the pitch, their number 8 and winger on the opposite side had no need to remain high, so they could instead move deeper and across the pitch towards the side of the ball.

In this second scenario, City began as a 4-1-4-1 before merging into a 4-4-2, with one of their number 8s moving high alongside Agüero, and the other number 8 dropping in alongside their pivot, as soon as it was clear the ball was going to remain one side. Of course, many teams played with a single pivot and two number 8s, the same as City, which meant City's midfield could not simply match them up naturally; City had only one midfielder deep, and two high.

However, City pressed in a similar way, again using the principle of keeping the opposition playing down one side. The principles of the two scenarios still applied; either Agüero bent his run when closing down to keep the centre-backs from passing to each other, or one of the number 8s released to close down, effectively forming a 4-4-2. However, in a single pivot system, the opposition pivot was in an awkward central position in between

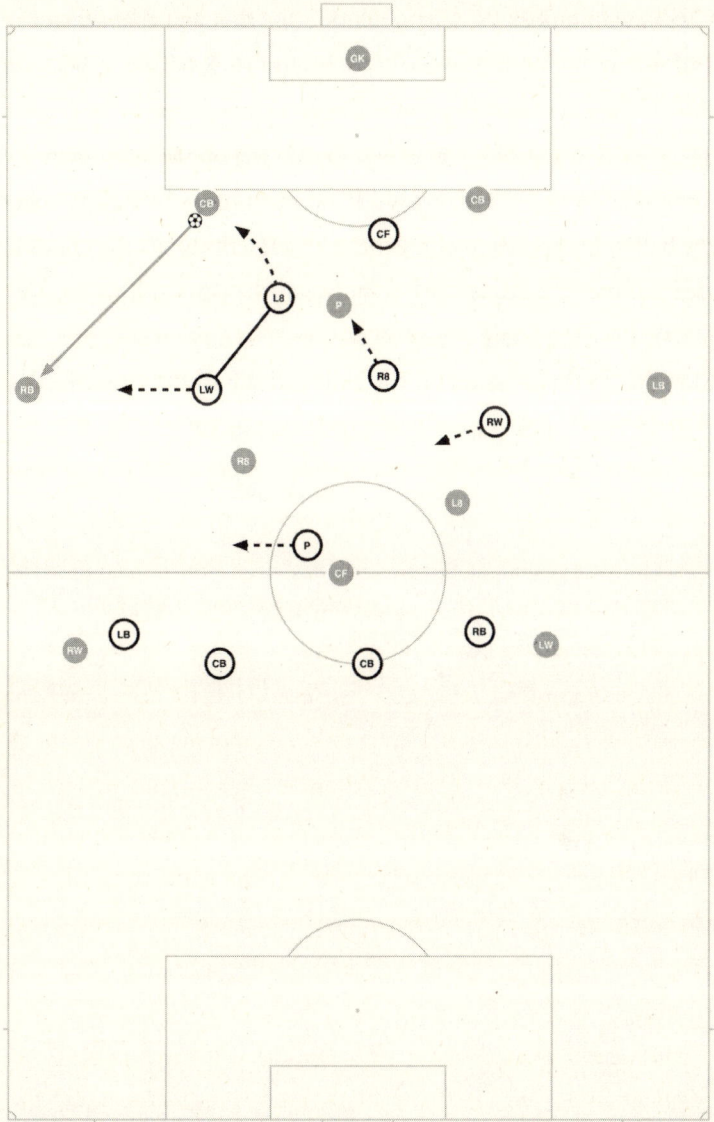

Figure 86. In this scenario, City's centre-forward has closed down the left-sided centre-back from a backwards pass, so is unable to prevent the pass to the other centre-back. City merge into a 4-4-2, with their ball-side number 8 releasing to close down the centre-back on the ball, and like in the last example, City's wide player remains narrow to prevent the pass into the pocket on his inside, inviting the pass to the full-back, before sprinting out to close down and trap him out wide. City's number 8 on the opposite side would move across on to the opposition pivot, helping to lock the opposition down the side of the ball

City's two number 8s. City's solution for this was that when the ball was with one centre-back, their number 8 on the opposition side of the pitch moved on to the opposition's single pivot (*Figure 86*). Again, the strategy here was to trap the opposition down the same side. When City's own midfield pivot moved across to cover the ball-side opposition number 8, City effectively left the opposite side number 8 completely free between the lines. However, this player was completely irrelevant as there was no available pass into him, due to the pressure on the ball, and the fact the centre-back was effectively being forced to play down one side.

Chapter 21

The counter-press: where Guardiola and Klopp's philosophies overlap

THE OTHER type of press which formed a large part of both City and Liverpool's games was the counter-press, which refers to the pressure a team applies immediately following a loss of possession. Let's reiterate its functions, which ultimately are two-fold: 1) To win the ball back near the opposition goal in order to create a goalscoring opportunity, with the counter-pressing team's offensive players remaining in attacking positions. 2) To prevent the opposition from either co-ordinating a counter-attack, or regaining their attacking shape so they can form their attacking patterns.

Counter-pressing is an interesting concept for the fact that it works in contrast to the belief that when a team loses the ball their players should retreat towards their own goal to protect it. Alternatively, when City and Liverpool lost the ball, their players behind the ball moved forwards towards it. This resulted in the teams transitioning from their players making the pitch as large as possible with their players spread out while in possession, to making it as small as possible with their players close together out of possession. The nearest players to the ball moved immediately to close down the player in possession, who usually found himself under pressure from behind, the side, and in front, with no obvious forward passing option, as the defensive line moved up to compress the space in front of them.

The philosophy from a defensive point of view was that the attack should be prevented at source, as far away from City and Liverpool's goal as possible. One Liverpool goal which highlighted how the counter-press enabled the defensive line to move up and compress the space for the opposition occurred against Bournemouth in March 2020. Bournemouth centre-back Jack Simpson intercepted a Liverpool pass just inside his own half and dribbled forward in an attempt to start an attack. However, he was immediately met by Wijnaldum and Fabinho, so made a five-yard pass to Jefferson Lerma, who was in turn closed down by the same two Liverpool players. Lerma scooped a short pass between them to Lewis Cook, but the pressure on the ball had been sufficient to enable the Liverpool defensive line to push up into an even higher position than when they originally lost possession, so Cook had no space to turn. At the point which Cook received the pass, there was a distance of approximately 15 vertical yards between the entire Liverpool team, ensuring that Bournemouth's space to pass the ball in was incredibly small. Immediately under pressure, Cook attempted a first-time pass which was intercepted by Van Dijk. In the time between Bournemouth winning back possession and Van Dijk intercepting, right-back Jack Stacey had begun to make a forward run. Mané was vertically close enough to Stacey to track him if necessary, but not too deep, and crucially, Mané was on Stacey's inside. This meant that as soon as Van Dijk intercepted,

Mané was in a fantastic position to run forward to receive a through ball on the inside of Stacey and score the resulting one-versus-one situation with the goalkeeper.

From an attacking point of view, the idea was to catch the opposition in their transition from a defensive to attacking shape. This is where Klopp's description of counter-pressing being the 'best playmaker' was applied. In an attempt to counter-attack, the opposition players would have to make an attempt to move forward or become more spread in an attempt to progress the ball. If City and Liverpool could win the ball back within the first few seconds of losing the ball, they were presented with a fantastic opportunity to counter-attack the opposition's own counter-attack, but crucially, not from deep. Instead, the counter-attack took place from near the location where City and Liverpool lost the ball, which was usually deep in the opposition half. The amount of space available to counter-attack following a counter-press simply isn't available when the opposition has been allowed to form their defensive shape; following a counter-press, there is no need to break down a compact opposition shape.

Perhaps the most notable counter-pressing goal scored by Liverpool during their record points seasons was their second goal in the famous 4-0 Champions League semi-final second leg victory over Barcelona in May 2019. Alexander-Arnold lost possession by heading straight to Barcelona's Ivan Rakitić, who was immediately pressurised by Divock Origi and Jordan Henderson, forcing him to quickly pass to left-back Jordi Alba. Instead of dropping back as wide player Philippe Coutinho made a forward run, Alexander-Arnold pressed Alba. With Alba not expecting pressure, Liverpool's right-back won the ball back deep in Barcelona's half and crossed via a deflection for Wijnaldum to score.

The chaotic nature of a counter-press scenario means that the desire and intensity is arguably the most important factor in its successful application. In an interview with *FourFourTwo* while Borussia Dortmund manager, Klopp explained, 'You can't tell the players, "You stand here and if this happens, you run there." Instead, it has to be an impulse to move into a ball-winning position immediately after losing the ball.' However, it's not true to say that City and Liverpool's counter-press wasn't organised. It was common practice for every Premier League team, once their attack had progressed sufficiently, to organise themselves in order to prepare for losing the ball. However, City in particular took it to the extreme, with their full-backs moving tight to the opposition wide players to prepare for the counter-attack. One factor which facilitated defensive organisation was their structure in possession. Although there was some element of freedom, City generally attacked with the same players performing similar roles. We have analysed the most common City attacking patterns in detail. For example, their wingers remaining wide, with their number 8s making runs from the pocket into the channel. Similarly, although Liverpool attacked with different players performing different roles, their shape was still based on a clear structure, carefully ensuring that either their full-back or number 8 one side was providing balance in terms of protection behind the ball. Due to this structure in possession, City and Liverpool tended to lose the ball in similar scenarios or following similar movement patterns. This meant there was consistency in terms of where their players were positioned when they lost the ball, which helped the process of winning the ball back.

However, it wasn't just that City and Liverpool had sufficient players behind the ball; just as essential was that they weren't deep marking space, but instead tight against the opposition players. This filtered forward from their deepest players. City and Liverpool went to great lengths to lock teams in their own half by using their centre-backs aggressively; at times when they were attacking deep in the opposition half you would see their entire team, and therefore the entire 20 outfield players of both teams, fairly deep in one half of the pitch. Once City and Liverpool had progressed deep into the opposition half, regardless of their system the opposition almost always only left one player up. In this scenario, both teams' strategy was for their two centre-backs to form a two versus one overload against the forward. The centre-backs defended in this two versus one in a specific way which enabled the whole team to perform the counter-press (*Figure 87*). They closed in tightly together with the opposition's forward, even if he was fairly deep inside his own half. The idea here was that when the ball was turned over, the tight marking from City and Liverpool's centre-backs made it very difficult for the opposition to find a pass into the forward, and even if they did, the receiving forward had a very difficult task to retain possession. Liverpool's winning goal against West Ham in March 2020 came from centre-back Joe Gomez aggressively winning the ball in front of centre-forward Sébastien Haller, deep inside the West Ham half, following a clearance.

For the opposition, key to counter-attacking was often their first pass into the centre-forward, whose aim was to hold the ball up; City and Liverpool's centre-backs were tight enough together so that when the ball was cleared or passed forward, one of them could attempt to get to the ball in front of the opposition's forward, while the other could cover in behind him should the pass be played into the space. They were occasionally caught out, but usually due to poor decision-making rather than a lack of organisation.

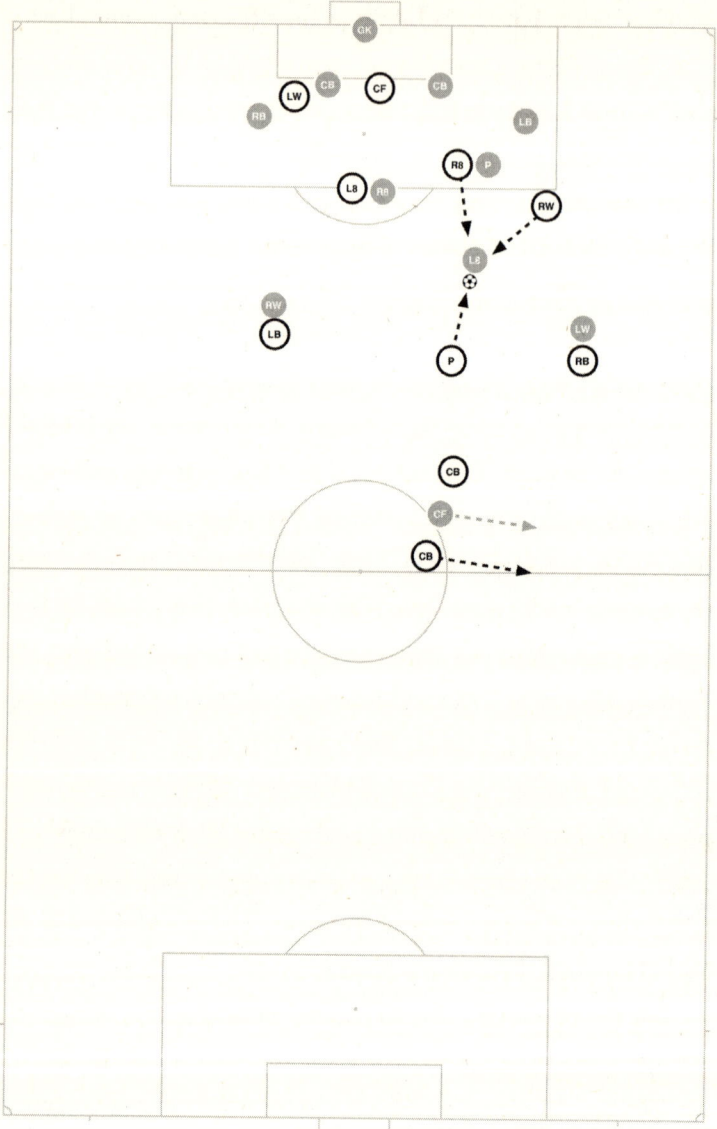

Figure 87. *City looked to suffocate teams by giving them no 'out ball' to bypass the press. As City's full-backs didn't tend to make runs beyond the ball, they were in place to push up closely behind the opposition wide players to prevent them receiving to feet. City's pivot would usually press the ball in front of him, and behind him, one centre-back would mark the opposition's centre-forward in front, and the other would cover behind should the pass be played into the channel*

Defending in this manner freed up City and Liverpool's pivot to press the ball further forward; there was no need for him to screen the pass into the centre-forward's feet. For example, for Liverpool's winning goal against Salzburg in October 2019, as a cross was cleared, Fabinho – with Van Dijk backing him up from behind – released to press on the edge of his opponents' box, enabling him to win possession. The ball fell to Firmino, who headed on for Salah to score. The relationship between the pivot and centre-backs worked both ways; the pressure from the pivot directly in front of the player on the ball enabled the centre-backs to be more aggressive with their line behind, as it meant the opposition player being closed down had to release the ball very quickly. This pressure from the pivot enabled one of the centre-backs to make his move to get in front of the centre-forward, as he knew when the ball was going to be passed forward.

Other than a pass into the centre-forward, the opposition's wide players were often key to counter-attacking. For City, as mentioned in an earlier chapter, their solution to prevent counter-attacks was for their full-backs to remain behind the ball, tight to the wide players, ready to get in front of them or apply pressure from behind if they received a pass to feet. This also meant City's full-backs were the correct side of the opposition wide players to give them an advantage should the wide player attempt a forward run in behind them or inside of them.

A great example of how this worked occurred for City's third goal against Arsenal in November 2017. After Arsenal won the ball back on the edge of their own box, Aaron Ramsey found wide player Alexis Sánchez on the left. Rather than being caught the wrong side, Walker was deeper than Sánchez, enabling him to force his opponent back as he attempted to turn. Sterling then joined in the counter-press from behind Sánchez, forcing Sánchez towards the touchline, where he eventually managed to offload the ball to the marked Sead Kolasinac, whom Fernandinho arrived to dispossess. Following a few quick passes, Jesus scored. The goal occurred after 74 minutes, highlighting the relentless pressure City and Liverpool put teams under throughout the whole game; late on in games you would often still see these two teams' front players relentlessly pressing. Another City goal which occurred against the same team (Arsenal) in February 2019 following a counter-press highlights that the key for City's full-backs was not only to be goal side of the opposition wide player but crucially to be tight behind them. Aymeric Laporte, effectively playing at left-back out of possession in a City formation which differed both in and out of possession, won the ball back off wide player Alex Iwobi as he turned on the edge of his own box, before crossing for Agüero to open the scoring.

As outlined, the key to City's counter-pressing success was their back four being in place behind the ball to 'lock' the opposition deep in their own half, preventing the opposition's 'out ball'. For Liverpool, however, having more players further forward than City enabled them to apply more pressure around the ball itself – Liverpool's counter-press could be described to a greater extent as *ball-oriented* (*Figure 88*). Perhaps only one full-back would be behind the ball as Liverpool attacked, but the number 8 that side was usually ready to cover. For example, Wijnaldum in particular would regularly cover for Robertson on Liverpool's left; the number 8 who was given the role of sitting deeper was always a suitable profile for this role; mobile, strong, and capable of making a tackle. In addition, on Liverpool's left, if the opposition wide player did escape Wijnaldum, Van Dijk, perhaps the most capable defender

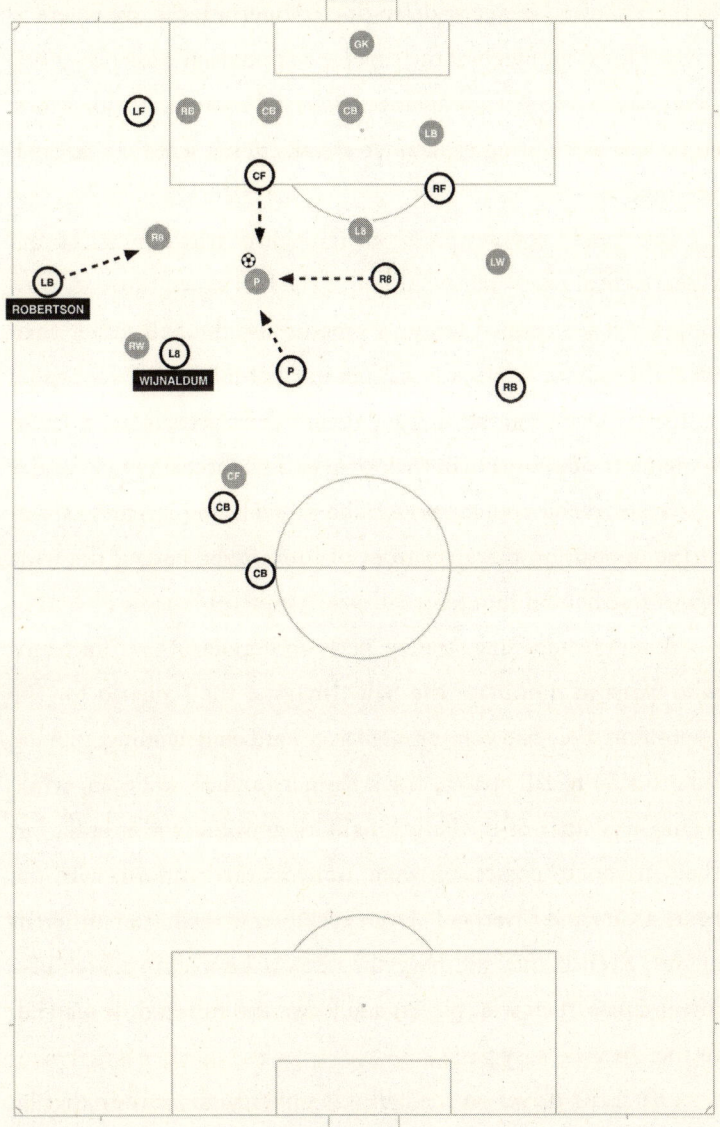

Figure 88. *Liverpool would usually have at least one full-back ahead of the ball, but one of the number 8s (Wijnaldum in this example) was usually covering behind. The full-back who was forward would often press the ball in front of him, with Robertson particularly effective at doing so*

in the Premier League at defending counter-attacks, was there to cover. However, much of the time, the opposition wide player was dragged deep to defend against Liverpool's advanced full-backs, so he was attempting to counter-attack from a less than optimal position.

Liverpool's counter-press was ferocious; their number 8s and Robertson in particular would hunt the ball down in front, with Liverpool determined to apply pressure on the ball rather than worrying about what was happening behind them. Liverpool suffocated teams by attacking and then counter-pressing relentlessly, trapping the opposition in their own half. Robertson in particular was a remarkable counter-presser; he would leave his man to sprint at the opposition player in front of him, often leaving the wide player free behind him to do so.

A counter-pressing strategy plays an important part for teams who want to dominate the ball. Imagine the scenario for the opposition; they had concentrated very hard on defending, moving side to side to fill spaces, track runners and close down, while seeing very little of the ball. Finally they would win it back, but their players in possession were immediately harassed, with the nearest City and Liverpool players sprinting at them from different angles. Even if they did have the time to look up in search of a forward pass, their wide players and forward(s) were tightly marked, so there was no easy pass.

Often the player on the ball was under such pressure that he couldn't even lift his head to assess the options in time. He would either simply clear the ball, attempt a very difficult pass which was often intercepted, attempt to run the ball out himself, drop a team-mate in trouble with a backwards pass, or simply hesitate for too long and be dispossessed. Even if he was able to execute a forward pass, the receiving player instantly had a City or Liverpool player aggressively attempting to win the ball back, preventing him from turning. This is how City and Liverpool wore teams down; when these scenarios occurred time and time again, with teams defending deep for long periods before immediately giving the ball back to City and Liverpool and having to repeat the cycle, opposition players would lose morale, especially once having gone a goal down. As soon as this occurred, City and Liverpool exploited the resulting lapses in concentration or effort. The automatic reaction of City and Liverpool's players to press when losing the ball could only have occurred with consistent training and the same message. If one or two players didn't do it, it would have been a risky strategy. Many Premier League teams contain players – especially attacking players – who don't work particularly hard to win the ball back, yet Guardiola and Klopp successfully trained some of the best players in the league to work remarkably hard, week in, week out.

A goal which demonstrated how Liverpool in particular wore teams down occurred for their first goal against Chelsea in April 2019, as it featured a long passage of play where they completely suffocated their opponents for a period of one minute and 30 seconds. It began with Liverpool defending a free kick on the halfway line, with Mané releasing to press the pass between centre-backs David Luiz and Andreas Christensen. This forced the latter to pass first-time to Jorginho, with Fabinho pushing up to press his fellow pivot and win the ball back. From the subsequent attack, Liverpool pushed both full-backs forward, with Alexander-Arnold attempting to find Robertson's run to the back post with a left-footed cross. The Robertson run forced right-winger Callum Hudson-Odoi all the way back into his own penalty area, which meant that when the cross was headed away, Chelsea had nobody to pick up the second ball, enabling Naby Keïta, who had covered for Robertson, to begin another attack. Liverpool moved the ball to their right side, with Chelsea defending well to prevent Salah and Firmino combining for a shot. The ball fell to number 8 Ruben Loftus-Cheek, who was immediately hounded by Henderson, Alexander-Arnold and Firmino on the edge of his box, with Alexander-Arnold making a block tackle. The ball fell to left-back Emerson, who partially cleared. Fabinho won a header ahead of very passive left-winger Willian, allowing Firmino to collect, and Liverpool to build another attack. Behind Fabinho, should the ball have been cleared to lone forward Eden Hazard, Joël Matip was tight to Hazard, ready to win the ball in front. Should it have been cleared over Matip's head, Van Dijk was in a position to pick up the loose ball. With Chelsea pinned in their own half, Salah and Firmino made another attempt to combine, with the ball falling to Henderson, who crossed for Mané to score.

Of course, some teams didn't lose morale, while others had a specific plan for how they were going to counter-attack, using players with the necessary attributes to exploit the space in behind, hold the ball up, or dribble or pass past City's pressure. However, often when teams did manage to play through or bypass the press, City in particular made a 'tactical' foul, with a player seeing a yellow card as a small price to pay for preventing a chance being created. They preferred to intercept or make a fair tackle, but at times when defending their aggression was such that they were either going to win the ball cleanly or foul the opposition player; being passive in order to not risk fouling was not an option. Guardiola has denied that this was a deliberate tactic, but when a team presses this aggressively, there doesn't actually need to be intent to foul; the aggressive manner of closing down, knowing that making a foul is a more favourable outcome than letting the player run by, is enough. For example, City's centre-backs wouldn't defend so aggressively in their own penalty area, risking conceding a penalty, but they were happy to higher up the pitch when defending counter-attacks.

Combining the ability to win the ball back as quickly as possible with City and Liverpool's outstanding in-possession strategies, they were able to dominate games to an extent that no other Premier League team could. This gave them control, but also the holy grail of every manager in the world; to create a large number of high-quality chances, while reducing the opposition to very few.

Conclusion

WHEN YOU implement an outstanding tactical framework with excellent, highly motivated players, a team capable of winning an unprecedented record points in a single Premier League season emerges. Remarkably, both Guardiola's City and Klopp's Liverpool managed to achieve this in the same era. Which team was better? The answer to that probably lies in the way you see football. If you're a purist, the mesmerising manner in which Manchester City played to win their 100 points is probably the pinnacle. However, if you favour a more varied or intense style of play, you probably admire to a greater extent the relentless nature with which Liverpool attacked in so many different ways to break teams down.

Let's leave it to these two great managers to judge each other's team. Guardiola has described Liverpool as, 'The toughest opponent I've faced in my career. When you let yourself be dominated and confined in your area, you don't get out. When you dominate them, they run into space like nobody else. They are very fast going backwards. They are very strong strategically. Their players have great mental strength. Klopp is the rival who has made me think about how to beat him the most.' Meanwhile, Klopp has said of City, 'Manchester City – I couldn't respect them more. Playing them is the hardest game in world football. The football they play, I really like it a lot. We are different, we have to be different. We cannot be like Manchester City. We probably celebrate different things when they happen. There are different ways of football and I like them both.'

This last sentence from Klopp sums up how I personally feel about these two greatest Premier League teams; over two-year periods they were both masters of their individuals philosophies, enabling them to win record Premier League points totals.

Acknowledgements

THANK YOU to StatsPerform for their permission to use their data, and to Bobby Shojai for the data visualisations.

Thank you to my sister Clare for her copy-editing, and to all those who made observations, most of all Adam Ridgewell, for his time, advice, support and encouragement.

Thank you to Nerea for her patience and support.

Bibliography

***HOW MUCH** influence do tactics have on the achievement of record points?*

Lijnders, Pep in Hunter, Graham: *The Big Interview* Podcast, 4 January 2021

Souness, Graeme, Virgin Media Sport, 30 April 2019

Pardew, Alan, *The Football Show*, Sky Sports, 6 May 2020

Perarnau, Martí: *Pep Guardiola: the Evolution* (Arena Sport, 2016)

Cox, Michael: *The Mixer* (Harper Collins, 2017)

Guardiola at City and Klopp at Liverpool

Klopp, Jürgen. *Monday Night Football*, Sky Sports, 26 September 2016

Klopp, Jürgen. spox.com, 14 December 2016

Klopp, Jürgen in McRae, Donald, 'Jürgen Klopp rallies neutrals to support "special" Borussia Dortmund'. *The Guardian*, 21 May 2013

Worville, Tom, The Athletic, 8 August 2020, 'Why ball retention matters'

Krawietz, Peter in Honigstein, Raphael: *Klopp: Bring the Noise* (Yellow Jersey, 2017)

Guardiola, Pep. 'Guardiola praises key impact of Juanma Lillo' www.mancity.com, 29 January 2021

Guardiola, Pep: canofootball.com, 7 August 2019, '90 minutes with
    Pep Guardiola'

Martín, Lu and Ballús, Pol: *Pep's City: The Making of a Superteam*
    (BackPage and Polaris, 2019).

City in possession overview

Henry, Thierry: *Soccer AM*, Sky Sports, 3 March 2018

Henry, Thierry: *Monday Night Football*, Sky Sports, 21 December 2015

Perarnau, Martí: *Pep Confidential: Inside Guardiola's First Season at
    Bayern Munich* (Arena Sport, 2014)

Guardiola, Pep: canofootball.com, 7 August 2019, '90 minutes with
    Pep Guardiola'

Liverpool in possession overview

Krawietz, Peter in Honigstein, Raphael: *Klopp: Bring the Noise* (Yellow
    Jersey, 2017)

Wilson, Paul, 'Pep Guardiola says he learned from Jürgen Klopp and
    praises attacking style'. *The Guardian*, 30 December 2016

Pearce, James, The Athletic, 'My game in my words. By Andy
    Robertson', 6 September 2020

The evolution of the full-back

Carragher, Jamie. *Monday Night Football*, Sky Sports, 16 September 2013

Guardiola, Pep. Sky Sports, 10 August 2018

Alexander-Arnold, Trent. BT Sport, 2 January 2020

Pearce, James, The Athletic, 'My game in my words. By Andy
    Robertson', 6 September 2020

Guardiola, Pep. *All or Nothing: Manchester City*, Episode 1. Amazon
    Prime, 17 August 2018

How City accessed one of modern football's key spaces

Guardiola, Pep: canofootball.com, 7 August 2019, '90 minutes with
    Pep Guardiola'

City's wingers versus Liverpool's wide forwards
Guardiola, Pep: canofootball.com, 7 August 2019, '90 minutes with
   Pep Guardiola'

City and Liverpool's final ball
Pearce, James, The Athletic, 'My game in my words. By Andy
   Robertson', 6 September 2020

City and Liverpool's 'final ball'
Pearce, James, The Athletic, 'My game in my words. By Andy
   Robertson', 6 September 2020

How did a back five match up against City's front five?
Guardiola, Pep. 'Pep Guardiola: Nothing is guaranteed in the Premier
   League', www.mancity.com, 29 January 2021

Goalkeepers starting attacks
Carragher, Jamie: *Monday Night Football*, Sky Sports, 15 January 2017

Why did City and Liverpool high press?
Stones, John: BT Sport, 5 February 2021

The counter-press: where Guardiola and Klopp's philosophies overlap
Klopp, Jürgen, *FourFourTwo*, 'Borussia Dortmund: Inside Europe's most
   happening club', 1 March 2013

Conclusion
Guardiola, Pep, DAZN, 31 July 2020
Klopp, Jürgen, *The Times*, 7 November 2020

Also available at all good book stores

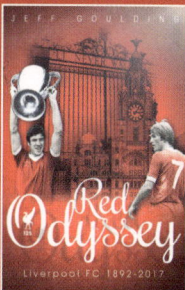

9781785313875

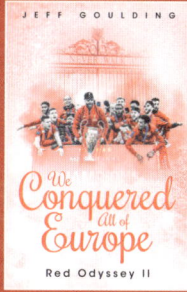

9781785315992

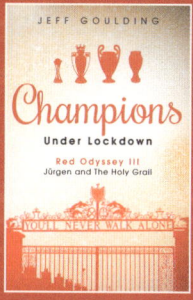

9781785317187

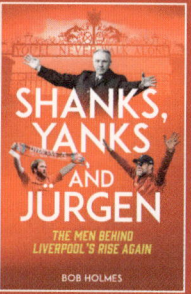

9781785316661

9781785313967

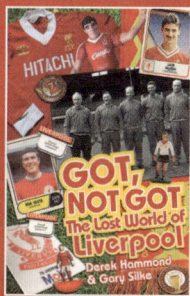

9781909626584

9781785313066

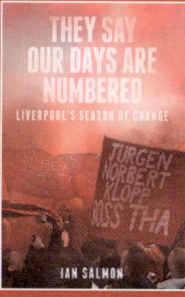

9781785311932

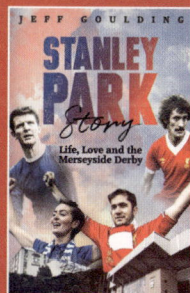

9781785314490